X60 18-693
Bexhill

THE GREYFRIARS GUIDE

THE GREYFRIARS GUIDE

A Comprehensive Who's Who,
What's What and Where's Where

by

Dr. Peter McCall

HOWARD BAKER

LONDON

THE GREYFRIARS GUIDE

A Comprehensive Who's Who,
What's What and Where's Where

by Dr. Peter McCall

ISBN: 0 7030 0226 0

A HOWARD BAKER BOOK

Published by Howard Baker Press Ltd.,
27a Arterberry Road, Wimbledon, London SW20.
Printed and bound in Great Britain by
SRP Ltd., Exeter.

THE GREYFRIARS GUIDE,

by

PETER McCALL.

**This Book
is
Dedicated**

by its Author to all Friars. Although a newcomer to their ranks he is, nonetheless, a member of another, slightly younger order – The Carthusians!

FLOREAT GREYFRIARS.

Floreat Greyfriars! Nulli secundus.
Quares qua ludus semper jucundus,
Et tanto victores nescium magistri.
Occulis nimis et classi electi.
Floreat! Veneat! Velum persuadeat.
Floreat Greyfriars! Semper Floreat!

(Frank Richards).

Long live Greyfriars, second to none.
Seek always to be joyful through games
And being the victors, become masters
                of the unknown.
So much looked up to and indeed chosen
                by worth.
Flourish! Endure! Truly prevail.
Long live Greyfriars;Flourish Forever!

(trans Peter McCall).

PREFACE.

Although I cannot claim to be anything other than a recent member of the Remove; or perhaps because of it, I felt the need for a much expanded version of Gosling's Greyfriars Guide, in which he showed visitors around the School. This New Guide can, I hope, claim to include all the people met and the places visited so far in Mr Howard Baker's Greyfriars Productions.

For the sake of brevity, (!), there are after all more than 2200 entries, I have excluded places mentioned but not visited. Also I have omitted slang expressions, as well as foreign terms and phrases met with during the holiday adventures of the Friars abroad. For obvious reasons this volume only includes that part of the School history as yet published by Mr Howard Baker.

I do not claim to be an expert authority but I hope that this book may help to pass a pleasant hour or two in reminding you, (as it does myself), of our old friends and enemies, whose everyday doings and extraordinary adventures give us so much pleasure.

ACKNOWLEDGEMENTS.

During the compilation of this book I have received much help and encouragement from many people.

To Darrell Swift who managed to find and lend me so many original Magnets for my research, I am deeply indebted.

To all those authorities on Greyfriars whose works I have perused - my thanks.

Perhaps the greatest debt due is to Ian Fullerton of Hewlett-Packard, an old and close friend. His help is such that is it certain that without it this book would never have seen the light of day. It is thanks to Ian and his company allowing me to use their facilities that I have first typed, and then set this book on their latest computer typesetting equipment. The time it has taken is vast, and my gratitude to him and both our wives for their forebearance during our long absences is immeasurable !

To Ian Ord-Hume, another old friend, who introduced me to the world of Greyfriars, and kept me to the task of finishing this labour, (albeit of love!), I owe a deep debt of gratitude.

To Mr Bill Howard Baker and his friendly helpers at the Greyfriars Press for their help at all stages of production, again my thanks.

Finally, to the man who cannot, unfortunately, see the fruit of his seed; a debt which we none of us can ever repay. To the Historian of Greyfriars - Frank Richards - Our Gratitude and Love.

NOTES.

In this book all entries are alphabetical. I have ignored titles in the classification, so that, for example, Colonel James Wharton FOLLOWS Harry Wharton. Where there are people with the identical name I have entered them in the following order:-

a) . People who appear throughout the history of Greyfriars.

b) . People who appear once or infrequently are entered in the order of: i) the volume in which they appear, and then, ii) in the order of Magnet number in which they appear.

After most entries is a number, or letters and a number. This refers to either Magnet number or Volume in which they appear.

Abbreviations used in this book include:-

BA	Bachelor of Arts
BSc	Bachelor of Science
Cantab	Cambridge University
GBC	Greyfriars Book Club Volume
GHA	Greyfriars Holiday Annual
GL	Greyfriars Library
HBA	Howard Baker Annual
HBE	Howard Baker Volume
JP	Justice of the Peace
MA	Master of Arts
OF	Old Friar
Oxon	Oxford University.

REFERENCES.

The Magnet. 1,000 numbers of which have been researched for this volume.

The Museum Press Publications which give so much scholarly insight into the school.

The Greyfriars Prospectus.

The Collectors Digest and The Collectors Digest Annuals, whose contributors have, for so many years, added so much to the knowledge of Greyfriars.

A

A-MENAH. See Golden Scarabeus of A-Menah.

ABBOT of GREYFRIARS. His ghost is said to haunt the cloisters at Christmas; although which of the venerable incumbents it is not vouchsafed for us to know. This legend was utilised by the Famous Five to make Bunter give up his misuse of Professor Sparkinson's Elixir. (1348).

ABBOT'S CELL. A modern shack for campers has been erected on the site of this ancient ruin situated within view of the School gates. According to legend it was used as a penitentiary by the monks; but in view of the secret passage leading between it and the School, it was more likely used as a place where, during the less holy times of the monastic age, orgies were held to the gratification of some of the monks. (1615).

ABBOT'S SPINNEY. A small wooded area near the School which used to be part of the monastic estates. After the dissolution of the monasteries it passed into lay hands, until, most recently, it became the property of Mr Pilkins, the Courtfield Estate Agent, who built the shelter. (1615).

ABBOTSFORD. A school, near St Jim's, against whom the First Eleven play matches. (417).

ABDULLAH. A Nubian slave, the property of Sheik Mustapha ben Mohammed. (806)

ABDURRAHMAN. Sheik of the Baggara, and a desert robber. Bribed by Kalizelos, he held up the Greyfriars party and took them into the desert to try to force Mauleverer to give up the Scarab of A-Menah. Maroudi, however, paid the sheik a larger sum than Kalizelos for their release. (1284).

ABRAHAMS, Mr. The local Rag and Bone man, who is also known to Greyfriars as "Old Clo". (729) .

ACHMET. A camel driver in the pay of Bou Saoud. When the Famous Five were searching for Marjorie Hazeldene and Clara Trevlyn he helped "Honest Ibrahim" to attempt their capture. In the ensuing fight he was shot and wounded in the shoulder by Harry Wharton. (866) .

ACID DROP. The nickname, not unfairly bestowed, on Mr Hacker.

ACTION AT GREYFRIARS. (Title GBC Volume 25) . When Hiram K. Fish cornered the market in pork and made a killing, (to us he secured a monopoly and got rich quickly!), his son Fisher T. Fish became the target for one of the top American crooks, Barney McCann, in order to extort ransom from father Fish. His efforts finally failed thanks to the intervention of Bunter and the Famous Five. By this time Hiram K.'s corner had collapsed so that McCann's efforts were in vain.

ADAMS, Ben. A boxing booth proprietor. Amongst the fighters at his charity promotion at Courtfield were Tom Belcher, Tommy Doyle, Slogger Sawyer and the Pixie Kid. The Famous Five, having had permission to go, were caught "out of bounds" by Loder. As he was determined to get them into trouble, the Removites let him do his worst ! (414) .

ADELAIDE. Parlourmaid to Miss Bull, aunt to Johnny Bull. (810) .

AESCHYLUS. Dr Locke spends many of his leisure hours preparing a new edition of the works of this 5th century B.C. Greek poet. This magnum opus is "intended to make some sensation among nine or ten gentlemen in quiet cloisters in Oxford !" (145) .

AGRA GOBLET. General Gadsby's most valued possession. Brought back from India by his father, it has since then been kept in the General's study. Pawson, a one time butler at Gadsby Croft, tried to steal it during his master's absence, with the intention of laying the blame on the Greyfriars party camping on the estate. (1339) .

AH FENG. A wealthy Chinese merchant of Singapore dealing in jade. A member of the Red Dragon Tong, his men captured Bunter and Nugent. The price for their release was to be the handing over of Wun Lung to the Tong. Nugent managed to engineer their escape unbeknownst to Ah Feng, thus enabling Ferrers Locke to bring Wun in safety to his father. (1180)

AHMED. The servant to Perez. He was a member of the Dinka tribe from the Nile region of Africa. (1230).

AHMED, Eye of. The insignia of power of the sheiks of the tribe of Yusef. Without it the hereditary ruler is unable to establish his right to govern. To gain possession of it, Mustapha ben Mohammed captured Major Cherry, Marjorie Hazeldene and Clara Trevlyn, in a bid to force Ali to give it up, and so cede his claims to the throne. (GBC 8).

AITOO. The South Seas word meaning Devil, and hence the name given, in fear, to Soames when he was working in that part of the world as a slave trader. (GBC 11).

ALBERT. The footman appointed to look after Bunter during his stay at Cavandale Abbey. In keeping with his aristocratic breeding, Bunter could never remember his name! (1191).

ALBERT. Footman at Gadsby Croft. (1339).

ALGERIA. The North African country which was the scene of the climax of Ali ben Yusef's struggle against Mustapha ben Mohammed. (GBC 8).

ALI. Half Arab, half Negro member of Krantz's slave trading gang. After being captured, Vernon Smith was in Ali's custody until his release by Bunter. (1229).

ALI. Servant to Hilmi Maroudi. Bribed the enormous amount of £800 to steal the Scarab of A-Menah by Kalizelos, his attempt failed after nearly throwing Harry Wharton into the sea while en route for Alexandria. (1278).

ALIENS. The nickname given to the boys of Herr Rosenblaum's short lived academy which was situated next to Greyfriars, separated only by the cloisters, through which one school would make raids upon the other.

ALLOTMENTS. To help the war effort, part of the school grounds, (in addition to the school garden), were made into allotments for each form to work in their spare time to grow vegetables for the school's consumption. (501; 508).

ALOHA. A South Sea Schooner belonging to Mr Vernon Smith's copra fleet. She was used by Tom Redwing and party in their search for Black Pete's treasure. Sunk on a reef off Caca Island, while they were trying to escape from cannibals, the Greyfriars party had to make their getaway in the ship's whaleboat. They drifted on the Pacific until picked up, by chance, by the Golden Arrow. (GBC 11).

ALONZO THE GREAT. The nickname given to Alonzo Todd while under the influence of Professor Sparkinson's "New Elixir". This is also the title of HBE Volume 21.

ALVARA, Carlos. A Spanish bandit who attacked and robbed Coker and friends while they were riding in the hills above Algeciras. (And he claimed to be a "Caballero !"). (1315).

AMADEO. A Neapolitan boatman hired by Tiger Bronx to help in his attempted kidnapping of Bunter while bathing at Posilippo. The Famous Five tried to hire the boat while the kidnap was in progress, and so, inadvertently, foiled the attempt. (1389).

AMELIA. The resident housekeeper to Mr Pickering, the tutor hired by Mr Vernon Smith to instruct Smithy during the holidays. Smithy, however, intended to pass the holidays with Ponsonby and Co. despite the knowledge that Mr Smedley was trying his utmost to get Smithy disinherited by his father. (1368).

AMPINGE. A small village, a few miles from Folkestone, on the Kent Downs; it is the home of Mr Pickering. (1365).

ANCHOR, The. The public house on the sea front at Pegg, near the end of the pier. Provided the licensed premises are not entered, Friars may take tea here on half holidays, when school bounds are extended to include the village and its facilities.

ANDERSON, James. The alias used by Soames when he visited Greyfriars to search for the cigarette case containing the clue to the whereabouts of the proceeds of a raid upon Lantham Post Office. (HBA 1).

ANDERSON, James. Valet to Bunter during his stay at Reynham Castle. As he said, "I usually call him George, because I can't remember his name is James !" So much for Bunter's pretensions to the aristocracy ! (157).

ANFRITH. A Saxon religious known as the Black Monk. Mr Quelch has traced the monastery back to his time, and is certain that he was the founder of the original Saxon buildings at Greyfriars. He was a "strange character who began his career as a soldier, and after became a hermit in the Romney Marshes. He acquired a sinister reputation as a robber chief wearing a black cassock and a hood. Years later he became a genuine monk".

ANGEL, Aubrey. Despite many close calls and warnings, he is still the same shady character who seems to revel in breaking school bounds and rules. Even the discovery of his younger, hero-worshipping brother, Maurice, seems to have had little or no effect on his character. Unfortunately, he is also an inveterate snob, which means that his friends are limited to his fellow Upper Fourth Form study mate Kenney and, worse, if possible, Skinner of the Remove.

ANGEL, Claude. Aubrey Angel's older brother. There is no mention of which school he attended. (821).

ANGEL, Denys. Late Colonel H.M. Armed Forces. Killed in action, he was the younger brother of Sir Philip Angel. While serving in his capacity as magistrate he incurred the enmity of Barengro who, in revenge, took a child he presumed to be the Colonel's son. In fact it was Maurice, Sir Philip's son, whom Colonel Angel had wished to make his heir as he was, himself, unmarried. (821).

ANGEL, Maurice. Youngest son of Sir Philip Angel, and heir to his late Uncle Denys' estate. Taken while a child by a gipsy, Barengro, he was forced to become a member of his band. During this time he was known as "Mick the Gipsy". Later he came into his inheritance and, after a short spell in the Remove at Greyfriars, he left school to continue his studies with a private tutor. (GBC 34).

ANGEL, Sir Philip, M.P., Bart., O.F., Governor, Greyfriars School. Father of three sons, Claude, Aubrey and Maurice. Until he learned that Mick, (the name by which Maurice was known at Greyfriars), had rescued him from an attack by Barengro, he had tried to persuade the Head to remove the boy from school. It was only after this that he learned that the Gipsy boy was, in fact, his youngest son. (GBC 34).

ANTHONY. Waiter at the Barley Mow Inn, Litle Puddleford. (1333).

ANTOINE. Major Domo at the mansion rented by Jarvish on Bunter's behalf in Paris. (1385).

ANTONIO, Brother. An Italian priest helped by the Famous Five after he had been attacked by footpads. Cardinal Colonna, on hearing of this, not only gave them a lift in his car after they had been stranded by a mixture of fate and Jarvish's machinations, but also put his car and his secretary at their disposal during their stay in Rome. (1388).

AOUDHA. An Indian Ayah engaged by Bunter thinking he was employing a manservant. He did not realise that she was in fact a nursemaid! (996).

APPEAL to the HEAD. The final court of appeal against punishment unfairly imposed. Rarely used due to the prevailing sense of justice in the school, it was on occasions unfairly used, as when Vernon Smith, shortly after his arrival, appealed to the Head after being caught smoking. Making use of his father's "Hold" over the Head, he escaped his just reward.

APPOLLO. One of Marco the Lion Tamer's pride of lions in Muccolini's Circus. (1483).

AQUILLA NERA, Osteria. A country inn in the Apennines at which Bunter and the Famous Five stayed after their plane had been forced to make an emergency landing. (1387).

A.R.P. The abbreviation for Air Raid Precautions. In the event of an attack by enemy planes everyone had to know what to do and where to go. Thus, ARP included, not only the evacuation of buildings, but also the practice of wearing gas-masks and the carrying of them at all times. The latter were not infrequently used as a device for misleading masters as to the true identity of boys !

ARCADE, The, Redclyffe. The rather grandiose name given to the main shops in Redclyffe, and hence the name of its Restaurant. (1631).

ARCHER, Norman. The Captain of Greyfriars from 1885 to 1888. (799).

ARTHUR. Footman at Wharton Lodge. (1491).

ARTOIS, Gaston. A member of Herr Rosenblaum's Foreign Academy.

ASHFORD. A town in Kent, "a good thirty miles" from Greyfriars, (1253), but only one hour by train, so that Colonel Wharton could invite Harry to tea with him here, prior to his going abroad. Harry's failure to keep the appointment led to one of his "Downfalls". (879).

ASHWOOD. Three miles from Cavandale Abbey, it is the nearest town. It lies in the County of Surrey. (1191).

AUNT BULL. See Bull, Aunt.

AUNT JUDY. See Coker, Miss Judith.

AUSTIN. The main town in the Rio Frio region of Texas, U.S.A. It was through lawyers in this town that Mr Vernon Smith bought the Kicking Cayuse Ranch. (1576).

AVIS. The code name by which Sir William Bird called himself when communicating with Wibley who impersonated him during the early days of the war while Sir William was absent on a secret mission. (HBE 41) .

B.

BADGER, Mr Fred. The stage manager of Mr Whiffles pantomime company at Lantham. To Nugent's chagrin, it transpired that he was affianced to Conchita, the leading lady. (409) .

BAGANDA. An African tribe from Uganda, men of which were employed on the Boa Vista Estate. (1230) .

BAGSHOT, Joe. A character created by Wibley as a parody of a "Racing Tough". He used this character to cure Bunter of any further desire to gamble. (1068) .

BAHADUR, Jam Munny Singh. Uncle to Hurree Singh, and Regent of Bhanipur during his minority.

BAJI RAO. Cousin to Hurree Singh and a pretender to the throne of Bhanipur. After several abortive attempts to kidnap Hurree Singh in England, he led an unsuccessful coup in Bhanipur itself, after taking Hurree Singh prisoner during a tiger hunt. After the failure of the coup, he escaped with a Russian agent provocateur, Lazaroff, who murdered him in order to increase his own chances of escape. (GBC 4) .

BAKER. The local miller operating Baker's Mill on the Sark, near Friardale. (1240) .

BAKER. Proprietor of Baker's Boatyard just below Friardale Bridge. "As good tempered as he was plump", he hired the Water Lily to the Famous Five for their summer cruise up the Thames. He shipped the boat to his nephew's boatyard at Kingston-upon-Thames where they started their holiday. (1643) .

BAKER STREET. Ferrers Locke's home address is, like many other famous detectives, to be found here.

BAKER'S MILL. On the River Sark above Courtfield, it is out of bounds to all Greyfriars below the Fifth Form because of the dangers of the nearby weir. The mill is water powered by a head of water supplied from Baker's pond, itself fed by a tributary of the Sark. Nugent Minor and his friends had a narrow escape from the mill race from which they were rescued by Eric Carlow. (1240).

BAKER'S POND. The reservoir supplying the water to Baker's Mill. The over-flow and spent water enters the River Sark below the mill, where the mill race is controlled by the weir.

BALDWIN. A parrot bought by Mr Green, the mate of the M.V. Silver Star. Said to be a talking bird, the only conversation it had was that put into its mouth by Bunter and his ventriloquism ! His attempted "con" of the mate of 15/- for the bird was foiled when caught in the act by the Famous Five. (1186).

BALOO. An Island near Kalua. While en passage for Kalua the Greyfriars party was attacked by the islanders. (1589).

BANBURY PET. A boxer trained by Bill Huggins, Drury's ex-manager. He took part in an illegal boxing tourney at the Three Fishers. (988).

BANCROFT. Sixth Form member of Greyfriars, and a member of the First Eleven football team.

BANE. Franz Kranz manservant. He helped his employer to kidnap Cherry, Vernon Smith and Mauleverer. He later received a jail sentence for his part in the crime. (1356).

BANKER. A card game of no skill with a fast betting action. The banker cuts the cards into a number of sections equal to the number of players. Each player bets blind on his cards. The piles are then turned over, and those players with the bottom card equal to or lower than the banker lose their bets. Higher cards receive an amount from the bank equal to their bets.

BANKS. A local bookmaker operating close to if not usually outside the law. He certainly takes bets from minors, which is illegal and, though he will probably not welch on a bet, he is unlikely to accept money on any prospect other than an outsider. He is an habitue of the Three Fishers. On one occasion he ran an illegal casino before being arrested while a game was in progress. Ponsonby had tipped off the police in an attempt to get de Courcy arrested and disgraced.

BANTHORPE. A timid Removite small for his age. He is only mentioned once when he did not become involved in a fight. Although there is no mention as such, there is a good possibility that he is, or was, a day boy. This would explain his non-involvement in school affairs, and the fact that he does not have a study. (251).

BARAK. A member of Ludwig Krantz's slave trading gang. After the capture of Vernon Smith and the Famous Five, he was killed by Kikolobo whilst they were being taken down the Congo to be sold as slaves. (1235).

BARCROFT. A minor Public School in Norfolk attended by Julian Devarney before he went to Greyfriars. After a short but eventful stay he returned to Barcroft. (1126).

BARENGRO. A petty criminal who, in revenge for a jail sentence, took a child he believed to be the magistrate's son in order to maltreat him and force him into becoming a criminal. His efforts failed as the boy ran away from the band, and went to Greyfriars for a time. Barengro recaptured Mick, and died by his own hand trying to prevent the rescue of Mick by a crowd of Greyfriars. (GBC 34).

BARGAIN FOR BUNTER. (Title HBE Volume 26). Bunter bought Mauly's bicycle after it had been stolen, amid the usual Bunterian wheeling and dealing! If any good could be said to have come out of this, it is that at least on this occasion crime did not pay!

BARKER, Mr. The mate in M.V. Fanny Jones. (964).

BARKER the BOOKIE. A theatrical part created by Wibley for a Remove Dramatic Society production. Later he modified the part to become Mr Bagshot, (cf). (1067).

BARLEY MOW INN, Little Puddleford. Visited by "The Greyfriars Hikers" while on a walking tour one summer holidays. On their arrival they discovered that it was the headquarters for a Tithe War. (1333).

BARNES. The Head's chauffeur, previously a junior lieutenant under Colonel Wharton's command. His real name was Arthur Poynings who, after serving a prison sentence for forging a cheque, entered service under an assumed name. Better known as "The Courtfield Cracksman", he used his position of trust to commit many daring robberies. He was eventually caught by Inspector Steele of Scotland Yard posing as a school master. (HBE 5; 4a).

BARNEY the BINGER. Skip the pickpocket's captor. Recognised by Miss Bullivant as Saul Crake, he was taken into custody on kidnapping and other charges. (HBE 62-63).

BARNEY HAYES. Lieutenant to Nosey Clark, he was the driver and strong man of the gang. He helped kidnap Harry Wharton. He is easily distinguished by his red hair, and moustache, (until he shaved it off!). He was finally captured by Inspector Grimes on information received from Vernon Smith. (GBC 9).

BARR. A one time member of Bulstrode's group of snobs and bullies, he was one of the crowd who bullied Linley on his arrival. (45).

BARRENGRO. One of the gipsies who kidnapped Marjorie Hazeldene on her first visit to Greyfriars. Harry Wharton was breaking bounds when he helped release her and capture the gipsies. The fact that he owned up to being out of bounds helped establish him in Mr Quelch's good books. After escaping from prison, Barrengro refused to gain revenge on Wharton, unlike his partner in crime, Melchior. (GBC 3).

BATES. A lesser light of the Upper Fourth, and a member of the Debating Society. (9).

BATES. The butler at Hogben Grange. (1215).

BATES. In league with the butler Pawson to rob Gadsby Croft. The blame was to be laid upon Harry Wharton and Co. The plan was frustrated by Vernon Smith falling out with Ponsonby and his friends, and so over-hearing the plot. (1339).

BATES, Joe. A fisherman and neighbour of Tom Redwing at Hawkscliff. (922).

BATESON. Johnny Bull's cousin. A Cambridge Rugby Blue who coached the Remove when they took the game up for a time as an alternative to football. However, the craze did not last long, and they soon returned to the school's main winter game - association football. (730).

BAYFORD CASTLE, R.M.S. A passenger liner of the Royal Mail Line travelled on by Bunter and the Famous Five on their return journey from Brazil. At the same time Putnam van Duck was a stowaway on board. (1468).

BAZAAR, Friardale. An annual event held in the Assembly Rooms, Friardale, in aid of the church funds. Several stalls are run by Greyfriars and Cliff House. On one occasion, Vernon Smith used the event to try to put Harry Wharton's nose out of joint. Successfully! (248).

BEAKY BILL. A local ruffian whose attempt to rob Coker with two accomplices was frustrated by Alonzo Todd, of all people - thanks to Professor Sparkinson's Elixir. (1345).

BEAN, Sandy. Hereditary piper to the McDiarmids, he farmed a croft on the Lochmuir estate. It transpired that he was the Wraith of Lochmuir in a pathetic and forlorn attempt to drive out interlopers and clear the way for the return of the Lairds. (GBC 34).

BEDE, The Venerable. The Saxon monk who wrote a History of England. He is said to be the author of some of the Manuscripts in the library at Cavandale Abbey. (1194).

BEECH HOUSE, Surrey. The country house of Sylvester Sugden, two hours by road from Greyfriars. Harry Wharton was held prisoner here, lest he reveal the identity of the crook known as the Wizard. (1219).

BEECHWOOD SCHOOL. The foreign academy run by Herr Rosenblaum which closed after going bankrupt. After this, Hurree Singh joined Greyfriars, and Herr Rosenblaum became the German Master. After a time he reopened his school next door to Greyfriars, (just through the cloisters). However, this proved too troublesome due to perpetual fighting between the schools, so that eventually Herr Rosenblaum was forced to move and open elsewhere; thanks to financial help from Dr Locke. (6).

BEGGAR of SHANTUNG. The disguise effected by Ferrers Locke when he was trying to help the Friars escape from Tang Wang. (1184).

BELCHER, Tom. A professional boxer of great fame. He befriended the Remove football team after they had been given 10,000 lines each by Loder for snowballing him and then playing football instead of doing the lines. Belcher beat Loder in a fight, the stakes in which were the Removites impots. Bob Cherry challenged Tom to a fight and managed a more than honourable draw in the Courtfield Assembly Rooms. (414).

BELKNAP, Professor. A supposed member of the Archaeological Association who was exposed in his true lights as Chick Chew thanks to Coker's inability to kick a football straight. (1478).

BELL, Paula. The leading lady of the Little Red Riding Hood Pantomime company giving a Christmas show in the Theatre Royal, Lantham. A close friend of George Wingate's, (he was in love with her), he was, for a time, distracted from keeping up his usual high standards as Head of School. (200).

BEN MOHAMMED, Mustapha. Pretender to the rulership of the tribes of the Oued Tahar, (whose rightful hereditary leader was Ali ben Yusef). However, thanks to Major Cherry and the Famous Five, he was prevented from obtaining the regalia of the tribe, (The Eye of Ahmed). (GBC 8).

BEN YUSEF, Ali. After his father's assassination he should have succeeded him as leader of his tribe. However, ben Mohammed had seized power and tried to dispose of Ali. Major Cherry, an old friend of his father, sent him to Greyfriars in an effort to protect him. Ben Mohammed tried to rule during Ali's minority but lacked the insignia of power, (the Eye of Ahmed). Captured from Greyfriars by Bou Saoud, Ali was taken to Africa. Under Major Cherry's command the Famous Five, and Bunter!, effected his release, as well as that of Marjorie Hazeldene and Clara Trevlyn. The last two had been taken to try to force Ali to yield his position. After putting down the insurrection Ali ruled as Sheik of his tribe. (GBC 8).

BENJAMIN, Uncle. Benjamin Todd, Esq. Uncle to the cousins Alonzo and Peter Todd. (See Todd, Benjamin).

BENSON. "The youngest and one of the cheekiest boys in the Remove". At least, during the time he was at Greyfriars. (46).

BENSON. A boatman living in Pegg. His boat is available for hire for trips up the river and along the coast. A friend to Harry Wharton and Co., his boat was stolen by a bank robber during the time that the Remove were "barred out" on Popper's Island. Inadvertently, Harry Wharton foiled the thief's escape by "hitching" a lift, not realising that Benson was not driving the boat, but instead was being used for a bank raid. After the robbery, Wharton recognised the man responsible and, taking the boat, made easier his capture by the police. (1380).

BENSON'S BOOTSHOP, Courtfield. Patronised by Bob Cherry on one occasion. It seems strange that he did not give his custom to Penfold's father, the cobbler in Friardale. (1275).

BENTLEY. A lesser light of the Sixth, and its debating society. (50).

BEPPO. Count Zero's chauffeur and confederate in the failed attempt to prevent Mr Vernon Smith purchasing Polgarth. (1453).

BEPPO. A Roman Bravo and member of a gang who tried to take Wun Lung captive on behalf of Mr O. (1543).

BHANIPUR. A country in the foothills of the Himalayas. It is the home of Hurree Singh. His uncle, the Jam Bahadur, rules the country as Regent during Hurree Singh's minority. An inaccessible spot only reached after a long and arduous journey, firstly by rail to Rawalpindi, and then by car to the bottom of the mountains; after this it is necessary to travel by elephant or horse. Being on the North-West Frontier, it is a good place for the Russians to support a revolution in order to gain a foothold in Asia.

BHANIPUR, Nabob of. The title of Hurree Jamset Ram Singh. (See Singh, Hurree).

BIDDULPH, Mrs. A widow who was employed as a resident nurse by Dr Pillbury on long and difficult cases, such as that of Mr Harrington. (807).

BIG BANG AT GREYFRIARS, THE. (Title HBE Volume 62). When Skip the Pickpocket came to Coker's aid, he little realised the implications. Taken from his East End roots, and thrust into the Remove at Greyfriars, he found himself "up against" Vernon Smith.

BIG SIDE. Although represented as First Team pitches for both cricket and football, it is obvious that they are in fact separate playing areas adjoining each other, called collectively Big Side.

BILL. A local petty thief and poacher who was the accomplice of Judson in the theft of the Moonstone from Popper Court, (1157). He was jailed by Sir Hilton Popper for poaching, (possibly in the preserves of Popper Court itself!). (1309).

BILL the BOOKIE. A play written by Wibley which gave the Famous Five the idea of how to mete out rough justice to Ponsonby and Co. after they had "sacked" Loder and used the Famous Fives' names to mislead the prefect. (See Huggins). (1587).

BILLIONAIRING WITH BUNTER. (Title HBE Volume 64). Thanks to the machinations of Jarvish who gave his entire, (non-existant!), fortune to Bunter, the Famous Five enjoyed a European holiday pursued by Tiger Bronx who had, himself, been excluded from his uncle Shook's will. The money eventually was discovered to have been left to an animals home !

BILLO, Professor. Bunter's stage name when performing a ventriloquial act in Muccolini's Circus. (1488).

BILLY BUNTER AND THE COURTFIELD CRACKSMAN. (Title HBE Volume 5). The country had been baffled by a series of daring and well executed robberies - the perpetrator leaving not a clue. It was not until the Head seemed always to have had an appointment in the area where a crime had been committed that Inspector Irons of Scotland Yard finally got the breakthrough to help him solve the case.

BILLY BUNTER AND THE TERROR OF THE FORM. (Title HBE Volume 4). Flip, while running away from his criminal past, encountered Bunter who persuaded Mauleverer to pay Flip's fees at Greyfriars. During Mr Quelch's absence with a chest infection caused by Bunter, Flip recognised the locum master as a previous associate and, as a result, was kidnapped to prevent his exposure. However, he was rescued by Bunter and, finding his father, he left Greyfriars to return to the home he did not recall.

BILLY BUNTER GETS THE BOOT. (Title GL Volume 1). Eggspelled (sic), for ventriloquial tricks, Bunter refused to leave the school. He stayed and formed a one man picket line outside the gates until eventually the sentence was rescinded.

BILLY BUNTER IN BRAZIL. (Title HBE Volume 44). With their share of the Polpelly Treasure the Famous Five and Bunter visited their old friend Jim Valentine on his uncle's estate in Brazil. Despite their being hounded by O Lobo, they helped Peter Valentine find his "treasure", a small but valuable cache of diamonds.

BILLY BUNTER IN CHINA. (Title HBE Volume 25). When Wun Lung's life was endangered by the Red Dragon Tong, he was escorted to the safety of his own home by Ferrers Locke and the Famous Five. (Bunter too!). The journey was fraught with hazards as Tang Wang made successive attacks on the Greyfriars party to try to make Wun Lung's father espouse his cause as pretender to the Emperor's Jade Throne. Finally, however, the threat was lifted and both Wun and the rest of the party returned in safety to England.

BILLY BUNTER IN THE LAND OF THE PYRAMIDS. (Title HBE Volume 1). Mauleverer invited the Famous Five to spend the holidays in Egypt. Bunter tagged along as usual! Kalizelos, a Greek antique dealer, tried many ways of stealing an ancient relic, the Golden Scarabeus of A-Menah. After he had been finally bested, he revealed that the scarab contained a massive diamond, known as the Eye of Osiris.

BILLY BUNTER OF BUNTER COURT. (Title HBE Volume 3). All the unbelieved boasts seemed to be true when Bunter took a party to his country house. With a total disregard as to cost, or the law of the land, Bunter was intent on giving his guests a good time. Until the exposure of the extent of the fraud, that is exactly what both the Friars and Saints in the party did!

BILLY BUNTER'S BANKNOTE. (Title HBE Volume 53). After an armed robbery at the Courtfield and County Bank, the proceeds, £7000, were hidden in the chimney of Study No 1 in the Remove passage. Carne discovered the loot and gave £50 to Joe Banks in settlement of a gambling debt. Banks threw the note away, suspecting it's origins. Bunter found it and boasted about the possession of a £50 note. This eventually led to the apprehension of the crooks.

BILLY BUNTER'S BLUNDER. (Title HBE Volume 76). Relates a series of unconnected incidents in the annals of the old school. ie. The robbing of the school by "Dick Chester"; Ponsonby and Co.'s feud against Linley - his expulsion and return; Bunter feuding with Harry Wharton with the aid of ventriloquism; Wibley coming to Greyfriars as Mr Mitchell; and Coker going speedway riding.

BILLY BUNTER'S CHRISTMAS. (Title HBE Volume 22). Persuading Lord Cavandale of his great courage, Bunter invited himself to stay at Cavandale Abbey for Christmas. (He then invited the Famous Five). Thanks to this, the several attempts on the Earl's life were foiled, and his race horse, Black Prince, was not withdrawn, as would otherwise have happened, from the Lantham 1,000 guineas race.

BILLY BUNTER'S CIRCUS. (Title HBE Volume 28). Escaping from detention and running away from school led Bunter into trouble. As usual Bunter made things worse when he persuaded the circus folk that he was Mr Whiffles, the proprietor, by wearing his wig and clothes that he had discovered by the banks of the river while Whiffles was taking a bathe. It transpired that Whiffles was being sought by one Huggins in revenge for the sack, and so the masquerade went on with the Famous Five being used as bodyguards. Bunter inevitably gave himself away, and was rewarded with the Order of the Boot Extraordinary!

BILLY BUNTER'S CONVICT. (Title HBE Volume 70). Convinced that Mr Gilmore was an escaped convict, Bunter caused quite a stir in the school! When the temporary master did not punish flagrant breaches of school rules it seemed strange. Then it came out that the convict was Mr Gilmore's half brother, and identical in appearance. Soon after this, Bunter bought a "new" bike from Mr Jobson. As it had been stolen from de Courcy, Ponsonby and Co. lost no time in accusing Bunter of the theft. However, the Caterpillar managed to outwit Pon. in quick time.

BILLY BUNTER'S CORONATON PARTY. (Title HBE Volume 40). Boasting that Lord Trant was his friend and had invited him for the Coronation, Bunter trapped the Famous Five into going up to London, only to discover that Lord Trant did indeed look upon Bunter as a friend, having been saved from the attack of a footpad by Bunter.

BILLY BUNTER'S EASTER TRIP. (Title HBE Volume 50) . After Jack Drake had solved the case of "The Mystery Man of Greyfriars", Vernon Smith fell out with the Famous Five and then Bunter. He had spoofed the Head with Bunter's aid. In revenge he invited them to stay with him at Blackrock Castle. Nothing loathe, they accepted, and were not amused to discover it was a ruin ! Marooned on Blackrock Island, they found themselves embroiled with Mr Rance, a dishonest Estate Agent, who kidnapped Mr Vernon Smith and Smithy to cover up his dealings. They were eventually freed by the Friars with Tom Redwing's help.

BILLY BUNTER'S HAIR RAID. (Title HBE Volume 41) . Discovering that Wibley had been given the job of impersonating Sir William Bird, Bunter invited himself and the Famous Five for the Easter holidays. Sir William had an important job involving state security, but the plan almost went wrong since Soames knew of the imposture which, but for the intervention of the Famous Five, could have well gone wrong.

BILLY BUNTER'S HAT TRICK. (Title HBE Volume 31) . Mr Vernon Smith lost a £100 note on the common near the school which was found by Hinks who hid it in the lining of the boater that Bunter was wearing while taking a snooze in the shade. This led to many misunderstandings as Hinks tried to find the correct boater in which the note had been hidden. Before his arrest, Hinks managed to destroy several hats – leading to a large bill for Billy at the school costumiers !

BILLY BUNTER'S LUCKY DAY. (Title HBE Volume 37) . Bunter took Mr Quelch's watch chain for a "lark". Unfortunately, Ponsonby obtained the chain and tried to frame Courteney for the theft. However, Bunter had seen Ponsonby's trickery and hid an imitation chain where Pon. had hidden the real one. Once discovered all was well.

BILLY BUNTER'S PRIZE. (Title HBE Volume 74) . Relates a series of unrelated incidents at Greyfriars: Mr Capper being arrested for theft; Fish searching for stolen plunder; Bunter trying to spend £500 he found at the station; and then trying to win a prize competition with part of Mr Quelch's History of Greyfriars.

BILLY BUNTER'S REBELLION. (Title GL Volume 4) . See The Persecution of Billy Bunter.

BILLY BUNTER'S TRAMP. (Title GL Volume 3) . The Famous Five rescued Ragged Dick from Pedlar Parker – a cruel lout. Sir Henry Compton found the waif and decided to adopt him as his grandson, to prevent Roger Compton, his spendthrift cousin, inheriting and disposing of the estates. Ragged Dick was sent to Greyfriars and, recognised by Bunter, blackmailed by him. Roger Compton's efforts to expose Dick were dashed when he discovered to Sir Henry's amazement that Dick really was a nephew: the son of his disowned brother.

BILLY JINKS. One of the "army" employed by Mr Carnforth to try to put down the Sixth Form rebellion during his short and disastrous headmastership. (GBC 36).

BINKS, George, The trapeze artiste in Swinger's Circus. (1160).

BIRD, Sir William. Uncle to Loder. The latter was furious to discover that Bunter and the Famous Five had been invited to stay for the holidays. What Loder did not know was that his uncle was in fact absent on a top secret mission, and that his place had been taken by Wibley! (HBE 41).

BIRD in HAND. A small and disreputable public house on the edge of Friardale sometimes frequented by Loder. (797).

BISHOP, Ron. A professional speedway rider with Lantham Speedway. (1220).

BITER. Mr Jenks' mastiff. (1187).

BITER. A professional burglar, expert in opening locked doors. He was employed by Jimmy the Fox when the latter was trying to kidnap Jack Drake. (1419).

BLACK, Mr Henry. The mathematics Master appointed in Mr Lascelles place after he had gone on active service. He turned out to be the man guilty of the crime for which Carne's father had been imprisoned. After Mr Carne had escaped from gaol, Black died helping the authorities search for the convict. (428).

BLACK BULL, Lantham. The Inn where Micky the Spratt and Skid stayed before robbing Popper Court. (1331).

BLACK EDGAR. See Ravenspur, Edgar.

BLACK GEORGE. A poacher in the Wimford area. He was caught by Harry Wharton and Co. after he had assaulted Wun Lung. (47).

BLACK MONK. See Anfrith.

BLACK PETE. See Bruce, Peter.

BLACK PIKE. A name used locally for the Pike. (46).

BLACK POINT. The promontory at the tip of the Pike.

BLACK PRINCE. Lord Cavandale's most famous race horse. In order to try to prevent it, (the favourite), running in the Lantham 1,000 guineas, several attempts were made on Lord Cavandale's life. (HBE 22).

BLACK ROCK CAVE, Polpelly. A large sea cave in Polpelly Bay. Through it smugglers could land their cargos hidden from excisemen. More recently, Count Zero used the secret passage from the cave to the house as a means of ingress in his search for the Polpelly treasure. (HBE 39).

BLACK ROCK ISLAND. A small rocky islet to the east of Black Point. The schooner Castille ran aground here and was discovered by Bunter and the Famous Five. (1077).

BLACK SHEEP OF GREYFRIARS. (Title HBE Volume 17). After Harry Wharton's identical cousin had been shown up in his true lights to the Remove, it still took a long time for the staff to learn the facts. But for Fish's blackmailing of Stacey being overheard by Mr Quelch, the truth might not have been revealed.

BLACKLEY'S STORES. A famous London department store whose label was used to disguise a bomb sent to Wun Lung hidden in a game of Mah Jongg. (1177).

BLACKMOOR PRISON. On the edge of Blackmoor, Devon, it lies half a mile from Hilton Hall. From this high security prison, Convict 33 escaped and terrified the Hilton's Christmas party. (1401). Later the wrongly sentenced Convict 22 also escaped from here. (1494).

BLACKMOOR PRISON. It seems most probably a typographical error, but Mr Carne was reported as having escaped from a prison of this name within a mile or so of Greyfriars. Most likely it was Wapshot Camp, which at one time was used for the internment of aliens; and, therefore, was likely used also as a prison. (428). George Waring escaped from a prison of this name in Surrey. It seems strange that there should be three institutions of the same name, but the evidence for two is overwhelming, since there is also the prison of the same name in Devon.

BLACKPOOL. The North of England's famous playground. It was visited by a large Greyfriars party one August Bank Holiday. Apart from one or two excesses indulged in by Vernon Smith and Bolsover, the excitement of the day was when Mossoo was recognised performing on the sands as a Pierrot! (234)

BLACKROCK CASTLE. A ruin in a poor state of repair on the island of Blackrock. It was to the castle that Smithy had invited Bunter and the Famous Five. (1626).

BLACKROCK ISLAND, Devon. Lying on the north coast of Devon, facing the Atlantic, about one mile from the mainland, the island was an ideal staging post for drug smuggling, until Mr Vernon Smith went to Devon to purchase land and inadvertently was instrumental in exposing the criminals. (HBE 50).

BLACKWOOD. A small country station on a loop line between Lantham and Redclyffe. It is only served by slow local trains. (947).

BLADES. At Highcliffe, where he is in the Fourth Form. On the whole a colourless youth who tends towards Ponsonby's group, rather than Courteney's. (571).

BLAGDEN, Mr Philip. He had been Captain of cricket at Greyfriars, but had been expelled for "wild and reckless conduct". After serving a prison sentence, he returned to the school and persuaded Dr Locke to give him a job as a cricket coach. In fact he was searching for the Greyfriars treasure. He was caught in possession of the stolen key to the vaults and assaulted Mr Quelch. Overpowered by the Famous Five, he was soon under arrest. (854).

BLAKE, Jack. A member of the Fourth Form at St Jim's.

BLAKE, Jad. A compulsive gambler who was forced to sell his ranch, the Circle O, which bordered onto Mr Vernon Smith's ranch, the Kicking Cayuse, in order to pay his debts. He tried, unsuccessfully, to "feather his nest" by a robbery committed while impersonating the Rio Kid, and was taken prisoner through the efforts of Vernon Smith. (HBE 32).

BLAND, Ernest. In the Fifth Form at Greyfriars, he is one of Blundell's closest friends, and is vice-captain of the form teams.

BLANE. A lesser light of the Upper Fourth. (10).

BLITZ, Herr. A German passenger on board the R.M.S. Comet in which Bunter and the Famous Five went to Brazil. Luckily for Harry Wharton, he was also riding up the Peak at Teneriffe, when O Lobo made an attempt on Wharton's life. (1462).

BLOGG, Jimmy. The Friardale butcher's boy. When Alonzo Todd was conducting a mission, he followed Blogg to preach his text. The butcher's boy, always ready for a fight, squared up to his pacifist opponent – and in the process lost the order he was delivering! (137).

BLOOMFIELD, Mr G. (Alias Herman Blumenfeld). He used to keep the music shop in Courtfield, and was the organist at the Free Church. He was also, for a time, the music master at Greyfriars after Mr Sharp had been called up. Although born British, he had retained his ties with Prussia, and tried to persuade Herr Gans to spy on behalf of Germany. This he refused to do, and was taken prisoner by Blumenfeld, to try to keep the latter's secret. (525).

BLUMP. The butler at Eastcliff Lodge. (HBE 41).

BLUNDELL, George. Head of the Fifth Form at Greyfriars, and Captain of the Form teams. He is also a "Blood". Despite not being over intellectually endowed, he is a firm favourite with his Form Master, Mr Prout. He shares study No 1 with Bland, his closest friend.

BLYTHE, Billy. The manager of the First Division football team of Tyneside Rovers. When they were in Kent, Dick Trumper tried to arrange a fixture with them. However, Wibley and the Remove tricked the Courtfieldians into playing against Greyfriars disguised as Rovers! (918).

BOA VISTA. The home of Senhor Caminho. It is a timber estate in Kenya, and was visited by Mr Vernon Smith and his party when "on safari". (1230).

BOA VISTA. The "fazenda" or estate belonging to Mr Peter Valentine. It lies in the Brazilian jungle, at least 100 miles from the nearest rail depot, and is accessible only by river. (HBE 44).

BOATMANS COTTAGE. Is about a quarter of a mile from the bridge over the stream in Friardale Woods, on the bank of the Sark. Loder, in one of his pogroms against Harry Wharton, fell into the stream and, after being hauled out of the water by Wharton, dried out in the cottage. (1295).

BOB CHERRY - SWOT. (Title GBC Volume 29). Major Cherry suddenly decided that Bob needed to show more academic acumen - an almost impossible request! However, the fiat went forth - win the Head's Latin Prize or leave Greyfriars. At the cost of losing all his friends and giving up his beloved games, Bob buckled down. The day before the exam he fought Ponsonby and Co. who had tied up Hurree Singh. As a result, his paper was a fiasco. Faced with expulsion, it took Hurree Singh all his persuasive powers to convince the major of the truth. Following this, Coker disappeared from school; abducted by Mr Poynings to prevent him going home for Christmas. Found and freed by the Famous Five, they spent the holidays at Holly House, exposing the blackmailing secretary who had for so long made Mr Henry Coker's life a misery.

BOB CHERRY'S BIG BARGAIN. (Title HBE Volume 36) . The Famous Five and Bunter set off on a walking tour helped, as Bob Cherry insisted, (hindered according to the rest of the party), by Bob's Big Bargain – an ancient Dionysius motor tricycle. Not only did they have trouble with the trike, but they were chased, harried and the trike stolen several times by Bill Harris and Alf Snooks, because a part of the trike was made of platinum.

BOGGS, William. Is well known to all Friars, past and present. He has been around Greyfriars as long as Gosling and that seems nearly as long as the buildings! He is the village postman who can be persuaded, on occasions, to turn a blind eye, not only to school rules, but also Post Office regulations.

BOKER. The pageboy at Cliff House School. (1528) .

BOLSOVER, Herbert, (Minor) . After a childhood spent in the slums of London, he came to Greyfriars. At first rejected by his brother, they soon became good friends – although, in true school tradition, major has little to do with minor during term. He is in the Third Form and is among its leaders.

BOLSOVER, Percival, (Major) . At one time an inveterate bully who tried to lead the form by strong arm methods. However, after he had been beaten in a boxing match, he calmed down to a great extent, although he is still somewhat inclined to be aggressive. He shares Study No 10 in the Remove with Napoleon Dupont, his one true friend – whom he protects from bullying! A keen games player, but of the rush and barge type, he is not usually selected for the form teams.

BOLSOVER COLLEGE. A school some distance from Greyfriars. They played two matches against each other. At first they did not realise that their footballs were of different shapes! (104) .

BOLTON, Oliver. A member of the Third Form who fancies himself as being of importance although, by comparison with Paget and Tubb, he does not shine in form matters. (1034) .

BOMOMBO, Prince of Bongoland. One of Wibley's many creations for the Remove Dramatic Society. On this occasion, Bunter took over the role and duped the school as to his true identity, while the real Bunter was "missing", trying to avoid trouble. For once, he actually was not guilty of the offence whereof he was charged! (1654) .

BOMOO. Mr McTab's chief Kanaka houseboy. (1590) .

BONIFACE, Abbot. The dispossessed Abbot of Cavandale at the time of the dissolution of the monasteries. Legend has it that his ghost reveals itself to all the earls immediately prior to their deaths. (1192).

BONITO. A macaw which befriended Bunter, or perhaps his sweetmeats! He was a wonderful mimic, and this talent led Valentine and the Famous Five to the rescue of Bunter after he had been captured by O Lobo. (1466).

BOONE. The trainer of Lord Cavandale's race horses. (1191).

BOSANGO. The Captain of Tofoloko's palace guards. (1235).

BOSANNEY, Mr Jonas. He used to be the late Earl of Portercliffe's private secretary before being discharged. When Mr Fish rented Portercliffe Hall he managed to persuade Mr Fish to employ him as his secretary, so that he could prosecute his own search for the late Earl's treasure. (HBE 34).

BOSS-EYE. One of the Lambury Pet's army hired by Mr Carnforth to put down the Sixth Form rebellion. (745).

BOU SAOUD. Son of Mustapha ben Mohammed and Lieutenant of Spahis. At his father's command he made several attempts upon Ali's life while the latter was at Greyfriars. Finally he captured Ali and took him back to Africa. Even while Major Cherry and party were on their way to Algeria, Bou Saoud kept up his work of trying to prevent the major aiding Ali. In his turn, Major Cherry was captured, as were Marjorie Hazeldene and Clara Trevlyn. Bou Saoud finally met his death in a fight with the Famous Five. (GBC 8).

BOUNDER, The. Nickname given soon after his arrival at Greyfriars to Vernon Smith.

BOUNDER OF GREYFRIARS, THE. (Title GBC Volume 18). Vernon Smith arrived at school and immediately gave warning that he held no brief for authority. Not only late in his arrival, he was also drunk! After a decidedly inauspicious start to school life, Vernon Smith took the Famous Four, (No Johnny Bull in those early days), as well as Wibley and Hazeldene on holiday to Switzerland. The following term was further brightened by the arrival of Alonzo Todd!

BOUNDER'S FEUD, THE. (Title GBC Volume 38). Kicked out of the team for blagging and refusing to reform, Vernon Smith's place was given to Tom Redwing. Furious at his best friend bagging his place, Vernon Smith stranded Redwing at Ashwood and played in the ensuing match, winning it for the Remove. A form trial brought out the facts, despite Redwing trying to keep them hidden. Vernon Smith tried to form a rival team but failed. Soon after this, the breach was healed.

BOUNDER'S REBELLION, THE. (Title HBE Volume 51) . See Teggers, Lucius.

BOWDSLEY, Lancashire. The home town of the Linley family.

BOWLINE, Sam. A near neighbour and friend to the Redwings at Hawkscliff. (1088) .

BOXER OF GREYFRIARS, THE. (Title GBC Volume 15). Richard Drury is a professional boxer. At one time he was at Greyfriars, thanks to his having helped Dr Locke. Even then, his size and weight meant that he could out-box any man at Greyfriars. This led to his becoming swollen headed, as a result of which he was shunned by the rest of the form. Unfortunately, he chose Hilton as an idol who was soon cast down, so disillusioning Drury, that he left school to return to the ring.

BRAITHWAYTE, Sir Henry. Uncle to Mauleverer, and one of his trustees, he has occasional charge of his nephew's affairs when Sir Reginald Brooke, (his brother-in-law), is absent.

BRANDER, Meyer. Of all the staff who ever were at Greyfriars, this man has to have been one of the most unpopular. A brutal and harsh man, who thought himself a just and fair disciplinarian, he turned a blind eye to the fact that his nephew had attacked Dr Locke in order to secure Brander's appointment as Head. (See Tyrant of Greyfriars) .

BRANDRETH, Arthur. Although only at Greyfriars for a short time, he was a popular member of the Remove after an initial division in the form as to whether his father was in fact a criminal. His generosity to Snoop, (who had been his chief adversary), after receiving "the knock", assured him of a good reception in the school. (288) .

BRANDRETH, Mr John. Wrongly accused of forgery and embezzlement, he was a fugitive from justice, hiding in a cottage in Pegg Lane, at the time his son came to Greyfriars. He was arrested after Snoop had informed the police, but his innocence was proved after the real culprit had confessed. (288) .

BRANDY FACE. The only "gentleman" known to Flip before meeting Bunter. A scholar who had taught Flip his letters, he never revealed his true name. (1247) .

BRASS POT. A waiter at the Marina in Lagos. (770) .

BRENT, John. Inspector of Scotland Yard. He was a dour, hard, embittered man, whose only son had been taken by Jimmy the One. Coincidentally, his tracking down and capturing the crook, also led to his finding his son. (1253)

BRETT, Mrs. Sub-postmistress at Friardale.

BRIGGS, Gunner. Has a long record of armed robbery and grievous bodily harm. Inadvertently, he gave Harry Wharton a lift from Popper Island to Courtfield, when he was on his way to rob the bank ! After the bank raid, he hid on the island prior to his being captured by the Remove. (1380-1381).

BRIGHT, Egdar. He was sent to Greyfriars by his father to search for the will of the late Mr Thorpe, who had been a master at the school. In it he had left a considerable fortune to the Levison family. By finding and destroying the later testament, Bright's father could keep the money left him by an earlier document. A son with a suspended court sentence for cruelty to animals was a suitably hardened character not to mind doing what was required of him. He was finally found out and expelled. (GBC 26).

BRIGHT, Mr Esau. A solicitor in Lantham, no longer in legal practice, (one wonders whether he had not been disbarred), but instead conducting a business purporting to deal in Real Estate and Mortgages. (A thinly veiled term for a loan shark). He had blackmailed Sir Hilton Popper to place his son at Greyfriars in direct opposition to the Headmaster's decision, in order that Edgar might find and destroy Mr Thorpe's last will. (GBC 26).

BRONX, Tiger. The nephew of Mr Shook and, as he thought, the real heir to his millions. To gain which he pursued Jarvish, and later Bunter, around Europe. Completely unscrupulous, (after all he was a Chicago ganster!), he was prepared to go to any lengths to obtain the fortune, only to disover at the end that it had been left to an animals home ! (HBE 64).

BROOKE, Lady. Wife to Sir Reginald Brooke, and aunt to Mauleverer. (1245).

BROOKE, Sir Reginald, Bart., O.F., Governor Greyfriars School. He is uncle and guardian to Mauleverer, as well as one of the trustees of his estate. Kindly and generous, he has on several occasions taken parties of Greyfriars men on holiday.

BROWN. (Alias Braun). A German spy whose mission was to obtain information on the secret work being carried out by Sir William Bird. He was also the paymaster of the spy ring. Soames disabled him and stole the money Brown was carrying, after which Harry Wharton and Co. effected his capture, which in turn led to the closing down of the spy network. (HBE 41).

BROWN. The foreman builder who directed the demolition of the hunting lodge at Ravenspur Grange in the search for a secret passage. The builders found both the passage and the Famous Five who had been trapped in it. (1124).

BROWN. Taxi driver from Reigate. Bunter, tired with the delights of Bunter Court, took Mr Brown's taxi from Reigate to Wharton Lodge and then, finding that Harry Wharton was staying with Mauleverer, hired the taxi to go on to Hampshire. He then did one of his disappearing tricks, leaving his host designate to pay the bill. The not inconsiderable sum of £11. (1244).

BROWN, Dr. Medical practitioner of Combermere who looked after Mr Pilkins, the Estate Agent, after he had been injured in a car crash on the way to show Bunter, whom he thought to be Lord Mauleverer, Combermere Place. (911).

BROWN, Mr. See Gentleman Pincher. (1264).

BROWN, George. A cottager living in Friardale Lane. While Mr Coote, the carrier, was making a delivery here, Edgar Caffyn catapaulted the carrier's horse, making it bolt. (1408).

BROWN, Farmer John. At their first camp site the Greyfriars Hikers were "done" twice. When the real farmer, (Mr Brown), came on the scene, he got a very unfriendly reception! (1332).

BROWN, Richard, (Dicky). At Courtfield School, he is a friend of Solly Lazarus.

BROWN, Tom. A New Zealander from Taranaki. He shares Study No 2 with Bulstrode and Hazeldene, with whom he has little in common. A good all rounder at games, and a quiet studious type, he is popular with the majority of the form. His chief hobby is that of a radio ham.

BROWN'S GARAGE, Friardale. Smaller than the Courtfield Garage, it is patronised occasionally by Greyfriars men.

BRUCE, Peter. Otherwise known as Black Peter, he was Tom Redwing's uncle, and made a fortune "blackbirding", (or kidnapping entire populations of islands to sell into slavery). He was killed by Silvio Xero in a beach brawl in the South Seas. He had hidden his treasure, and left a map showing the whereabouts of the treasure which he gave to Ben Dance to take to Tom Redwing in England. (1017).

BRUTUS. One of Marco the lion tamer's pride of lions in Muccolini's Circus. (1483).

BRUTUS. Colonel Bullock's bulldog. (1644).

BUBU. Prime minister to Tofoloko, king of the Moteli. He spoke English after a fashion, having worked on the boats out of West Africa. After the Greyfriars party overpowered the king, he escaped from the village with them, rather than face the king's rage. (1235).

BUCK, William, (Buckskin Bill). The chief cowhand on the Kicking Cayuse Ranch in Texas. He was sent to England to meet Mr Vernon Smith with details of the ranch, and when Mr Vernon Smith decided that Smithy and a party of Greyfriars men should go to Texas, Bill escorted them. Described by Mr Vernon Smith as an honest, simple man, he was not "in" with Barney Stone's cattle rustling schemes. And after the latter had been exposed and caught, he was made foreman in the latter's place. (HBE 31–32).

BULKELEY, George. Head of School and Captain of Games at Rookwood School.

BULL, Miss. Aunt to Johnny Bull, she looks on him as her favourite and is always ready with a sizeable tip or supply of tuck in the form of excellent home made cakes. A spinster, she lives in the Home Counties, within easy reach of Reading. (810).

BULL, Mr. Father of Johnny. Majority shareholder in Bull Ltd. He lives at Moor Fell, Yorkshire.

BULL, Mrs. Mother of Johnny Bull.

BULL, Johnny. The last to arrive of the Famous Five, he hails from Yorkshire. His father owns a large mill, Bull & Co., which Johnny is expected, and expects, to take over some day. Mediocre in class, he is a good all round sportsman. He is frequently stubborn to the point of pig-headedness, full of the knowledge of his own rightness. This stems from honesty, rather than anything else. Although this leads to arguments within the Famous Five, they naturally present a united front to the world, and often "bump" him for being right, and especially when he delights in saying that he "told them so"! The same honesty means that he does not suffer fools or wrong doers gladly, and he is not slow to say so, although he rarely speaks without measuring his words, and never uses two where one would do.

BULL, Lucas. Some years older than Johnny, he is his first cousin, and manager of the works at Bull Ltd. A true Yorkshireman, he is about as stubborn, pigheaded and right as Johnny! The two of them were at daggers drawn until, one holiday, when Lucas was placed in loco parentis to Johnny, they each came to realise the others worth, and are now firm friends. (1491).

BULL LIMITED. The textile mill belonging to Mr Bull, Johnny's father. It produces high quality yarns and woollens. (1491).

BULLIVANT, Miss Amelia. Deputy headmistress at Cliff House School, and mistress in charge of the mathematics department. An austere lady, she hides a warm heart under a cold, forbidding exterior. Before coming to Cliff House, she taught at Ridings School, Brighton, and brought up her younger brother, Richard, until he was taken by a man called Crake.

BULLIVANT, J. At Oakshott School, Essex. Stephen Price had a feud against Jim Warren and, in order to prove that Warren was an imposter, Price brought Bullivant down to Greyfriars to see a First Eleven match. However, Warren had been "crocked", and did not play. Bullivant took this as another example of Warren's behaviour, which, at Oakshott, was not of the best. Nor did he play in the First Eleven at his previous school. (1444-1445).

BULLIVANT, Richard, (Dicky). See Skip.

BULLOCK, Colonel. Lives at Bullock Court, up river from Old Windsor Lock on the Thames. The Famous Five and Bunter had planned to camp on his meadow, but the Colonel turned them off. When Ponsonby and Co. raided the erstwhile camp site, they were chased off at some cost to Pon.'s trousers by the colonel's mastiff, Brutus. (1644).

BULLY OF GREYFRIARS, THE. (Title HBE Volume 69). Loder never loses a chance to tilt at Wingate. To get Wingate out of, and himself into, the First Eleven, Loder sent a telegram saying that Mr Wingate had been seriously injured. Luckily the Famous Five knew and had given Wingate the details in writing before the event. Loder was unmasked, and received a sound drubbing from Wingate in secret – in front of nearly all the school! Loder then turned his attentions to the Famous Five, whose guile is greater than Loder's cunning! Instead of catching the Famous Five, Loder found himself caught out by his old enemies. Finally Linley, desperate for money to send home, helped Uncle Clegg with his income tax return. The cads of the Remove tried to accuse him of stealing the hard earned cash from Stewart of the Shell.

BULSTRODE, Mr. Father to George and the late Herbert. Initially a roman parent, unforgiving of any fault – especially when George was accused of theft, he softened considerably after Herbert's death.

BULSTRODE, Mrs. Amelia. Mother of George Bulstrode. A somewhat colourless lady, she is much in awe of her overbearing husband. (177).

BULSTRODE, George. Was Captain of the Remove when Harry Wharton arrived, and was soon supplanted by him; apart from a short spell when he again took over as Captain. He used to be a bully but, after the tragic death of his younger brother, Herbert, he improved radically. Although not exactly a leading light in the form, he is at least now a useful member of society. He shares study No 2 with Brown and Hazeldene.

BULSTRODE, Herbert, (Minor). Thinking that his brother was as dissolute as ever, Bertie came to Greyfriars intending to pass the time in the Cross Keys. However, one night was all he had. After breaking out of the school by a makeshift rope, which broke, he was caught in a rainstorm and spent much of the night in the open. His death from pneumonia caused the final reform in his brother, who left Greyfriars for a time after the tragedy. (178).

BUN SHOP, Courtfield High Street. A favourite rendezvous of all Greyfriars on half holidays, it was, and is, the scene of many celebrational parties, when the funds don't allow for Chunkley's! To sit outside on the pavement, shaded by the ancient trees on a summer's afternoon makes it an exceedingly popular haunt.

BUNCE, Farmer. The tenant of Oak Tree Farm near Courtfield, (part of the Popper Court Estate), he has an especial "down" on poachers. Indeed, when he caught "Mick the Gipsy" roasting a chicken there was quite a rumpus! (819).

BUNCE, Robert, (Bobby). Ex Royal Navy seaman, and now a boatman on the Thames at Lechlade. Having lost a leg in action, he found his wooden stump very useful in "repelling boarders" when the Greyfriars Hikers were attacked by Herbert Higgs! (1334).

BUNCH of GRAPES, The. A pleasant country Inn half a mile from Wharton Lodge. It was while he was staying here that Dick Lancaster met the Famous Five and Coker. (1209).

BUNCHY. A boxer employed by Archie Valence as a sparring partner when he thought that Mr Lascelles was going back into the ring. (1322).

43

BUNCOMBE, Mr. The "Head Master" employed by Mauleverer at High Oaks School to try to bring some semblance of order to the establishment. The plan misfired as Ponsonby had seen the advertisement for a Head and turned up disguised as an M.A. (1048).

BUNNY, Mr. The curate at Friardale Church. (248).

BUNTER, Mrs. Amelia. Mother of William, Elizabeth and Samuel. A plump good natured lady who is blind to most of the faults in her children, in particular William. This is perhaps understandable as she is the only person for whom Billy has any regard, (except himself!). To what extent this is true was shown after she had pneumonia. Billy gave her all his remaining reward money, (earned after he had given information leading to the arrest of smash and grab raiders at Chunkley's), so that she could convalesce at Bournemouth. (1532).

BUNTER, Elizabeth Gertrude, (Bessie). The unlovely sister of Billy and Sammy. She is the bane of the Fourth Form at Cliff House School. As greedy as the rest of the family she may be but, at least, she is not as devious as her older brother. Like Billy, she has a talent for ventriloquism. She has no opinion of men, and usually thanks a knight errant with complaints! Altogether she is a worthy member of the Bunter Clan!

BUNTER, Mr George. Uncle to Billy. He lives in a residential hotel in Folkestone. A dutiful relative, he has tried on several occasions to persuade Bunter to mend his ways. An attempt at morality teaching through the example of Dicken's Christmas Carol did have the desired effect for a brief time, (1036). But efforts to spur Bunter to academic success or sporting prowess have failed dismally. The promises of largesse did not produce the effort but rather an increase in dishonesty. (1359; 1555).

BUNTER, Margaret. The Bunters' Aunt Peggy. When Sammy came to Greyfriars she sent Billy a tip to give to his minor. Needless to say it all went in the tuck shop to Billy's delectation. (144).

BUNTER, Miss Rebecca. Sister to Mr Bunter. One of the few members of the Bunter clan who are not overweight. She prefers Sammy to Billy, (to the latter's mystification and chagrin!). (513).

BUNTER, Mr Samuel. The Head of the Bunter clan is a stockbroker who lives at Bunter Villa, Redgate, Surrey. He seems to suffer more downs than ups in his fortune making. He is, on the whole, about as self centred as the rest of his family and so, it is no wonder his offspring are as they are when one considers the facility with which he can rid himself of his children on holiday, without so much as enquiring into the veracity of their stories. (Surely he must know that they are without exception as far removed from truthful as it is possible to be?) .

BUNTER, Samuel Tuckless.   The youngest of three children. Indistinguishable from his brother, Billy, except in stature and, if possible, a greater affinity for dirt ! He leads the Second Form, of which he is a dubious ornament, about as much of a dance as his brother leads the Remove.   The acquisition of knowledge is as anathematous to him as the schism was to the Roman Popes !

BUNTER, Walter, (Wally) .   Cousin to William George and looked down upon by him because he had to leave school early to work for his living.   It is almost impossible to credit that two people so identical in appearance should be so diametrically opposite in character – but such is the case.   Wally has none of his cousin's vices, (although, as a trencherman he is, given the chance, his equal!) .   After preventing a robbery at his employer's office, he was sent as a reward to St Jim's School.   When WGB suggested a change of identity, Wally, believing his cousin's reasons, willingly agreed; only to discover that William had made Greyfriars too hot for himself ! When Wally left school for the second time, he returned to his office before being posted to the firm's Paris branch, where he now works.

BUNTER, William George.   How it is that this most unattractive specimen has remained at Greyfriars has to be a mystery as great as that of the Marie Celeste ! Leaving out his personal appearance – unwashed, with food smeared hands and face, and with clothes so ill-fitting to the point of the ludicrous, he hides what good he has behind a thick pair of spectacles, through which he peers near sightedly at the world.   He excels at eating, sleeping and talking, of which the first is by far and away his favourite.   To realise this ambition he will beg or borrow money; or borrow the food having forgotten to ask ! When caught, as he invariably is, his lies and distortions justify, to his entire satisfaction, that: 1) he never had it; 2) he was nowhere near the scene of the crime; 3) there was not enough to go round; and 4) he never had it ! When it comes to talking, malicious gossip is his forte.   He is never at a loss to twist facts, and to keep a secret by ensuring that the entire world knows all the details, luridly and fallaciously distorted beyond all recognition.   To obtain material for his vast fund of knowledge, he will listen at any key hole, hide behind any convenient pillar or curtain and, again, distort the facts he hears.   Frequently he acquires information of great import but, as he is pathologically incapable of telling a straight story, his reports are never believed.

Wiliam George Bunter is the eldest of three children of Mr and Mrs. Bunter of Bunter Villa, Redgate, Surrey.   He never fails to delight in boasting of his aristocratic connections and relatives, from each and every one of whom, (whose names and styles change by the minute),

he is, Micawber-like, in daily expectation of something to his credit -
an imaginary Postal Order. This is a regular source of income from
new boys, whose loans to the exact value, (!), of the postal order are
never repaid.

WGB is one of the nasties, meanest snobs in the school and will conde-
scend to the sons of cobblers, fishermen and solicitors, all of whom are
so immeasurably superior to Bunter as to make his "Kontemt", (sic),
laughable.

Convinced of his nobility of geniture, deportment and looks, he cannot understand why it is that any girl upon whom he condescends to
bestow a look of admiration is bowled over - not by instant admiration but by hysterics !

The one talent he does possess is ventriloquism. It is rarely used for
entertainment but reserved for the creation of discord and strife
amongst friends. To be fair, it has on occasions proved of use. He has
an animal cunning and is so cowardly that it is incredible that he
should ever be of use; but such is the perversity of nature that having
caused havoc by blackmail, stupidity or greed, he is almost inevitably
instrumental in putting straight blunders of his own making. Thus it
is he more often than not escapes his just rewards.

Lazy to the point that makes a hibernating dormouse look active, he
has a medical history as to make the playing of games fatal - plum-
bago, pneumonia of the legs, treble pneumonia, etc ! When it comes to
the acquisition of knowledge, the anathemata of Torquemada are
nearer to love than the desires of Bunter to learn !

Of the Seven Deadly Sins, he is the living embodiment of pride, envy,
avarice, greed, sloth, wrath and gluttony; and no doubt soon will add
lust to complete the list !

With a make up as it is, the only reason for his remaining at
Greyfriars is that, with all his faults, he is so obtuse that those in
authority do not hold him responsible for his actions !

BUNTER AND THE GREYFRIARS MUTINY. (Title HBE
Volume 10) . When Mr Quelch was dismissed by the Head after
Skinner had made it appear that the Form Master despised the Head,
the entire Remove walked out of Greyfriars under the leadership of
Mauleverer. They formed High Oaks School. This was a disaster, but
eventually justice was done and Mr Quelch reinstated, thanks to
Colonel Wharton acting as peacemaker.

BUNTER AT ST. JIMS. (Title HBE Volume 67) . After making
Greyfriars "too hot" for himself, Bunter found a perfect escape by

swapping places with his cousin Wally, who was supposed to be going to St Jims. He would, however, have preferred Greyfriars, but his benefactor was an Old Saint. Unfortunately, Wally had to suffer a great deal because of his cousin's dishonesty. He had just about persuaded Greyfriars that Bunter was a reformed character when he had to leave.

BUNTER COURT. As befits an aristocrat, Billy Bunter lives, not in a suburban semi, but a ducal palace ! No one at Greyfriars believes this, (except Billy!), but when he conned the estate agent into renting him Combermere Lodge, all the world had to admit the existence of such a place. Until the fraud was exposed ! (HBE 3) .

BUNTER TELLS THE TRUTH. (Title HBE Volume 38). Jim Warren entered the Fifth Form in place of his thoroughly unlikeable cousin James. Price tried his utmost to discredit Jim after hearing him talking to Harry Wharton. To do this he stole a letter and when Bunter did "tell the truth", (mirabile dictu!), he was, not surprisingly, not believed. Eventually weight of evidence told against Price.

BUNTER THE BAD LAD. (Title GL Volume.2) . Caught ordering a massive amount of tuck from Chunkley's, Bunter had a "brainstorm" to try to avoid the consequences. Inevitably he gave himself away. Then, after a visit to the cinema, he dreamed of being Bunter the Bandit. A cold night with his food stolen soon cured that fantasy ! When Bunter claimed to have rescued a gipsy child from the railway line, it was taken to be another "whopper" - but - mirabile dictu - it was true !

BUNTER THE HYPNOTIST. (Title HBE Volume 52) . Bunter convinced Coker that he had "the power". A conviction that cost Coker dear ! (See also Teggers, Lucius) .

BUNTER THE LION TAMER. (Title HBE Volume 55) . After discovering that Caesar, one of the circus lions, was in fact exceedingly tame, Bunter fooled the school into believing that he was brave. However, when Loder was hunting for him, the sang froid soon evaporated, and Bunter ran away from school to join the circus at the invitation of Marco the lion tamer. As usual, Bunter caused as much unpleasantness as possible with his ventriloquism. Later, he found out that Muccolini, the circus owner, was in fact spying on military establishments and, as usual, Bunter finished up a hero instead of being expelled from school !

BUNTER THE VENTRILOQUIST. (Title HBE Volume 13) . This does not retail a complete passage of the history of Greyfriars, but rather a series of incidents.

47

BUNTER VILLA. Sited near the town of Redgate, in the county of Surrey, a few miles from Reigate. Unfortunately for Harry it is within easy reach of Wharton Lodge, so that Wharton is constantly being pestered and conned into paying taxi fares, as well as Bunter's holiday expenses. Redgate is within walking distance of Wimford, by most people, (although there is a train service). (1664).

BUNTER'S CHRISTMAS CAROL. (Title HBE Volume 58). Bunter having fallen under the spell of Dicken's Christmas Carol was moved to uncharacteristic generosity toward a tramp. He lent him his umbrella. The tramp turned out to be an eccentric millionaire – Mr Skilton. Bunter was invited for Christmas, but his visions of splendour rapidly vanished when it transpired that the intention was to spend the season in giving presents to less fortunate people. Mr Skilton was persuaded to go on holiday, and Bunter was kicked out of the house, (literally!).

BUNTER'S CHRISTMAS PARTY. (Title HBE Volume 48). Bunter inveigled his way on board Captain Compton's yacht for Christmas and, as was his wont, he invited his own guests – the Famous Five. Only when on board did they discover that the boat was being used for smuggling. Compton himself was trying to escape from the web of deceit, but it seemed in vain, until Mr Vernon Smith came to the Captain and his nephew's rescue, (they had been marooned), after an eventful Mediterranean cruise.

BUNTER'S FUNNY TURN. (Title HBE Volume 56). See Bunter the Lion Tamer.

BUNTER'S ORDERS. (Title HBE Volume 63). Bunter, in order to get into the Remove football team, and so get a large tip from his Uncle George, descended to blackmailing Harry Wharton after he had seen Nugent and Vernon Smith beating Walker.

BUNTER'S RICH RELATION. (Title HBE Volume 59). Arthur Carter was expelled from his previous school and sent to Greyfriars as a last chance to earn his Uncle Joe Carter's approval. Failure to do so would have meant that Bunter, (another nephew), would become the chief beneficiary under Mr Carter's will. Carter was above no chicanery in his efforts to get Bunter expelled, but instead was expelled himself. Thus he was finally excluded from his uncle's will.

BUNTER'S SEASIDE CAPER. (Title HBE Volume 34). Hiram K. Fish, in search of a "quick buck", rented Portercliffe Hall to search for a hidden fortune. Bunter, as usual, found out the truth behind Fish's holiday plans and asked himself to stay. Needless to say, it was Bunter who, while hiding from a deserved bumping, literally fell into some of the money! Luckily, the rightful owner of the house, and heir to the fortune, arrived from abroad in time to prevent the Fishs', and other would be thieves, escape with the money.

BUNTO the BOY TAMER. The stage name taken by Bunter when helping Marco with his act in Muccolini's Circus. (1482).

BURGLAR OF GREYFRIARS, THE. (Title HBE Volume 30). See The Mystery of the Moat House.

BURKE, Ulick. After picking Coker's pocket, to the tune of $50, Burke decided to kidnap Horace and ransom him for the sum of $10,000, which Mr Fish refused to pay. It was left to Bunter to lose his way in New York and so rescue Coker from this Bowery Tough. (1094).

BUSTER, The. He was employed by Jimmy the One to kidnap Flip to try to stop him giving information to the police. (1251).

BUZZARD. One of the aliases used by Tighe, a confidence trickster. Under this name he was employed by Miss Judith Coker in the capacity of private secretary, and was able to make quite "a pile". (1133).

C.

CACA ISLAND. The island in the Pacific whereon Peter Bruce, (Black Peter), hid his treasure. He made a map of the hiding place and entrusted it to Ben Dance to deliver to Tom Redwing in England. While Mr Vernon Smith was on business in the Islands, his son and a party of his friends went to the island to search for the treasure. Soames, (Mr Vernon Smith's valet), proved to be a rascal and did his utmost to steal the treasure for himself. (GBC 11).

CACTUS. One of the ranch hands on the Kicking Cayuse Ranch. (1577).

CADGER, The. A tramp who, in company with Beaky Bill and Soapy Jones, attacked Coker. To the amazement of all, Alonzo Todd knocked out all three assailants, thanks to the effects of Professor Sparkinson's Elixir. (1345).

CAESAR. Marco the lion tamer's chief lion in Muccolini's Circus. Bunter discovered how tame he was and hoodwinked the school and Cliff House when the lion escaped from the circus and entered Cliff House grounds. (HBE 55-56)

CAFFYN, Edgar. (The Snipe). A thoroughly nasty piece of work who was sent to Greyfriars through the plotting of Mr Sarle, (Miss Judith Coker's solicitor at the time), and thanks to the generosity of Miss Coker. His brief was to use any method necessary to disgrace Coker and so persuade Aunt Judy to alter her will in Caffyn's favour. However, all his efforts failed for one reason or another, and finally, Caffyn changed his ways, confessing his intent to Aunt Judy. (HBE 9).

CALEB. An old beggar of Wharton Magnus. When Wun Lung gave him a guinea he thought a mistake had been made and tried to give it back. (47).

CALLING MR QUELCH. (Title HBE Volume 15). Gilbert Tracy did not want to go to Greyfriars and so, when his uncle and guardian, Sir Giles Oakwood, asked his old friend, Mr Quelch, to try to see if he could reform the boy, Tracy vowed he would stop at nothing to get himself expelled from school. Mr Quelch, however, did not allow this to happen, and eventually Tracy setled down, after he found out that his invalid father was fit enough to leave his nursing home and take him abroad.

CAMINHO, Senhor Manoel. The Portugese concessionaire of the Boa Vista Estate in Kenya. His intention was to sell the concession to Mr Vernon Smith, but the Senhor was kidnapped by Perez in order to obtain the purchase money for himself. Bunter, hiding from Smithy, saw Perez practising Caminho's signature and so led the Greyfriars Safari party to effect his release. (1230)

CANALETTI. Muccolini's contact and messenger in the passing of military secrets. (1490).

CANTON. A large Chinese city in the south of China. It is the home town of Wun Lung and his family. Ferrers Locke and a party of Greyfriars visited the city when helping Wun Lung against the efforts of Tang Wang. (HBE 25; HBE 25a).

CAPPER, Mr Algernon J., M.A., Oxon. Master of the Upper Fourth Form. A mild sufferer from asthma, he once gave Vernon Smith some asthma cigarettes so that Smithy could lead Mr Smedley into "catching him smoking", (1369). Not so strict in class as Mr Quelch, he is easily distracted from the subject under discussion into talking about his hobbies of mountaineering and stamp collecting. On one occasion there was trouble when it was thought that he had been over-indulging in the bottle. Mr Capper ended up in court, but it proved to be someone identical in appearance, (although the name of his double was never revealed). (974).

CAPTAIN of SCHOOL. The Head of Games, George Wingate, (Major).

CARBERRY. A one time Sixth Former and a prefect. He was a bullying blackguard, whose money went on unplaced horses, whiskey and cigarettes. He was expelled afer taking Dicky Nugent to the Waterside Inn. Believing that he had been seen by the Head, Carberry made up a tissue of lies to evade trouble. Instead, trapped in the net of his own weaving, he was caught out and expelled. After his departure, Loder was promoted to become a prefect.

CARBOY. A member of the Junior Team at Rylcombe Grammar School. (118).

CARBOY, Christopher Clarence. Expelled from Oldcroft, his previous school, for a succession of practical jokes. (Carboy was incapable of controlling his propensity for light hearted mischief). Much trouble was caused and, it was not until Bunter, prying as usual, found out that Carboy had in fact taken the blame for the Head Master's son, cleared the way for his return. (HBE 23).

CARDEW, Ralph Reckness. A member of the Fourth Form at St Jim's School. He affects a superior air, but when thought or action are required he is a most useful man to have around. As happened when Sir Jimmy Vivian disappeared from Pengarth. It was Cardew who found him and the other captive Friars.

CAREY. A Second former. He joined in the efforts to rag Sammy Bunter on his arrival at school. (144).

CARFORD MAJOR. A member of the Sixth Form. (925).

CARFORD MINOR. Younger brother of the above, and in the Upper Fourth Form. (925).

CARKER'S RENTS. A tenement area in the East End of London. It is a thieves kitchen, and was the home of Sir Jimmy Vivian before his coming to Greyfriars. (491).

CARLO. A Venetian gondolier employed by Tiger Bronx in one of his abortive attempts to kidnap Bunter. On this occasion the Famous Five and a party of St Jim's men were on hand to effect a rescue. (1386).

CARLOW, Eric. Rescued Sir George Cheyne from drowning, who, in gratitude, adopted the lad. As the first step in preparing him to take over his iron works, Carlow was sent to Greyfriars, where he fell foul of Nugent, who thought Carlow was bullying his minor. Repaying good for ill, Carlow rescued Nugent Minor from the mill race at Baker's Mill. He did not stay long at Greyfriars, but instead took up his indentures as an apprentice at Sir George's foundry. (1239–41).

CARLTON. A one time member of the Remove who was, if possible, lazier than Bunter ! (184).

CARLYLE'S. Tobacconist's shop in Courtfield.

CARNE, Arthur. In the Sixth Form and a prefect. His only friends are Loder, Walker and Price. A bully and a coward he may be, but he is not so forceful as Loder. He can be mean, spiteful and dishonest, as on the occasions he has taken a more than usually powerful dislike to someone; ie Valentine Compton. But at least he usually realises, before it is too late, exactly what he is doing, and stops in time.

CARNE, Mr Hubert. Father of Arthur, who believed his father to be working in Africa. When he recognised an escaped convict as his parent, he was appalled. However, Mr Black, fatally injured in the manhunt for the convict, made a death bed confession to the crime for which Mr Carne had been imprisoned. (428).

CARNFORTH, Mr James, M.A. A minority of the governors, under the impression that a state of slackness existed in the school, persuaded Dr Locke to resign. In his place they appointed James Carnforth, previously Head Master of St Bede's School. His belief in corporal punishment was so strong that he even attempted to cane Loder. Upon this, Wingate, against his better judgement, led the Sixth Form, (later joined by the Remove), into a revolt against the new Head. Unable to control the situation, Mr Carnforth hired a gang of local ruffians and then, after their defeat in a pitched battle, was dismissed from his post and Dr Locke reinstated. (GBC 36).

CART & HORSES INN. Having conned a lift out of Mr Wilmot, Bunter fled when he next saw him in Wimford Wood. He wandered lost, until he came upon this inn, some six miles from Wharton Lodge. Having fortified the inner man, he then rang Harry Wharton and demanded a lift back to the Lodge ! (1208) .

CARTER, Inspector of Police, Lantham. He was involved with several cases in which Greyfriars men were material witnesses. ie the Courtfield Cracksman's robbery at Lantham Chase, as well as the smash and grab raiders whose arrest Bunter was instrumental in achieving. (1146; 1531) .

CARTER, Arthur. Expelled from St Olaf's for smoking and gambling, Carter was given one last chance to regain his uncle, Joseph Carter's good opinion. Failure to do so would mean that Bunter would become the chief beneficiary under his new will. In order to prevent this, Carter under the guidance of Gideon Gooch, (his cousin and a solicitor), tried to get Bunter expelled. Initially, no one believed Bob Cherry who had over-heard the plotting, but events changed the rest of the Famous Five's minds. Carter was eventually expelled for theft, after a plan to "frame" Bunter failed and the money actually found in Carter's possession. (HBE 59-60)

CARTER, Bud. The bank messenger at Prairie Bends. While taking the purchase money for the Kicking Cayuse Ranch to Packsaddle, the stage coach was held up by a masked thief who turned out to be the vendor, Jad Blake. (1580) .

CARTER, Cyrus. A New York detective of police employed by Mr Fish to protect his son against Barney McCann. Using forged credentials, McCann impersonated the detective and successfully abducted Fishy. (1164) .

CARTER, Mr Joseph. Uncle to Arthur Carter, and a relative of the Bunters'. Disgusted by his nephew's behaviour and subsequent expulsion from St Olaf's School, he threatened to exclude Arthur from his will, unless he could mend his ways. After Carter's expulsion from Greyfriars it is not mentioned in whose favour he did draw his will. It certainly was not Bunter ! (HBE 59-60)

CARTER, Peter. A detective from Los Angeles and fiance to Miss Leanora La Riviere. On the trail of a gang of bootleggers, he was visiting the film set of the Greyfriars Film when he solved his case. (GBC 21) .

CASCO, Pedro. A Spanish adventurer who tried to stop Captain Kit Corkran, (Bob Cherry's cousin), from finding a hoard of ivory. (GBC 12) .

CASEY, Captain. Captain in the M.V. Fanny Jones, a tramp steamer, in which Colonel Wharton and party travelled from Port Said to Bombay. (964).

CASTILLE, Schooner. Picnicking on Black Rock Island one day, the Famous Five and Bunter found a stranded schooner, all of whose crew, with two exceptions, were dead. Pedro Montana had, as he thought, murdered all the crew, to obtain the valuable cargo of smuggled diamonds. After a horrifying afternoon, the Friars and Chawson, (the second survivor), managed to escape from the mad Spaniard who, in trying to evade the Customs and Excise, drowned. (1077).

CASTLE. A somewhat impecunious member of the Upper Fourth who tries, without success, to ape Temple. (120).

CASTLE, Thomas. A member of the Second Form. (571).

CASTLEWOOD, Sussex. The town nearest to Reynham Castle. (1557).

CATCHAM, Captain. A card and billiards sharp who frequents the hotels in Margate. He had no trouble in relieving Bunter of a large amount of money on an occasion that Bunter actually had any to lose ! (1384).

CATERPILLAR. The nickname given to Rupert de Courcy of Highcliffe.

CAVANDALE, Abbot of. Legend has it that the ghost of the Abbot is seen walking the abbey prior to the death of the earl. Parker, the Earl's secretary, tried to make Bunter leave by dressing up as the abbot, but he was exposed by Ferrers Locke. (HBE 22).

CAVANDALE, Colonel. Nephew and heir to the present earl. He is on active service with Colonel Wharton's old regiment. (1191).

CAVANDALE, The Right Honourable, The Earl of. An Old Friar and friend of Colonel Wharton who saved his life in battle, and a contemporary at school with Major Cherry. His life was threatened and attempted several times. Unwittingly saved by Bunter, the Earl invited him, and the Famous Five, to stay for Christmas at the Abbey, where they were able to play a large part in aiding Ferrers Locke solve the problem. (HBE 22).

CAVANDALE, Sir Giles. An ancestor of the present earl. He was a cavalier during the Civil War and was killed during the siege of Cavandale Abbey by Cromwell's Ironsides. Sir Giles expected his death as he had seen the ghost of Abbot Boniface the night before it happened. (1192).

CAVANDALE ABBEY. The seat of the Earls of Cavandale. It lies near Ashwood in Surrey, and is about 15 miles from Wharton Lodge, although there are obviously short cuts reducing the distance considerably, since Bunter, on one occasion, bicycled as far as the Abbey while staying with Wharton. (HBE 22).

CAVE on the PIKE. A favourite picnic spot for Greyfriars and Cliff House. It has been used as a hiding place, as when James Loder escaped from Blackmoor prison. Discovered by the Cliff House girls, there was a fight between the convict and Mr Lascelles, as a result of which the master fell and sustained a broken leg. Rather than leave him, James Loder carried Larry to the road where he could be placed in a cart and taken for treatment. (1493).

CECILIA. Aunt to Mauleverer, and sender of frequent generous tips, one of which was intercepted by Loder who had the intention of using it for placing a bet. Luckily for himself, he changed his mind. (1399).

CHALKE. A small village in Kent served by a branch railway line. It is the nearest station to Hawkscliff, being about two miles therefrom. (1416).

CHANDOS. The butler at Portercliffe Hall. So far from being the perfect butler he was prepared, (and did), go to extremes to find the late Earl of Portercliffe's hidden gold; even to the extent of imprisoning Mr Fish and Fishy. He escaped from the Hall before the police arrived but was later apprehended and sentenced to prison. (1334).

CHANG KO. The leader of a crew of Chinese river pirates who attacked the Greyfriars party while on board the Silver Star. They were driven off by Ferrers Locke who used a steam hose to repel the attack. (1181).

CHAPEL. Greyfriars was founded as a school on the site of a religious house. Thus it follows that the School Charter insists on a Christian curriculum. As a regular part of this, every member of the school has to attend a short chapel service each morning in the week, and at least one full church service on Sundays. The Chapel is an integral part of the main buildings, and dates in part from monastic times.

CHAPEL in FRIARDALE WOODS. An ancient ruin of a small mediaeval wayside shrine. It possibly lay just on the boundary of the old monastic estate in what is now known as Friars Wood. (9).

CHAPMAN. Inspector of Police, Ashwood, Surrey. With the aid of Ferrers Locke he solved the case of the attempts on Lord Cavandale's life. (1192).

CHARLES. Footman at Eastcliff Lodge. (1680).

CHARLEY. One of the gipsies in whose caravan Coker sheltered in an effort to avoid punishment after refusing to be caned. When Mr Prout called upon Coker to return, the gipsies attacked him, and the fact that Coker came to his Form Master's rescue meant that he did escape punishment. (1042).

CHARLEY. One of the rogues employed by Cyril Rackstraw to kidnap Tatters. Carne had sent him to the post office to register a letter, and Tatters was to be taken on the way there. Unfortunately, (for Carne), Tatters was playing football and had bribed Bunter to run the errand in his place. (1200).

CHARLEY. One of the pugilists employed by Archie Valence to take Mr Lascelles prisoner so that Archie could force him to re-enter the ring. (1322).

CHARLEY. A poacher in Berkshire who, while trying to enter Sir Giles Frump's preserves, caused Ponsonby's capture by Sir Giles' keeper while Ponsonby was on his way to raid the Famous Fives camp. (1338).

CHARLEY. The ostler at The Old Oak Inn, near Wharton Lodge. (1367).

CHARPENTIER, M. HENRI, (Mossoo). The French Master at Greyfriars. He is usually dismissed as a "good-natured little ass". This thoughtless, but well meant compliment, does not do him credit. He is the proud uncle to numerous nephews and nieces to whom he sends home more of his income than he can readily afford. Because of this he is mocked by Skinner and cronies for his worn out clothing. If anything, Mossoo is too good-natured. It is easy to rag him in class – and this happens regularly, unless Mr Quelch is on hand to mete out the punishment Mossoo will not. Unfortunately, when he does punish it is indiscriminate and without regard for the innocent or the guilty!

CHAWKER, Charley. The leading actor in Mr Whiffles' pantomime company. He walked out of the production without notice, leaving them "in the lurch". Harry Wharton who, with his friends, was looking for a job to raise money to buy comforts for the troops, got the part. (409).

CHAWSON. The only crew member of the Castille not murdered by Pedro Montana. He was found and released by Bunter. (1077).

CHE-KIANG, River. The Canton River flows from Canton to Hong Kong. While in China the Greyfriars party sailed a part of their journey on the river, before being taken by Tang Wang. They escaped from Pan Shan down the canal which connects that city with the Che-Kiang. (HBE 25; HBE 25a).

CHEQUERS, The. An inn some 25 miles from Greyfriars at which Vernon Smith sometimes spends a half holiday out of bounds playing banker and billiards. (1414).

CHERRY, Mrs. Wife of Major Robert, and mother of Bob, Cherry. She is devoted to both men in her life, and puts up with their boisterous chatter and pranks with great good humour.

CHERRY, Robert, (Bob). The only child of Major and Mrs. Cherry of Cherry Place, Dorset. He is one of the acknowledged leaders of the Remove at Greyfriars, jointly called the Famous Five. A cheery, restless athlete, he is only down hearted when it is impossible to be active – in class! Even on the worst of days, he will look for a rag rather than be idle. Perpetually in trouble for sliding down the bannisters and shuffling his feet in class, he is usually accepting of the fate meted out. When he and Harry Wharton first met they fought, but settled their differences, and decided the Form captaincy, by a cricket match. Although Bob was more popular, (and possibly still is), he realised that Harry is a born leader. The Famous Five tend to be a complete unit but Bob, with his natural bonhomie, has friends outside – notably his study mates in No 13 Wun Lung and Linley.

CHERRY, Major Robert, O.F., Governor of Greyfriars School. He is the younger brother by at least ten years of Sir William Cherry, and the father of Bob Cherry. An ex-army officer, he is completely honest and straightforward – almost to the point of simplicity. He is deeply attached to his wife and son. At heart a boy, he delights in Bob's prowess at games, and normally does not care about his mediocre showing in class. Bob's friends are always assured of a warm welcome at Cherry Place, the Major's Dorset home; especially as it gives the major a valid excuse to forget his years! For all his boyish enthusiasm, he can be stern and strong-willed – as Heath discovered after he had forged Bob's name to a postal order and Bob faced unjust expulsion. As one would expect of an officer, he is fearless, no matter what the odds, and faced what must have seemed like certain death when captured by Bou Saoud. His only regret being that he had failed, as it then seemed, to fulfil his mission for Ali ben Yusef.

CHERRY, Sir William, Bart., O.F. Uncle to Bob Cherry, he spent his working life in China. After his return to England he was poisoned by a Corsican secret society, the Rafia. The price of the antidote was his entire fortune as payment for his father having many years previously, discovered their secrets. Thanks to Bunter, the gang were identified, captured and Sir William's life saved. Had they failed with

Sir William, their next target was to have been Bob Cherry as Sir William's heir. (1108).

CHERRY PLACE. The home of the Cherry family. It is a small country house set in a large garden, rather than an estate. It lies some miles outside Dorchester, in the county of Dorset.

CHESTER. After moving from Surrey, where they used to live near Wharton Lodge, the Wingate family moved to this ancient Roman City.

CHESTER, Richard, (Dicky). An Old Friar who had been one of the greatest goalkeepers in the history of the school. After one Old Boys match it was discovered that Chester had in fact died in action and that the man purporting to be Chester was actually his ex-batman – Cunningham. (844).

CHEW, Hannibal, (Chick). A Chicago ganster, and one of the most successful kidnappers in the U.S.A. He had marked out Putnam van Duck as a victim and spared no expense in his efforts. Following from Brazil to England, Chew tried several times – unsuccessfully – until, in the guise of Mr Saloman, (a locum for Mr Quelch who had suffered a head injury), he managed to get van Duck out of Greyfriars. Only to find that Poker Pike was present to foil the kidnappers. (1468; HBE 45).

CHEYNE, Sir George. Governor of Greyfriars. While holidaying at Brighton, he was saved from drowning by Eric Carlow, the bootboy at The Regency Boarding House. In gratitude, Sir George adopted Carlow and sent him to Greyfriars to prepare him for entering Sir George's iron foundry. (1240).

CHEZ NOUS. The holiday bungalow at Rottingdean taken by the Famous Five for a few days at the end of their summer holidays after they had left Muccolini's Circus. (1486).

CHICK. The choreman, (or "odd-job" man), at the Kicking Cayuse Ranch. (1575).

CHICK, Bill. The leader of the "army" of ruffians employed by Sir Hilton Popper to end the Barring Out resulting from Meyer Brander's rule at Greyfriars. (1174).

CHICK CHEW. See Chew, Hannibal.

CHICO O CACADOR. The Brazilian native jaguar hunter employed by Mr Peter Valentine to capture O Lobo. By chance, Bunter earned his good opinion, when accidently he let off his rifle and shot a jaguar ! His admiration knew no bounds when Bunter, later saved him from certain death. (HBE 44) .

CHINESE CHARLEY'S SALOON. A waterfront bar in Kalua frequented by Brian Mauleverer before he finally reformed his ways. (1590) .

CHIPPY. The porter at Friardale station. (18) .

CHIRPY, Mrs. While her husband was absent on active service, Coker used to take her food, (all too often past its best!) . (528) .

CHISHOLM, Dr., D.D. The Headmaster of Rookwood School. He is a stern and unyielding man who is rarely lenient to offenders. (1328) .

CHOLMONDLEY, Arthur. The late, third son of Sir George Cholmondley, and father to Tatters. (1195) .

CHOLMONDLEY, Arthur Cecil. The son of Arthur, and grandson of Sir George Cholmondley. He is better known to his friends as Tatters. (cf) . (1195) .

CHOLMONDLEY, Sir George, O.F., Governor of Greyfriars School. An irrascible gentleman, much of whose temperament may be put down to his desire to manage his estate and ensure the succession. Unfortunately his eldest son died in a riding accident; his second son also died without issue; the youngest was expelled from his home and disappeared. Later he died in poverty, leaving a son, Arthur Cecil. Despite the other grandson, (Cyril Rackstraw), who hindered the search, he was found and restored to his rightful place. (GBC 19) .

CHOLMONDLEY CASTLE, Hants. The seat of Sir George Cholmondley. It is a large and ancient castle. It has all the features of late fortifications; ie Moat, Keep and Bailey, etc., and is in a remarkable state of good repair.

CHOWNE, Chomondley. A member of the Shell at Greyfriars.

CHRISTMAS DINNERS ASSOCIATION. A charitable trust set up to raise money for the purpose of providing Christmas Fare for the aged and infirm. Bunter heard of the trust and tried to obtain money of them so that he could feed, not the needy of Friardale, but himself ! (148) .

CHU, Mr Impersonating Wun Lung's uncle Chung, he was sent to Greyfriars by Tang Wang with orders to carve the Szi Wang, (or sign of death), on Wun's face. The intention was to coerce his father into contributing to Tang's campaign to become Emperor of China. (1173) .

CHUGGY. Turf accountant of Shaftesbury Avenue, London. Bunter had seen an advertisement in a racing paper and tried to open an account with him. As a minor this was of course refused. Instead, Barker the Bookie, played by Wibley came into Bunter's life ! (1068) .

CHUNDER RUN. A Bengali merchant of Nairobi. He kidnapped Bunter in mistake for Vernon Smith and demanded a ransom of £10,000. During Bunter's rescue by Kikolobo, the Indian shot at the Kikuyu but himself received a severe wound. (1231) .

CHUNG. Uncle to Wun Lung. (1175) .

CHUNG LO. One of Tang Wang's coolies, distinguishable by a scar on his arm. He was in charge of the captured Greyfriars men, (Wharton, Cherry and Bunter), and had orders to deliver them to Tang Wang. They managed to escape twice, the second time only to fall into the hands of Tang himself. As punishment for the second escape Chung was executed. (1183–84) .

CHUNKLEY'S DEPARTMENT STORE, Courtfield. A large department store wherein one can purchase most goods. Although expensive, they are renowned for the quality of their merchandise. The chief appeal of the shop to Greyfriars is its first class restaurant.

CHUPE. A country town in Yorkshire near the Lancashire border. While on a hiking holiday, Harry Wharton and Co. spent some time in the vicinity while searching for Bob Cherry who had been kidnapped at Ponsonby's behest by some gipsies. (1137) .

CHURROCK, Mr Albert. Sir Gilbert Frump's head keeper. He captured Ponsonby in mistake for a poacher while Pon. was trying to make a night raid on the Greyfriars Hiking party. (1338) .

CHURROCK, Mrs Emily. Wife to Mr Albert Churrock. (1338) .

CIRCLE O RANCH, Rio Frio, Texas. The neighbouring spread to the Kicking Cayuse. It was bought by Vernon Smith as an investment, on his father's behalf while the Greyfriars party was staying in Texas. Smithy discovered that the Circle O was for sale, and promptly showed his business acumen ! (HBE 32) .

CLANCY. A "black sheep" in the Shell at Greyfriars. He usually has both playing cards and smokes hidden in his study. (988) .

CLANCY, Mike. An American gangster of Irish extraction in the employ of Barney McCann. Bunter tricked him by ventriloquism so that he was able to escape after being captured by McCann in mistake for Fisher T. Fish. (GBC 24) .

CLARK, Compton, (Nosey). The boss of a gang of crooks. He had "a hard hawkish face which was thin and cold, with a prominent nose like a vulture's beak", (hence the soubriquet). He was guardian to Jim Valentine, whom he was loathe to lose – not as a ward, but as a master forger and, therefore, of use to him. When Jim fled, Clark kidnapped Harry Wharton to force Colonel Wharton to return his ward, (about whom he knew nothing). When Valentine refused to return to the fold, Clark threatened and blackmailed to no avail. His efforts at disgracing Valentine also failed. This ruthlessness of his led to his arrest, for a trap, set to catch Valentine, caught Clark and the rest of the gang, after Vernon Smith had tipped off the police. (GBC 9).

CLAVERING, Leonard. Orphaned after his father was killed in action, he was begrudgingly helped by Sir Hilton Popper who had in effect blackmailed his father into signing up. Clavering did not wish to go to Greyfriars and so, when the opportunity arose, changed places with a chance acquaintance, Tom Redwing. Clavering then joined up, (by lying about his age), and after his initial training at Wapshot was posted abroad. Not, however, before he had thrashed Sir Hilton for his attitude to his father. (517).

CLAVERING, Oswald. A widower with a son and no prospects, he was in effect blackmailed by Sir Hilton Popper into "joining up". He did so on the understanding that Sir Hilton would be responsible for the boy should he fall in action, as indeed he did. This moral obligation was not felt strongly by Sir Hilton, who only helped grudgingly. (517).

CLEGG, Mr. Tutor hired by Sir Hilton Popper for his nephew Cecil Popper, (Pop). (1166).

CLEGG, George, (Uncle). Proprietor of the confectionary shop in Friardale which is known to everyone at Greyfriars as "Uncle Clegg's" or "The Tuckshop in the Village". Outwardly he is a gruff man who, at heart, is a kindly soul who is very lonely.

CLERE, Abbey of, Normandy. The father house of Greyfriars when a monastery. (1191).

CLIFF COTTAGE. Some two miles from Greyfriars on the cliffs overlooking the English Channel, it is the home of Mr Jenks who derives an income from letting the cottage and doing much of the housekeeping for the guests. On one memorable occasion, Mr Prout, after acquiring a black eye, stayed here in a forlorn attempt to hide the disfigurement, until discovered by Coker. (1187).

CLIFF GARDEN. A restaurant specialising in summer teas for tourists in their adjacent garden overlooking the cliffs at Pegg. (1417).

CLIFF HOUSE SCHOOL. A famous girls Public School situated between the villages of Pegg and Friardale in the county of Kent. Several of the girls have brothers at Greyfriars, and there are many firm friendships between the members of the two establishments.

CLIFF PATH. One of the routes between Greyfriars and Pegg lies along the cliff tops. With a sheer drop of some 60 feet to the sea below and the cliffs rising sheer above, the path is only passable on fine days.

CLIFTONVILLE, near Margate, Kent. A suburb of Margate with an excellent sandy beach. It is a favourite place for holiday makers and is often visited by Greyfriars men. (757; 1437).

CLIVE, Sidney. A South African Junior at St Jim's and a friend of Ralph Cardew.

CLOISTER FIELD. Adjoining the cloisters and more an unkempt lawn than a field. It is used for bonfires and Guy Fawkes celebrations rather than agriculture.

CLOISTERS. A relict of monastic days the cloisters are original and in a good state of repair. Situated at the back of the main school buildings they abut onto the wall around the the school, affording a widely known "secret" way out of the school on illicit trips. Secluded as they are, they are an ideal spot for many nefarious activities, including smoking.

CLOSE. An enclosed quadrangle behind the main facade, (unlike the quadrangle itself which is open on one side). It is surrounded by the gymnasium, chapel, and kitchen quarters.

CLYFFE. The village nearest to Hawkscliff. It is served by a branch railway line, and is some twelve miles from Greyfriars by main road. Unless going to Hawkscliff by road, it is an out of the way spot for Greyfriars.

COBB, Ben. The landlord of the Cross Keys Public House, Friardale. As disreputable as his house has a bad name, he is an associate of both Jerry Hawke and Joe Banks, (when the latter is not at the Three Fishers).

COCK OF THE WALK, THE. (Title GBC Volume 16). Relates the arrival of Percy Bolsover and his failure to establish himself as leader of the Remove; the arrival and subsequent death of Bulstrode Minor; and one of Vernon Smith's many expulsions and reinstatements.

CODDER'S PLACE. A near derelict farm cottage half a mile from Wharton Lodge. While staying here in training, the Game Kid met and saved Dr Locke from footpads. (985).

CODGERS, Farmer. He lives in the Vale of the Kennet in Berkshire, and met Harry Wharton and Co. while they were on a hiking holiday. They had just taken Ponsonby prisoner to prevent further raids on their camps. Convincing him that Pon. suffered from delusions the farmer relayed this information to the magistrate after Pon. was accused of poaching. (1338).

COFFIN. The butcher's boy from Pilverton, Devon, whose round includes deliveries at Polpelly. (1454).

COKE, Captain. Captain of the M.V. Hope, a tramp steamer chartered by Colonel Wharton in the search for Major Cherry who had been shipwrecked on his way to India. (179).

COKER, Mr Henry. Brother to Miss Judith Coker and Uncle to Horace. He lives with his sister at Hollywood House. Extremely fond of his nephew he could hardly show his gratitude after Coker had freed him from the continued threat of blackmail by his secretary Poynings. (929).

COKER, Horace James, (Major). He shares study No 4 in the Fifth Form with Potter and Greene. For a long time the butt of the Shell, his Aunt Judy, convinced that he was discriminated against, forced the Head at umbrella point to accede to his promotion. After all, the Head reasoned, he might as well be a fool in the Fifth as the Shell!

Horace is the most self-possessed and self-confident of mortals. He is not convinced, he simply knows, that no-one can do things like him. And he is right! What he cannot realise is that try as he will, (and try he most certainly does), he is incapable of doing anything – let alone well! Although he has a rough way with fags, woe betide anyone he catches bullying them. (As Loder will bitterly attest). He has to be the most obdurate of scholars, but at least he tries. What ever he does, (and that is all things), he puts his entire energies into it. Where he scores over the other duffers is his honesty, loyalty and dignity. His generosity knows no bounds. Whether is it is as the founder of a feast to which all are invited or the purchaser of a replacement horse for the local carrier, he provides largely and open handedly, and without thought of reward for himself. His ploys to get himself elected Head of Games and a place in the First Eleven are not according to Cocker! But again, his intentions are entirely honest. He is convinced that he is worthy of the position.

His impenetrable bubble of dignity and eccentric self-esteem lead him to be one of nature's clowns but, with nothing of the hypocrite about him, he loftily ignores the slings and arrows. It is this dignity which saves him from bootings and bumpings.

In fact, he is a potential leader, if only he would listen to advice and learn according to the system - but a non-conformist to the bitter end, he can never hope to attain the heights to which he could be worthy.

COKER, Mr James. Uncle to Horace, after whom Coker was named. He is careless in money matters and, being a younger son, is not so well endowed as his brother and sister. (145).

COKER, Miss Judith, (Aunt Judy). A spinster of great wealth, it is she who seems to pay all the family bills. She is more of a mother and father to Horace than his parents, and he seems to spend at least as much, if not more, time with her than at his own home.

Her over-weening pride in her beloved Horace is perhaps the root of his problems, for if she did not so roundly announce his perfections, he might not be as he is. She is as convinced to-day, now that Horace is in the Fifth Form, as she was when he was in the Shell, that her nephew is misunderstood, (true!), unfairly reviled by his teachers, (false!), to such an extent as to prevent him reaching his full potential.

She is cranky, quirky and one of the most eccentric of characters ever to visit Greyfriars. Her ancient bonnets, (no hats for Aunt Judy!), her bombazines and her umbrella are trade marks that make her identifiable at a great distance. However odd a picture she may present, cast no slur on her in Horace's hearing - his fist is ever ready in her defence.

COKER, Reginald, (Minor). Horace's younger brother. Undoubtedly one of the brainiest scholars at Greyfriars, he is the youngest member of the Sixth Form, but is something of a misfit and a nonentity in the school as he does not take part in other activities or games.

COKER LODGE. Referred to in error as the home of his aunt, (1405), it is in fact the home of Horace and his parents.

COLLINSON, Miss Kitty. The daughter of a coastguard at Pegg. After nearly running her down with his motor cycle, Coker developed a "crush" on her. Discovered writing "poetry of the mushiest sort", he was banned from going to Pegg. Disobeying his Form Master's orders, Coker went to see her again and, on his way to the tryst, saved a motorist who had been involved in a serious accident. (1058).

COLOMBO. A Venetian felucca hired by Tiger Bronx to take him and Bunter, (after the latter's capture), away from the rest of the Greyfriars party in a forlorn attempt to regain his late uncle's fortune. Luckily for Bunter, D'Arcy and his friends were cruising with Lord Conway and were able to come to his rescue. (1386).

COLONNA, Cardinal. A prelate of the Church of Rome. After saving Brother Antonio from footpads while they were stranded outside Rome, the Cardinal gave the Famous Five a lift back to their Hotel, and later lent them his car to see the city under the guidance of his secretary. (1388).

COLOURS. Greyfriars School blazers and representative sports shirts are in alternate vertical stripes of blue and white. The change strip is red shirts, while intra-school matches are played between blue- and red-shirted teams.

COMBERMERE, Kent. Asked by Mauleverer to view the house on behalf of his guardian, Bunter persuaded the estate agents that he was Mauly; and the butler that he was taking the place on behalf of his father, (Mr Bunter). He then changed the name to Bunter Court and invited a party to stay for the holidays. (HBE 3).

COMET, R.M.S. The Royal Mail Line passenger-cargo liner on which Harry Wharton and Co. travelled out to Brazil on their way to visit Jim Valentine. Leaving Tilbury, the ship calls at Boulogne, Lisbon, Madeira, Canary Islands, Pernambuco and, finally, Rio de Janeiro. (1462).

COMPTON, Sir Henry, O.F. An autocratic landowner whose bitterness and overbearing manner was due to the untimely death of his son and later his grandson. A sufferer from heart trouble, he suffered a minor stroke when his cousin Roger confronted him on one occasion. Since his nephew, Richard, has been found, he has mellowed a great deal. (HBE 80; GL 3).

COMPTON, Captain James, (Jim), O.F. The one time owner of the M.V. Firefly, a yacht which was used extensively for smuggling. He sent his nephew Valentine to Greyfriars with the intention of his using the secret passage between the school and Pegg to land contraband. The plan went sadly awry when Vernon Smith discovered their secret and intercepted each cargo, which he then sent to the police annonymously. While the Famous Five and Bunter were on a cruise in the Firefly, Valentine persuaded his uncle to give up smuggling. This he tried to do, but a mutiny on board led to uncle and nephew being marooned on an island near Corsica without food or water. Vernon Smith, despite his cynical outlook on life, was sufficiently convinced of the Captain's intentions as to persuade his father to give Captain Compton the command of a new ship - The S.S. Eastern Queen. (HBE 47-48).

COMPTON, Richard. The grandson of Sir Henry Compton. He died in childhood of either T.B., or possibly Still's Disease. (HBE 80; GL 3).

COMPTON, Richard. See Ragged Dick.

COMPTON, Robert. The younger brother of Sir Henry Compton. He left home after his brother had refused to help him. Later, after the death of his wife, he took to the road and became a tramp. He died at an early age, leaving one son - Richard. (HBE 80; GL 3).

COMPTON, Roger. An inveterate gambler and an alcoholic. Deeply in debt, he tried to raise money on his expectations as heir to his cousin, Sir Henry Compton's, estates and title. Enraged by the appearance of a "grandson" Richard, he did his utmost to prove that the boy was an impostor, only to prove to Sir Henry's amazement that Richard was indeed the rightful heir. Roger then left the country, fleeing from his numerous creditors. (HBE 80; GL 3).

COMPTON, Valentine. The nephew of Captain James Compton who was sent to Greyfriars so that he could act as carrier for contraband. He was placed in the Fifth Form. His reputation was already assured, as he had rescued Billy and Bessie Bunter who had drifted out to sea in a boat without oars. A first class footballer, he was soon in the First Eleven in Carne's place. Carne conceived a hatred for the Fifth Former and, convinced that he was going out of bounds into the secret passage, and not as supposed studying in the library, tried to catch him out. All to no avail. When trapped in the passage, Compton climbed the Shoulder to avoid being discovered in rule breaking. Trapped on the cliff face, it was Bunter who helped him to safety. On the strength of this, Bunter invited himself, and the Famous Five, on a cruise for the Christmas holidays. Compton, who had already tried to persuade his uncle to give up smuggling, tried again - this time successfully after Rawlings had made use of Bunter to carry goods ashore. The crew mutinied rather than give up the easy pickings. Valentine and his uncle were rescued through Vernon Smith from a certain death having been marooned on an island. The Captain took the post of Captain of the Eastern Queen and took Valentine with him to study to become a mercantile officer. (HBE 47-48).

COMPTON HALL, Kent. Lies six miles up the coast from Greyfriars and is the home of Sir Henry Compton. (HBE 80; GL 3).

COMPTON WOODS. Surround a large part of the estate of Compton Hall.

CONCHITA. The leading lady in Mr Whiffles' Pantomime Company. Her looks belied her 37 years and, as a result, convinced that she was 17, Nugent fell in love with her; to her amusement, and the annoyance of her fiance, Mr Badger. (409).

CONCHY. The nickmame given to Richard Hilary's father because of his pacifist views. (571).

CONROY, Kit. In the classical Fourth Form at Rookwood. He comes from Australia, and is a member of the Colonial Co.

CONVICT 19. See Waring, George.

CONVICT 22. Falsely imprisoned for theft, James Loder escaped from Blackmoor Prison to try to clear his name. Discovered hiding in a cave on the Pike, he fought with Mr Lascelles; the latter sustaining a broken leg. Fate then played into his hands when Mr Stephen Lagden, the temporary replacement for Larry, was critically injured in a road accident. James Loder took his place at Greyfriars and was able to prove, not only that he was innocent, but also that Lagden was the real thief. All the while Gerald Loder was going to all lengths to prove that Convict 22 was not his cousin ! (HBE 47).

CONVICT 27. See Carne, Mr Hubert.

CONVICT 33. Bunter had blackmailed Cedric Hilton into an invitation to stay at Hilton Hall over Christmas for himself and the Famous Five. While they were staying here, a convict escaped from the nearby Blackmoor Prison. The party was much interrupted until he was recaptured and the reason for his remaining so close to the Hall explained. He was the half brother to the butler, Walsingham. (HBA 6).

CONWAY, The Right Honourable the Viscount. The heir to Lord Eastwood, and older brother of Gussy D'Arcy. Luckily he was in Venice at the same time as Bunter and the Famous Five, and was able to rescue Bunter after one of Tiger Bronx' efforts to kidnap him. Conway's yacht, the Silver Foam, easily ran down the felucca in which Bunter was being held. (1386).

COOK, Inspector. Stationed at Leyford, Oxfordshire. He was in charge of the investigation into the attempted murder of Sir Henry Ravenspur. When he was close to solving the crime, he was murdered by a gun shot from the house. (HBE 36).

COOK, Clarence. A weak and dissolute young man who took the tenancy of Popper Court during one of Sir Hilton's absences. He invited a dubious crowd of youths to stay with him, amongst whom was James Warren. (1446).

COOK, Capt. George. First cousin to Bunter on his mother's side of the family. A kindly, cheerful, gregarious soul, he had sold everything to buy his yacht, "The Sea Nymph", with the object of chartering her to parties of tourists. The Famous Five, together with Coker and friends, were passengers on her first cruise. They had been invited by Bunter who forgot to mention one thing – the price ! (HBE 61).

COOMBE, Hants. The village nearest to Rookwood School. It is served by a branch railway line.

COOPER, Ralph. A gipsy boy who ran away from Michael. He hid in the grounds of Wharton Lodge, and so was able to save Bunter after he had disobeyed orders and gone skating. Bunter tried to help the boy, and his efforts caused much misunderstanding and friction among the Famous Five until the boy was discovered hiding in one of the attics. (1038).

COOT, Colonel & Mrs. Joint proprietors of the Long Beach Boarding House where the Greyfriars Film Stars stayed while filming in Hollywood. (GBC 20-21).

COOT, Ezra. A close friend of Mr Van Duck. Chick Chew made use of Mr Coot's visit to England to try to kidnap Putnam Van Duck through a spurious invitation to tea. Thanks to his greed, Skinner was the one kidnapped. (HBE 36).

COOT, Peter. A longshoreman of Potkelly, Devon. He was employed by Mr Rance to keep the Famous Five and Bunter away from the smugglers' cave, wherein were imprisoned Mr Vernon Smith and his son. (HBE 50).

COOTE. The carrier of Friardale. Friendly with many of the Greyfriars men, he has on several occasions been helped by them. One time when stuck in a ditch, the Famous Five pulled him out, and then made use of the fact that they had "backed a horse" to jape Mr Hacker who was convinced that they were up to no good. (1617). Coker's cousin Caffyn bolted Coote's horse with a catapult, and almost caused Coker's expulsion when it was discovered that he required money "to pay Banks for a horse"! (1408).

COOTE. A fag in the Third Form at Highcliffe. (1418).

COOTS, Mr. The Postmaster of Friardale Post Office. (133).

CORCORAN, Pete. The chief of the cattle rustlers in the Valley of the Rio Frio. He used to buy cattle from any dishonest foreman and share the profits. Before Mr Vernon Smith bought the Kicking

Cayuse Ranch, he had a very profitable arrangement with Barney Stone. (HBE 32).

CORKER. Colonel & Mrs. They visited Greyfriars one day and, while they were watching the Remove at work, "Pop" made as many "howlers" as possible to try to force his expulsion from school. (1167).

CORKRAN. A swindler who had tried to "con" Colonel Wharton when he was serving in India. Determined upon revenge for his past failures, Corkran made several attempts to thrash the colonel. He was finally thwarted by Bunter who was hiding in Wharton Lodge, having invited himself for Christmas. (1351).

CORKRAN, Capt. Christopher, (Kit), O.F. He is Bob Cherry's cousin. He invited the Famous Five to accompany him to Africa in the search for a hoard of ivory. The most important member of the party was to be Bunter who was required for his ventriloquism. The Captain is a famous Big Game Hunter and lives in West Africa. (GBC 9).

CORTOLVIN, Mr. Distantly related to Harry Wharton through his paternal grandmother, he had known both Colonel Wharton and Wharton's father. When, in the course of duty, the colonel had prevented a robbery, Mr Cortolvin made Harry Wharton his heir in preference to his nephew, Captain Marker. (1065).

COTSWOOD, Kent. On the western border of the county, it was the home of Leonard Clavering before he was sent to Greyfriars. (517).

COTTON KING. A nickname given to Mr Vernon Smith by his acquaintances in the city and later adopted by the press.

COUNT ZERO. See Zero, Count.

COURTENAY, Frank. The Junior Captain of Highcliffe and implaccable enemy of Ponsonby and Co. He has, since his arrival, salvaged some of the pride Highcliffe must have had before it became so decadent. His strength of character is such that he has withstood the snobbery of the knuts and the fact that he has the misfortune to be Ponsonby's cousin. The Junior Team, so long the laughing stock of the neighbouring schools, has, under his tutelage, become a force to be reckoned with. And with the re-emergence of self-respect, many of those who went with the tide, have joined Courtenay and his greatest friend, de Courcy, in actively opposing the arrogant attitudes of most of the school.

COURTFIELD, Kent. A market town of some size, lying on the River Sark some four or five miles from the coast. It is three miles from Greyfriars School and is on the main railway line to London in one direction and Dover in the other. The name is derived from the Anglo-Saxon – Curta's Feld, (or the field of Curta's people).

COURTFIELD COMMON. Lies between the town of Courtfield and Greyfriars School. Designated as common land in the middle ages, it has helped to keep the rural nature of the district. It stretches for nearly three miles in one direction and almost one mile in the other, and is an area of natural beauty, characterised by many fine stands of ancient trees, as well as open expanses of ling and gorse.

COURTFIELD CRACKSMAN, The. The nickname given to an elusive and daring burglar who managed to avoid the police for a long time. (See Billy Bunter & The Courtfield Cracksman).

COURTFIELD EMPORIUM. A large shop in Courtfield which deals exclusively in furniture and household fittings. (1344).

COURTFIELD EXPRESS. Like so many local newspapers with limited circulations, this paper enjoyed only a short life. It took over from the Courtfield Times as the local organ. On one occasion they ran a competition for the best essay on local history which was won by Bunter who submitted a part of Mr Quelch's "History of Greyfriars"! (1054).

COURTFIELD FINANCE COMPANY. A shady loan company from whom Bunter tried to borrow money against his expectations!

COURTFIELD GAZETTE. After the Courtfield Express had ceased publication a new company was formed to produce a new local paper with the title of "The Courtfield Gazette".

COURTFIELD HALL. A large country house on the outskirts of town. Although it seems to have avoided the interest of the Courtfield Cracksman, it was, nonetheless, robbed by Slim Jim. (1660).

COURTFIELD HALL, The. Part of the Courtfield Institute, it is used for lectures open to the general public.

COURTFIELD HIGH STREET. The main thoroughfare of the town. In it are situated most of the businesses of local importance, from the Bank to Chunkley's and Mr Lazarus' Shop.

COURTFIELD HOSPITAL. Lies near the edge of the town. It boasts facilities for all but the most serious of cases, (which are referred to Lantham Hospital).

COURTFIELD JUNCTION. Is an important railway station. It lies on the main line to London and Dover, as well as branch lines to Friardale and other places in the surrounding district.

COURTFIELD POST OFFICE. Lies in one of the side streets about half way down the High Street.

COURTFIELD RANGERS. A junior football team composed mainly of fellows from the local Grammar School, (formerly the County Council School). The team is captained by Dick Trumper. Their ground is on the outskirts of the town on the common. (1343).

COURTFIELD ROAD. Runs between Greyfriars and Courtfield itself, skirting the common. Entering the town, it becomes the High Street. At the junction of Oak Lane, near the school, it becomes the Redclyffe Road.

COURTFIELD SCHOOL. Previously known as the Courtfield County Council School, the name has been changed to Courtfield Grammar School.

COURTFIELD TIMES. The original local newspaper which later became the Courtfield Express, and latterly the Gazette. (748).

COURTFIELD WOODS. Lie between the town and Highcliffe School. It is possible to get to Highcliffe from Greyfriars, avoiding Courtfield, by following the bridle path through the woods. (1418).

COURTNEY, Arthur. A close friend of George Wingate's who also befriended Rupert Valence becaue he was in love with his sister, Violet Valence. He died tragically in a fire at the Cross Keys, when trying to save Valence. (520).

COUTTS, Mr. A motorist badly injured in a car accident at Pegg. He was dragged from his car by Coker. As he was out of bounds at the time, Coker left no name; but a clue to the identity of the rescuer was found in a cap. It belonged to Bunter, who tried to take the credit! (1058).

COW & BULL INN, Hawkinge, Kent. After running out of petrol while on a motoring holiday, Coker and friends met Bob Cherry who filled their spare can with water! Signor Muccolini came past but refused to help. Eventually they were directed to this pleasant country Inn, where they were able to restore their tempers! (1488).

COW & SHEEP INN, Nr Cricklade, Wiltshire. Ponsonby stayed here for a few nights when trying to steal Bob Cherry's Holiday Annual which held the clue to the whereabouts of the proceeds of a large robbery. (1334).

COW LANE. A little used road three miles beyond Lantham. Vernon Smith stranded Bunter here who, while trying to find his way to Lantham, came across the getaway vehicle of a smash and grab gang. (1531).

COWGATE, Surrey. Some five miles to the west of Wharton Lodge, it was chosen as the starting point of their summer hike by the Famous Five. It lies twenty miles from Bunter Villa and about 100 miles from Greyfriars. (1332).

COWLEY, James, & Co. A factory at Ashton, whose payroll was stolen by the cashier. (955).

CRAKE, Barnabas. Better known as Barney the Binger, he had, while working at Brighton, abducted Miss Bullivant's young brother. (1551).

CRANE, The Honourable & Ancient. The name of the Sampan travelled in by the remainder of the Greyfriars party from Canton to Pan Shan to rescue their friends captured by Tang Wang. (1185).

CRAVEN, Inspector. Stationed at Lantham, he was the officer in charge of the investigation into the robbery at the Lantham and County Bank which had been witnessed by Vernon Smith, who later saw the robber without his disguise. (1008).

CRAVEN PRIZE. Is open to any scholar of the Junior School. The prize is awarded to the entrant who gains most marks in an examination paper set in Latin prose. The prize is monetary and is derived from the Craven Bequest. (1107).

CRAWJAW, Professor. One of the "shark" film studios visited by Bunter in his bid for stardom. His interest rapidly dwindled when he discovered that he was expected to pay for the privilege of appearing in a film ! (1107).

CRAWLEY. The real culprit responsible for the theft for which Eric Wilmot had been expelled from Topham School. He managed to hide his guilt until the pressing need for £5 to settle a bet forced him to use one of the stolen notes. (1469).

CRAWLEY, Mr. The private secretary to the inventor Sir William Romayne. It transpired that he was not only spying for the Germans, but also sheltering escaped prisoners of war. His refusal to help a party of Friars and Saints, stranded in a blizzard, led to his exposure and capture. (461).

CREEPER & CRAWLER. The nickname given to Lucius Teggers while at Greyfriars posing as Mr Smedley. (1364).

CREWEY, Devon. A small fishing village about one mile from Polpelly where the Greyfriars party stayed after leaving Polpelly House in a ploy to trap Count Zero. (1454).

CROCKER, Randolph, (Sportsman Crocker), O.F. Expelled from Greyfriars for theft, he had spent many years drifting from one place, (and almost certainly prison), to another. Finally, he returned to Kent with the express intention of causing havoc in the school. In this he most certainly succeeded. Indeed, it was not until Jack Drake came down, on Ferrers Locke's instructions, that Crocker was discovered to be the one who was causing so much damage to person and property in the school; in addition to the annoyance caused by setting up as a bootmaker in the Abbot's Spinney near the gates! (HBE 49-50).

CROOK, Rupert. An escaped convict from Highmoor Prison with a long record of burglary and other offences. It was not until after his capture that it was realised that Crook was in fact the alias of Randolph Crocker. (HBE 49-50).

CROSS KEYS INN, The. Lies on the outskirts of Friardale in its unkempt garden, and presided over by its evil genius Ben Cobb. Apart from the illegality of drinking under age, the place is, not without reason, out of bounds as the landlord and his cronies are only too ready to fleece any unsuspecting innocent who thinks himself a man. Whether by the use of marked cards or not, it is rare indeed for the winner to be any other than Cobb or his friends. More recently, since the tragic death of Courtney, the place has been less patronised by the black sheep of Greyfriars in favour of The Three Fishers.

CRUMM, Mr. Owner and star of "Crumm's House of Magic". He made use of his extraordinary powers of hypnotism to persuade Dr Locke to admit his son Henry to Greyfriars. Although a flamboyant and extrovert man, he is in fact kindly and good natured. (HBE 73).

CRUMM, Henry Christopher. Although used to a life on the road appearing in his father's show, "Crumm's House of Magic", he was sent to Greyfriars. At first looked upon as an outsider because of his different ways, he also perplexed the school by the way in which he could make anyone do his bidding. (Including Mr Quelch, Vernon Smith and Sir Hilton Popper). Mauleverer realised that it was an hypnotic power and made him promise not to use it any more while still at school. (HBE 73).

CRUMP, P.C. A member of the local constabulary who sometimes works in Friardale during P.C. Tozer's off-duty. (1055).

CUNHA, Vasco. A Portuguese living in Macao where he earned a precarious living by enticing "gulls" into Fan Tan dives where they could be relieved of their money; as happened to Bunter who had ignored Ferrers Locke's orders not to go to Macao. (1182).

CUNNINGHAM, Mark. Batman to Dick Chester. Cunningham used to impersonate him after his death in action. On one occasion he even came to Greyfriars on the day of the Old Boys match in this role so that he could rob the school. Luckily, he was recognised before he could escape. (844).

CUTTS. A member of the outdoor staff at Cliff House School. (1415).

CYCLISTS REST, Woodend. A bicycle shop which not only supplies and repairs cycles, but also provides a safe lock up for machines. (1160).

D.

da COSTA, Arthur. He was sent to Greyfriars by Captain Marker with orders to ensure the expulsion of Harry Wharton so that the Captain might inherit the fortune left by his late uncle Mr Cortolvin, who was also distantly related to the Whartons. In the belief that he would be sneered at as a half caste, da Costa was prepared to try any trickery to achieve this end, before fully realising the criminality of his activities. Especially as he had been accepted at Greyfriars on his own merits as an equal. (HBE 27).

da SILVA. The true name of O Lobo. (1463).

DABNEY, William Walter. He shares study No 2 in the Upper Fourth with Temple and Fry. A weaker character than Temple, he usually follows rather than waste time arguing with his dandy leader. He is good at games and is a regular member of the form teams.

DACOITS. Followers of the goddess Kali, they are a caste of robbers in India, many of whom allied themselves with Nally Das in his efforts to seize the throne of Bhanipur. Colonel Wharton and his party were attacked by a large crowd of Dacoits on their way to Bhanipur. (GBC 4).

DAK. The Indian messenger service and, hence, rest bungalows placed at intervals along such routes as they operated. These bungalows are also used by travellers. Colonel Wharton's party had to make use of such accomodation on the way to Bhanipur. (967).

DALLAS, Mr James, (Jim), O.F. A contemporary of Colonel Wharton at Greyfriars. He is aged about 40. At one time he lent Mr Vernon Smith £1,000 to help him over a financial crisis. After his presumed death in South America, Mr Vernon Smith helped his son, Paul, by way of repaying the debt. After his return to England and finding his son, they went to Brazil where he became a partner in a coffee plantation. (GBC 6).

DALLAS, Paul. The only child of Mr Jim Dallas. Taken out of a "charity" school by Mr Vernon Smith and sent to Greyfriars, he promptly earned the enmity of Smithy, who could only believe that Dallas was an "interloper" after his father's fortune. It was not until Mr Dallas' unexpected return to England that Smithy ceased to try to down one he had looked upon an enemy. (GBC 6).

DALTON, Mr Richard, (Dicky). The Fourth Form Master at Rookwood.

DANBY, Sir George. A relative of Loder's. He lives at Danby Croft. His home was burgled one holiday while Dick Lancaster was among the house guests. Loder was convinced that Lancaster was guilty of the crime. (1211).

DANCE. The assistant ring master of Whiffle's Circus. An inveterate gambler, he saw his chance of unlimited funds when he recognised Bunter as an imposter. (HBE 28-29).

DANCE, Ben. A one legged seaman who had been the shipmate of "Black Peter". He had promised Black Pete on his deathbed to deliver a map to his heir, Tom Redwing, which showed the whereabouts of his treasure. Despite the efforts of Silvio Xero to capture the map, he fulfilled his mission, and later helped Tom find the treasure. (GBC 11).

DANDY, The. The leader of a gang of "Crooks, coiners, and cracksmen". After being captured by Ferrers Locke, his lieutenant,

Jimmy the Fox, threatened Locke through attempts on Jack Drake's life, to try to secure his release. (1419).

DANDY DEVARNEY. See Devarney, Howard.

DANDY JIM. An American railway robber whose gang was arrested thanks to the marksmanship of Hurree Singh. Dandy Jim was captured later while trying to gain revenge on Inky. (1096).

DANDY PETER. The nickname of Capt. Parsons, (cf).

DANDY SANDERS. See Sanders, Dandy.

DANDY SUGDEN. See Sugden, Dandy.

DANE, Clifton. Son of a North American Indian mother and an English father. He shares a study with Noble and Glyn at St Jim's, where he is a member of the Shell.

DANNY. The native cook in Ken King's ketch the Dawn. (1598).

D'ARCY, The honourable Arthur Augustus, (Major), (Gussy). The second son of the Earl of Eastwood. He is in the Fourth Form at St Jim's School. An aspirant to fashion, he affects a lisp and a monocle. His impeccable manners are rarely ruffled, except when Bunter exceeds even his normal degree of boorishness. He is a ready butt for his form and invites raggings by the fatuousness of his suggestions, and an ill-becoming dignity. Bunter managed to persuade "his old friend" to stay at Bunter Court as a profitable source of income to provide tips for the voracious staff. When Gussy discovered the trick played by his host he left, furious that he should have been made a party to such goings on. But he still gave Bunter a lift out of the danger area.

D'ARCY, The Hon. Walter Adolphus, (Wally), Minor. The third son of Lord Eastwood. He is in the Third Form at St Jim's, of which he is the acknowledged leader. He is a typically scruffy fag, full of humour and fun, especially when it comes to his older brother Gussy! His closest friend is Levison Minor.

DARKE, Philip. A distant relative of Mr Quelch who used to work in a variety show called "Magicland", until he hypnotised the manager and stole £4,000. He used his hypnotic powers on Mr Quelch to make him believe that he, Darke, was James Watson. Unfortunately for Darke, he had been recognised by Harry Wharton and so was taken by the police. (1517).

DARRELL, George Richard Bruce. Prefect at St Jim's. He is the closest friend of the Head of School, Eric Kildare.

DATCHETT. A member of the Sixth Form. He used to be one of Carberry's crowd before the latter's expulsion. (46).

DAWES, Mr Jim. Landlord of the Feathers Inn which is situated up the towpath from Greyfriars. It seems likely that he lost his licence, as he was always running close to, if not actually foul, of the law. (795).

DAWN, The. The ketch owned by Ken King, (cf). (1593).

DAY BOYS. Although there is no mention of Greyfriars taking day boys, there are many members of the school who do not appear on the study lists, and yet are mentioned fairly frequently. It is a well known fact that many Public Schools do take day boys, and there is no reason to suppose that Greyfriars is any different.

de BONTERRE. Answering the advertisement of a dishonest heraldist, Mr Bunter was convinced that he was in reality Sir Samuel de Bonterre ! On his father's instructions, Bunter looked in the school library for Stodge's "Cavalier Reliques" of 1724 in which he found the ancient Norman family of de Bonterre. Unfortunately, it did not mention that the original de Bonterre had died without issue ! Sic transit gloria ! (897).

de CERNAY, Le Compte. A French nobleman living at the Chateau de Cernay, La Fontaine, in France, and a life long friend of Sir Reginald Brooke. It was while the Silver Scud and a party of Friars were visiting his home that Poynings was exposed as a blackmailer. (759).

de CERNAY, Le Viscompte Louis. Son and heir to the Compte de Cernay. He is a close friend of Mauleverer. As a keen cricketer he founded the Fontaine Cricket Club which played a match against a team drawn from the Friars on board and some of the crew of the Silver Scud. (759).

de COURCY, Cecil. The stage name of Mr Thompson who played the Wicked Baron in Little Red Riding Hood. (200).

de COURCY, Rupert, (The Caterpillar). In the Fourth Form at Highcliffe and a one time associate of Ponsonby and Co. He changed his ways under the influence of Courtenay. His langourous, graceful ways earned him his nickname. But for all that, he is a good sportsman when he can be stirred. He is particularly a good bowler.

When his ire is roused he makes a formidable opponent with the gloves on – as Ponsonby has found out to his cost more than once.

de VERE, Algernon. The name by which Timothy Perkins preferred to be known when at Greyfriars, masquerading as a sprig of the nobility. (GBC 35).

de VERE, Edmond. The stage name of Mr Jack Brown who played the Wolf in Little Red Riding Hood. (200).

DE VERE AND THE SILVER SCUD. (Title GBC Volume 35). Relates the arrival and the downfall of Algernon de Vere, (cf); and the almost ill-fated cruise of the Friars on the M.Y. Silver Scud.

DEL REANO, Captain. The murdered skipper of the schooner Castille. A diamond smuggler for many years, he finally met his end, (together with all but one of his crew), at the hands of the crazed Pedro Montana. (1077).

DELANEY. Almost certainly a misprint for Dabney. He is in the Upper Fourth, and is mentioned as the "usual trio of Temple, Delaney, and Fry". (862).

DELAREY, Piet. A South African whose mother was English. His arrival at Greyfriars coincided with the death of General Delarey, a rebel against British Colonial rule and, although no relation, it did mean that his early days at school were difficult. He shares study No 12 with Mauleverer and Vivian. Above average in form, he is a keen sportsman who rarely makes the form teams.

DELHI. Visited by Colonel Wharton and his party on their way to Bhanipur. While there, Bunter astounded the natives by first employing an Ayah, (a children's nursemaid), in the belief that she was a manservant, and then walking the streets unaware that Cherry had fixed to him a paper hat adorned with kite tails ! (966).

DEMPSTER. Member of the Sixth Form and a leading light of its debating society. (50).

DENHAM. Chauffeur to Sir Peter Lanchester. (1556).

DERWENT, Philip, (Flip). Twin brother to Philippa. Their home is in Tasmania. He is in the Fourth Form at Highcliffe. Although somewhat reckless, he is a supporter of Courtenay rather than Ponsonby.

DERWENT, Philippa, (Flap). Twin sister to Philip, she is in the Fourth Form at Cliff House School.

DESERTED WING. At one time a derelict part of the school reached through the Remove box room. One of the many secret staircases lead out of the wing down to the vaults. Situated at the back of the school it has been converted into use in recent years.

DESMOND, Michael, (Micky). He shares Study No 6 in the Remove with Wibley, Morgan and Rake. He is a cheerful Irishman, fond of practical jokes, and, therefore, a good study mate for Wibley, helping him with his impersonations. A fair sportsman, he is among the substitutes rather than the Form teams. He is a keen stamp collector and, for one blissful moment, thought he was the proud possessor of a Sandwich Islands 2c stamp. Had this been true it could have been worth a small fortune. Sadly, it was only a facsimile.

DEVARNEY, Mr Duncombe. Father of Julian, he is the 25th of that name to live at Devarney Court. For a time his income was lost due to the schemings of "Shem Isaacs". He sent his son to Greyfriars for a while. While visiting him one day he was attacked by an accomplice of "The Dandy", from whom he was saved by Newland. A proud man, his poverty, short lived though it was, was unbearable to him, and he tried all he knew to "keep up appearances". (HBE 72).

DEVARNEY, Howard, (The Dandy, Alias Shem Isaacs). He escaped from Dartmoor prison while serving a long sentence, double crossing his accomplice Ledgey. He then disguised himself as a businessman, Shem Isaacs, working in the City. Mr Devarney went to London to "make his Fortune" and, meeting Isaacs, was defrauded of everything. Eventually, however, he was caught thanks to the Greyfriars Scout Troop. (HBE 72).

DEVARNEY, Julian. After his father lost what moneys he had, Devarney left Barcroft for Greyfriars. Blaming "The Jews" for his father's bankruptcy, he barred Newland, until the discovery that Isaacs was in fact his father's cousin. (HBE 72).

DEVARNEY COURT, Sussex. The home of the Devarney family since Norman times. For a while they were forced to leave but, since the restoration of their fortunes, they have been able to return. (HBE 72).

DEVERILL, Richard, (Dick). A legendary Old Friar who in one school match took 10 wickets for 20 runs. (795).

DHOOLAH DAS. A close friend of Hurree Singh. He is at Southgate School. He brought a team over on one occasion to play football. Unfortunately, neither Greyfriars, nor Southgate, realised that they play different forms of football ! Greyfriars play Association, Southgate Rugby ! (306).

DIAZ. A Peruvian mining engineer who was tricked by Mr Vernon Smith into parting with a mine he had discovered. His revenge on Smithy enabled the latter to lie about the affair, leading to the expulsion of Wharton. When Diaz later confessed, Wharton was reinstated. Vernon Smith escaping, as usual, from "the Chopper". (253).

DIAZ, Senor Don Guzman. Picked up from the sea off Cartegena, thanks to Bunter's ventriloquism, while escaping from Franco's forces during the Spanish Civil War. He was wearing a money belt with several thousand pounds in it. Rawlings and Swain, (two of Capt. Compton's crew), tried unsuccessfully to steal it. (1507).

DICK, Ragged. See Ragged Dick.

DICK the PENMAN. The name by which a master forger was known to the criminal fraternity and the police. He reformed his ways and went to Greyfriars under his true name of Jim Valentine. (GBC 9).

DICTATOR OF GREYFRIARS, THE. (Title HBE Volume 43). See Greyfriars Secret Society, The.

DICTIONARY. A nickname given to Alonzo Todd because of his propensity for grandiloquent circumlocution!

DIEGO. A member of Gomez' bootlegging and smuggling gang whose voice Bunter imitated in order to create confusion and so escape fom the gang. (1102).

DIEGO. The only hired hand kept on at the Circle O Ranch after the remainder had been fired by the impoverished owner. (1580).

DIGBY, Robert Arthur. A member of the Fourth Form at St Jim's. He shares Study No 6 with D'Arcy, Blake and Herries.

DIGGS. A member of the Second Form who was incensed when Sammy Bunter, on his arrival at school, made disparaging remarks about his kippers! (144).

DIN DAS. A member of the Jam Bahadur's suite. He had seen Hurree Singh hide Harry Wharton and Co.'s Christmas presents, (a diamond apiece), in a set of candles. His theft of the gifts was discovered, and they were recovered by Jack Drake. (723).

DIXON. A chauffeur from the Courtfield Garage who often drives Smithy out on his various escapades.

DODD, Tommy. In the Modern Side at Rookwood, sharing Study No 5 with Tommy Doyle and Tommy Cook. They are in the Fourth Form and Dodd is the recognised leader of the Modern Side. He is a regular member of the Form Team.

DODDS. A Sixth Former who is a rare member of the cricket eleven. He is not one of the brighter lights of the school. (121).

DOLLAR DUCHESS. The luxuriously appointed yacht belonging to Mr Van Duck. Putnam, his son, was on a cruise to avoid being kidnapped when he met the Greyfriars party returning home from Brazil. He left the yacht to stowaway on the R.M.S. Comet. (1468).

DOMINGO. Steward to Mr Peter Valentine's household at the Boa Vista plantation. (1465).

DON POMPOSO. The very apt nickname given to Mr Prout by the Fifth Form.

DOOLAN. Butler to Sir William Romayne. He found himself in a cleft stick when trying to allow a party of Friars and Saints shelter from a blizzard, while Crawley, Sir William's secretary, was trying to prevent their entering the house. (461).

DORCHESTER, Dorset. The county town. It is the nearest station to Cherry Place, which is about 10 miles outside the town (1142).

DOST HAMID. An Afghan horse dealer who met Colonel Wharton's party on their way to Bhanipur. Under the pretence of conducting Bunter back to civilisation, he robbed him of 100 rupees before Pandy Din killed the horse trader while rescuing Bunter. (967).

DOWNFALL OF HARRY WHARTON, THE. (Title HBE Volume 6). Seeing a letter in his uncle's hand which referred to his nephew as "a selfish, ungrateful burden", Harry Wharton decided to win a scholarship. He fell out with everybody – friends as well as those who were trying to help. He resigned the captaincy of the form, to which Vernon Smith was elected in his place. After the truth about the letter was revealed, (it was from Colonel Wharton to Major Cherry about Paul Tyrrell), some of the rifts were healed, but Vernon Smith continued to fight Harry Wharton during the holidays. Staying at Riverside Bungalow, near Wharton Lodge, Vernon Smith planned to maroon Wharton on Monk's Eyot, but instead Ponsonby captured Tom Redwing. As a result of his exposure, Tom missed much of the following term.

DOYLE, James K., (Jimmy). A boxer in Ben Adams' boxing booth. He fought, and was beaten by, Tom Belcher – knocked out in the third round, to the chagrin of Fish, his compatriot. (414).

DRAKE, Jack. He left Greyfriars, where he had been in Study No 3 in the Remove, to become assistant to Ferrers Locke. He is a close friend of the Famous Five. On many occasions he has been an honoured guest, either at their homes, or in their studies. Most visits are memorable for the adventures he brings upon his friends. As one would expect of an embryo detective, he is a master of disguise, and extremely astute, level-headed and brave.

DREW, Jerrold. An industrial spy who attempted to steal the details of a new dyeing process in order to blackmail Mr Kerr for their return. Harry Wharton, however, managed to let him steal a phoney set of notes, while safely delivering the real notes to Edinburgh, and Drew to the Police. (672).

DRIVER, Ulick, O.F. A hard bitten crook, aged about 40, who had sent his cousin and ward to Greyfriars with explicit orders to befriend the wealthy, obtain invitations to their homes, and spy out the land, so that Driver could later rob them. He also forged bank notes, which his cousin, Jim Lee, unknowingly passed for him. A vicious, cruel man, he beat his ward to try to make him obey orders. The result of this treatment was that he was trapped and arrested by Inspector Grimes. (GBC 37).

DRURY. One of Ponsonby's lesser satellites at Highcliffe.

DRURY, Richard, (Dick). A professional boxer of some fame, despite his youth, who spent some time at Greyfriars as a protege of the Head's in reward for saving Dr Locke from a party of footpads. He was placed in Study No 3 in the Remove. His conceit was so great that he soon fell out with the entire form, and unfortunately was befriended by Hilton of the Fifth. An idol who soon proved to have feet of clay, when he asked Drury to "throw" a fight. The entire school was amazed to learn that he had not been expelled for knocking down Wingate. Soon after, he knocked out Loder, who had caught him out of bounds, and left the school of his own accord to return to the ring. (GBC 15).

DUBBS, Dr. A dishonest trichologist who answered an advertisement placed by Vernon Smith, to restore Mr Prout's bald head. The "Doctor's" magnificent mane was claimed to be the result of his own treatment. As it was a wig, this may well have been true! (763).

DUBOC, M. Gaston. A Frenchman Harry Wharton and Co. met while caravanning in France. Like the Greyfriars party, he was on the road for his holidays. The delicious supper he cooked them was enjoyed by all; especially Bunter, until he discovered it was prepared from frog legs and snails! (706).

DUCK, James. The part played by Jack Drake while at Greyfriars to unmask "The Mystery Man of Greyfriars". Outwardly a duffer, it became apparent that he was no such thing, and his disguise was penetrated by several members of the Remove. (HBE 49).

DUCK & PARTRIDGE, The. An Inn on the outskirts of Courtfield. At an auction here, Coker bought an old autobus, (at least Bunter did the bidding in Coker's voice!). Fish, with an eye to the main chance, bought the vehicle from Coker, and founded Fishy's Travel Agency. (993).

DUCLOS, Captain. Leader of the party of French Cavalry that set out with Major Cherry to find Marjorie Hazeldene and Clara Trevlyn. Attacked one morning by Bou Saoud, all the Frenchmen were murdered, leaving Major Cherry as the only survivor. (866).

DUFFER. One of the nicknames given to Alonzo Todd.

DUNK, Hunk. P. An American patent medicine seller from whom Fisher T. Fish stole a formula which he thought was a hair restorer. It turned out to be a corn cure! But not before most of the Remove had suffered from its effects! (920).

DUNMORE, Lord. The past owner of the palatial yacht The Skylark. He sold her to Mr Samuel Hunter. Skinner, in one of his flights of wit, changed the newspaper report so that it appeared that Mr Samuel Bunter was the new owner. For a time, William George's head reached the skies! (955).

DUPONT, Napoleon. The French Junior who shares Study No 10 in the Remove with Bolsover. A more unlikely combination is hard to imagine! Nap is an excitable, but gentle soul, who is protected from bullying by his study mate. Willing, but hopeless on the games field, (with the exception of fencing at which he excels), he is not a great deal better in class. His greatest talent is cooking. The dishes he prepares are enjoyed by all until they discover the ingredients – for some reason the Remove do not like snails and frogs' legs!

DURANCE, Arthur. Following the recent death of his mother, and his father's departure for South America, he left Devon, his home, for Greyfriars. On his arrival at Courtfield he was kidnapped by Stone whose son went to school in his place. This was part of a plot to embezzle Durance mother's fortune. Vernon Smith recognised Stone as an imposter and exposed the plot. (1130-1131).

DURIE, Captain. Captain of M.V. Sundabund. Vanderpeck tried to murder him for his money but, thanks to the Famous Five, his attempt failed. (1186).

DUTCH SAM. The owner of the hideaway on the East Side of New York where Vernon Smith and Bunter were imprisoned after their capture by Two Gun Sanders. (1574).

DUTTON, Thomas, (Tom). He shares Study No 7 with the Todds and Bunter in the Remove. He is somewhat deaf - a recipe for misunderstanding! But the advantages of not hearing Bunter's incessant squeaking, and Alonzo's perpetual philosophical circumlocution and morality, must make hardness of hearing a blessing in that study! He is an excellent footballer and usually plays at full back for the Form Team.

E.

EASTCLIFF. The village near Eastcliff Lodge. It lies between Eastcliff Lane and the North Foreland. (1678).

EASTCLIFF LODGE, Eastcliff, Kent. It is the home of Sir William Bird, a high ranking Civil Servant. The house lies within easy walking distance of the North Foreland which can be reached by walking through the village. During Sir William's absence on a secret mission, Wibley impersonated him and invited the Famous Five and Bunter as guests. (HBE 41).

EASTERN QUEEN, S.S. A passenger cargo ship built by Mr Vernon Smith to serve his oriental interests. After his retirement from smuggling, (largely through force majeur!), Captain Compton was given the command of her. (1509).

EASTHORPE, Hants. A village near D'Arcy's home. (1074).

EASTWOOD HOUSE. The home of Lord Eastwood, Gussy D'Arcy's father.

EGERTON, Mr. One of the water pirates on the Thames who make good living out of letting other people's paddocks to unsuspecting tourists. The camp site at "Egerton Lawn" turned out to be Majo

Loder's home. His nephew, Gerald, was staying at the time, and so it is not surprising that trouble ensued. (1645).

ELIZA. House maid at Cliff House School. (749).

ELLIOTT, Ninian. A member of the Remove who figures only rarely in the affairs of the form - either academic or sporting. He shares Study No 8 with Smith Minor. He is so retiring as to be one of the few members of the form about whom very few personal details are known.

ELM WALK. Lies between the school buildings and the boundary wall. It is a peaceful secluded spot, popular with all the school for strolling in. Hopefully the trees will survive the ravages of Dutch Elm Disease. If not, the school will lose a famous landmark.

ELMBRIDGE, Surrey. A village close to Wharton Lodge. It boasts a racecourse which nearly caused the final downfall of Vernon Smith during the time that Mr Smedley was trying to discredit him. Luckily, Smithy recognised that Smedley was following him, and decided not to go the races. (1367).

ELMDALE, Surrey. The village lies only half a mile from Wharton Lodge. It is served by a branch railway line which goes to Woodgate, or Elmbridge in the opposite direction.

EMILY. At one time House maid to Mrs. Locke. (49).

ENTERPRISE FILMS. One of Mr Hiram K. Fish's rivals in Hollywood. They tried to steal Mauleverer from Perfection Films. Bunter who was wearing Mauly's hat was happy to sign with them! (1097).

ERROLL, Kit. Shares study No 4 in the Classical Side at Rookwood wih Mornington. A good all round athlete, he is also a restraining influence on his study mate.

EUCHRE. One of Pete Corcoran's gang of cattle rustlers. (1576).

EVERS, Albert, (Bertie). A friend of Coker's at Uppingham School. He sent an invitation to Greyfriars to play a rugby match which Coker was going to arrange. His plan fell through because the Remove had the only set of rugby posts in the school, and the Head would not allow the Fifth to use the Remove pitch. (730).

EVERSLEY SCHOOL. A nearby school against whom Greyfriars First Eleven used to have matches. In recent times, however, there has been no record of fixtures against them. (200).

EXPELLED FROM GREYFRIARS. (Title HBE Volume 57). After being caught impersonating M. Charpentier, Wibley was expelled. Rather than go home and face the wrath of a Roman parent, he returned to school disguised as Sir Hilton Popper's nephew Archie. At the same time, he was trying to persuade Mossoo to put in a word for Wibley; the while the Remove were ragging Mossoo "bald-headed" in retaliation for Wib's expulsion ! Eventually Wibley earned remission through rescuing M. Charpentier from a footpad.

EYE of OSIRIS. A priceless diamond lost for millenia. Kalizelos had discovered the secret of its whereabouts and pursued Mauleverer to obtain the Scarab of A-Menah, wherein was hidden the diamond. (HBE 1).

F.

FAGGING. The Second and Third forms have to hold themselves ready at all times to run errands and take messages for the prefects. In addition to this, each prefect has a fag whose duties are to prepare his tea, wash the dishes, as well as generally keeping his fag-master's study tidy.

FALL OF THE BOUNDER, THE. (Title GBC Volume 24). After being suspected of smoking, and in fact covering up for Skinner, Vernon Smith's recent good behaviour took a turn for the worse. He took to "blagging" again and then broke detention and prevented the form eleven from playing a match. His decision to reform was almost spoiled by Skinner, but Smithy eventually got the better of his evil minded study mate.

FAMOUS FIVE, The. The collective name given to the leaders of the Remove, who are friends through thick and thin, with rare lapses of harmony. The group consists of Harry Wharton, Bob Cherry, Johnny Bull, Hurree Singh and Frank Nugent.

FANE. The Junior Captain of Redclyffe School.

FANFAIR, William Napoleon, (Nap) . When his uncle, William Gosling, received the profits on a life insurance policy, he at first cheeked everybody, from the Head down, until he was sacked. Eating humble pie, he was reinstated, and paid the school fees for his sister's son, Nap. Bunter found out the truth and, telling the whole world the facts, got both Gosling and Nap the sack. However, after they had picked Sir Hilton Popper out of a car crash, the one was again reinstated, and the other "adopted" by Sir Hilton, and his school fees paid at Rookwood. The Remove were sad to lose him, a likeable hard working man who also excels on the sports field. (1152) .

FANGS. Colonel Wharton's bulldog. He helped in the apprehension of a gang of poachers, who were trying to harm Wun Lung. (47) .

FANNY JONES, M.V. The vessel chartered by Colonel Wharton to convey Hurree Singh and friends from Port Said to India. (964) .

FAULKENER. A lesser member of the Sixth Form.

FAWCETT, Miss Priscilla. Tom Merry's one time nurse maid, but now in loco parentis. She originally caused much embarrassment when she made Tom arrive at St Jim's dressed in out dated clothing. However, she is a kindly, caring soul, whose one aim in life is to help Tom Merry in all possible ways.

FEATHERS, The. An Inn up river from Greyfriars. It is sometimes patronised by Greyfriars men.

FELICITA, Madame. A somewhat fiery French lady who was a member of Mr Whiffle's pantomime company. (409) .

FERGUSON, Mr. The chief engineer in the Firefly and an active member of Captain Compton's smuggling gang. However, he would not have agreed to the treachery proposed by Rawlins, had he known of it. (HBE 48) .

FERNBRIDGE. A small village near Wharton Lodge. It boasts one of the stations which serve the area.

FERRERS, Captain. An army officer stationed at Rawalpindi, with whom Colonel Wharton and party stayed en route for Bhanipur. (966) .

FERRET. Employed by Captain Reynham to kidnap Lord Reynham. His efforts failed, and he was eventually captured, thanks to Bunter. (HBE 14) .

FERRET, The. A member of Dandy Sanders' gang. An expert with locks, he tried to retrieve the loot hidden in Greyfriars after a bank raid. His first effort failed thanks to Coker's blunderings – the second, thanks to Bunter and his greed, led to his arrest. (1271-72).

FERRYDALE, Kent. A small village a few miles from Greyfriars. It lies on the road to Braye. After escaping from some gipsies, Marjorie Hazeldene spent the night here at the Green Man. (5).

FIELD, Sampson Quincy Iffley. He shares Study No 14 in the Remove with Bull and Fish. His home is in New South Wales, Australia and, true to his country's sporting traditions, he is a fine sportsman, shining especially on the cricket field. On the whole he is a firm friend and supporter of Wharton & Co. but he has, on occasions, listened to the opposition; although he is man enough to admit it when he is wrong.

FILER, Mrs. The sub-postmistress and proprietress of a general shop in Greenleaf, Bucks. (1120).

FILEY, William, (Bill). A poacher and tramp who Coker decided was dodging conscription. His ludicrous efforts to make Filey enlist earned him more kicks than ha'pence ! When it finally came out that Filey had three times tried to enlist, and been turned down as many times, Coker received a massive impot from the Head ! (429).

FILIPPI, Madame. The stage name of the lady who played the Grandmother in the Courtfield pantomime, Little Red Riding Hood. (200).

FILMER, Mr. One time Master of the Second Form. It is not made clear whether he was a temporary master or the predecessor of Mr Twigg. (117).

FINN, Buck. An American from Arizona in the Fourth Form at St Jim's. A somewhat bombastic braggart, he made an unpopular member of the party which stayed at Greyfriars one Christmas. (513).

FIR LANE. Runs alongside the Cloisters outside Greyfriars to join Friardale Lane.

FIREFLY, M.V. Captain Compton's yacht which was used for smuggling until Valentine, the Captain's nephew, persuaded him to stop. The rest of the crew mutinied and marooned the Comptons. (HBE 47-48).

FIRS, The, Stacliffe by Sea. A holiday house rented by Ponsonby and Co. to which Mauleverer was invited, as a lamb to the slaughter. Having met the Famous Five while trying to find the house, Mauly was more than glad when they came to his rescue, as he faced the knuts who were trying to make him pay non-existent debts. (706).

FISH, Fisher Tarleton.   An indescribably repellent specimen.   He is tolerated, (barely), in Study No 14 by Bull and Field.   An entrepeneur of no mean ability, (as he is convinced), no chance of making a buck or two is lost.   Whether it be usury amongst the fags at a penny per week on a bob, or buying unwanted items at ridiculous prices to sell when required at inflated prices, any scheme is meat to Fishy.   An arrant snob, he cannot understand that only he cares about profit.   Any one else is happy to share his last crust.   Not Fishy.   He sells it, and it takes the ingenuity of Mauleverer to get the better of him.   When barred out on Popper's Island, Fishy had bought supplies to sell. Mauly bought the entire stock and sold Fishy a portion at the price of all the goods !

FISH, Hiram K.   The father of Fisher T., he has proved an able teacher to his son of business shenanigans.   His home address is 1150, 299th Street, New York, U.S.A.   A financier with fingers in many pies, he is at his happiest "doing" some one, as when he "cornered pork", or trying to find the Portercliffe treasure.   Incapable of a straight action, he fooled the Headmaster, and his charges, when he took a party to America on an "educational trip".   It turned out to be a visit to Hollywood to make a film on the cheap, with the Friars taking most of the parts.

FISH, Vanderbilt.   A somewhat unkind nickname give to Hiram K. Fish because of his pretensions to great wealth. (150).

FISHER, Arthur, (Art).   A member of Lantham Speedway. (1220).

FITZGERALD, Terrence.   A member of the Fifth Form who shares Study No 2 with Smith Major.

FIX, Inspector.   A member of the C.I.D. who came down to Greyfriars after receiving an annonymous letter accusing Wun Lung of being a spy.   The Inspector discovered that Levison's animus had led him into mistaking the moves in a game of postal chess for a cryptogram ! (43).

FLAMINGO.   A schooner of some 20 tons burthen normally used in the copra trade.   She was hired by Mauleverer to take him and his friends for a trip from Kalua to Suva, (in Fiji).   They also had to take two prisoners, Ysabel Dick and Capt. van Dink, who managed to escape from their irons and take over the ship.   As the Greyfriars men would not surrender, Ysabel Dick scuttled the craft rather than have them harmed. (1593).

FLASH, Captain. Probably the nickname of a crook who used a caravan to tour the country and then hide his booty therein. After his arrest, Mr Lazarus bought the van and rented it to Harry Wharton and Co. Their tour was interrupted by Stokes and "The Rabbit" who tried to steal the van. (GBC 22).

FLATT, Mr. The part time music master at Greyfriars.

FLIP. A waif from Puggins Alley in London. He was on the run from the police and, having helped Bunter, found himself at Greyfriars, courtesy of Mauleverer. A tearaway, he was the despair of Mr Twigg. For all that he was intensely loyal to his hero, Bunter. Flip would have taken the blame when Bunter landed Mr Quelch in the sanatorium by dropping a pail of water on him. The temporary master of the Remove was known to Flip – he was a Mr Lagden, better known as a master thief, Jimmy the One. Although Flip would never have "grassed", Lagden kidnapped him. Inspector Brent was sent down from Scotland Yard in charge of the search and not only arrested Jimmy the One, but also discovered that Flip was his son. (HBE 4).

FLOGGING JUDGE JEFFREYS, THE. (Title GBC Volume 27). During Dr Locke's absence, Mr Jeffreys was appointed temporary Headmaster at Sir Hilton Popper's recommendation. He was a harsh, sadistic bully, who immediately earned the hatred of the Remove by ordering them to fag. They got their own back by spending an entire history lesson animadverting upon Judge Jeffreys and the Bloody Assizes ! Harry Wharton was sentenced to bread and water in the punishment room, and Mr Quelch was dismissed for standing up to the new Head. To counter the brutality of Mr Jeffreys, the Remove founded the "Greyfriars Inquisition", and ragged Loder, Mr Schwartz, (Mr Quelch's replacement), and finally Mr Jeffreys himself. The Remove finally barred themselves out and, in a pitched battle, defeated the "army" put into the field against them. Following this, Jeffreys was drummed out of the school, with his face painted with soot and gum !

FLOOK, Phineas. A business friend of Mr H.K. Fish, and a member of the combine which "cornered" the pork market. Barney McCann telephoned Greyfriars in his name, but Fishy guessed who was calling, thus forestalling McCann's kidnap attempt. (1163).

FLOWING BOWL, The, Wimford. The Inn frequented by Muccolini's circus hands when they were pitched in Wimford. Tippity Tip was convinced that the ale was extra strong when he saw Bunter's face after it had been painted by Bob Cherry ! (1485).

FLYNN, Patrick O'Donovan. A member of the Classical Side at Rookwood. He shares Study No 6 with Oswald and Hooker.

FOLKESTONE, Kent. Situated on the coast, it lies some distance from Greyfriars on the Lantham side of the school. It was near here that Vernon Smith was supposed to spend his holiday studying with Mr Pickering. And it was while Muccolini's Circus was pitched here that Ferrers Locke got the breakthrough in solving the spy case against Muccolini.

FOO LO. Dr Sin's pilot who was under the influence of opium while flying the "Ancient & Honourable Pigeon" with Wun Lung and friends on board. (1544).

FOR EVER BUNTER. (Title HBE Volume 80). Retails the story of Ragged Dick, (abridged in GL Volume 3).

FORBES. A member of the Lantham Speedway. (1220).

FORMS. Greyfriars School is divided, broadly speaking by ages, into several forms. These are, from the senior down:-
Sixth,
Fifth,
Shell
Upper Fourth,
Lower Fourth, (usually called the Remove),
Third,
Second.

There used to be a First Form when Public Schools took boys from the age of 11 years. Since this practice stopped, the First Form has ceased to exist, but the tradition remains of naming the lowest form as it has been known for the last 200 years.

FOUNDER'S PRIZE. An annual prize for Greek awarded upon the results of a paper in that language. The prize value is £50. Originally intended for poor scholars to enable them to "pay their way" it has, of recent years, become more open. Nonetheless, for people like Mark Linley, it means the difference between staying at school, and having to work for his living. So much so, that on one infamous occasion, Vernon Smith cheated to win the prize so that Linley had to leave for a time. (180).

FOUNDERS SCHOLARSHIPS. Endowed from the inception of the school they are awarded annually to candidates who satisfy the examiners and Board of Governors of their merit. They are to the amount of the tuition fees, and are intended for scholars whose parents are unable to meet the fees. Current holders include Linley and Penfold of the Remove, and Wilkinson of the Upper Fourth. Harry Wharton entered one year, (they are awarded to outside entrants or present scholars in the Junior School), when he mistakenly thought that he had become a financial burden to his uncle. (1256).

FOX, Jimmy the. "The right hand man, factotum, and jackal" to The Dandy. After the latter's arrest and imprisonment, Jimmy the Fox tried to kidnap Jack Drake as a hostage for the release of The Dandy. After several abortive attempts he was himself captured in the midst of the Jubilee celebrations in Oxford Street, London. (HBE 33).

FRAZER. The chemist and pharmacist of Friardale. Ionides, while still at school, made Bob Cherry run an errand for him. Instead, Wun Lung went and "doctored" the face lotion ordered, so that Ionides' face turned dark! (49).

FRED. A member of a gang of poachers whose leader had been jailed by Sir Hilton Popper. In revenge, Fred and his accomplices tried to beat Sir Hilton, but were foiled by the Famous Five. By way of reward, Sir Hilton gave £5, which was most unpopularly used as prize money in a French exam to prevent ragging against Mossoo! (1301).

FREDDY. Porter at Friardale Station.

FREDERICK. Footman at Seahill Park. (1525).

FRIAR. Any member of Greyfriars School. Old Boys are known as Old Friars.

FRIARDALE. The nearest village to Greyfriars. It is about one mile distant. It is an ancient settlement which grew up around the monastery, and from which the village took its name.

FRIARDALE ARMS. An Inn which also has a few rooms to let. It is situated in the main street of the village. A pleasant establishment, it does not receive the custom of the shady characters of Greyfriars. (569).

FRIARDALE BRIDGE. Crosses the Sark on the edge of the village. Near it are the boatyards of Mr Jones and Mr Baker. This bridge is not to be confused with the bridge over the tributary of the Sark which it is necessary to cross to get from the village to Greyfriars. It was at the latter that Harry Wharton saved Frank Nugent on his arrival at Greyfriars.

FRIARDALE CHURCH. Is one of the oldest buildings in the county. In part, (the crypt and the nave), it dates back to the early twelfth century. (178).

FRIARDALE GAZETTE. The village newspaper. Unlike the Courtfield papers which have changed hands three times, the Gazette has managed to continue publication despite all uncertainties. A photographic competition, open to all readers, produced much interest at Greyfriars. The eventual winner was Penfold, who had inadvertently taken a picture of Price at the Three Fishers. Bunter used this snap to invite himself to tea for several days. Needless to say the rest of the Remove showed him the error of his ways! (1221).

FRIARDALE GRANGE. The home of Mr Walsh. It is a large house lying off the Friardale Road, on the far side of the village, and bounded by the Highcliffe Road. On his way to rescue Alonzo Todd, buried in snow by Pon. and Co., Mark Linley was caught on the horns of a dilemma when he heard a girl's voice calling for help. Electing to save the girl, (for he knew other Friars were at hand to look after Lonzy), he then promised to keep her rescue a secret, (she should not have been skating), and left himself open to accusations of cowardice. (939).

FRIARDALE GREEN. Lies at the centre of the village, and is barely a mile from the school. On it are held fetes, fairs and circuses. (1168).

FRIARDALE ROVERS. The village junior team. They play occasional football matches against the Remove. (100).

FRIARDALE STATION. Is only a branch line station, but is, of course, of importance as the nearest station to Greyfriars. It makes connections with the main line services at Courtfield.

FRIARS OAK. An ancient oak tree midway between the school and the river. While being chased by the Famous Five, Ponsonby took refuge in the tree and discovered that, not only was it hollow, but also that a secret passage ran between it and the school. In fact the entrance was in the Remove box room. Pon., in typical fashion, used the passage to cause as much harm and damage as possible before he was found out. The passage has now been sealed up. (HBA 10).

FRIAR'S SPINNEY. The part of Friardale Wood where the Friar's Oak stands. (781).

FRIARS WOOD. Is the name given to the part of Friardale Wood wherein stands a ruined chapel. A secret passage connects the school vaults with the ruin. (8;9).

FRIO, Valley of. The river of the same name meanders through the valley, producing a fertile cattle country. On the river is the town of Packsaddle, itself fifteen miles from the Kicking Cayuse Ranch. (HBE 31-32).

FRIO PETE. A cow puncher on the Kicking Cayuse Ranch. (1577).

FROST, Detective Sergeant. Stationed at Courtfield. He arrested Mr Capper in mistake for a drunk who had burgled Major Thresher. Angel was out after lock up, and had seen "Capper", and so identified him to the police in revenge for a punishment, (justly received, it should be said!). However, the burglar, whose name we were not told, was caught and Capper freed. (974).

FROZEN MUTTON. A nickname given to Tom Brown in memory of the New Zealand meat imports to this country.

FRULO, Joao. The manager of the Boa Vista plantation in Brazil. He was sent to England to invite the Famous Five and Bunter for a holiday. On his way, he was attacked by O Lobo and, fortuitously, taken to the sanatorium at Greyfriars. He then escorted the party to Brazil, where he soon became a firm friend of the Famous Five. (Bunter, however, with his Chesterfieldian manners, was not a favourite!). (HBE 44).

FRUMP, Sir Gilbert. The owner of Frump Park, Berkshire, on whose water meadows Harry Wharton and Co. camped, believing it to be "Egerton Lawn"! Ponsonby did not know that they had been moved off and tried a night raid on the erstwhile camp site. Instead of "getting the Holiday Annual", he was "got" by Sir Gilbert's dog! (1338).

FRY, Edward. In the Upper Fourth, he shares Study No 2 with Temple and Dabney. He is a good sportsman and less of a cypher than Temple's other lieutenant, Dabney, but lacking drive, he is content to be led rather than lead.

FU LONG, Mr. Sent by Tang Wang to kidnap Wun Lung, he instead caught Bunter who had dressed up as a Chinaman, by way of a jape upon Wun Lung! Ferrers Locke, luckily for Bunter, was on the scene and was able to arrest Fu. (1176).

GABLES, The. At one time the home of the Wingate family before their removal to Chester. This house lies within walking distance of Wharton Lodge in Surrey. (931).

GADSBY. A one time member of the Shell at Greyfriars, he was expelled for theft.

GADSBY, General. Father to Reginald and his elder brother. A somewhat blind gentleman who seemed to be unaware of his butler's dishonesty. He also seems to have no idea of the worthlessness of his two sons.

GADSBY, Major, (recently promoted from Captain). Expelled from Highcliffe, he seems to have made no effort to reform his life style. He encourages his younger brother and friends to gamble. On one occasion he even persuaded Mauleverer. After leaving school, he studied chemistry and has even used this knowledge to evil ends. To aid Ponsonby win a bet, he made up a mixture to make the Greyfriars Team feel off colour. (147; 706).

GADSBY, Reginald. He is not quite as nasty a piece of work as his Fourth Form colleague, Ponsonby, at Highcliffe. Nonetheless, he rarely feels any compunction in aiding his leader in any escapade, including the frankly criminal.

GADSBY CROFT, Bucks. The home of General Gadsby and family. Not realising it to be the home of one of their arch enemies, Harry Wharton and Co camped here one holiday. They were warned by Vernon Smith, who was staying in the house, that the butler, Pawson, was intending to frame them for a robbery. (1338-39).

GAME CHICKEN. A well known professional boxer who Mr Lascelles' cousin, Archie Valence, proposed matching against Larry. Valence would not believe that Larry did not wish to re-enter the ring, but his efforts to stage the fight came to naught. Shortly after this the Chicken met the Lantham Pet at the Three Fishers. Vernon Smith attended the fight and was caught out of bounds by Mr Smedley. (1321-22; 1373).

GAME KID, The. See Drury, Richard.

GAMES. Most sports are played at Greyfriars to a high standard. Major sports are football and cricket; all others being "minor". Each boy must play the seasonal sport on Wednesdays and Saturdays for two hours, (unless there is a match for which he is not required), and is expected, although not forced, to play for half an hour on other days.

GAMES ROOM, The. The Fifth Form Common Room. A somewhat statelier appartment than the Rag, since the Fifth never riot - unless constrained to deal with their shady members, Price and Hilton; or unless it seems good to them to boot Coker !

GANS, Herr Otto. The Greyfriars German Master. He hails from Bavaria. Despite his hatred of Prussians making it obvious that he was not a spy, Skinnner did accuse him of being one.

GANSO, M.V. The coastal vessel chartered by Captain Corkran to take him and his party from Lagos to Banana in the Congo. (770).

GARNISH, Inspector. A member of the C.I.D. who was sent down from London to investigate the murder of Jim Lane at Ravenspur Grange. A laconic man, he appeared to be making no progress with the case. In fact he had solved it, and was murdered to prevent the murderer's exposure. (1124).

GARTH CLIFF. Is situated in Pengarth Cove. There is a large cavern within the cliff, wherein the Famous Five and Vivian were imprisoned. Their rescue was effected by Cardew of St Jim's. (812).

GATTY, George Adelbert. He is one of the acknowledged leaders of the Second Form. He is large for his age and on the elderly side for the form. His closest friends are Myers and Dicky Nugent. The three of them are willing to, and do, take on all comers if the occasion demands !

GAUNT, Gideon. The pseudonym under which Edgar Poynings wrote to Mauleverer and Sir Reginald Brooke, threatening Mauly's life unless a large sum of money was paid. (GBC 33).

GAY, Gordon. Hails from Australia and is at Rylcombe Grammar School, where he is Captain of the Junior elevens. A consumate actor, on his first meeting with Greyfriars he made up as Gussy D'Arcy of St Jim's, in which guise he took in, not only Greyfriars, but also St Jim's !

GEDGE, Mr J. A solicitor of Chancery Lane, London. He was Captain Marker's London representative in the plot to get Wharton expelled from Greyfriars. It was he who did his utmost to persuade da Costa to continue with his campaign against Wharton when his resolve was weakening. (HBE 27).

GENTLEMAN JIM. A crook who kidnapped Mr Sutcliffe, a temporary master to the Second Form, when on his way to the school. He took his place so that he could rob the school. However, he was unmasked after the Famous Five had rescued the real Mr Sutcliffe. (992).

GENTLEMAN PINCHER. A confidence trickster who worked the London hotels. He met M. Sarrail, an old friend of Mr Quelch and, having locked him up, impersonated him with the intention of robbing Greyfriars. Vernon Smith, however, had met the real Sarrail and so was able, not only to expose the imposter, but incidentally, avoid expulsion! (1264).

GEORGE. A poacher who with Squinty, after failing to rob the Famous Five, attacked Sir Hilton Popper. The Famous Five were out of bounds on Popper Island at the time and, after saving Sir Hilton, expected to get into trouble. Instead, Sir Hilton presented £5 as a prize to the Remove. Mr Quelch decided it would be for French. A sarcastically humourous way of preventing further ructions in Mosoo's class! (1309).

GEORGE. The waiter at the Golden Pig Inn, Hoad. (1335).

GEORGE. Assistant salesman in the cycle shop at Kennet End, where Mauleverer hired a machine to stop one of Ponsonby's raids on the Greyfriars Hikers camps. (1338).

GEORGE. The ostler at the Anchor Inn, Pegg. It was he who drove Mr Lascelles to the doctor after he had sustained a broken leg fighting with Convict 22. (1493).

GEORGE. Farm hand on Redmays Farm. (1566).

GEORGE. The candy seller on the train Smithy and friends travelled on to Texas. Bunter had bought nearly $25 worth of sweets and when Smithy refused to pay the bill, he used his ventriloquism to cause a fight beween the candy seller and Smithy! (1574).

GEORGE. Footman at Monson Chalet. (1648).

GEORGE, Uncle. An occasionally used familiar name for Mr Clegg of "The Tuckshop" in the village. (9).

GHOST of HOAD CASTLE. The local legend of a haunted castle was utilised to the full by Watkins, the local estate agent, so that the vendor, in desperation, would take a price well below market valuation. (1335).

GHOST OF POLPELLY, THE. (Title HBE Volume 39). Mr Vernon Smith bought the old Devonshire house of Polpelly to search for tin. According to local history a Captain from the Spanish Armada had been a prisoner in the house while his release was being negociated. His ship was said to have been the treasury of the fleet, and he was supposed to have hidden the payroll somewhere in the nearby caves. The squire's ghost is said to walk the house searching for the treasure. The legend was traded upon by Count Zero to try to frighten Smithy and his friends away. Bull and Nugent were captured and, in trying to tunnel out of the dungeon wherein they were captive, found the treasure.

GHOST of REYNHAM CASTLE. Is said to haunt the King's Room in the castle where he had met his death in mysterious circumstances. Some say by the hand of the cousin he murdered to succeed to the title. Each Christmas Eve bloodstains appear on the floor of the chamber and the wicked earl walks the castle until the New Year. (1558).

GHOSTLY MONK, The legend of. Downstream from Greyfriars, near Friardale, is an island which used to support a small holy order. When dissolved, one monk refused to leave. The new landowner murdered the monk and threw his body into the river Sark. As his body was not laid in consecrated ground the monk haunts the island. (149).

GHOSTLY SPANIARDS. Legend has it that the ghosts of the drowned seamen from a ship of the Spanish Armada, sunk in Pengarth Cove, haunt the cove. Most of the locals claim to have heard their voices. (811).

GIACOMO. A charcoal burner and bandit from near Perni in the Apennines. His partner Tiriddu kidnapped Bunter, stole all his possessions, (which at that time were considerable), and then demanded a ramsom of £10,000 for his release. However, the Famous Five were able to secure it for nothing! (1587).

GIDDY. A member of the Upper Fourth.

GILBERT. A member of the Shell.

GILDED JIM. Skinner, thinking he was onto a good thing, took five gold sovereigns from a man as pay for rowing him across the river He sold them for 25/- each, the value of the gold in a sovereign, and this led to trouble. They were forgeries with about 10/- of gold in them. Gilded Jim had no trouble in selling his coins to the greedy who saw a quick and illegal profit. Skinner was lucky to get off with a flogging, once Gilded Jim had been arrested. (846).

GILES. Gamekeeper at Wharton Lodge. (1038).

GILES, Mr. The owner of Shepcote Farm, some five miles from Wharton Lodge. Mr Quelch and Jim Valentine spent the night here after Valentine had "rescued" Mr Quelch who was lost in a fog. (1297).

GILES, Mr. The owner of Giles' Farm in whose cowshed Jervish spent the first night after meeting Bunter while on the run from Tiger Bronx. (1383).

GILES, Herbert. A retired carrier living in Little Puddleton. (1333).

GILES CORNER. A hamlet on the Lantham side of Redclyffe Woods. (1566).

GILES FARM. Is situated on the Courtfield side of Friardale just out-side the village. (1383).

GILES LANE. Near Greenleaf in the Chilterns. The Famous Five camped here for a night while Bob Cherry tried to get his motor tricycle repaired. During the night, Harris and Snooks tried to steal the trike. Coker, vowing revenge for an egged face, raided their camp while the trike was being taken, and prevented its loss. (1120).

GILES MILL. Is about a mile from Greyfriars in the direction of Friardale.

GILES POND. Lies half way between Wimford and Wharton Lodge. Lucas Bull was thrown in it by Harry Wharton and Hurree Singh when he persisted in pestering them about Johnny Bull's whereabouts after he had run away from Yorkshire. (1491).

GILMORE, Eric, M.A., Oxon. Took over the Second Form during the absence of Mr Twigg while he was ill. Bearing an uncanny likeness to his half brother, George Waring, he was mistaken for the latter by Bunter. Making his way towards Dover, Waring met Gilmore and, having his appeals for help refused, struck him down and stole his passport with the idea of fleeing the country. Luckily, the Famous Five knew of the double and were able to rescue Gilmore. (1039-41).

GINGER. One of the gang of toughs hired by Mr Hacker to put down the Tuckshop Sit-in Strike of the Remove. (HBE 35).

GINKER'S GOLDEN FOOTBALL POOLS. One of Bunter's get rich quick schemes was to do the pools. Despite it being against the rules, he raised the shilling stake money, posted his coupon and, full of ex-pectations waited for his cheque when he found his results were correct. Sadly, so were many other punters. His winnings? One shilling ! (1456).

GLENN. A one time member of the Remove. (3).

GOBANGO. Native boy who guided the Famous Five part of their way to look for Vernon Smith after his capture by Krantz. The Famous Five left Gobango with Bunter to guard their canoe, but they were overpowered by the slave trader. Gobango escaped and carried the news to Kikolobo. (1234).

GOLDEN ARROW, M.Y. Mr Vernon Smith's yacht in which the Greyfriars party, searching for Redwing's treasure, travelled from Southampton to the Marquesas Islands. After their shipwreck they were drifting in the Pacific when the Golden Arrow picked them up. (GBC 11).

GOLDEN FLEECE INN, Friardale. Backing onto the towing path, the inn was out of bounds. It is possible from its description and location that it was renamed the Cross Keys. (119).

GOLDEN LION, The. An hotel in Courtfield, patronised by Skinner and his cousins. (513).

GOLDEN PIG INN, Friardale. The Inn where Carne usd to buy his cigarettes. This esablishment is not mentioned in the later histories, and so the place either lost its licence or was forced to close down due to lack of trade. The latter is the more likely, since the village seems to have supported a large number of licensed houses. (121).

GOLDEN PIG INN, Hoad. Caught in a downpour of rain, the Greyfriars Hikers were glad to take rooms in this inn. Ponsonby and friends, also stranded, spent a night here after they had been scared by the ghost of Hoad Castle. (1335).

GOLDEN SCARABEUS OF A-MENAH. An ancient Egyptian relic. It is made of gold and Mauleverer, in whose collection it was, did not realise its importance. In fact it housed a priceless diamond known as the Eye of Osiris. (HBE 1).

GOLDEN TROUT. A waterside Inn on the Thames between Wallingford and Oxford. The Famous Five and Bunter lunched here and, Bunter, liking the table, tried without success, to make the Famous Five stay by pretending he had disappeared. (1649).

GOLOPPI, Signor. Dancing Master to Mr Whiffles' pantomime company. He coached Wharton for his part. (409).

GOMEZ, Jose. A Mexican bootlegger. The titular head of a gang of smugglers whose real boss was Myron Polk. At the latter's orders he assaulted Coker, and later Harry Wharton. His final act was the attempted murder of Wharton while engaged in a film stunt. Luckily Bunter had overheard the plan and warned Peter Carter, a detective, so that Gomez arrest could be effected in time. (GBC 20-21).

GOOCH, Dr. Medical practitioner of Friardale. When Bunter had his ears boxed by Walker he pretended to be deaf and claimed to have consulted Dr Gooch, instead of Dr Pillbury, the school medical officer. Bunter then blackmailed Walker until, in desparation, Walker saw Dr Gooch himself, who denied ever seeing a Greyfriars man. (689).

GOOCH, Gideon. Cousin to Arthur Carter. He is a disreputable solicitor who saw the disgracing of Bunter as an easy means of lining his own pockets. He would, therefore, suggest ways and means to Carter, by which his object might be attained. However, after being pitched into a muddy ditch and later locked in the woodshed for the night, he lost interest in the project. (HBE 59-60).

GOOLIGAN, Mike. A New York tough employed by Two Gun Sanders to kidnap Vernon Smith. His plans went awry and he got Bunter instead! (1574).

GORDON, Stuart. A cousin of sorts to Harry Wharton. Monty Newland had decided that Wharton had a "down" on him, and persuaded Wibley to impersonate Mr Gordon; in the process making him ultra Jewish! The plan was working marvelously, much to Wharton's discomfort, when Colonel Wharton and Mr Gordon arrived, exposing the jape. (1498).

GOSLING, William. The Greyfriars School Porter who has grumbled at more generations of Friars than history records! Well over retirement age, he is not yet, as many aver, 100! A crusty man with an inherent hatred of all members of the school, there is nothing he likes better than to lock the gates as some perspiring Friar comes into sight, almost in time for calling over, and to greet him with a "which as 'ow I'll 'ave to report yer" – unless it is his bottle of gin! He does, however, have a more than slight affection for his sister and her son, William Fanfair.

GOUJON, Jean Pierre Paul. Convinced that he was a bank robber in disguise, this Gendarme arrested Bunter. In fact, Wibley had made an intentional hash of making up Bunter so that he would not be able to get into a casino! (316).

GOVERNORS of GREYFRIARS SCHOOL. To whom the Headmaster is directly responsible for the running of the school. The chairmanship is rotational. Present members of the board are:-
> Sir Hilton Popper, Chairman,
> Major R. Cherry,
> Colonel J. Wharton,
> Mr Wingate,
> Sir Reginald Temple,
> Sir George Cholmondley,
> Sir George Cheyne,
> Sir Reginald Brooke,
> Sir Philip Angel.

GOVERNORS STATUE. There is a statue of the founder on the plinth of the fountain in the quadrangle. It was erected by the Governing Body, hence its name. (1623).

GRABBETT, Mr. A solicitor of Courtfield briefed by Mr Coutts after his accident. In the belief that Bunter had saved his client, he questioned Bunter. Since it was actually Coker who had performed the deed, it is not surprising that Bunter could not answer the questions put to him! (1058).

GRABBLE, Farmer. Bunter, convinced he was going big game hunting, borrowed Mr Prout's gun for a bit of practice! The first shot hit Mr Grabble's donkey. The damage was probably greater to Bunter after the irate farmer had finished. But to judge by the uproar, they were both at death's door! (1091).

GRACE, Edward. In Study No 2 in the Classical Side at Rookwood School. His real name is Edward, but is commonly known as "Putty" because he is so soft!

GRAFTER, Joseph. A turf accountant with whom Loder had an account. Loder had asked Wharton to post a letter, but it was lost. Bunter found it and started to blackmail Loder. (1090).

GRAHAME, Walter. A Junior at Courtfield County School. His friends are Trumper and Lazarus. He is a good sportman, and is a member of the school's Junior teams.

GRAND PACIFIC HOTEL, Pita. The hotel at which Mauleverer and friends stayed after they had been searching for Mauly's cousin, Brian, without success. Instead they had been shipwrecked, and met cannibals and pirates! (1597).

GRANT. A member of the Third Form.

GREAVES. Valet to Captain Lankester. (1193).

GREEN, Mr. The mate in the Silver Star. (1178).

GREEN, Mr. Lives in a cottage at the top of the hill in Friardale Lane, between the village and the school. (1408).

GREEN HEDGES. A village on the railway line. It is equidistant from Greyfriars and Courtfield, and lies in the Lantham direction.

GREEN MAN, The. The village Inn at Ferrydale. (5).

GREENE, Captain. The Captain of the M.V. Golden Arrow. (1020).

GREENE, William Frederick. He shares Study No 4 in the Fifth Form with Coker and Potter and, while he is one of the main body of the form, appearing regularly in Form and First Elevens, he does not take the same manners to his study. He looks on Coker as the butt that he may be but, so hypocritical and cavalier is his attitude, that one is forced to the conclusion that he is only there for the feasts provided by Aunt Judy. This is borne out by the rarity of occasion that Greene will ever stay to support his self-appointed leader.

GREENFORD, Surrey. A village lying two-thirds of the way between Redgate and Wharton Lodge. (1661).

GREENGATES, Chester. The home address of the Wingate family after their removal from Surrey. (1570).

GREENLEAF, Buckinghamshire. A village in the Chilterns. The Famous Five on a hiking holiday with a motor tricycle, met Coker here while he was on a motoring holiday. Despite having to contend with his aggressiveness, they managed to prevent yet another attempted theft of the trike. (1120).

GREENLEAF, Surrey. A village some ten or fifteen miles from Wharton Lodge. Whiffle's Circus pitched camp here, as did the Famous Five on a cycling holiday. While here, Huggins tried to assault Bunter who was saved by the Famous Five. As a result of this, they were invited to join the circus as bodyguards. (1072).

GREENOAKS, Wiltshire. A village lying near the county border. Whiffle's Circus had a pitch here just after Bunter's imposture was discovered. (1075).

GREENWOOD, Surrey. The station next down the line from Wimford.

GREYFRIAR. The correct name of a member of Greyfriars School. In practice this is usually abbreviated to Friar.

GREYFRIARS ADVENTURERS, THE. (Title HBE Volume 12). One summer holiday Mauleverer took a party on his yacht to the Pacific to search for his cousin, Brian Mauleverer. He had sunk to the depths of alcoholism and beachcombing after an appeal for help had received no reply. (In fact Mauly had offered assistance but his offer had not reached Brian). While searching the islands, the Greyfriars men were shipwrecked, and Bunter became chief of a cannibal tribe for a time, thanks to his ventriloquism. Rescued by Ken King, they eventually found Brian who had been instrumental in their misfortunes.

GREYFRIARS BOUNDER, THE. (Title HBE Volume 75). Vernon Smith in one of his regular campaigns against authority cut a detention short. The only thing that saved him from a flogging was return-ing some money stolen from a bank at Lantham. No-one believed his descripton of the bank robber, let alone his accusation against Captain Spencer. However, he was finally vindicated when Spencer was indeed proved to be the robber. Soon after this, Hazeldene had the gambling fever and Vernon Smith, using his own peculiar methods, saved both Hazel and his money.

GREYFRIARS CHUMS IN CHINA. (Title HBE Volume 25A). See Billy Bunter in China.

GREYFRIARS COWBOYS, THE. (Title HBE Volume 32). Mr Vernon Smith had bought a ranch in Texas. Being too busy to go himself, he sent his son with some friends to examine the place. They found that the livestock was being rustled by the foreman, who had also murdered the previous owner. With the help of the Rio Kid, they put things to rights.

GREYFRIARS CRUSADERS, THE. (Title GBC Volume 7). Vernon Smith had vowed to get the Famous Four and Mark Linley expelled. One by one he succeeded. Lastly, Bob Cherry was expelled but, refusing to go, he barricaded himself in the Old Tower and called his friends back to join him so that they could get their names cleared.

GREYFRIARS DOUBLE, THE. (Title HBE Volume 18). The correct title of the volume commonly known as "The Stacey Special". (cf).

GREYFRIARS FILMSTARS, THE. (Title GBC Volume 21). See Harry Wharton & Co. in Hollywood.

GREYFRIARS HERALD. The newsheet edited by Harry Wharton which takes an irreverent and humourous view of life at Greyfriars.

GREYFRIARS HIKERS, THE. (Title HBE Volume 19). Following a smash and grab raid on Mr Lazarus' shop, Mickey the Sprat, before he was arrested, put a clue to the hiding place of his loot in Bob Cherry's Holiday Annual. Ponsonby discovered this and tried to steal the Annual so that he could claim the reward. The summer holidays ensued and the Famous Five, Mauleverer and Bunter went on a hiking holiday which, pursued as they were by Pon., meant that their holiday was frequently disrupted. Finally, at the beginning of the next term, Inspector Grimes broke the code and recovered the loot. None of the contenders for the reward received anything.

GREYFRIARS IMPERSONATOR, THE. (Title HBE Volume 60) . Wibley took in all and sundry with his impersonations of Vernon Smith's cousin Ginger, Mossoo and Mr Twigg. As usual he ended up the worse for wear when his japes were discovered.

GREYFRIARS MYSTERIES, THE. (Title HBE Volume 81) . Narrates some of the happenings at Greyfriars shortly before the Famous Five went to India.

GREYFRIARS ON SAFARI. (Title HBE Volume 65) . Visiting Kenya, on business Mr Vernon Smith took the Famous Five and Bunter as company for his son. Soon after their arrival, Smithy fell foul of one Krantz, a slave trader who, one by one, captured the members of the Greyfriars party and sold them into captivity in the Congo. There they were enslaved, except for Bunter who was destined for the cooking pot ! After much hardship they were rescued by Kikolobo, the Kikuyu hunter.

GREYFRIARS PLOTTERS, THE. (Title GBC Volume 30) . Nugent Minor celebrated his arrival at Greyfriars by only just avoiding expulsion. Carberry and Ionides, two of the greatest blackguards unhung, had accused Harry Wharton of stealing a valuable diamond pin which Bunter had borrowed. Wun Lung fell through the ice and did not reappear. Convinced he had caused his death, the bully of the Remove was stricken with remorse – unnecessarily as Wun Lung was indulging in one of his practical jokes. Wun followed this by locking Bulstrode in the vaults. Dicky Nugent continued his defiant behaviour by going to the Waterside Inn with Carberry and Co. Thinking they had been seen by the Head, Carberry tried to lie his way out of trouble, but was caught out and expelled.

GREYFRIARS PRETENDER, THE. (Title HBE Volume 7) . Dick Lancaster was sent to Greyfriars by his guardian, Slimy Sugden, the leader of a gang of crooks. Lancaster was placed in the Sixth Form and proved immensely popular, both as a scholar and a first rate cricketer. As Sugden's main asset, he was known by reputation to the police as The Wizard, a master safe cracker. His experiences at

Greyfriars led him to reform, but Sugden tried to blackmail him into continuing as a crook. However, he eventually escaped both Cops and Robbers to make a new life for himself.

GREYFRIARS SCHOOL. A famous Public School near Friardale in Kent. There was a monastic foundation here from Saxon times – almost certainly Benedictine, since Anfrith, the founder of the first house is known to have become a "Black Monk". He cannot have been a member of the Augustinian order, since they did not come to this country until about 1100 AD. At what date the house changed its allegiance to St Francis, (or The Grey Friars), is not clear, but it was at its earliest 1224. Following the Acts of Succession, Treason, and Supremacy, the rift between King Henry VIII and Rome was complete. The reign of terror began with the Franciscans being the first to suffer. We can safely say, that being so close to Canterbury, Greyfriars would have been one of the first houses to be suppressed in 1534. In 1551 a school for "poor boys" was established by King Edward VI. The Foundation prospered until a new wing and two-thirds of the original buildings were destroyed by fire in King Charles time. Some fifty years later an extensive college for "the sons of gentlemen" was built on the site. The original buildings fell into disrepair. The School Charter, still valid today, was granted by King George Ist in 1716.

GREYFRIARS SECOND ELEVEN, THE. (Title HBE Volume 71) . Relates a series of unconnected happenings at Greyfriars: ie, Vernon Smith leaving school to make his own way in the world and finding himself in borstal, being just one of the histories recounted.

GREYFRIARS SECRET SOCIETY, THE. (Title HBE Volume 42) . After the Head and Wingate had been injured in a motor accident, Mr Prout was appointed temporary Head in Dr Locke's place. His first action was to make Loder head of school, whose tyranny, together with the blindness of Mr Prout to the situation, led Vernon Smith to form the Secret Society to combat Loder's bullying. The Head returned just in time to prevent the wholesale slaughter of the Remove by Mr Prout after they had gone out of bounds – albeit with Loder's permission, having persuaded him to reform his rule.

GRIGGS, Mr. Rescued from the sea by Captain George Cook who was cruising with a party of Friars. He had escaped from Folkestone in a small boat after robbing a bank. Thinking that the police were after him, he gave himself away; in fact it was Coker in a speed boat chasing the Sea Nymph, after literally missing the Boat ! (1314) .

GRIME'S AUCTION ROOMS. Off the High Street in Courtfield. Bunter bought a four poster bed here, and conned the Famous Five into paying both the carriage costs as well as the purchase price. When destroying the mattress as ordered by Mr Quelch, the Famous

Five recouped their costs by finding several sovereigns hidden therein. Bunter was incensed when Mr Quelch did not allow him some of the treasure. (729).

GRIMES, Inspector Henry. The senior police officer at Courtfield. He is also in charge of the local station at Friardale. He is a first class policeman of the slow, steady type, who never makes brilliant, intuitive guesses, but instead, by slow, methodical work, solves his cases. He is known to all Friars, as he is always one of the first on the scene if there is a local crime.

GRIMSLADE WATER. A river on the Yorkshire moors. While on a hiking holiday the Famous Five camped here only to lose Bunter who had "done a bunk". While searching for him, Bob Cherry was kidnapped by gipsies on Ponsonby's instructions. (1337).

GRIMWADE, Dr. Headmaster of Greyfriars School during Cromwellian times. Meyer Brandon was likened to him as one of the worst tyrants who had controlled the school. (1170).

GRUBBI, Signor. Patron, (or owner), of the Albergo Oriente. (1386).

GRUNTER of GREYHURST. A parody of Bunter written by Wibley for the Remove Dramatic Society. Bunter made use of his "double" to escape trouble for a while. The end result, which he should have foreseen, was a flogging for both himself and Wibley who had played the part of Grunter. (1652).

GUGGS, Jimmy. A tramp who tried to rob Bunter, (he actually had £1!). Marco, the lion tamer, of Muccolini's Circus came to the rescue and Bunter joined the show. Guggs later encountered Bunter on tour, and robbd him of 35/-. Muccolini learned of his attacks on Bunter and offered him money to beat up W.G.B. His various attempts were thwarted. (HBE 55-56).

GUGLIEMO. The stage name adopted by Bunter when running a side show as a crystal gazer in Muccolini's Circus. He had obtained the cystal by fraud from Zara, making her believe that he, Bunter, had the "power", and could make her hear her father's voice. (1485).

GUISEPPE. A Neapolitan who tried to steal the Scarab of A-Menah from Wharton at the behest of Kalizelos. (1278).

GUISEPPE, (Beppo). A diminuitive Roman and a member of the underworld, employed by Tiger Bronx to kidnap Bunter. Ponsonby was engaged in a prank against the Friars, and so was kidnapped for his pains! (1388).

GUISEPPE. An Italian crook who was engaged by Dr Sin to hold up the Famous Five so that Dr Sin could take Wun Lung back to China. (1543).

GUNMEN AT GREYFRIARS. (Title HBE Volume 45). On their return trip from Brazil the Famous Five befriended Putnam van Duck, the son of an American millionaire, who had been threatened with kidnapping by Chick Chew. With a Chicago ex-gangster for a bodyguard, the scenes are better imagined than described when Pike insisted on attending Mr Quelch's classes. Despite Fisher T. Fish and Chew's insistence on this being a sleepy little show, it was over here, in England, that Chew's enterprises were finally halted with his arrest.

GUNN. A member of the Second Form.

GUNNER, Bert. When on a caravan holiday, the Famous Five were joined by a one-legged ex-serviceman. Jack Drake fell in with the party and soon saw through the charade, realising that "Wilkinson" was actually Gunner. (707).

GUNNER, Peter Cuthbert. In the Fourth Form at Rookwood, he is on the Classical Side, where he shares Study No 7 with Dickinson.

GWYNNE, Patrick. A Sixth Former and a prefect. Since the death of Courtney he has become Wingate's closest friend. He is a regular member of the School teams. An Irishman of the more level headed sort, he is consistent in his actions, and popular with all the school, (except the black sheep!).

H.

HACK, Mr Joshua. The American storekeeper on Kalua. (1594).

HACKER, Mr Horace Manfred, M.A. Known as the Acid Drop on account of his sarcastic, bitter, mean and spiteful nature. He is a humourless man with no friends amongst the staff, and who is perhaps the most unpopular member of staff as far as the school is concerned. During the Head's absence he was, mistakenly, promoted to acting Headmaster by the governors. His petty tyranny led to the expulsion of seven of the Remove, followed by the "Sit in Strike".

HAIR TRIGGER. An almost perpendicular path down the side of Jack Rabbit Canyon. Harry Wharton stood in for Myron Polk to do a film stunt which entailed riding a horse down the canyon's side. As it was considered impossible, Polk saw it as an ideal opportunity for murdering Wharton, (through the offices of Gomez). But for Bunter overhearing the plans, his death would have been taken for accidental. As it was, Peter Carter was able to arrest Gomez in the act and prevent a catastrophe. (1104).

HALL, Barney. The owner and Captain of a lugger trading out of Tonga, who was not averse to smuggling. He brought Van Dink to Kalua, only to have to deport Ysabel Dick for an assault on Mauleverer. Later he took the Greyfriars party from Pita to Kalua, after they had made a safe landfall following a shipwreck. (HBE 12).

HALL, Captain Jim. Serving in the Texas Rangers and nicknamed "Mulekick" because of the strength of his punch. He was engagd in hunting the Rio Kid when he was caught himself by the Kid who had no trouble in escaping from the Captain. Vernon Smith freed him from his ignominy and persuaded him to help entrap Barney Stone. (1579).

HAMMERSLEY, Vincent. A member of the Sixth Form and in the form teams.

HAMID. An African guide who instead of taking Marjorie Hazeldene and Clara Trevlyn on a ride to a nearby oasis led them into the clutches of Bou Saoud. He received a large bribe for his efforts. (867).

HAMZA. An Arab camel driver in the pay of Mustapha ben Mohammed. He attacked the Famous Five while they were searching for Major Cherry. (864).

HAMZA. A steward on board the steamer of the Messageries Maritimes from Marseilles to Port Said. He was in the pay of Nally Das and prepared a drugged drink for Hurree Singh which Bunter consumed, thus preventing Inky's capture. To avoid arrest after being discovered, he jumped ship. (964).

HAMZA. In the pay of Kalizelos, he tried to steal the Scarab of A-Menah from Mauleverer - who luckily had left it behind in his hotel ! (1279).

HANK. The cook at the Kicking Cayuse Ranch. For most of the time that Vernon Smith and his friends were here the cooking was done by Chuck the Choreman. (1575).

HANKEY, Rat. The confederate with whom Soames robbed the Post Office at Lantham. There was a lot of snow at the time, and he injured himself falling from his motor cycle. He was arrested by the police, but not before he had left a cigarette case with a message scratched inside it to guide Soames to the stolen money. (1609).

HANSON. A deck hand on board the M.V. Hope. (179).

HANWAY. The host at the Riverside Inn to which Loder and Carne took Nugent Minor soon after his arrival at Greyfriars. (107).

HARD TACK. A cow-town downstream from Packsaddle on the Rio Frio, Texas. (1575).

HARKER, Big Bill. One of young Mr Rance's henchmen who tried to turn the Famous Five off Blackrock Island. He later helped Peter Coot kidnap Vernon Smith. A brutal ruffian, he was no match for the combined strength of the Famous Five. (HBE 50).

HARKER, Bill. A tramp who encountered Bunter after he had run away from school to become a bandit. He was hiding in his lair in Friardale Woods which, after having all his food eaten by Harker, ceased to be so attractive ! (1137).

HAROLD. There had been a split in the Famous Five over Johnny Bull's birthday. Harry Wharton had sold his camera to provide a feed. As Bunter had eaten it, Bull did not believe that his friends had remembered his birthday. To try to heal the breach, Bob Cherry hired Harold and his friend Huggins to attack Hurree Singh. The idea was that Bull would save Inky and so repair the rift. Unfortunately, both Harold and Huggins were drunk so that the scheme came to naught. (497).

HARPER. Head keeper at Wharton Lodge. (47).

HARRINGTON, Mr Henry. Suffered from shell shock and as a result was convinced that he would explode at any minute! Mauleverer, inadvertently, heard about the case and tried to raise £500 to pay for the necessary treatment. He was unable to borrow or raise the cash on his possessions. His guardian, Sir Reginald Brooke, when he heard about the case, agreed with Mauly's intentions and paid for the treatment himself. (807).

HARRINGTON, Mr Jasper. The alias assumed by Mr J.J. Hazeldene when fleeing from the police after some money had been stolen from the bank at which he works. (1415).

HARRIS. The make up artist at Perfection Studios. (1104).

HARRIS. Valet to Lord Cavandale. (1192).

HARRIS, Bill. The accomplice of Alfred Snooks. They tried throughout the Famous Five's holidays, (spent hiking with a motor tricycle), to steal the trike for the platinum used in its construction. (HBE 36).

HARRIS, George. Pressed into helping Harold Hinks recover the boater worn by Bunter wherein Hinks had hidden a £100 note; he was as unsuccessful as his friend in finding the correct "lid"! (1326).

HARRIS, Hubert. His attempted burglary of Mr Prout's study was foiled by the Famous Five. He soon after assaulted Mr Prout and bloodied his nose. When Harris attacked Coker, Mr Prout tried to come to the rescue, and for his efforts received a second black eye, (the first had come from Coker!). (1187-88).

HARRY WHARTON AND CO. IN AFRICA. (Title GBC Volume 12). Captain Kit Corkran, Bob Cherry's cousin, knew of the whereabouts of a hoard of ivory. To find it was not the problem. To actually get the ivory, Bunter and his ventriloquism were necessary to make the African village idol speak. However, the Famous Five and Bunter were taken prisoners by the villagers and for a time Bunter became their chief by the same ventriloquism! Bunter found the ivory and felt that, as he had found it, it should all belong to him. The rest of the party agreed, so long as Bunter carried it home himself! At that point he relinquished title to the treasure!

HARRY WHARTON AND CO. IN HOLLYWOOD. (Title GBC Volume 20). Mr Hiram K. Fish saw that there was a "killing" to be made in the production of a film about a British Public School, especially if one of the cast was a real live earl. To this end Fishy plotted and planned to get a large party from Greyfriars to go to the United States, ostensibly for educational purposes. Had the real reason for their trip been known, permission would never have been granted. (Mr Fish could never understand why it was that all the schools he had approached with the truth had refused the offer!) . After a eventful trip the party arrived in Hollywood. Bunter conned a rival studio into believing that he was Lord Mauleverer, and for a time thought that he had found fame and fortune ! Wharton earned the enmity of the leading man, Myron Polk, a self-opinionated bootlegger, as well as an accomplished actor. Polk attempted Wharton's life, and was actually arrested, to the fury of the studio director. But, as the police had rounded up the rest of the gang, he was set free.

HARRY WHARTON AND CO. IN INDIA. (Title GBC Volume 4) . The life of Hurree Singh was threatened by Baji Rao. Colonel Wharton, who stands in loco parentis in England, felt that it would be safer for Inky if he were in Bhanipur. After several attempts to kidnap him, both in England and on the high seas, the party, (the Famous Five, Bunter and the Colonel), arrived safely in Bhanipur to quell the insurrection of his cousin. Baji Rao was murdered by Lazaroff, a Russian agent provocateur, during their escape after the failure of the coup.

HARRY WHARTON'S ENEMY. (Title HBE Volume 16) . Ralph Stacey, cousin to Harry Wharton, was sent to Greyfriars. Identical in appearance, it was hard to tell them apart, even when together. However, in character they could not have been more different. Wharton would never tell a lie to save his life. Stacey on the other hand, never minded how far he went to achieve his ambition - which was to disgrace Wharton. His plotting was so clever that it took a long time for the Remove to see through the new boy. However, by that time, Stacey had persuaded those in authority to make him both Head of the Form and Form Captain. The truth was eventually revealed when Mr Quelch inadvertently overheard Fish blackmailing Stacey, who was expelled and Wharton reinstated. (See also HBE Volume 17, and HBE Volume 18) .

HARRY WHARTON'S FEUD. (Title HBE Volume 77) . Following the excitement of Pedrillo's appearance, kidnapping and rescue, Harry Wharton had a row with Mossoo which developed into a full scale feud. When Wharton discovered that Mossoo was being blackmailed by Mr Rigg, a moneylender from Lantham, he changed his tune and with Mauleverer's help paid the outstanding account.

HARVEY'S SHOP, Friardale. A sports shop at which Greyfriars men occasionally purchase goods. (46) .

HASSAN the SON of SULEIMAN. A dragoman, or guide, in Egypt. Foisting himself upon Sir Reginald Brooke's party, this "splendidly rascally guide" showed the Friars the sights after, by force majeur, he had become one of the party. Hilmi Maroudi, realising that Hassan had been bribed by Kalizelos, threatened him with death should harm come to his charges. And so, for the rest of the trip, this likeable rogue was their mentor, friend and confidant. (HBE 1).

HATCH. The owner of a racing power boat which Coker hired to catch up with the Sea Nymph after she had been hijacked by Griggs. (1314).

HATCHET. A cow-town 30 miles south of the Kicking Cayuse Ranch. To reach the town, it is necessary to cross the Squaw River. Barney Stone, the then foreman, gave Vernon Smith the wrong directions, (as indeed he did to the previous owner), so that he almost lost his life in a quicksand from which he was rescued by an Indian, Running Water. (1576).

HAUNTED ISLAND, The. Lies a short distance downstream from Greyfriars. There is an old monastic ruin on the island which was once used by Joe Banks for an illegal casino. The island is said to be haunted. (See Ghostly Monk). (149).

HAUNTED MANOR, The. A ruined house on the Pike where Captain Holsten kept Colonel and Harry Wharton captive. (1053).

HAWES. A member of Scaife's drug smuggling gang operating out of Pengarth. When Scaife came up to Greyfriars, Hawes played the part of his chauffeur. (GBC 33).

HAWKE, Captain. The Captain of the Silver Scud. For a time he was suspected by Harry Wharton of being Gideon Gaunt. (756).

HAWKE, Jerry. Mr Cobb's chief crony. Working mostly out of the Cross Keys, but also frequenting race tracks, he is a bookmaker who is, if possible, worse than Joe Banks. Hawke will not only take IOU'S, but will also use them to gain a hold over any unsuspecting would-be gay dog. If that fails, he has even been known to use photographs to gain the same end.

HAWKINGE, Kent. A village near Folkestone. Its airfield was a target for Muccolini's spying, and so his circus made a pitch here. It was while he was here that his activities became known to the Famous Five. (1488).

HAWKINS, Cecil. The alias used by Skinner in his attempt to con Mr Punter into giving him details of the whereabouts of the Greyfriars Treasure. (952).

HAWKSCLIFF, Kent. A small fishing village sited high on the cliffs overlooking the English Channel. It is two miles from the nearest village, Chalke, and its railway station. By road it is fifteen miles from Greyfriars, although the short cut along the cliffs reduces the distance to ten miles. It is the home of Tom Redwing and his father, John.

HAWKSCLIFF HOUSE. Lies just inland of the fishing village of the same name. The house was rented by General Skeppleton for a season. (693).

HAYES, Barney. Lieutenant to Nosey Clark. He usually drove for the gang. After they had lost Jim Valentine, Hayes and Clark kidnapped Harry Wharton. When the gang set a trap to catch Valentine, Hayes, together with the rest of the gang, was arrested by the police who had been tipped off by Vernon Smith. (GBC 9).

HAYES FARM, Near Friardale. A tramp was arrested here on suspicion of sending threatening letters to Mr Quelch. As the Remove Master received another letter posted while the tramp was in custody, his innocence was proved, and he was released. (420).

HAZELDENE, Colonel, (Retired). Grandfather to Peter Hazeldene and his sister Marjorie, and father to their father and uncle. A stiff peppery gentleman, he has a soft spot for Marjorie. When her Uncle John, was suspected of robbing the bank at which he works, the Colonel came over from his home in the South of France to help clear his son's name. On his first day in Kent, Coker accused him of being the bank robber! (HBE 33).

HAZELDENE, Mr. The older son of Colonel Hazeldene. His home is Brighton where he is in holy orders. His two children are Peter, at Greyfriars; and Marjorie, at Cliff House School.

HAZELDENE, Mrs. It is from her mother, Mrs. Hazeldene that Marjorie gets the gentleness predominant in her character.

HAZELDENE, John James. The younger son of Colonel Hazeldene and a clerk in a bank at Brighton, where he lives in Prince Regent Mansions. When the bank was robbed, although he had nothing to do with the crime, he fled rather than be interrogated by the police - thus giving rise to the suspicion that he was indeed the guilty man. Only his niece Marjorie and his father believed in his innocence, although the stolen money was being passed in the Courtfield district where he was hiding. (HBE 33).

HAZELDENE, Marjorie. In the Fourth Form at Cliff House, she is the sister of Peter Hazeldene of Greyfriars. She is one of the gentles and kindest of souls, and never refuses to help even the worst of characters, no matter what the circumstances. She manages with great skill to be friends with, and not to divide, her two most staunch admirers - Bob Cherry and Harry Wharton. On the whole she probably favours Bob the more; though with her tactful nature, this is a dangerous statement !

HAZELDENE, Peter. The brother of Marjorie, and the son of a clergyman. He is perpetually hard up, and too often in debt to Joe Banks or one of his cronies, and it is to be feared that Peter is one of those men who will never have the courage of his convictions. He will gamble feverishly, but cannot take with a good grace, the losses he inevitably incurs. When "done", he always appeals to the Famous Five for help. Requests that amount to blackmail for he knows that they will never refuse him, since that would mean him pestering his sister. Worse than the financial hardships it would cause, is the worry his excesses cause his sister. If only Peter would give up blagging he would be an excellent member of the Form Team, who could possibly keep Field out of his place in goal.

HEAD of SCHOOL. The position enjoyed by the senior prefect, who at present is George Wingate, (Major) . As Head of School he is responsible to the Headmaster for most of the day to day affairs of the school, as well as much of the discipline - unless an offence is committed which cannot be ignored by masters or Headmaster.

HEAD'S LATIN PRIZE. Is held each year and the prize awarded to the scholar, (junior to the Fifth Form), who presents the best paper on an examination based on set books. The winner receives a medal.

HEAD'S STUDY. The inner sanctum of the school. Situated at the end of one of the wings it overlooks Little Side. It is a quiet panelled appartment on a corridor, (The Head's Corridor), leading between the school and the Head's House. It is here that the malefactor most fears to be summoned; and it is here that the most condign punishment, (short of a public flogging or expulsion), is meted out.

HEADMASTER. The present incumbent is the Reverend Henry Locke, (cf) .

HEADMASTERS PAST. In the past, men such as Drs. Rudge, Sterndale, Grimwade, and Trumpington have gained an immortality not to be envied. Their tyranny and cruelty was a byword. The last named was directly responsible for the High Oaks Rebellion of the Remove. Skinner gave Dr Locke a piece of Mr Quelch's research about Trumpington, which the Head took as a personal affront.

HEARD, Daniel. The caretaker at Polpelly. An ex-seaman with a wooden leg, he is also as deaf as a post. As a result of this affliction he was unaffected by the wailings of Count Zero's so called ghost ! (HBE 39).

HEATH, Esau. A thoroughly nasty youth who was thrashed by Bob Cherry soon after arriving at Greyfriars. In retaliation, Heath stole a postal order of Nugent's and, forging Cherry's signature, cashed it at the post office in an effective disguise. Expelled for the crime, Major Cherry threatened the school on his son's behalf with a law suit. However, as Bunter had found Heath's practice signings the truth was revealed and Heath expelled. (173-174).

HEDGE, Albert. Soon after his return from Australia he met the Famous Five and, telling them that he knew Black Edgar, they took him up to Ravenspur Grange. However, before they had reached the house, he was killed by a shot from within. (1125).

HENRY. The nickname give to Mr Quelch by the Remove. It derives from his first forename.

HENRY. Bulstrode had been locked in the vaults by Wun Lung. D'Arcy, over from St Jim's for the day, convinced that he was a detective, vowed to find him. Seeing two tramps, he determined that they were the culprits. In fact Henry and his mate, Herbert, were merely enjoying a poached rabbit. (103).

HENRY. One of the staff at Tipton Lodge, Mapledurham, Berkshire. (1646).

HERBERT. A tramp who, with Henry his mate, was accused by D'Arcy of kidnapping Bulstrode. (103).

HERRIES, George. A member of the Fourth Form at St Jim's School.

HEXHAM SCHOOL, Northumberland. The school which "Ginger" Vernon Tracy, Smithy's cousin, attends. (1308).

HIGGINS, Mr. A farmer on the Wessex Downs. After he had refused permission for the Famous Five to camp on his land he fell in the river. Having been rescued by them he then gave his consent, and later played a part in the arrest of Bert Gunner. (707).

HIGGINS, Mr Josiah. Uncle to Snoop. After his brother-in-law had been imprisoned he took responsibility for Snoop's schooling and continued to do so after Mr Snoop was parolled. After the latter' demobilisation from the army he took him to his home in Canada to give him a fresh start in life. Snoop respects his uncle, but also fear him. For no-one else will he stop his "doggish" behaviour; even then it is not for long.

HIGGINS, Ted.   Assistant Stage Manager of Mr Whiffle's pantomime company. (409).

HIGGS. A member of the Fifth Form at Greyfriars. He was friendly with Coker for a short time after his promotion. (145).

HIGGS. A member of the estate staff at Ponsonby Park. (1336).

HIGGS, Herbert.   A tramp who tried to hold up the "Greyfriars Hikers". After coming off very much the worse in the ensuing fight, he needed little persuasion to join forces with Ponsonby in trying to steal Bob Cherry's Holiday Annual. He was foiled on several occasions - once by Bobby Bunce and another time by a bulldog hired by Mauleverer for the night ! (1334).

HIGH COOMBE SCHOOL.   The school attended by Roger, Mr Quelch's nephew. He left for a time to attend Greyfriars. (994).

HIGH HOAD. The neighbouring village to Hoad, where Mr Timothy Watkins had his office. (1335).

HIGH OAKS. A large country house on Courtfield Common. It had been on the estate agent, Stummer's, books for years since the owner had been forced by rising taxation to live abroad. It was bought by Mauleverer for use as a school, after the Remove had left Greyfriars in protest at Mr Quelch's dismissal. After they returned to the fold, the estate was developed as a housing project by Mauleverer. (HBE 10).

HIGH TOR. Some miles from Hilton Hall, it is the highest point on Blackmoor. The Famous Five, trying to receive distant stations, had taken a wireless set up there. Bunter stole it, convinced that the knapsack contained a picnic ! An escaped convict from the nearby prison thus only got Bunter's clothes ! (1403).

HIGHCLIFFE SCHOOL. A lesser Public School situated on the out-skirts of Courtfield, Kent. At present it is very run down, due to lack of direction from the Headmaster, Dr Voysey, who ought to have retired some years ago. His dispirited disinterest in the school means that the school is generally slack and most men do pretty much as they please. Ponsonby and company with their smoking and gambling are merely following the example of many of the Sixth Form. Despite this, the Junior Eleven, led by Courtenay, is a force to be reckoned with and always gives the opposition a good game. The School colours are yellow and black.

HIGHMOOR PRISON. The prison from which Rupert Crook, (alias Randolph Croker), escaped in order to plague Greyfriars, and to where he was returned after his recapture by Jack Drake. (HBE 49-50).

HILARY, Richard, (Dick). In the Remove where he shares Study No 5 with Kipps. At first he was a pacifist, (or conscientious objector), like his father, but he soon changed his ways as befits a normal member of the Remove! He is not in the vanguard academically or in sporting matters but is a typical "middle of the form" type.

HILLCREST. Little more than a mile from Cliff House, it is a bungalow sited on the cliffs. It is part of a recent development of holiday homes. Mr Poynings hired the place and kept Coker prisoner here while he, Poynings, was blackmailing Coker's Uncle Henry. (929).

HILLIGAN, Mike. The Deputy Sheriff of the town of Packsaddle, Texas. (1578).

HILTON, Lady. Wife of Sir Gilbert Hilton and mother of Cedric. (HBA 6).

HILTON, Cedric. The son of Sir Gilbert Hilton, of Hilton Hall, Devon. He is in the Fifth Form where he shares Study No 6 with Stephen Price. If only he was not so well endowed with pocket money, he could be a most useful member of society. Certainly, if he tried, he would be on the verge of a First Eleven place. Instead, with a slightly cynical outlook on life, he gambles and breaks bounds, letting his evil spirit, Price, take him where he will. He is, for all his faults, a very likeable chap. Except that is for the occasion that he lowered himself to asking Drury to throw a fight.

HILTON, Sir Gilbert, Bart. Father of Cedric Hilton, he is always glad to see his son's guests filling his home. Unfortunately, he has been too easy going in the upbringing of his son. (HBA 6).

HILTON HALL, Blackmoor, Devon. The home of the Hilton family. Situated on the edge of Blackmoor it is also within a short distance of the prison. This often leads to alarms, (as happened one Christmas when Bunter blackmailed Hilton into inviting himself and the Famous Five for the holidays). Being on the edge of the moor means that there are many splendid walks and rides with panoramic views of the surrounding country. (HBA 6).

HINKS, Harold. A tramp who "found" a £100 note belonging to Mr Vernon Smith. He hid it for safe keeping in the lining of Mauleverer's boater which Bunter had borrowed. His ludicrous efforts to regain the hat and the note led to the destruction of several straws before the recovery of the money and its safe return to Mr Vernon Smith. (1325-26).

HISTORY of GREYFRIARS, The. Mr Quelch's magnum opus to trace and record the entire history of Greyfriars from its foundation as a religious house to the present day. Cynics maintain it will never see the light of day, but in fact the author has actually reached the middle of the nineteenth century, and so its completion must be assured.

HOAD. A village in Oxfordshire. Although off the beaten track, it receives many visitors because of its historic castle. (1335).

HOAD CASTLE. Situated two miles from the village the castle is partly habitable although mostly in ruins. It is open to the public who visit it in large numbers, at least in part because it is said to be haunted. It was on the market for many years but the ghost put off many would-be buyers, particularly as there had been many recent sightings before the "Greyfriars Hikers", as well as Ponsonby and Co., arrived in the area. The Greyfriars men discovered that the ghost was in fact the local estate agent trying to lower the price so that he could buy it himself to develop it at a handsome profit. (1335).

HOBSON, James. Head of the Shell at Greyfriars and Captain of the Form teams. He used to be Coker's best friend before the latter was promoted to the Fifth Form. Since then Coker has been too superior to talk to "juniors". He shares Study No 5 with Hoskins and looks on his friend's musical ability with something akin to reverential awe! Not over endowed intellectually, he is a roughly good natured man who is not above entering into rags.

HOBSON, Sir James, Bart. A second son, he had no expectation of succeeding to the title and so, when the opportunity arose to come into a fortune, he arranged his young nephew's abduction by an unscrupulous circus owner. Succeeding to the title he latterly "saved" his nephew, (with some coercion from Wharton), and made full retribution. Despite his criminal act, or maybe because of it, he appears a hard uncompromising man who is in fact a fond and caring parent. (HBE 77).

HOBSON, Peter. See Pedrillo.

HODGE, Mr. Landlord of The Old Oak Inn, Wharton Magnus. He is an unsuspecting soul whom Vernon Smith had no difficulty in convincing that Mr Smedley was a criminal wanted by the police. (1367).

HODGE, Will. The assistant to Mr Sandeman, the Friardale grocer, and a volunteer member of the Friardale Fire Brigade. (48).

HOFFMAN, Fritz. One of the leaders of the "Aliens". His good natured feuding and ragging with the Remove were, in a large part, responsible for Herr Rosenblaum having to move his Foreign Academy away from Friardale. (6).

HOGBEN, Sir Julius. The owner of Hogben Grange, where he lives.

HOGBEN GRANGE. About one mile from Greyfriars, it is the home of Sir Julius Hogben. Set in a park of some 300 acres it is a local landmark. It has on several occasions been the target for well known crooks. ie, The Wizard, The Courtfield Cracksman and Slim Jim.

HOLLOW GREEN. A small country village with a railway halt on the line between Chalke, (the halt for Hawkscliff), and Courtfield. It was at this station that Clavering and Tom Redwing changed identities. (517).

HOLLOW OAK. A tree of great antiquity in Friardale Woods. It is also known as The Friars Oak, (cf).

HOLLY HOUSE. The house at which "de Vere" was pageboy and his father the butler before the latter, speculating with success on the Stock Exchange, made his fortune. Mauleverer had visited the house and later recognised de Vere at Greyfriars, but said nothing. (752).

HOLLY HOUSE. The shortened name by which Miss Judith Coker's home, Hollywood House, is called. (982).

HOLLYWOOD FILM LEDGER. The American Newspaper taken by all aspirants to stardom or those having dealings with the film world. Bunter saw a cutting from the paper relating to Mr Fish's plans for a film about British Public School Life. He then blackmailed Fishy into letting him join the party his father was taking to Hollywood. Detective Peter Carter inserted a paragraph in this paper hinting at Myron Polk's cowardice on the film set to force him into criminal acts so that he could arrest him. (GBC 20-21).

HOLLYWOOD HOUSE. The home of Mr Henry and Miss Judith Coker. It is sometimes affectionately called Holly House.

HOLMES, Dr Richard, M.A. The Headmaster of St James' Collegiate School, (better known as St Jim's).

HOLROYD, Dr. The Headmaster of Oldcroft School, and a man with the reputaton of being a tartar. His son, Dick, could not face him when accused of a practical joke, so Christopher Carboy, his best friend, took the blame and had to leave. Later, when the truth came out, Carboy returned there from Greyfriars. (1082).

HOLROYD, Richard, (Dick). The son of the Headmaster of Oldcroft School. As so often happens, he suffered more for his sins than the sons of lesser mortals! Fear of his father led him to allow Christopher Carboy to take the blame for a jape he had perpetrated. (1082)).

HOLSTEN, Captain. Court-marshalled for, and found guilty of, manslaughter, he held Colonel Wharton responsible for his twenty year prison sentence. He, therefore, kept the Colonel and Harry Wharton prisoner in the "Haunted Manor" for a ransom of £30,000. Bunter, in search of the reward money, managed to overcome his fear and effect their release. (1053).

HONK, Darius. The director of Magic Films, Hollywood, one of the main rivals to Perfecton Films. Bunter imitated Myron Polk's voice when telephoning the director and so got himself into the films – for a time! (1099).

HONOURABLE SOCIETY of the MONKS of FRIARDALE. Cobb, the landlord of the Cross Keys, ran an illegal gambling casino in the crypt of the ruin on the Haunted Island. Somewhat euphemistically, the members went by this grandiloquent title! (149).

HOOGER, Cato R. Better known to the American police as Slick Flick he visited Greyfriars to kidnap Fish at gun point. Harry Wharton, who had been sent to the head for sliding down the bannisters, was able to knock out the gangster, (who had the Head at gun point), with his cricket ball. (1163).

HOOKER, Mr. Conned the Greyfriars Hikers' into paying him, and not the real land-owner, the fee for camping on the first night of their holiday. (1332).

HOOKEY. A confederate of Dandy Saunders who searched Greyfriars for the plunder hidden there by Jerry the Rat. (HBE 53).

HOOKEY, Jim. One time porter at The Regency Boarding House, Brighton, from where he was dismissed for theft. He met Carlow, with whom he had worked there, in Friardale and tried to blackmail him. He was soon after arrested for assaulting Sir George Cheyne. (1239-40).

HOP HI. The younger brother of Wun Lung. Placed in the Second Form he soon bought his way into popularity. Although he was no toady he realised that this was an easier way than a ragging! He used to be bullied by some of the Remove until they realised that they could not get away with it.

HOPE, M.V. The vessel chartered by Colonel Wharton in the search for Major Cherry after he was posted missing when the ship on which he was returning to England was wrecked in the Red Sea. (179).

HOPKINS, Mrs. The postmistress at Wimford. (1105).

HOPKINS, Alfred, (Alf). A tramp who came upon Bunter preparing breakfast while the Famous Five were taking a morning dip in the Thames. Alf demolished breakfast in a quite Bunterian style, leaving Bunter disbelieved when he protested his innocence! (1644).

HORROCKS, Mr. The butcher in Combermere. His arrival at the house at 10:30 a.m. actually disturbed Bunter's sleep! Although the "owner's son" did not seem to be worried by the enormous amount owed on his account. (914).

HORROCKS, Mr. The assistant to Dr Woods of Leyford. (1123).

HOSCOT, Hampshire. A town a few miles from Mauleverer Towers. Bunter scornfully left the Famous Five at Cherry Place, to stay as he thought with Mauleverer, in a car purporting to come from the Hoscot Garage. In fact he was being taken to Devon by Jimmy the Fox's gang as a step in the kidnapping of Jack Drake. (1034).

HOSKINS, Claude. He shares Study No 5 in the Shell with Hobson. Convinced of his musical genius, he almost scares the music staff with compositions that make a sound synthesiser seem like a Brahm's lullaby! Only Hobby loyally stands up for his genius. To Mr Hacker the appearance of "tadpoles" on a latin prose means the opportunity for sarcastic vituperation. Hoskins looks upon all this vilification as evidence of the vandal!

HOTHAM, Inspector of Police at Woodford. He was in charge of the hunt for Convict 19 who had escaped from Blackmoor Prison and made his way to Surrey where he encountered a frightened Bunter and robbed him of his coat and cap. (1039).

HOUSEKEEPER. See Mrs. Kebble.

HOWELL, Archie. The brother of Phyllis Howell of Cliff House School, he was in the Remove for a time.

HOWELL, Phyllis. In the Fourth Form at Cliff House, she is a close friend of Marjorie Hazeldene and Clara Trevlyn, and is a member of the Cliff House-Greyfriars coterie.

HUBBARD, Walter. A member of Lantham Speedway. (1220).

HUDSON. Chauffeur to Lord Cavandale. (1191).

HUDSON, Kit. Ken King's partner, and mate in the Dawn. (1598).

HUGGINS. The character assumed by Wibley to pay back Ponsonby after the Famous Five had been forbidden to see him. They were trying to get even with Pon. having been condemned for "sacking" Loder. Wibley's idea was to go to Highcliffe as a bookmaker's runner collecting a debt. When Mr Mobbs discovered "that man" Ponsonby's fear and panic can well be imagined! (1587).

HUGGINS, Bill. A tramp who was paid by Cherry and Nugent to fake an attack on Hurree Singh. The idea was for Bull to come to the rescue and so heal a rift in the Famous Five. Sadly, Huggins drank the "payment in advance" and so could not fulfill his part of the bargain. (497).

Later, after a short spell in prison, he followed Whiffle's Circus vowing vengeance on the owner, as it was due to him that he had been "inside". Bunter would never have taken the proprietor's clothes and identity if he had realised this! He received another prison sentence for robbery with violence after this episode. (HBE 28).

He was imprisoned yet again for assaulting Mossoo. Wibley, who had been expelled for "guying" Monsieur Charpentier, came to the rescue, and so was reinstated. (HBE 57).

HUGGINS, Bobby. An ex-boxer who had lost an eye in a drunken brawl. Unable to keep off the drink he is a frequent attender at the magistrates' courts and equally a frequent guest of the Crown! After leaving the ring he became a boxing manager and trainer. One of his proteges is Richard Drury who was at Greyfriars for a time. Basically a good natured man, he bore Drury no ill will for the thrashing he received from him after attempting to hold up Mr Quelch. (GBC 15).

HUGHES. A Welshman and one time member of the Remove. He was the only person who stood up for Harry Wharton on his arrival at Greyfriars. (3).

HUNG SHING. After Harry Wharton, Bob Cherry and Bunter had been captured by Chung Lo, on behalf of Tang Wang, Ferrers Locke disguised himself as a beggar of this name to aid his search for them. (1184).

HUNKER, Mr. The bailiff of Chupham, in Sussex, who had orders to distrain William Wuggs' farm for non-payment of tithes. After a "Tithe War", Mauleverer secretly paid the dues. (1333).

123

HUNT. Ex-batman and now manservant to Captain Vernon. While Vernon Smith was captive in Lantham Chase, Hunt made a perfect jailer, being both strong and loyal. (HBE 54-55).

"HUNTED MAN, The". The title of a play by Wibley. James Loder had escaped from Blackmoor Prison at the time the Remove were rehearsing the piece. Wibley took the opportunity of japing Loder in a convict suit, only to discover that the convict was a relative of the bullying prefect! (HBE 47).

HUNTER, Mr Samuel. A self-made millionaire who, on retiring from the Stock Exchange, bought a luxury yacht - The Skylark - from Lord Dunmore. With carefully applied ink to the "H", Bunter was persuaded it was his father's yacht! (955).

HUNTER, Tom. A member of Lantham Speedway. (1220).

HUNTER'S BEECH, Near Wimford. An old beech tree and a well known landmark. Joe Banks had made an appointment to meet Vernon Smith here to receive payment for an old debt. Mr Smedley made use of the meeting to accuse Smithy of betting. Luckily, Bunter overheard the conversation and so was able to clear Smithy of the slander. (1368).

HURREE SINGH, Minor. While Hurree Singh was in India for the Durbar he wrote to say that his younger brother was coming to Greyfriars. Dicky Nugent had been expelled and so impersonated "Inky Minor" to win a bet that he would not leave the school! The discovery that Inky's brother was not going to arrive led to the exposure of the jape. (183).

IBRAHIM, Honest. An Algerian Arab. He is a rascally guide who makes as much as possible out of his "gentlemen". When Harry Wharton and Co. were searching for Major Cherry, Ibrahim was employed as their guide. Unbeknownst to them, he was in the pay of Mustapha ben Mohammed. However, he was found out and, after being saved from a lion, changed his allegiance to become a most useful ally of the search party. (GBC 8).

IKE. He was employed by Roger Compton to capture Ragged Dick in what was almost the last effort made to prevent Dick coming into his inheritance. (GL 3; HBE 80).

IKE the WEASEL. One of Mr Hacker's army hired to put down the Tuck Shop Rebellion. He is a small wiry man with a foxy face. A fierce fighter who has been known to "chew a bobby's ear off".

Shortly after the rebellion he was employed by Coker to hold Wingate captive so that Coker could, as he thought, play in the First Eleven. (HBE 35).

INKY. The nickname given to Hurree Singh by his friends on account of his "dusky skin".

INQUISITION, The Greyfriars. Vernon Smith's scheme for ridding Greyfriars of Mr Jeffreys. By punishing in turn the new Headmaster, his deputy and Loder, (the Head of School), the idea was to force them, in the manner of Torquemada, to recant. (927).

IONIDES, Heracles. A Greek who was for a time in the Sixth Form at Greyfriars. Foppish, scented, and above all a bully, he was for a short time a prefect who was soon demoted. Although he had no real friends in the school, he was closest to Loder and his cronies. Ionides somehow managed to avoid expulsion, but was almost certainly asked to leave.

IRONS, Inspector. See Steele, Richard.

ISAACS. An habitue of the Cross Keys who scrounges his drink by marking, or scoring, at billiards. (923).

ISAACS. A "fence" in Puggins Alley, and an aquaintance of Flip before he came to Greyfriars. (1250).

ISAACS, Mr. Was robbed of a valuable diamond by Sniggerson who sold it to Bunter for 1/-, intending to get it back after he had avoided the police. Bunter, however, sold it to Fish, whose efforts to sell it to Mr Lazarus led to a painful interview with Mr Grimes! (1352).

ISAACS, Shem. The name assumed by Howard Devarney when posing as a business consultant in the City. He successfully bankrupted Mr Duncombe Devarney. As a result, the latter's son, Julian, hated Jews and picked a quarrel with Monty Newland. After the imposter was caught, Devarney admitted his behaviour had been more than unreasonable. (HBE 72).

ISLANDS in the SARK. There are two islands in the river near the school. The so-called "Haunted Island", and "Popper's Island". (cff).

ITO. A Japanese manservant to Mr Cyrus Parker. (1097).

IVES, Seth. A poacher operating in the Wimford area. He is a brutal ruffian with a record of grievous bodily harm. (47).

IVYDENE. The Linley's house in Bowdsley, Lancs. It is a semi-detached house lying on the outskirts of this industrial town, in a "tree-lined street". (952).

J.

JACK RABBIT CANYON. Thirty miles from Hollywood in the Santa Monica Mountains and facing the Pacific Ocean. It is a beautiful but lonely spot used by the Perfection Film Studios for location work during the Greyfriars visit. At the landward end of the canyon is the notorious "Hair Trigger". (GBC 21).

JACKSON. A keeper at Popper Court. (954).

JACKSON. Chauffeur to Lord Mauleverer. Unknown to the "Greyfriars Hikers", he followed them to provide creature comforts and a car ride, should Mauly have tired! He was mistaken for

Ponsonby, (who was trying to steal Bob Cherry's Holiday Annual), and ragged before Mauly received the same treatment to make him send his driver home ! (1332).

JACKSON, Mr Henry. Dandy Sanders, trying to recover his hidden plunder, came to Greyfriars in the guise of a reporter from the Lantham Advertiser. He chloroformed Mr Quelch prior to searching Study No 1 in the Remove, but was discovered before he could repossess himself of the stolen money. (1271).

JACKSON, Philbert. A member of the Shell.

JACKSON'S of COURTFIELD. The local music shop from whom Bunter obtained a gramophone "on approval". He then proceeded to raffle it ! Fish, with an eye to the main chance, bought all the tickets. He had barely "won" the machine when it had to be returned, leaving Fishy sadder, poorer, (and hurt), but none the wiser ! (753).

JACKSON'S GARAGE, Courtfield. Situated off the High Street in Courtfield it is patronised by several Greyfriars men who hire cars for outings. Some, Vernon Smith in particular, hire cars for illegal nocturnal expeditions.

JACKY. The Kanaka boatswain in the Aloha. He was murdered by Soames during the taking over of the vessel by the Sea Lawyer, as a show of strength. (HBE 12).

JACOB. A gipsy to whom, (with Charley, his mate), Coker offered 10/- if they would allow him to hide in their caravan. Coker had refused to be caned ! When Mr Prout came on the scene they attacked him. As Coker came to the rescue he had his punishment rescinded. (1042).

JACOBSTEIN. A second hand clothes dealer in Waterloo Road, London, to whom Vernon Smith sold his belongings when he left Greyfriars after his father was, for a short time, bankrupt. He gave Smithy 15/- for the clothes he was wearing, and charged him 12/6d for a second hand suit. (GBC 33).

JAM DAS. An Indian rickshaw boy in Nairobi. In the pay of Chunder Run he was to kidnap Vernon Smith so that Chunder could extract a ransome. Unfortunately, Chunder had mistakenly assumed Bunter to be Mr Vernon Smith's son ! (1231).

JAMES. Footman at Bunter Court. (HBE 4).

JAMES. Manservant to the Reverend Lambe. (413).

JAMES. Footman at Hollywood House. (984).

JAMES. Footman at Portercliffe Hall. (1436).

JAMES. Footman at Popper Court. (1480).

JAMES. Footman at Trant Elms. (1526).

JAMES. Footman at Monson Chalet. (1648).

JAMRACK, Captain. Captain of the Brig Mindanao, the vessel the Greyfriars party travelled in from Suva to Kalua. (1589).

JANE. One of the housemaids at Greyfriars. (1356).

JANE. One of the dolls used by Tippity Tip, the clown, for his ventriloquial side show. Bunter used his ventriloquism to cause havoc in Muccolini's Circus by making the doll insult all and sundry ! (HBE 55-56)

JANETH the GIPSY. Mother of Minna, the little girl saved by Bunter from the path of an approaching train. (1016).

JARRAM, Mr. An Indian planter of Butiaba on the shore of Lake Albert. Mr Vernon Smith and his party of Friars were visiting him when Krantz's theft of a canoe led to his capture. Bunter was forced to free him, and Krantz then took Smithy prisoner. (1233).

JARVIS. A name given in error to Joyce the woodcutter. (1135).

JARVIS. The butler at Cherry Place, Dorset. (1142).

JARVISH, James. One time manservant to Mr Shook, he had persuaded his late master to leave him his fortune. Tiger Bronx, nephew of the deceased multi-millionaire, determined to gain his rightful inheritance, and so threatened Jarvish's life. To save himself, Jarvish gave his fortune to Bunter, so long as he, Jarvish, was manservant to Bunter. In order to avoid pursuit, Jarvish suggested a European trip for Bunter and the Famous Five. After many attempts to "get" Bunter, (aided by Jarvish), it was discovered that the money had in fact been left to an animals home ! (HBE 64).

JASMOND. Butler at Reynham Castle. Although an old family retainer, he did not recognise Bunter as an imposter who had been introduced to save the real Lord Reynham by Sir Peter Lanchester. (HBE 14).

JASON, Farmer. In the search for a prizewinning photograph, Bunter "borrowed" Mr Wiggins' camera. While taking a snap of Wiggins himself, asleep by the Sark, Bunter, trespassing on Farmer Jason's meadow, was tossed by the bull to the detriment of the camera ! (1221).

JEEVES. Butler to Major Thresher. (974).

JEFFREYS, Mr. See Flogging Judge Jeffreys. (GBC 27).

JELKS. An American share swindler who tried to sell Walker's Aunt worthless stock. To prevent this, her solicitor took the cash entrusted to him for this purpose and, obviously, found himself wanted for embezzlement. (954).

JENKINS, Pete. See Lariat.

JENKINS, William. A plumber and glazier employed by Chunkley's Stores. He had been sent to Greyfriars to repair a window broken by Dandy Sanders. He was held up by Sanders so that he himself could get into the school. As the window was in Study No 1 in the Remove, Sanders had the opportunity of searching the appartment for Jerry the Rat's hidden plunder. (1272).

JENKS. A keeper at Compton Hall. After the discovery of the truth about Ragged Dick, he was given a job on Sir Henry's Scottish estate in order to avoid any of the facts becoming known locally. (HBE 80; GL 3).

JENKS, Mr. The owner of Cliff Cottage which he lets to holiday makers while he himself acts as factotum to his guests. Mr Prout stayed there to try to hide a black eye from the world. Coker, playing at detective, saw Mr Prout's topcoat and, convinced that his Form Master had been kidnapped, caused quite a furore. (1187).

JERMYN. Valet to Sir William Byrd. He was of necessity in the secret of Wibley's impersonation of his employer. Bunter and the Famous Five recognised him as Soames who confessed to having taken the position in order to obtain, for himself, a German spy ring's treasury. (HBE 41).

JERRY the PUG. A local ruffian who was hired by Joe Banks at Vernon Smith's request to thrash Harry Wharton after they had fallen out. Luckily for Wharton, Vernon Smith repented of his actions and was able to come to the rescue, before too much damage had been done. (1013).

JERRY the RAT. After stealing Coker's motor cycle, (registration No KK 66606), he used it to rob the Courtfield & County Bank. As unreliable as ever, he had to abandon it and make his getaway on foot. When pursuit became uncomfortably close, he climbed into Greyfriars, and hid his loot, £7,000, in Study No 1 in the Remove. He was then arrested. Following this, the school was disturbed on many occasions, as Dandy Sanders tried to recover the stolen money. Carne, desperate for funds, found the cache and tried to pay off Joe Banks who, suspecting the origins of the money, would not take it. Bunter then found the discarded note and bragged about "Billy Bunter's Banknote". (HBE 53).

JERVIS. Chauffeur to Ponsonby. He had the distasteful job, (to himself at least), of following the "Greyfriars Hikers" while Ponsonby tried to steal Bob Cherry's Holiday Annual. (HBE 19).

JERVIS. Valet to Sir Richard Ravenspur. (1123).

JESSOP. Keeper at Wharton Lodge.

JIM. A Friardale bus driver. It is part of his duties to drive the bus between school and station on the first and last days of term.

JIM. A boatman who works for Mr Baker of Baker's Boatyard, Friardale. (1643).

JIM LEE'S SECRET. (Title GBC Volume 37). Sent to Greyfriars by his crooked cousin, Ulick Driver, Jim Lee had orders to befriend the wealthy and, having gained access to their homes, he was to "case the joint" so that his cousin could rob them. Determined not to do this, Lee went out of his way to be as unpleasant and unco-operative as possible. As a result he gained unpopularity amongst his form mates, and thrashings from his cousin for not obeying orders. Eventually, Lee confided in Harry Wharton, who persuaded him to see Mr Grimes. Successful in trapping the criminal, Mr Grimes let Lee go free.

JIMMY the FOX. See Fox, Jimmy the.

JIMMY the ONE. A pail of water, intended for Walker, had got Mr Quelch instead, landing him in the Sanatorium. Mr Lagden was appointed locum tenens and recognised by Flip as Jimmy the One, a notorious thief who had been sought by the police for twelve years. He kidnapped Flip to try to preserve his secret, and kept him prisoner in Mr Joyce the woodcutter's cottage, rented for that purpose. This act led to his downfall and arrest by Inspector Brent of Scotland Yard (HBE 4).

JIMMY the PINCHER. One of the "army" hired by Mr Hacker to try to put down the "Sit In Strike" in the tuckshop. Shortly after that fiasco, Coker hired him, together with Ike the Weasel and Albert Juggins, to hold Wingate prisoner for the afternoon of the St Jim's match so that he, Coker, could be selected for the First Eleven ! Wingate was released in time to play, and Coker had his wallet stolen when he foolishly showed the tramps his wealth. (1516).

JIMMY the PUG. See Juggins, James.

JIMMY the RAT. The ruffianly accomplice of Skip. Their "lay" was for Skip to feign injury and pick the pockets of anyone who came to his aid. Having played this trick on the Famous Five, they failed with Coker who, instead, thrashed Jimmy the Rat. Bent on revenge, Jimmy the Rat entered Greyfriars one night, but Skip, who was out of dormitory bounds, was able to save Coker. (HBE 62).

JOBLING, Mr. Alias Shifty Spooner. He towed the Water Lily up to Rushey and then managed to steal the boat wherein he had hidden the proceeds of his robberies. The officer in charge of the case recognised Spooner and returned the boat to Harry Wharton and Co. (1650).

JOBSON, Mr. The owner of a livery stables in Friardale who hires out horses and traps for those desirous of "taking a tool" round the country side. (4).

JOBSON, George. A bicycle thief who stole de Courcy's machine and sold it to Bunter. Ponsonby made out that it was Bunter who had stolen the bike – and caused much unpleasantness until de Courcy catching Pon. making bets with Jobson, forced a retraction out of him. (1056–57).

JOE. The school boatman who, when the Remove were training for a race against Highcliffe, discovered Skinner's handkerchief in the racing shell. This proved that Skinner was, in league with Ponsonby, trying to ruin the Remove's chances. (918).

JOHN. One of Tippity Tip's ventriloquial dolls. (HBE 55–56).

JOHN. Man servant to Dr Locke. (49).

JOHN. Footman at Wharton Lodge. (1038).

JOHN. Footman at Gadsby Croft. (1339).

JOHN. Footman at Portercliffe Hall. (1436).

JOHN. Footman at Popper Court. (1480).

JOHN. Footman at Seahill Park. (1525).

JOHN. Footman at Eastcliff Lodge. (1677).

JOHNSON. Keeper at Compton Hall. (GL 3).

JOHNSON, Alf. A waif befriended by Vernon Smith after he had left school to make his own way, having learned that his father was bankrupt. With some of his precious last few pennies, he bought a snack for the two of them, only to be rewarded by being accused of the theft of a watch stolen by Johnson and placed by him in Smithy's pocket. Sentenced to three years Borstal it took Dr Locke and Tom Redwing to uncover the truth. Luckier than Smithy, Johnson was bound over and discharged from the court. He then left England for Canada and made a fresh start thanks to the generosity of Mr Vernon Smith. (933).

JOHNSON, George. Of 16, Bank Buildings, Courtfield. The phoney name and address of a passer of forged £5 notes. Coker, against advice, changed one for him; discovered it to be a forgery and threw it away. Bunter picked it up and placed it in his wallet to show the chaps that he too had money. Arthur Carter then tried to make out that Bunter had stolen the note. Smithy promised Bunter £1 for the fiver, (to protect the duffer), and being Bunter, he, as usual, came out best ! (1564).

JOHNSON, Smiley. Together with "Nosey", he kidnapped Coker on Poynings instructions to prevent him going home for Christmas. Johnson then held Coker prisoner at Hillcrest, whence he was rescued by the Famous Five. (982–983).

JOKER OF GREYFRIARS, THE. (Title HBE Volume 23). Christopher Clarence Carboy had to leave his previous school because he had taken the blame for his friend's prank. Addicted to practical joking, he never failed to enliven any situation. Bunter, trying to get his own back for one of these japes, unintentionally discovered the truth about Carboy's "expulsion". Thus his stay at Greyfriars was short, and anything but uneventful.

JOLIFFE. The landlord of the Red Cow Inn, Friardale. Carberry used to patronise the place, and also sent fags to get his smokes and whisky On one occasion Bob Cherry performed this errand for Carberry and then wetted the cigarettes and doctored the drink ! (46).

JOLLY SAILOR, The, Pegg. A boarding house on the front at Pegg where the Tyneside Rovers Football Team stayed before their match against Lantham Argyll. (919).

JONES, Major. A member of the Shell and its teams.

JONES, Minor. A one time member of the Remove. (200).

JONES, Sports Outfitters of Courtfield. Bunter claimed to be "collecting a blazer" for Walker as an alibi against being caught out of bounds on Popper's Island. (954).

JONES, Detective Inspector. He was the officer in charge of the Spooner case. After Spooner had been released from prison, Mr Jones followed him to try to recover property stolen by the former. Ponsonby was almost arrested one night when he tried to steal the Water Lily. After this fright he gave up harrassing the Famous Five. Mr Jones finally got his man, and the stolen goods, which Bunter discovered hidden in the Water Lily. (1650).

JONES, Inspector. Mr Grimes' predecessor at Courtfield. It was he who arrested Mr Brandreth, only to find out that Mr Snoop had confessed to the crime of which the former had been accused and found guilty. (288).

JONES, Mr. The greengrocer of Combermere, and one of the many tradespeople owed vast amounts by the "Son of the Owner" of Bunter Court. (917).

JONES, Mr. Auctioneer from Chupham who had the unenviable task of holding a tithe sale at Little Puddleton on William Waggs' distrained livestock. As these had disappeared there was no sale and Mr Jones finished up in the Horse pond! (1333).

JONES, Mr. A builder of Margate who was employed by Mr Fish to aid his search for the Portercliffe treasure. He was to lift floorboards and remove panelling to find any secret hiding places. (1439).

JONES, Mrs. Proprietress of a teashop on the cliffs between Margate and Broadstairs. After Zara had fallen off her horse, Harry Wharton fetched Mrs. Jones to render first aid. (1489).

JONES & CO. The false name painted on the side of a Pantechnicon, supposedly from Weymouth. The van was used as a rendezvous, (and repository for the stolen goods), after smash and grab raids. Bunter, lost, asked the men for a lift which was refused. Later he recognised them, and earned a £50 reward for the information leading to their arrest. (1531).

133

JONES & CO. Bootmakers of Courtfield. (1551).

JONES & SMITH. Estate Agents of Radcot, Oxfordshire. (1650).

JONES, Andy. The driver of the twice weekly hack, (or stage coach), between Prairie Bends and Packsdaddle. The journey takes a day in each direction. (1575).

JONES, Bert. The chief of the Volunteer Fire Brigade in Friardale. When not so engaged, he is the assistant in the local draper's shop. (48).

JONES, George Albert. Bunter had been caught stealing a cake from Coker. To avoid a stumping he confided to Coker that Jim Warren was in reality G.A. Jones, the son of a keeper at Wharton Lodge. Needless to say, there is no keeper at Wharton Lodge of that name! (1442).

JONES, Joe. An alias used by Jack Drake while he was being pursued by Jimmy the Fox. (1419-21).

JONES, Soapy. Together with "Beaky" Bill and the Cadger he attacked Coker, only to be knockd out by Alonzo Todd of all people! (1345).

JONES, William. A steward on the R.M.S. Comet. He found Bunter in a life boat where he had been hiding all night from Bob Cherry dressed up as O Lobo! (1463).

JONES, Mr William. A boat builder near Friardale Bridge. He often hires out his boats to Greyfriars and Cliff House boating parties. Marjorie Hazeldene and friends were picnicking on Popper's Island when Ponsonby stole the boat, stranding the girls. As Bob Cherry's hat was in the boat when it was recovered, the Cliff House girls thought Bob had played a thoughtless trick on them. It took Mauleverer all of his tact and guile to make Ponsonby confess the truth and so heal the rift. (1340).

JOOCE, Janet. The Perfection Film Studios leading Lady. She is billed as "The World's Winsome Witch". (GBC 21).

JORROCKS. The motor cycle dealer in Lantham from whom the Famous Five bought "Methuselah" the Dionysius motor tricycle they used on a hiking holiday. (1118).

JOSE. A member of O Lobo's band of bandits. While Bob Cherry was trying to avoid capture, Jose was killed by a herd of peccaries. (1466).

JOSEPH. The father of Minna, the gipsy child snatched from the path of an oncoming train at the level crossing at Pegg by Bunter. Joseph, who had just sold him a bad coconut, was full of remorse and could not show his gratitude enough. (1010).

JOSEPH. A gipsy and a "man of education" who had been expelled from his tribe for exceeding their code of conduct. When Ponsonby met him and Michael, his associate, he found a pair of willing helpers to kidnap Bob Cherry and steal his Holiday Annual. The Famous Five rescued Bob and thoroughly ragged their caravan, so that they might be said to have earned their pay ! (1337).

JOYCE. The head keeper at Popper Court. He is a long suffering man who has to put up with a lot of abuse from his employer. He is brother to Joyce the woodcutter, and both are great friends to most of Greyfriars. As keeper Mr Joyce often has to chase Greyfriars parties off Popper's Island.

JOYCE. The local woodcutter. He is married with two sons. His home is in Lantham Woods, but he camps out in whichever part of the county he is working. When working away from home he lets out his cottage; his lessees have included Hazeldene's uncle, and Jimmy the One.

JOYCE. An under keeper at Wharton Lodge. (1038).

JOYCE, Michael. The younger son of Mr Joyce the woodcutter. Snoop who was under the threat of having to leave Greyfriars unless he could impress his uncle, saved the lad from drowning. As Snoop had lied as to his whereabouts he could not tell his uncle about the rescue. Luckily for Snoop, he and his uncle met Joyce who, in thanking Snoop for what he had done, enabled him to stay at school. (1135).

JUD. After Herbert Higgs had failed to get Bob Cherry's Holiday Annual by himself he went in force. Jud was one of the team. They were routed by the Famous Five who were helped considerably by Bobby Bunce. (1334).

JUDD, Kicky. See Kicky the Pincher.

JUDE, Inspector. He was sent down from Scotland Yard to take over the Ravenspur case after the murders of Inspectors Cook and Garnish. His contempt for "poor Locke" received quite a jolt when it was Ferrers Locke who solved his case for him ! (1125).

JUDKINS. The steward in the M.Y. Silver Scud. (759).

JUDSON. A gardener at Wharton Lodge. (1176).

JUDSON, Joe. After the theft of the Popper Court Moonstone by Dandy Sugden, Judson was sent down to Greyfriars to get the stone from Wharton to whom Sugden thought he had given it for safe keeping. In fact it was Bunter taking his usual liberties! Judson then kidnapped Harry Wharton to try to force the return of the diamond. This was found by the Famous Five and returned to Sir Hilton Popper. Judson, like the rest of the gang, escaped arrest. (1157-58).

JUGGINS, Albert. A tramp who, after attempting to rob Mr Hacker, was astounded to be employed by him to bring six or seven helpers to break the "Sit In Strike". It cannot be said that any of "Hacker's Army" enjoyed themselves, nor covered themselves with glory, as they were, time and again, repulsed by the Remove. Juggins ended up a prisoner in the coal cellar! However, he seemed not to have learned his lesson because, a few weeks later, he tried to rob Coker. After which he was employed by his prospective victim to kidnap Wingate so that Coker could play in the First Eleven, (some Hope!). Juggins received a thrashing from the Famous Five and Smithy; as well as Coker's wallet which he managed to steal. (HBE 35).

JUGGINS, Albert. Brother to Alfred, the High Oaks Caretaker. He was employed as chauffeur to High Oaks School, (despite the absence of cars!). (1046).

JUGGINS, Alfred. The titular head of the Juggins "Clan". He used his position as caretaker at High Oaks to find employment for all his relatives from "Aunt Martha who's 69 down to Algernon who's 12"! In spite of his nepotism, he was a good porter-cum-butler who took with equanimity all the vagaries and excesses of the Remove while in residence at High Oaks. (HBE 10).

JUGGINS, Algernon Cecil. The youngest member of the clan. He was employed as pageboy at High Oaks. (HBE 10).

JUGGINS, James. Known as Jimmy the Pug, he used to be employed as doorman and bouncer at the Courtfield Picture Palace. After a misunderstanding he was fired and came to High Oaks as Mauleverer's method of enforcing discipline! For a while the "school" was peaceful until Vernon Smith persuaded Bunter to create a fracas by means of his ventriloquism - as a result of which Jimmy left. (HBE 10).

JUGGINS, Martha. Aunt to Alfred and employed as cook to High Oaks School. (HBE 10).

JUGGINS, Percival. Younger brother of Alfred he was another supernumerary chauffeur to High Oaks. (HBE 10).

JULIUS CAESAR. Not to be confused with the Roman general and Bane of the Second Form with his "de Belli Gallico", this Caesar is the African servant of Professor Sparkinson! (1344).

JUNIOR COMMON ROOM. Sometimes also called the Junior Day Room by those in authority it is more usualy simply known as "The Rag".

K.

KA-AHA-HUA-HINA. Known simply as Ka for short, he comes from Raiatea and was the Captain of the Flamingo, one of Mauleverer's copra fleet. He took the Greyfriars party from Kalua to Suva to prosecute their search for Brian, Mauly's cousin. He was clapped in irons by Ysabel Dick and Van Dink when they took over the vessel and was taken off with the rest of the crew, when Ysabel Dick scuttled the schooner. (1593).

KALASHTI. The Kanaka Bosun's mate in the Aloha. He was promoted to bosun after the murder of Jacky. When the cannibals of Caca Island attacked the boat, he escaped onto the island where it is probable that he perished, either in the cooking pots of the Malaita or in a volcanic eruption. (GBC 11).

KALIZELOS, Konstantinos. A Graeco-Egyptian antique dealer from Alexandria with an extensive knowledge of the mythology and theology of Ancient Egypt. From his study of ancient papyri he had learned the hiding place of "The Eye of Osiris". In his efforts to steal the Scarab of A-Menah, in which the diamond was hidden, he stuck at naught. He was finally brought to book with the help of Hilmi Maroudi. (HBE 1).

KALOUTH. Confidential servant to Nally Das, with whom he thought he had captured Hurree Singh as the first stage in the overthrow of the throne of Bhanipur. It was in fact Wibley masquerading! Once in India, Bunter fell into their hands and, at the point of torture, was persuaded to reveal Inky's whereabouts. Luckily this came to nothing. Kalouth met his end when Bunter left the party in a huff and discovered an ambush which was reversed by Pandy Din. In the skirmish that ensued, Kalouth was killed. (GBC 4).

KALOUTH. The Major Domo of the Jam Bahadur's household. When the Jam came to England, Kalouth accompanied him to make all necessary arrangements. (723).

KALUA-ALUA-LALUA. Known as Kalua for short it is an island lying some 1,000 miles from Sydney, and about 350 miles from Suva in Fiji. The island was bought by the late Earl of Mauleverer on a whim when cruising in the area. Under the jurisdiction of Fiji, the main product is copra. The major area of population lies to the south of the island where access to the harbour is gained through a break in the coral reef. The eastern side, exposed to the prevailing winds, is almost deserted. Mauleverer brought a party of friends here to search for his cousin Brian. (HBE 12).

KALULA-ULULO. A Kanaka boy from Papalagi. He had been saved from a shark by Soames to whom he became a servant. They came to England together so that Soames could make Redwing hand over his fortune. However, just when success seemed certain, Soames who had hit the boy for not obeying orders, was himself struck down by the Kanaka. As Soames had a gun on the Famous Five at the time, they were able to escape. Because of this act, Kalula was held blameless in Soames' crime and so allowed to return home. (1089).

KAMINEGO. The cannibal chief of the Island of Baloo which lies in the same group as Kalua. While the Flamingo was becalmed off Baloo, Kaminego led an attack on the vessel which was repulsed with no loss to the crew or passengers of the schooner. (1589).

KANG. One of Tang Wang's assassins. He attacked the Greyfriars men while they were staying in Macao, and again while they were sailing up the River Canton. His last attempt was in Mr Wun's house where he was captured and beheaded. His severed head was sent to Tang Wang marked "This side up, with care!" (HBE 25).

KASI JEE. One of the Naukars in the palace of Bhanipur. He was chosen by Bunter as his own body servant while staying with Hurree Singh. Mistreated as all men are by Bunter, he gained his final revenge for his twice daily kicks by stealing the gold chain given to Bunter by Hurree Singh. (GBC 4).

KEARNERY, Mr. A producer for Enterprise Films. When he saw "Lord Mauleverer", as Mr Parker believed Bunter to be, he was not impressed with the impact such a figure would have on the cinema going public! (1097).

KEARY, Tug. A member of Chick Chew's kidnapping gang. Bunter had answered the telephone and, believing that Mr Ezra Coot had invited Fish to tea at the Courtfield Hotel, accepted intending to go himself. Sharing the news with Skinner, Bunter found himself locked in his study while Skinner set out for Courtfield. The chauffeur awaiting Fishy was in fact Tug who took Skinner, not to tea, but to Chew's headquarters! (1474).

KEBBLE, Mrs. A widow who, for many years now, has combined the positions of housekeeper and house matron at Greyfriars School. A fanatic about clean linen, she is heartily disliked by most of the fags, and Bunter especially, because she will insist they wear clean collars!

KEELEY, Black. The caretaker of Pengarth. After the death of the previous owner, he remained to look after the property. He was generally disliked in the community and had few acquaintances. The house being empty made it an ideal landing site for smuggled drugs, and Keeley was an active member of Scaife's gang. After the smuggling ring was broken, he was arrested with the other members. (GBC 33).

KEENE. A one time member of the Remove. He was inclined to the Skinner school of cruelty and took an active part in ragging Linley on his arrival at Greyfriars. (180).

KELLY, Mr. One time Master of the Second Form at Greyfriars. He gained Sammy Bunter's undying hatred for making him wash his hands when he arrived at school. After all, he had already washed them that day! Mr Kelly left Greyfriars for the army; his place being taken by Mr Toodle. (144).

KENNEY, Paul. He shares Study No 6 in the Upper Fourth with Aubrey Angel. He is a mean, vicious character who breaks all the rules and somehow has so far escaped expulsion.

KENYA. The East African country visited by Vernon Smith and his friends "On Safari". (HBE 65).

KERR, George Francis. The son of Mr George Kerr of Edinburgh, he is in the Fourth Form at St Jim's School. As well as being a good all round sportsman, he is a first class actor.

KERR, Mr George F., (Senior). The father of Kerr of St Jim's. He is an industrialist and lives at No 24, Castlegate, Edinburgh. He negociated the rights to a revolutionary new dyeing process with the inventor, Mr MacAlpine. Jerrold Drew, an industrial spy, was determined to steal the plans and sell them abroad. After MacAlpine had been injured in a train crash it seemed to him as though he would succeed. However, Bob Cherry and Harry Wharton were able to outwit him and bring the papers safely to Mr Kerr. (672).

KICKING CAYUSE RANCH. A large spread in the Rio Frio Valley in Texas, some fifteen miles to the west of the town of Packsaddle. It was bought by Mr Vernon Smith as a speculative investment. While visiting the place Smithy and friends were instrumental in putting an end to the cattle rustling that had plagued the area. While out there, Smithy extended the ranch by buying the neighbouring ranch – The Circle O. (HBE 32).

KICKY the PINCHER. One of Nosey Clark's gang, he was, as his name suggests, a pickpocket. Using his skills, he picked the pockets of the Famous Five, Vernon Smith and Jim Valentine. He then replaced Valentine's money with counterfeit, and allowed himself to be taken by the Friars. Valentine earned Smithy's enmity when forced by circumstance to let Kicky go. The counterfeit money caused a great deal of trouble in the school, until the mystery was solved. Kicky was eventually arrested, along with the rest of the gang. (GBC 9).

KID, The Game. See Drury, Richard.

KIDNAPPED SCHOOLBOYS, THE. (Title HBE Volume 24). See Mysterious Mr Kranz, The.

KIKOLOBO. A Kikuyu chief from Masalindi. On his way to Nairobi to lay a complaint against Ludwig Krantz, he met Vernon Smith and the Famous Five. When Smithy saved him from a wounded lion he earned himself a friend for life who crossed rivers and jungle to rescue him and his friends after Krantz had sold them into slavery. To this end, Kicky even allowed himself to become a slave. (HBE 65).

KILLIP, Mr Joe. The owner of a garage in Friardale who hired a motor cycle to Hazeldene who, having crashed the machine, found himself in dire need of cash to pay for repairs. To raise the ready, Hazel almost sank to depths unplumbed, even by him. (949).

KING. A one time member of the Remove. One of Bulstrode's toadies he seemed ready to join in bullying anyone weaker than his leader. (4).

KING, Ken. Known as King of the Islands, he is the owner and Captain of the ketch Dawn. After Ysabel Dick had scuttled the Flamingo, the Dawn sailed past the drifting Friars, but did not sight them. After Van Dink had pitched Harry Wharton into the sea, it was King who picked him up and, learning of the "Adventurers" predicament, went to their aid. (1598).

KINGSGATE, Kent. A seaside resort visited by the Famous Five while staying with Fishy at Portercliffe Hall. (1438).

KINGSTON-upon-THAMES, Surrey. An ancient market town on the River Thames from where Harry Wharton and Co. started their cruise up the river in the Water Lily. (1653).

KIPPERS. The nickname of Oliver Kipps.

KIPPS, Oliver. He shares Study No 5 in the Remove with Hilary. He is, like his father, an accomplished conjuror. A talent he usually reserves for practical joking but, which, on occasions, proves to be of use in more serious matters. Apart from his theatrical stunts, he plays little part in form life, although occasionally turning out as a reserve for the Form Teams.

KLACK, Mr. The musical director, conductor and singing master to Mr Whiffle's pantomime company. (409).

KNOWLES, Mr. Father to Ulick Stone, he rented the Old Red House to use as a prison in which to keep Arthur Durance while his son impersonated him at Greyfriars. The purpose of the charade was to gain control of the fortune left to Durance by his mother. (HBE 68).

KO-KO. The local deity of a Congo village. Bunter made the idol speak and thus had himself appointed, for a time, their chief. His reign was brief as, when Pedro Casca arrived he was able to show the natives that it was all trickery and not their god talking. (GBC 12).

KOKO. A crewboy in the Ketch Dawn. (1598).

KOLOLOO. The chief of police in Kalua. His badge of office was, like the rest of his men, his lawyer cane. (1590).

KOMOO. A native of Koo Koo's island. He was friendly towards the Friars and helped them capture the Sea Cat to aid their escape. (HBE 12).

KONSTANTINOPOULOUS, Mr. A Greek friend of Colonel Wharton who was unable to translate the "Greek" message inside Soames' silver cigarette case. (HBA 1).

KOO-KOO-KOOLOO-KULULO. The cannibal chief of the island whereon the Greyfriars party was shipwrecked. Bunter displaced him for a time as chief by using his ventriloquism. For the duration of the usurper's reign the cannibalistic practices of the tribe were halted. (HBE 12).

KOTOO. A crewboy in the Sea Cat, Captain Parson's boat. (1595).

KOUMI RAO. The Jam of Bundelpore. He is at St Jim's and is a close friend of George Figgins.

KRANTZ, Ludwig. A slave trader of Germano-Arabic parentage. Vernon Smith fell foul of him shortly after arriving in Nairobi and, by way of revenge, Krantz captured the Greyfriars Safari party and sold them into slavery in the Congo. They were rescued by Kikolobo, after he had killed Krantz. (HBE 65).

KRANZ, Mr Franz, O.F. He left school under a cloud. An airman by profession, he had heard of Major Cherry's invention, and determined to possess it. To this end he kidnapped Bob Cherry. Vernon Smith, under threat of expulsion, found out what was happening, but he too was kidnapped, as was Tom Redwing. Mauleverer, castigated as a lazy fool by Kranz, solved the mystery and Kranz found himself behind bars. (HBE 24; HBE 24a).

KURI DIN. A friend of Hurree Singh's from Bhanipur at St Jude's School. Shortly after he arrived there he took up gambling with Jerry Hawke and Cobb at the Cross Keys. He had to borrow a large sum from Inky to settle his debts. Skinner, who had taken a photograph of him, managed to get Mr Quelch to accuse Hurree Singh of "Pub haunting". (GBC 27).

KWANG SI. A province of China which was effectively under the control of Tang Wang since he held a position there under its Tu-Chun, or War Lord. (1183).

L.

LA FONTAINE. A small port and fishing village in Northern France which is near the Chateau de Cernay. The Silver Scud anchored here when visiting the chateau. (GBC 35).

LA RIVIERE, Leonora. The stage name of Jane Snookson. She was one of the extras in "The Lord of the Desert". Mauleverer fancied himself in love with her, rescued her from a fire in the studios and, when he saw her in the clutches of a strange man, rushed to the rescue yet again. He then discovered, to his intense embarrassment, that he was Peter Carter, her fiance! Having given up her stage career, she is now happily married to Mr Carter. (GBC 21).

LACY. A one time Removite. He used to share Study No 12 with Russell and Wun Lung. Linley was later placed in the same study, to Russell's disgust. Lacy was a weak character who was easily led, which may acount for his leaving Greyfriars. (45; 118).

LAGDEN, Mr Rupert, M.A., Oxon. A qualified schoolmaster who supplemented his meagre pay as a "supply teacher" by theft. He was sought by the police for twelve years, and was known to the criminal fraternity as "Jimmy the One". As such he was recognised by Flip. Lagden, therefore, in order to keep his secret, had Flip kidnapped. He was kept prisoner in Mr Joyce the woodcutter's cottage, hired for that purpose. This act, unnecessary as it was, (for Flip would never have "grassed"), led to his arrest by Inspector Brent of Scotland Yard. (HBE 4).

LAGDEN, Mr Stephen. He left his previous school under something of a cloud, and gained a temporary post at Greyfriars in Mr Lascelles' absence. While on the way to the school, he was knocked down by a hit and run motorist. James Loder saw the accident and changed clothes with Lagden to take his name and place at Greyfriars. There was quite a sensation when it was discovered that the unconscious man, picked up at the roadside in prison clothes, proved not to be the escaped prisoner but, by an incredible coincidence, the man guilty of the theft for which Mr Loder had been imprisoned. (HBE 47).

LAIRD of LOCHMUIR, The. Amongst the clans almost obliterated at the Battle of Culloden was the MacDermids of Lochmuir. Angus, the hereditary piper to the lairds, would walk the battlements playing his laments, vowing to keep the place safe for the return of the laird. (GBC 34).

LAKME. The chief dancing girl in the Palace at Bhanipur. Bunter formed a crush on her and made an assignation which was kept by the palace executioner and the Famous Five to pull Bunter's leg. (968).

LAL CHUNDER. A subadar, or Captain, in the palace guard in Bhanipur. He remained loyal to the Nabob throughout the attempted coup by Baji Rao. (969).

LAL JANG. In the pay of Chunder Run, he helped in one of his master's abortive attempts to kidnap Bunter in mistake for Vernon Smith. (1231).

LAMB, Mr. An arty man in his early thirties, he was "a rather pale young man with gold rimmed glasses, a sleepy looking face, and hair worn a little long", Soon nicknamed The Pet Lamb, he belied both appearance and soubriquet. In fact he was Slim Jim, a much sought thief, whom Mr Quelch saw without his mask and was, therefore, kidnapped. Ferrers Locke was called in to look for him and took the post of Chauffeur to the Head. Vernon Smith took a dislike to Mr Lamb and, in the course of a running battle, discovered his secret. He, too, was kidnapped before Ferrers Locke finally trapped Mr Lamb, using the Head's Bearer Bonds as bait. (HBE 29-30).

LAMB, Mr. A professional boxer known as The Lambury Lamb. He was the leader of the "army" hired by Mr Carnforth to put down the "Sixth Form Rebellion". (744-745).

LAMBE, Reverend Orlando Beale. The vicar of Friardale. He is an old friend of both the Head and Mr Quelch, (with whom he often plays chess).

LANCASTER, Mr. Uncle to Dick. He was an accomplished safe breaker and taught his nephew well. He died prematurely as a result of alcoholism. (1209).

LANCASTER, Mr George, (Handsome). Killed in action, he was in the same regiment as Colonel Wharton. His surviving son is Dick Lancaster. (1209).

LANCASTER, Richard, (Dick). An orphan, (who possibly has relatives abroad). Educated for the most part privately, he was sent to Greyfriars at the orders of Slimy Sugden. Revolting against his past and trying to go straight, Lancaster, (known to the police as The Wizard), became a mainstay of the cricket team, as well as being a classicist of no mean ability. Harry Wharton admired him but discovered his secret and caused a furore by "cutting" him in the quad. Kidnapped by Sugden and his associates, Harry escaped with the help of Lancaster who, as the net woven by Ferrers Locke closed around him, was injured saving Locke from a murderous assault by the gang. Reprieved for this act, Lancaster emigrated to start a new life. (HBE 7).

LANCASTER, Captain William. The son of Lord Trant's oldest friend was reading a letter when Bunter rode him down and appropriated the letter. Using this missive, Bunter invited the Famous Five to see the Coronation from Lord Trant's London house. (1526).

LANCHESTER, Sir Peter, Bart. "A very distant connection" and guardian of Lord Reynham. Following attempts upon his life, from which Bunter saved him, Sir Peter had the idea of installing a phoney Lord to try to entrap the would-be kidnappers. Bunter managed to annexe the post, having given Sir Peter a false impression of his bravery. (HBE 14).

LANE. A Junior at Rylcombe Grammar School. (118).

LANE, Jim. While searching for Ravenspur Grange, the Famous Five were held up at gunpoint by a man with a deeply scarred face. Telling them of his past and his quest for "Black Edgar", they had barely parted when a gun shot rang out killing the one time member of Black Edgar's gang. (1122).

LANG. A member of the Sixth Form. (50).

LANGLEY, Arthur de Bohun. The Head of School and Captain of Games at Highcliffe School. A pleasant enough chap, his job is not made any easier by the prevailing air of disinterest in the school, and so he joins in the regular evening bridge fours, rather than exercise his authority.

LANGTON. A misprint for Langley, the Captain of Highcliffe School. (939).

LANKESTER. In the Second Form at Greyfriars and a member of the Form teams.

LANKESTER, Captain Gerald. A close friend to Lord Cavandale who had served under Colonel Wharton in the army. While staying at Cavandale Abbey, Lankester attempted the Earl's life, to try to prevent his horse running in The Lantham 1,000 Guineas. Exposed by Ferrers Locke, he left the country disgraced, and financially ruined by his gambling. (HBE 22).

LANTHAM. A county town some ten miles from Greyfriars by road; although, by using bridle paths, two miles can be cut off the journey. It is a town of some size, lying on the main London road. Amongst its facilities it boasts a fine shopping centre – The Lantham Arcade. Its hospital is the main centre locally catering for all specialities. On the sporting front, the town supports two football teams. Lantham Argyll is a professional team and a member of the Football League; while Lantham Rovers is an amateur club against whom Greyfriars play regular matches. There is a combined greyhound and speedway stadium and, also, just outside the town, a famous race course where the highlight of the January meeting is the Lantham 1,000 Guineas.

The town is served by Lantham Junction, an important railway junction in the South East.

LANTHAM CHASE. A large country house some two miles outside the town in the Greyfriars direction. It is surrounded by park and woodland. Squire Luscombe, the owner, has been forced to live abroad by high taxation, and rents the house and its shooting. Captain Vernon rented the place in a bid to substitute his nephew Bertie for Vernon Smith. (HBE 54-55).

LANTHAM 1,000 GUINEAS. One of the classic races in the calendar. It is run during the January meeting at Lantham. Lord Cavandale's famous horse, Maharajah, was one favourite who won, despite attempts to get the horse withdrawn. (HBE 22).

LANTHAM PET. A professional boxer based in the town who fought the Game Chicken at the Three Fishers. Vernon Smith planning to go, was followed by Mr Smedley. Luckily, Tom Redwing was able to warn Smithy in time. (1373).

LARIAT. The horse wrangler at the Kicking Cayuse Ranch. It was his job to break in new horses. After giving Bunter an almost unbroken horse, he had a fight with Bill Buck, giving Stone the excuse he wanted to fire Buck. Soon after, he put cactus thorns under Vernon Smith's saddle and, but for Bill Buck, Smithy might well have been killed. Smithy fired Lariat after a shoot out, thus reducing Stone's allies on the ranch. (HBE 32).

LARKIN. Butler to Mr Vernon Smith at his house in Courtman Square.

LARKIN. One of Sir Gilbert Frump's keepers. He helped in the arrest of Ponsonby thinking he was a poacher! (1338).

LASCELLES, Mr Lawrence, (Larry). He combines the duties of mathematics and Games Master. Before coming to Greyfriars, he was a professional boxer, but promised not to re-enter the ring after taking up teaching. He is arguably the most popular master in the school, not only for his athleticism, but also his fairness.

LATCHAM. One of the stations at which it is necessary to change on the journey from Greyfriars to Rookwood. Convinced that Tom Redwing had done him out of his place in the team, Vernon Smith stranded his best friend here so that he, Smithy, could play in the match. (858).

LATHAM, Mr Philip G. The Fourth Form Master at St Jim's. He is not the strongest of characters but he is popular with his form, despite his interests in archaeology and prehistoric man !

LATIN VERSE PRIZE. An examination for which Mr Quelch gives a prize of a copy of a classical author. Bunter, spurred by the vision of £5 from his Uncle George, entered the exam, and was most upset to be caned for presenting a paper stolen from Linley. He did not realise that it was one of the Odes of Horace ! (1159).

LAURELS, The, Bayswater. After Vernon Smith had been expelled for persistent rule breaking, he was disowned by his father who made arrangements for him to stay with the family at this address. This harsh treatment of a boy, already punished severely, was sufficient for Dr Locke to give Smithy another chance. (1362).

LAVEROCK. A town at least five miles from Greyfriars. Bulstrode and Skinner sent Bunter several Postal Orders for 1/-. One of them required to be changed at Laverock - the return fare for which was at least 1/- ! (133).

LAWRENCE. A member of the Sixth Form at Greyfriars, and a member of the First Eleven.

LAZAROFF, Sergei. A Bolshevik agent provocateur operating in the North West Frontier region of India to foment trouble, and so gain a foothold for Russia in Asia. In Baji Rao he found a willing tool who raised his standard in an attempt to usurp the throne of Bhanipur with the aid of Lazaroff. The coup failed; Lazaroff murdered Baji Rao, stole his jewels, and tried to run for it. However, Mahbub, one of Hurree Singh's Shikarees, caught up with and executed Lazaroff. (GBC 4).

LAZARUS, Mr. The owner of the second hand shop in Courtfield. Dealing in everything, he is also an adept at stage make up and often helps Wibley with some of his more difficult characterisations.

LAZARUS, Solomon, (Solly). The son of Mr Lazarus, the second hand dealer. He is amongst the leaders of the juniors of Courtfield Grammar School who, in between the inter-school rivalries and feuds, is a good friend to the Famous Five; but perhaps never so opportunely as when the Famous Five were accused of "sacking" Loder. Luckily Solly had seen Ponsonby and Co. in the act of putting the sack over Loder's head !

Le BOSQUET-dans-le-FORET. A small select seaside resort near Boulogne. Like its neighbour it too can boast a casino. Vernon Smith visited the place several times when the gambling fever was upon him.

On one of these illegal trips he left Ponsonby and Co. after a row, and so was on the spot when his father was attacked by a footpad. (758; 1365).

LEARY. A small time New York gangster. He worked for Two Gun Sanders and helped to kidnap Bunter in mistake for Smithy in a bid to prevent the Friars going to Texas. (1574).

LEBON, Louis Joseph Marie Pierre. A waiter at the Paris Exhibition who was not amused by Bunter's attempts to speak French. Cochon cannot be considered a polite name to call any man - no matter what his origins - except perhaps Bunter himself ! (1543).

LECCHI, Giovanni. The leader of a gang of toughs in the Calabrian Mountains of Italy. His gang captured the Famous Five so that Dr Sin could take Wun Lung home to China. As Bunter had lost himself in the forest he was not captured, but instead freed the Famous Five. (1127).

LEDGEY, George. A one time member of the "Dandy's" gang of crooks. After being double-crossed by his leader, he determined upon revenge. In error he assaulted Mr Devarney to whose assistance came Newland. A somewhat ironical situation since Julian Devarney had declared war on Newland ! (1127).

LEE, Jim. An orphan who was brought up from infancy by his cousin, Ulick Driver. It was not until he was sent to Greyfriars that Lee discovered the truth about his cousin. Appalled at the prospect of making friends so that his cousin could rob their homes, he made himself, (completely uncharacteristically), as unpopular as possible. For this he received several thrashings from his cousin. Torn between not becoming embroiled in dishonesty and his liking for many of the Remove, he confided in Harry Wharton. Acting on his advice he went to Inspector Grimes who trapped Driver, and allowed Lee to go free, since he had not, in fact, committed a crime. Jim Lee left Greyfriars, and was helped by the Head, Colonel Wharton and Major Cherry to make a new life for himself. (GBC 37).

LEECH. A hanger on at The Three Fishers. He indulges in illegal bookmaking and also acts as billiards marker. (1329).

LEECH. Dismissed from his position as footman at Popper Court, he stole the Popper Court silver that same night. Coker, out of bounds on Popper's Island, recovered the stolen goods, and so avoided an otherwise certain flogging. (1479).

LEGGE. A fag in the Second Form at Greyfriars. (1248).

LEGGE, Mr Benjamin. The Headmaster of Courtfield School. (146).

LEGGETT & TEGGERS. A scholastic agency of Regent Street, London, W.1. A long established firm with an impeccable reputation for supplying teaching staff to the best schools. After many years, Mr Leggett took a junior partner, Mr Lucius Teggers, who turned out to be a thoroughly unscrupulous man in his dealings with Vernon Smith, (his cousin). He appears to have escaped without penalty, for the firm continued as Leggett & Teggers, and it is inconceivable that Mr Leggett would permit a man to be his partner with any stain on his character.

LEIGH. A one time member of the Remove. (200; 249).

LENNOX, Captain William. Captain of the Aloha, one of Mr Vernon Smith's copra carrying fleet. When Soames took over the ship, he pitched the Captain overboard to his death. (1022).

LEOFRIC. A Saxon monk who built a cell for himself on Monk's Island in the River Wyme. (1261).

LEVISON, Ernest. The older son of Mr John Levison, he was, for a time, in the Remove at Greyfriars. Expelled for persistent rule breaking, he was allowed to go to St Jim's where he reformed his ways, to the disbelief of Skinner and Co. whenever they see him! He is now a stalwart of the Junior Team at St Jim's School, and has become a good friend to the Famous Five.

LEVISON, Frank, (Minor). The younger brother of Ernest, he is in the Third Form at St Jim's School. He ran away from school on one occasion and, arriving in Kent, was sheltered in the Old Tower by the Famous Five. As a result of this, he landed in the Sanatorium, and his brother allowed to stay at Greyfriars during his recovery. (GBC 14). He came to Greyfriars again when Mr Bright laid claim to the family money, and returned to St Jim's after the correct will had been proved. (GBC 26).

LEVISON, Mr John. Father of Ernest and Frank. He had been left some money by his uncle, Mr Thorpe, (a late member of staff at Greyfriars), but Mr Bright laid claim to it by presenting an invalid will. Ernest found the last will of his great uncle, while at Greyfriars for that purpose, and so restored the family fortunes. (1031).

LEVISON'S RETURN. (Title GBC Volume 14). When Levison Minor ran away from St Jim's accused of a theft he had not committed, he was found near Greyfriars by the Famous Five who sheltered him, unwisely, in the Old Tower. As a result, he caught pneumonia and had to be placed in the sanatorium. Because of the seriousness of his condition, his brother, Ernest, was allowed to stay at Greyfriars for a time. Skinner and Co., his old cronies in blagging did not believe in his reform. They thought it all a part of a deep plot. A ragging or two later and they were forced to believe! Helping Hazeldene led Levison into deep trouble from which, but for Vernon Smith, he might not have escaped. Finally, Ponsonby, another crony of the old days, tried to frame him for a theft. This time Levison was saved by Bunter. Then, his minor cured, they left Greyfriars to return to St Jim's.

LEXHAM. A town on the main railway line beween St Jim's and Courtfield. (569).

LEY, Oxfordshire. The village about one mile from Ravenspur Grange. (1122).

LI WING. Ferrers Locke disguised himself as a gardener of this name in Tang Wang's household, so that he could free Wharton, Cherry and Bunter, who were being held prisoner there. (1185).

LI YI. Mr O's personal servant. (1543).

LIBRARY. The school library contains many rare volumes and manuscripts, many of which relate to the history of the school and the monastery before. It is out of bounds to all but the Sixth Form without permission from a member of staff. It is a secluded room at the end of one of the wings of the school buildings.

LICK, Sheriff. The Law Officer of Packsaddle, Texas. He was unwilling to believe that Barney Stone was guilty of cattle rustling but, when Vernon Smith and the Famous Five produced the necessary proof, he acted quickly to arrest him. (HBE 32).

LIMBURGER, Wilhelmina. A German girl who was, for a time, at Cliff House School. Slow witted and greedy, she was, to Bunter, the embodiment of femininity. (59).

LING, Mr. The deputy governor at H.M.P. Stoneville. (933).

LINKY. A tattermedallion from Pegg who delights in cheeking the Remove, especially when there can be no retribution. He is a bully and has been known to obtain money with menaces from the elderly.

LINLEY, Gerald. Younger brother to Mark. He used to be an inveterate snob, and persuaded his parents to raise the money so that he too could go to Greyfriars. He saved Mauleverer who had fallen through the ice, and took money for a reward. After a hard time, he realised that Greyfriars was not the place for him, and he returned home a happier and wiser man. (468).

LINLEY, Mabel. Sister to Mark, she is a gentle soul.

LINLEY, Mark. Winning a scholarship to Greyfriars, Linley had a dreadful time to start with. He was scorned by the snobs - after all, he had actually worked for his living before going to school! Most men, however, treat their peers on merit, and the majority of Greyfriars is no exception. Linley has plenty of sterling qualities. He is always top of the form, (he actually likes work!), and he is a useful member of the Form teams. To the rest of the form his quiet studiousness is inexplicable but, at the same time, they understand the need for him to win all the prizes he carries off termly in order to help the family finances, which are often in a parlous state due to his father's ill-health. Mark is the oldest of the family, having one brother and a sister.

LINLEY, Mr Thomas. Father of Mark, and looked down upon by some of the Remove because he is a working man. He is enormously proud of his oldest son, and goes through many hardships willingly so that he can help with his schooling. A sufferer from ill-health, he is not too proud to receive help from Mark in the form of half the amount he wins in prize money if times are hard.

LITTLE PUDDLETON, Sussex. A village on the Downs visited by "The Greyfriars Hikers". They arrived to find the village in a turmoil over the prospect of an enforced auction of Wlliam Waggs' goods, distrained for non-payment of his tithes. (1333).

LITTLE SIDE. The Junior teams playing fields for both practice games and matches.

LOBO, O. The popular name, given in fear, to a Brazilian bandit. He had somehow heard of Peter Valentine's diamond find and tried many ways to lay claim to it himself. While the Famous Five and Bunter were in Brazil they had a running battle with O Lobo who was wounded several times in skirmishes. He met a gruesome end, mauled by an alligator. (HBE 44).

LOCHMUIR. An ancient castle in the Highlands of Scotland to the north of Inverness. It was formerly the home of the MacDermids, but now belongs to Angel's young brother, Mick. Visiting the house for Christmas, the Friars were haunted by Angus the piper who still dreamed of the old days, (before the Battle of Culloden!). (GBC 34).

LOCKE, Mrs. Alice. The Headmaster's wife. She is a shy unassuming lady who plays little active part in school life.

LOCKE, Miss Amy, B.A. The Head's youngest sister. She is a graduate of Girton College, Oxford, and is a forthright commanding young lady. A schoolmistress by profession, she has even taught the Remove on occasion. She, was for a time, a mistress at Cliff House School.

LOCKE, Mr Ferrers. The world famous detective and cousin to the Head. His home is in Baker Street, London, from where he conducts his cases with the help of his assistant, former Removite, Jack Drake. He is often at Greyfriars, and has helped the police with many famous cases – such as the Courtfield Cracksman; and Slim Jim. He has also been instrumental in solving the attempted murders of Lord Cavandale and Sir Richard Ravenspur. When Wun Lung's life was threatened by Tang Wang, he escorted him to China to the safety of his father's house.

LOCKE, The Reverend Herbert Henry, D.D., (Cantab) . The Headmaster of Greyfriars School. Giving the appearance of un-wordliness, he is infallibly courteous and fair. Sometimes ridden over roughshod by Sir Hilton Popper and some of the Governors, he will employ men of less than sterling worth or admit boys who are not of Greyfriars calibre. In these circumstances he often appears indecisive, but his innate desire is to be just to all. A first class Headmaster he leaves the running of the school to his staff and prefects, and only becomes involved when the gravity of the situation demands. His two great loves, after his family and the school, are his garden and the classics – in particular the Greek author Aeschylus.

LOCKE, Molly. The Head's youngest child who idolises Harry Wharton. She had taken a favourite doll to him for repair when she was trapped by a fire, (Bunter had been too enthusiastic with his cookery!) . But for the bravery of Wharton she would have perished. (48) .

LOCKE, Percival, (Percy), O.F. The Head's only son. After a tempestuous youth of rebellion, no doubt due to being at his father's school, he has grown into a personable young man.

LOCKE, Rosie. The elder daughter of Dr and Mrs. Locke.

LODER, Major. The owner of Thames Nook on the Buckinghamshire side of the Thames below Henley, and uncle to Loder. The Famous Five and Bunter camped here, believing they had permission from a Mr Egerton. After a battle royal with Loder, Hilton and Price, they retreated in good order. (1645) .

LODER, Gerald Assheton. One of the few mistakes Dr Locke has ever made was the elevation of Loder to a prefectship after the expulsion of Carberry. He is a past master of all the vices, not the least being his dissimulation. A compulsive gambler and smoker, and a regular breaker of bounds, he relieves his nocturnal activities by a daily round of bullying. He wages perpetual war on the Remove, and the Famous Five in particular, and any excuse for excessive punishment is seized upon. On one occasion he was threatened with demotion, but was saved by a severe injury received by the Head. And, so far from demotion, was actually promoted to Head of School by Mr Prout, whom he "stuffed" successfully until finally bested by the "Secret Seven". He even takes his ruffianly ways onto the football field where, if things are not going his way, he will hack and foul opponents unmercifully – and still be convinced that he is worthy of a place in the team. Not surprisingly he has few friends – and they are fair weather friends – Carne and Walker.

LODER, Major, H. Father to Gerald and, like his younger brother, an ex-major. When James Loder escaped from prison, he was quick to refute any relationship.

LODER, Mr James. Falsely accused of theft, he was sent to Blackmoor Prison where he became known as Convict 22. Escaping in an attempt to clear his name, he met Stephen Lagden, an old associate from Okeham School, Devon. Lagden was seriously injured in a hit and run accident. Loder, therefore, changed clothes with him and went to Greyfriars as Games Master, (Lascelles had been injured in a fight with James Loder). There was great excitement when it was discovered that the temporary beak was an impostor; and greater still when it came out that the man he was impersonating was guilty of the theft for which Loder had been convicted. Throughout this time, Gerald Loder could not have been said to have enjoyed himself. (HBE 47).

LODER FOR CAPTAIN. (Title GBC Volume 2). Loder has always hated Wingate. He is jealous of his popularity and his ability on the games field. His fury at not being selected for the First Eleven knows no bounds. When the opportunity arose to force Wingate's resignation through leading his wayward and headstrong younger brother astray, he made the most of his chance. After Wingate had resigned, Loder, by bribery and false bonhomie, got himself elected as Captain. Although no one was appointed Head of School, Loder acted as though he had been. Bullying all and sundry – from Wingate downwards, he raised a hornet's nest when he tried to make the Remove fag. Wingate Minor confessed the truth to the Head who announced a new election and Loder, in an effort to keep his new found power, tried to hold up Wingate in the holidays. The result of this was that Wingate had to rescue Loder from a snow storm – and so with some show of graciousness, Loder conceded defeat.

LODER PARK. The home of the Loder family. (1494).

LODGEY, Joseph. Known as Joe, he is a shady horse dealer, bookmaker and an habitue of the Cross Keys. He ensnared Caffyn into betting with him. Caffyn refused to pay his debts, instead trying to blackmail his way out of trouble. Lodgey, by way of reply, thrashed Caffyn who, snipe that he was, accused Coker of the crime. Luckily, Mr Joyce, the woodcutter, had seen the assault for which Lodgey received a six month prison sentence. (HBE 9).

LONG BEACH BOARDING HOUSE, Sunset Boulevard, Hollywood. Run by Colonel and Mrs. Coot, the "Greyfriars Film Stars" stayed here while filming in Hollywood. (GBC 20-21).

LONGLEY. A member of the Sixth Form. (50).

LORD of the DESERT. A film made by Perfection Studios. It stars Myron Polk and Janet Jooce. Harry Wharton was brought in to double for Polk in some of the riding scenes – including the famous descent of The Hair Trigger. (GBC 20-21).

LORNE. A member of the Upper Fourth.

LOVELACE. A famous past head of School in the nineteenth century. He led the "Great Rebellion" against the tyranny of Dr Trumpington, the then Headmaster. Skinner found a scrap of paper referring to this Head's actions, and gave it to Dr Locke to mislead him about Mr Quelch's feelings towards him. Thus began the High Oaks Rebellion. (HBE 10).

LOUIS. A Marseilles longshoreman who was paid by Rawlings, (the steward on the Firefly), to kidnap the Famous Five in the hills above the port. Rawlings then announced they had left for England. However, Bunter had not been taken and was able to get help from Valentine Compton – and in the process expose Rawlings plans. (1508).

LOUIS le COUTEAU. A Parisian Apache employed by Tiger Bronx to kidnap Bunter in an effort to gain control of his late uncle's fortune. Coker had had a row with Bronx and, returning to Le Chat Noir to continue his fight, he found Bunter a prisoner and freed him. (1385).

LOVELL, Arthur Edward. One of the "Fistical Four" at Rookwood. Although one of the world's non-intellectuals he is well above average at games.

LOWER FOURTH. The correct name of the Remove at Greyfriars. It is, however, rarely used, even by Mr Quelch, the Form Master – unless he is feeling unusually starchy!

LOWTHER, Montague, (Monty). One of Tom Merry's closest friends at St Jim's, where he is a member of the "Terrible Three".

LUCAS, Mr. Private secretary to Mr Skelton, he took a dim view of Bunter's philanthropy, and was certain that he was after the main chance. By arranging for his employer to go abroad, he was able to remove Bunter from the house at the toe of a boot ! (1037).

LUKWE. The Polynesian island that is the home port of Captain Parsons and his vessel the Sea Cat.

LUNN. The Junior Captain of St Jude's School.

LUSCOMBE, Squire. The owner of Lantham Chase. Impoverished by ever increasing taxation, he has been forced to leave his home and live abroad. By renting out the house and the shooting on the estate, he is able to keep the place in the family.

LUTZ, Karl. A member of Herr Rosenblaum's Foreign Academy, and a close friend to Fritz Hoffmann. (6).

LYNTON, Devon. Dr Locke received a letter from Mr Quelch postmarked from this town. It was an attempt that failed by Slim Jim to mislead Ferrers Locke in his search for the kidnapped master. (1662).

M.

MACAO. A Portuguese colony on the Chinese mainland. It is renowned for its casinos and so, when on his way to Canton, Bunter decided, against explicit orders, to try his hand here at Fan Tan. "Picked up" by Senhor Vasco Cunha he was taken to a hell which soon relieved him of his cash. The Famous Five followed Bunter to try to bring him back to Hong Kong but, as there were no night ferries, they had to stay the night, giving Tang Wang's assassin a chance to attack them. Luckily without success. (1182).

MACAW ISLAND. Lying in the Rio Rexo near the Valentines' Fazenda in the back country of Brazil, this small island was the head-quarters of O Lobo. It's name derives from the enormous flocks of scarlet parrots inhabiting the place. O Lobo had taken Bunter prisoner and was holding him here. Luckily Bonito, a parrot taught to speak by Bunter, was with him when he was captured. Flying back to the plantation he gave the Famous Five the clue as to his master's whereabouts. (1467).

MACK. The Rookwood School porter.

MADDISON. A member of the Shell. (49).

MAGIC FILMS. By using Myron Polk's name and mimicking his voice, Bunter conned this film company, (one of Perfection's main rivals), into giving him an acting role. It did not take long for the director to discover both the lack of talent and the fact that he had been "had"! (1099).

MAGICLAND Ltd. A variety show composed of illusions and magic. Philip Darke, (a relative of Mr Quelch), worked in the show. After hypnotising the boss, he fled with the contents of the safe. (1517).

MAHARAJAH. The famous race horse belonging to Lord Cavandale. It was the favourite for the Lantham 1,000 guineas. To get the horse withdrawn, several unscrupulous men attempted the Earl's life. (HBE 22).

MAHBUB. The chief Shikaree, (or hunter), to Hurree Singh. After Baji Rao's coup failed, he fled; Mahbub tracked him down and, after beheading him, brought his head back to court to claim the reward money for Baji's capture. (GBC 4).

MAKING OF HARRY WHARTON, THE. (Title GBC Volume 3). On his return home to England from service in India, Colonel Wharton found that his nephew had been allowed to do as he pleased. As a result he had become thoroughly spoilt and selfish. To cure this, Harry Wharton was sent to Greyfriars where he made a really unpopular start - fighting all and sundry and refusing overtures of friendship from Nugent whose life he had saved. It did not take long before he realised that conformity was the best path to a comfortable life. Then, with his innate sense of loyalty and honesty, he changed his outlook on life. So much so, that apart from occasional lapses from grace due to impulsiveness and pride, he became the Head and Captain of the Remove.

MALAITA. The cannibal tribe on Caca Island who proved a potent threat by Soames against any insubordination by the Kanaka crew of the Aloha. Better the brutality of the Sea Laywer than the cooking pots. So warlike a tribe were they that even Soames, in his Blackbirding days, had not dared to try to enslave them. (GBC 11).

MALEK. One of the camel drivers hired by "Honest" Ibrahim, and in the pay of Bou Saoud. His orders were to prevent the Famous Five finding Major Cherry after he had been captured in a bid to force Ali to give up the rulership of his tribe. (866).

MANNERS, Henry, (Harry). In the Fourth Form at St Jim's. He is a close friend of Tom Merry, and is a member of "The Terrible Three". He is a keen photographer.

MARBLE HALL, Courtfield. The rather grandiose name given to one of the public buildings in Courtfield. Built in what is fondly imagined to be the Palladian style of architecture, it is used for films and lectures. (1137).

MARCHBANKS. As stately as his name, he is butler to Lord Trant at Trant Elms. (HBE 40).

MARCO. The lion tamer, and one of the main crowd pullers, in Muccolini's Circus. Taken in by Bunter, he invited him to join the circus as "Bunto the Boy Tamer", thinking he had enough courage to enter the lions' cage ! As usual, the fiction was soon seen through, and Bunter dismissed his post. Marco is now married to Zara, the Bareback Rider, in his real name of Bill Williams. After Muccolini had been arrested, Marco took over the running of the circus. He is a simple honest soul who had difficulty in understanding Bunter's duplicity and cunning, and so was easily led to believe that Bunter had permission to join the circus, (in reality he had run away from school!).) He soon became a firm friend to the Famous Five. (HBE 55-56).

MARCO. One of the Calabrian bandits hired by Dr O to imprison the Famous Five so that he could take Wun Lung back to China. A drunken lout, Marco was soon overpowered, when in his cups, by Bunter who had stumbled on the cave wherein the Famous Five were being held. (1544).

MARGARET, Aunt. Sister to Colonel and Miss Amy Wharton. She is possibly the eldest of her generation, since she does not enjoy good health, and on one occasion at least, the Colonel and Miss Wharton had to go to Bournemouth, where she lives, in order to look after her; leaving Harry Wharton and his friends to fend for themselves. That holiday the Famous Five spent Christmas at Cavandale Abbey at Bunter's invitation, later endorsed by the Earl. (1192).

MARGATE, Kent. The famous seaside holiday resort. While staying here one holiday, the Famous Five stumbled on Muccolini's secret and were able to help Ferrers Locke bring him to justice. (1490).

MARKER, Mrs. Mrs. Kebble's deputy house keeper and house matron.

MARKER, Captain Eric. A dissolute spendthrift and inveterate gambler who had blotted his copy-book – as a result of which his uncle, Mr Cortolvin, left his fortune to Harry Wharton, (a distant relative through his grandmother). To redress the balance, Marker sent da Costa to Greyfriars with express orders to get Harry Wharton disgraced and expelled, (as had happened to Marker). However, his plot failed as da Costa, realising that Wharton was, contrary to his expectations, no snob and a basically decent fellow, refused to continue with the scheme. Captain Marker came to England and tried to persuade da Costa to continue, but to no avail. So he tried himself and, meeting Bunter wearing Wharton's hat, thought he had an easy prey! Ponsonby proved a keen ally, but again, they failed. At last, defeated, he fled the country. (HBE 27).

MAROUDI, Hilmi. A rich Egyptian landowner and a long standing friend of Sir Reginald Brooke. When the latter took a party of Friars to Egypt, Maroudi played a large part in saving Mauleverer from Kalizelos. First he doubled the bribe offered to Hassan, and thus ensured his loyalty; and later when all seemed lost, Maroudi came to the rescue by his claim of friendship on Sheik Andurhaman. (HBE 1).

MARSDEN. Private secretary to Sir William Cherry. After his employer was poisoned, he fled the house, giving rise to the suspicion of complicity in the crime. It transpired, however, that he had been embezzling his employer's money. (1108).

MARSDEN. A fag in the Second Form. (1248).

MARSEILLES. The French sea port on the Mediterranean. It is the steamer port for the East and, as such, was visited several times by Greyfriars parties. It was also from here that Rawlings set into motion his plan for mutiny to try to prevent Captain Compton giving up smuggling.

MARY. One of the domestic housemaids at Greyfriars.

MARY. One of Miss Wharton's housemaids at Wharton Lodge.

MARY BEATRICE WINIFRED. Mrs. Locke's housemaid in the Head's house at Greyfriars.

MASALINDI, Kenya. The district in which Mr Milsom has his plantation. While staying here, Vernon Smith killed a lion that was about to attack Kikolobo. This earned him the Kikiyu's friendship. As a result of this bravery, Kicky made every effort to free the Friars after their capture by Krantz. (HBE 65).

MASON, Mr. Personal secretary to Mr Vernon Smith. (1525).

MASON, Richard Harcourt. A legendary past Captain of Greyfriars in 1880. In that season he scored ten centuries on the cricket field and, in the Old Boys match, he scored 226 not out.

MASTER'S GATE. A side gate near the Main Gate. It is closed and locked by a spring lock to which masters and prefects each have a key so that they may enter and return to school after "Lock Up".

MASTER'S PASSAGE. Lies on the ground floor overlooking the Quadrangle. In it are all the staff studies with the exception of the Head's. The Master's Common Room is at the Hall end of the corridor and, at the same end, is a staircase leading up to the masters' bedrooms.

MATRON. The day to day health of the boys is under the supervision of the House Matron who combines these duties with those of Housekeeper. In cases of greater seriousness, boys are sent by Mrs. Kebble, or her deputy, Mrs. Marker, to the Sanatorium where a nursing sister is in charge, under the direction of the School Medical Officer, Dr Pillbury.

MATTER, Watts. D. An American patent medicine seller. When he and his partner, Hunk. P. Dunk, met Fisher T. Fish they were in the hair restorer business. Fishy found what he thought was the formula and went into business himself making "Growo". Unfortunately, it turned out to be "Killemkwick", a corn cure! By the time this was discovered the Remove had plastered their hair and, apart from the agony it caused, they also attracted a swarm of bees ! (920) .

MAULEVERER, Herbert Plantagenant, The Right Honourable the Earl. Usually dismissed as "his lazy Lordship", this vastly wealthy nobleman seems on the surface to sleep his way through life. In fact nothing can be further from the real Mauly. Possessed of a fine mind he is often the one to come up with the solution to an imponderable problem. It was he, for instance, who worked out that Kranz had kidnapped Cherry, Vernon Smith and Redwing. As a man of action he took command of the "Sit in Strike". When the occasion demands, and he can be got out of his study, he is by no means useless on the games field. There is nothing mean or spiteful about Mauly, and he counts all men, (worthy of the title), his friends. He cannot stand snobbishness at any price, nor will he permit ill-manners – he even apologised before waving a red hot poker in P.C. Tozer's face ! He was orphaned in infancy and has been brought up by his uncles and co-trustees, Sir Reginald Brooke and Sir Henry Braithwaite. The kindest and most forgiving of natures, he even searched the Pacific for his wayward cousin, who had previously made several attempts on his life.

MELFORD. The home town of Walker's Aunt, and the business address of Mr Simmons. (953) .

MELOAH. A gipsy woman, possessed of the "sight" who warned Harry Wharton of the impending attack on his uncle and himself by Captain Holsten. (1053) .

MERRILL & SIMMONS, Solicitors of Melford. A warrant was issued for the arrest of the junior partner, Mr Longford Simmons, on charges of embezzling client's moneys. This charge caused much trouble at Greyfriars between Walker and the Remove. (HBE 81) .

MICK THE GIPSY. (Title GBC Volume 34) . Taken while a child from his uncle's house, in the belief that he was his uncle's son, by a gipsy, Barengro, he was brought up in great hardship as a member of the tribe. Beaten for not stealing, he ran away. Saving Sir Hilton Popper from the river, he was sent to Greyfriars as a reward Barengro took Angel in mistake for Mick and it was discovered that they were brothers – hence the mistake – after Angel had plotted against him. United as a family, they spent Christmas with the Famous Five, at Mick's Highland property, Lochmuir – haunted by the piper Angus.

MICKY the SPRAT. With his accomplice, Skid Smith, he staged a daring daylight smash and grab raid on Mr Lazarus' shop under the amazed eyes of Mr Quelch and Mr Prout, and a petrified Pon. and Co Micky managed to avoid capture long enough to hide the booty on

Popper's Island; and then borrow Bob Cherry's Holiday Annual from Bunter. In this he concealed a message which WGB took to Lantham. Too late to give the book to Skid, it became the centre of attraction for Pon. and Co., and reason enough for them to rag the 'Greyfiars Hikers'. (1331).

MIEL. The son of Meloah, a gipsy woman. (1053).

MIKE. Arrested Ponsonby in Sir Giles Frump's woods for poaching while he was trying to steal Bob Cherry's Holiday Annual. (1338).

MILES, Samuel. In the Shell at Greyfriars. He is a member of the Form teams. Otherwise he is quiet and studious. He shares Study No 1 with Carr.

MILLERAND, Monsieur. The predecessor of M. Charpentier as French Master at Greyfriars.

MILSOM, Mr. A Planter in Kenya with whom Mr Vernon Smith, his son, and friends stayed while "on safari". While on a lion hunt Smithy saved Kikolobo's life. (1228).

MIMBLE, Mr Alfred. The gardener at Greyfriars School. Probably more of necessity than inclination, he is at least on drinking terms with Gosling ! Although ostensibly the school gardener, he in fact does perhaps more than his fair share of the work in the Head's garden – which is, as a result, looked upon in the area as a showpiece. It cannot be said that Mimble particularly likes the boys.

MIMBLE, Herbert Henry George. Son of Mr and Mrs. Mimble. By all accounts he is a greedy and dishonest youngster.

MIMBLE, Mrs. Jessie. The manageress of the school tuckshop. Efficient and extremely businesslike she has plenty of captive custom. Her home baked produce is particulary popular, (both pies and cakes). The only caveat she enters is that Bunter may not have credit – strictly CWO !

MINDANAO. The brig in which the "Greyfriars Adventurers" travelled from Suva to Kalua. (1589).

MINNA. The gipsy child saved by Bunter from the path of a train. His more than usually untidy clothes earned him trouble from Mr Quelch and, needless to say, his story was taken as the normal Bunterian flight of fancy ! However, when the Remove met the grateful family, the fantasy became reality. (1016).

MITCHELL, Mr Wilfred. The locum appointed in Dr Locke's place while he was absent on holiday. Only Wibley knew that Mr Mitchell had been delayed and so impersonated him successfully, until confronted by Coker's Aunt Judy – before whom all men tremble! (1153).

MIX, George. One of the hands in Whiffle's Circus. (1069).

MOAT HOUSE, The Old. A ruined property near Wharton Magnus. The Famous Five were intrigued by stories of ghosts and so, with Jack Drake, they explored the ruins – only to discover that Mr Quelch had been held prisoner there. He had been removed before they could rescue him, but Bunter remained! (HBE 29).

MOBBS, Mr. The Master of the Fourth Form at Highcliffe. Mean and spiteful by nature, he victimises all those not possessed of titled relations, (except for Courtenay, whom he thoroughly loathes). His dear Ponsonby can do no wrong and, even with overwhelming evidence, he will protect him against Greyfriars' accusations. He is an ardent stamp collector. His collection was largely destroyed by Ponsonby to incriminate Courtenay and de Courcy. However, he was seen by Bunter who transplanted the evidence to Pon.'s study. Mobbs had great difficulty in believing his dear Pon. on that occasion!

MOFOBO. Captain of the Palace Guard to King Tofoloko. (1235).

MOLE. A member of the Shell.

MOLES, Inspector. After an attack on Cardew of St Jim's had been reported to the police at Easthorpe, the inspector took charge of the hunt for Huggins. Although it was to be several weeks before he was arrested, there was a feeling of greater security in Whiffle's Circus knowing the ruffian was being sought. (1074).

MONTANHA FRIA. Literally meaning "The Cold Mountain", this peak lies some distance up river from the Valentines' plantation in Brazil, followed by twenty gruelling miles cross country. By some geological freak, there is a diamond bearing gravel at the foot of the mountain. This was discovered by Mr Valentine, who worked it with the help of the Famous Five, despite attempts by O Lobo to steal the gems for himself. (HBE 44).

MONK, Dr. The Headmaster of Rylcombe Grammar School.

MONK, Black. See Anfrith.

MONK, Frank. A Junior at Rylcombe Grammar School, and a keen member of their cricket team. He is in the unenviable position of having his father as Head.

MONK, Ghostly. See Ghostly Monk.

MONK'S CELL. Most of the priory in Friardale Woods is in ruins. One fair sized chamber is intact, and is known locally as The Monk's Cell. It lies underground and is most likely a remains of the vaults or crypt. It was in here that Harry Wharton and Co. japed Fisher T. Fish into believing that the Head's plate had been hidden after a robbery. To their amazement, this is exactly where it was! (HBE 70).

MONK'S EYOT. Some three miles downstream from Wharton Lodge this small island is a favourite picnic spot for boating parties on the River Wyme. The Famous Five were doing exactly that when they saw Vernon Smith being kidnapped by Nessuno in an efort to blackmail Mr Vernon Smith over a land deal in East Africa. (1524).

MONK'S HILL. A small village a mile or so from Greyfriars. (974).

MONK'S ISLAND. A local variation on the name of Monk's Eyot. While holidaying at Riverside Bungalow, (about half a mile up stream from Wharton Lodge), Vernon Smith fell in with Harry Wharton and Co. and continued a wrangle begun before the end of term. Intending to "sack" Wharton and maroon him on the island, Smithy's plans were foiled by Tom Redwing warning Wharton. Instead, Vernon Smith got Redwing. As a result of this, he missed a good part of the next term – ill. (HBE 6).

MONROE, Dr. A general medical practitioner of Courtfield. He was called in when Sir William Cherry was poisoned by the Rafia. (1108).

MONSON. A fag in the Second Form at Greyfriars.

MONSON, (Major). Older brother of Richard. He succeeded in being expelled from Highcliffe. When one thinks of what passes for normal behaviour at that establishment, he must be a very polished rogue.

MONSON, Mr. Father of Richard. He was robbed by Captain Oakshott. The Famous Five came to the rescue. Knowing how the land lies between Friars and Highcliffe, Mr Monson, by way of thanks, made his son welcome "the enemy". One good result of this episode was that Monson saw through Ponsonby, and eschewed his company, for a time at least!). (1648).

MONSON, Richard, (Dick). One of Ponsonby's intimates at Highcliffe. He is not quite as bad as Gadsby or Vavasour and he can,

GREYFRIARS GUIDE

at times, see the evil in his leader. As he will never persuade him to stop, he does at least, sometimes, walk away from trouble.

MONSON CHALET, Near Wallingford, Oxfordshire. The home of the Monson family. While staying here with his friends, Ponsonby introduced Captain Oakshott to the house. A thief who robbed his host, but was foiled by the Famous Five. (1648).

MONTANA, Pedro. A crazed deck hand in the schooner Castille. He murdered all the crew but one to gain possession of the smuggled diamonds on board. When he was discovered, he escaped on a Customs vessel, only to lose his life in a collision at sea. (1077).

MONTE CARLO. The famous capital of Monaco. Harry Wharton spent a miserable Christmas here with Vernon Smith. Wharton, in one of his periodic paddies, had fallen out with his friends and, as Wharton Lodge was closed for the holidays, he accepted, but soon regretted, Smithy's invitation. (880).

MONTMORENCY, Phyllis. When Coker fancied himself in love with Phyllis Howells, he wrote her a letter. To teach him a lesson, Wibley dressed up as La Montmorency and claimed to be his fiancee. Needless to say this caused quite a stir! (419).

MOOKERJEE, Mook. The wise Moonshee of Bhanipur who has the distinction of having taught Hurree Singh his inimmitable flowery and highly idiosyncratic version of the English tongue! For all Bunter's rudeness, (inevitable), to him, the English members of the Famous Five found him a delightful old gentleman with a great fund of knowledge, philosophy and wisdom - a worthy tutor to a prince. (GBC 4).

MOON, Mr. Sporting a black eye, Mr Prout was absent from school. The temporary master was impersonated by Wibley who proceeded to "lick and line" the Fifth in a very successful retaliation for insults heaped upon the Remove. (1190).

MOON, Mr. The manager of The Bun Shop, Courtfield. (1416).

MOONSTONE, The. A famous and fabulously valuable diamond belonging to Sir Hilton Popper. It was stolen by a recently dismissed footman, Sugden, who gave it to Bunter for safe keeping. As he had given his name as Wharton, there was confusion for a time, until the stone was found and returned by the Famous Five. (HBE 68). It was stolen a second time by Nosey Clark's gang, and sent to Jim Valentine as a birthday present in the manner of the Trojan Horse. Again the Famous Five were able to recover the gem safely. (1306).

MOOR FELLS, Yorkshire. The home of the Bull family. It is a large house, solidly-built against the winds off the fells, with a character not unlike its owners !

MOOSEY, VINEY, & MOOSEY, Lincoln's Inn Fields, London. Solicitors to The Earl Mauleverer. (807).

MORGAN, David. A Removite who is in Study No 6. He is a typically excitable Welshman, and is a keen but merely adequate sportsman.

MORNING PRAYERS. Held in Hall each morning, with the exception of Sundays, immediately after rising and before breakfast. Attendance is compulsory. After the Roll has been called, a brief prayer is offered. After breakfast comes Chapel.

MORNINGTON, Valentine. He is at Rookwood, and shares Study No 4 with Kit Erroll on the Classical Side. Formerly wealthy, snobbish and vice-ridden, he has to some extent reformed.

MORNY, Monsieur. Assistant to Herr Rosenblaum in his Foreign Academy. While the school was at Greyfriars he taught French - assisting M. Millerand. (6).

MOSES, Mr. A second hand dealer in Friardale who also hires out and sells theatrical costumes. He trades on an altogether smaller scale than Mr Lazarus. It was Mr Moses who sold Heath a blond wig so that he could impersonate Bob Cherry forging a postal order and so cause his expulsion. (174).

MOSES, Isaac. The proprietor of the Courtfield Finance Company, of whom Bunter tried to borrow money. (955).

MOTELI. The cannibal tribe in the Congo to whose king, Tofoloko, Krantz sold Vernon Smith and the Famous Five as slaves; and Bunter to provide a feast ! (HBE 65).

MOTANGO. From the Mabode country in the Congo, he brought news from Kikolobo to Mr Vernon Smith about the enslaved Friars. (1235).

MOWBRAY, Bishop. A Governor of the School in Edward VI times. He founded the Mowbray Scholarship, which Linley won to gain entry to the school.

MPOCA. One of the elders of the village which the Famous Five and Bunter visited when searching for Captain Corkran from whom they had become separated. Mpoca acted as interpreter to the village idol, Ko Ko, conveying "King" Bunter's orders. After the ivory cache, for

165

which they were hunting, had been found, Mpoca led an attack on the Friars party in which he was killed. (GBC 12).

M'TOKO. The wise man and Witch Doctor to Tofoloko's tribe. A practised murderer by slow, painful methods, he was to have "operated" on Vernon Smith who had struck the king. Kikolobo freed him in the nick of time. (HBE 65).

MUCCOLINI, Signor Pietro. Proprietor of "Muccolini's Magnificent Circus & Menagerie". He was a loud-mouthed bully to everyone in the show, from the main artistes to the junior roughneck. Bunter conned Marco the lion tamer into letting him join the circus and, once he had been shown up for what he is, he blackmailed Muccolini into letting him stay. The circus tour was a "front" for spying on military establishments in the South of England and, Bunter had, of course, guessed something of the truth. But for Ferrers Locke and the help he received from the Famous Five, a great deal of classified material would have left the country. (HBE 55-56).

MUFFIN, Reginald, (Tubby). As his nickname suggests, he is the "Bunter" of Rookwood. He shares Study No 2 in the Classical Side with Higgs, Jones and Grace. He is not quite as greedy as Bunter; he is more honest; and certainly has less cunning than his Greyfriars counterpart.

MUGG, Peter. One of Cobb's cronies at the Cross Keys. (149).

MUIRLAND. Lying some three miles from Lochmuir, it is the nearest village to the estate. (GBC 34).

MULBERRY, Mr Jack. A card sharp and gambler who used to frequent the Feathers. Hazeldene got in a panic beause he owed the man £10. He borrowed the money from Vernon Smith, but was too scared to return it himself. Levison went in his place and was caught out of bounds. Levison, who was at Greyfriars while his brother was ill in the sanatorium, was asked to leave. It took all of Smithy's guile to clear Levison, using Mulberry as a witness. (795).

MULE KICK. The nick name of Captain Jim Hall of the Texas Rangers. It derives from the strength of his punch. (HBE 32).

MUSTAPHA. An Arab member of Ludwig Krantz' slave trading gang. He was left behind to guard the base camp, while the rest of the gang took the captured Friars to the Congo. He was killed by Kikolobo. (1234).

MUSTAPHA. A donkey boy in Alexandria from whom Bunter insisted on hiring a mount, against all advice. His journey was short, eventful, and disastrous ! (1279) .

MY LORD BUNTER. (Title HBE Volume 14) . Misled into believing that Bunter possesses courage, Sir Peter Lanchester accepted his offer of help in impersonating his young ward, Lord Reynham, who was being sought by a kidnapper. An eventful Christmas with the Famous Five invited by "His Lordship" to protect him, ended with the culprit caught and, to Bunter's fury, the real lord in his seat !

MYERS, Edwin, (Teddy) . A fag in the Second Form at Greyfriars. He was, with Gatty, the acknowledged leader of the form, until the arrival of Dicky Nugent. The three of them are close friends, boisterous and cheekily cheerful.

MYSTERIOUS MR KRANZ, THE. (Title HBE Volume 24a) . Mr Kranz kidnapped Bob Cherry to try to get his father to give him a secret process relating to flying. He took Bob, in view of the entire school, by plane on a long roundabout route to keep him prisoner in the vaults below Greyfriars. When Vernon Smith became suspicious, he too was taken prisoner, as was Tom Redwing in his turn. Mauleverer, however, playing the village idiot as usual, was not. And Mauly it was who solved the mystery and, inadvertently in the process, saved Smithy from the sack.

MYSTERY MAN OF GREYFRIARS, THE. (Title HBE Volume 49) . Randolph Croker had been expelled from Greyfriars. At that time he had vowed to get his own back. Setting up shop as a cobbler in the Abbot's Spinney, opposite the main gates, he firstly annoyed the Head by his very presence ! When there were assaults upon persons and property, the situation looked serious for Vernon Smith who was under threat of expulsion - presumed guilty of assaulting Loder by virtue of being out of the dormitory. Jack Drake was called in to help solve the problem. After a lot of trouble, including Mr Quelch losing faith in him, he managed to "get his man", who was also wanted for escaping from prison.

MYSTERY OF PENGARTH, THE. (Title GBC Volume 33) . The news that Sir Jimmy Vivian was to be allowed access to his Cornish property - just released from Chancery- caused dismay to Scaife and his associates. Efforts to stop Sir Jimmy going to Cornwall having failed, the drug-smuggling gang operating from Pengarth kept Sir Jimmy and his friends prisoners in the nearby caves. Cardew of St Jim's and a party of Saints visiting the area, did not believe Keeley's story, and so freed the Friars.

MYSTERY OF THE MOAT HOUSE, THE. (Title HBE Volume 29).
Mr Woose had been called away from school, and Mr Lamb appointed
in his place. A well known thief, Slim Jim, was working the
neighbourhood. Mr Quelch, having seen the crook without his mask,
was kidnapped. The Pet Lamb, (as the Remove called their new master), was a real misnomer. Vernon Smith soon started a feud against
him, which led, in the end, to Smithy's own disappearance. This in
turn led to the capture and arrest of Slim Jim, and the release of
master and pupil.

MYSTERY OF WHARTON LODGE, THE. (Title HBE Volume 8).
Bunter was supposed to spend Christmas with his Uncle George, but
problems recurred over missing food! So, Bunter, after being refused
admission to Wharton Lodge, hid in the attic. While on a grub raid
one night, he disturbed Corkran who had broken into the house to assault Colonel Wharton. By way of reward, Bunter was invited to
spend the remainder of the holidays at Wharton Lodge. However, he
outstayed his welcome, and left. On the train home, he bought for 1/-,
a real diamond pin, stolen from a Mr Isaacs by Sniggerson. Once back
at school, Fisher T. Fish determined to make a profit out of the
diamond. Instead he burned his fingers. He was interviewed by the
police to explain his possession of the stone; and worse, he lost the
£2-0-0 he had paid Bunter for it!

Mc.

McALPINE, Angus. An inventor who, on his way to Edinburgh, was
injured in a train accident. To prevent the details of a new dyeing
process falling into the hands of Jerrold Drew, he asked Harry
Wharton to carry the papers to Mr Kerr. (672).

McCANN, Captain. A former African game hunter. He was engaged
in hunting for Ludwig Krantz when Mr Vernon Smith and party arrived in Nairobi. He did capture his man once, only for him to escape.
Krantz was killed by Kikolobo during the Friars escape from the
Congo which had been masterminded by the Captain. (HBE 65).

McCANN, Barney. The leader of an American kidnapping gang who came to England with the express intention of holding Fisher T. Fish to ramsom. $500,000 was to be the asking price, levied on the fact that Mr Fish had "cornered pork". McCann did kidnap Fishy, only for the Famous Five to rescue McCann's "meal ticket", and Mr Fish's corner to collapse ! (GBC 25).

MacDERMID. The past hereditary owners of Lochmuir. The "Old Laird" had been slain at the Battle of Culloden, since when the Beans, the hereditary pipers, have been awaiting the arrival of the new laird – a forlorn hope since the old Laird died childless. (GBC 34).

McLAREN, Boy. A rider with Lantham Speedway. When invited to join in Joe Banks' scheme for "fixing" the races, he refused. Coker overheard a plan to damage McLaren's bike. Joe Banks and friends were soon put out of business! (1220).

MacLAREN, Ken. Cousin and manager to Boy MacLaren. (1220).

McNAB. The man hired by Sir Philip Angel as butler at Lochmuir. However, he left the house with all the staff once the "Wraith of Lochmuir" had started to walk the castle. (GBC 34).

McTAB, Mr Angus. The manager of Mauleverer's plantations on Kalua. He is also the resident magistrate on the island. Mauleverer was not best pleased when, in his capacity of magistrate, McTab made Mauly do as he was told, and refused to rescind his sentence of deportation on Ysabel Dick. (HBE 12).

N.

NADESHA, A gipsy woman who warned Harry Wharton of Melchior and Barengro's escape from prison, and their intended revenge on him. (9).

NAIVASHI. The area in Kenya, where Mr Milsom's plantation is to be found. (HBE 65).

NALLY DAS. An associate of Baji Rao. It was Nally Das who came to England with orders to kidnap Hurree Singh. Failing several times – including capturing Wibley dressed as Hurree Singh ! – he followed Colonel Wharton's party to India. Continuously throughout the insurrection, Nally Das tried to capture the Nabob. His success, when it came, did not last long for, through Bunterian errors, Hurree Singh was soon free. Nally Das fled with Baji Rao and Lazaroff. When pur-suit was close at hand, Nally Das gave his life to save that of his master. (GBC 4).

NALAU. One of the crewboys in the cutter Sea Cat. (HBE 12).

NATTY. A petty crook in Chicago whose job it is to rob the gulls Van Schuyler picks up. They are taken for a car ride and, when the car conveniently breaks down, it is held up. (1095).

NEMO. Literally meaning no-man, it was the nom-de-guerre adopted by Franz Kranz. (HBE 24 & 24a).

NESSUNO. An Italian who tried to persuade Mr Vernon Smith to give up his interest in the N'gombo concession in Kenya. To this end, after threats had failed, he tried kidnapping – but was eventually captured at Seahill Park by Vernon Smith and the Famous Five. (HBE 37).

NETHERBY SCHOOL. The first English school to which Hurree Singh was sent. It was forced to close during an epidemic, and did not re-open. (6).

NEW ACADEMY. Herr Rosenblaum's ill-fated second attempt at opening a school for foreign boys. His first was Beechwood School but that was a financial disaster. The New Academy was established just through the cloisters from Greyfriars. Not surprisingly this led to a great many fights between schools. For several reasons, Herr

Rosenblaum was forced to move away and the New Academy buildings were taken over by Greyfriars. (GBC 3).

NEW BOYS AT GREYFRIARS. (Title GBC Volume 13). For Mark Linley, arriving at Greyfriars was bad enough, without the snobbishness of many of the school. Once he had proved himself, he became accepted on his own merits by most people, especially if he had fought them ! He is now the acdemic delight of Mr Quelch. Soon after Linley's arrival, several more notable Removites arrived, and Levison was expelled.

NEW ELIXIR. A discovery by Professor Sparkinson that made the puniest into the strongest, and probably also conferred longevity on the taker. (HBE 20).

NEW YORK. On their way to Hollywood, Mr Fish' party of Friars had an eventful stay here during which Coker was held to ransom; and Bunter lost himself and rescued Coker, (both mistakes!) . Th Famous Five and Bunter visited the city again with Vernon Smith when on their way to Texas. On this occasion "Two-Gun" Sanders kidnapped both Bunter, in mistake for Vernon Smith, and Vernon Smith himself, after realising his error. Both victims had little difficulty in escaping. (GBC 20; HBE 31).

NEWCOME, Arthur. One of the Fistical Four at Rookwoood. He shares Study No 8 in the Classical Side with Silver, Lovell, and Raby. Like his friends, he is a good all-round sportsman.

NEWLAND, Montague, (Monty). The son of Sir Montague Newland, he shares Study No 9 with Penfold, Trevor and Treluce. Well endowed with pocket money, he is never permitted by his closest friend, Penfold, to pay more than his share of study expenses. He is a quiet studious fellow, on good terms with all but the cads of the Remove, and puts up with as good a nature as possible with the taunts about his Hebraic origins.

NEWLAND, Sir Montague. An exceedingly wealthy city banker, and the father of Monty Newland. His home is at Newland Croft. He readily helped Mr Penfold, without the Penfolds knowing about it, after Mr Penfold had lost his savings in a phoney share scheme.

NEWLAND CROFT. The home of the Newland family.

NEWMAN'S POOL. Sited on the Highcliffe side of Friardale, this secluded pond is a favourite skating place during the winter months. (938).

N'GOMBO, Kenya. Lies to the north of the country, near its border with Abyssinia. It is a potentially rich tin mining area. To obtain this tin for his country, Italy, Nessuno went to all lengths to try to persuade Mr Vernon Smith to give up the options he held on the region. (HBE 37).

NIXON, Nutty. A member of Nosey Clark's gang. A master lock-pick, he entered Greyfriars several times to try to frame Valentine for theft. For one reason or another, all his planted evidence did not come to light. His final act was to steal Valentine's "Insurance Policy", (a letter of confession addressed to Mr Quelch). Clark quite thought that he now could force Valentine back to the fold; but, before he could bring pressure to bear, the gang was arrested. (GBC 9).

NOBBS, Nobby. The Clown in Whiffles' Circus. (HBE 28).

NOBLE, Harry. An Australian in the Shell at St Jim's School; he is an excellent all round sportsman.

NOBLE PRIZE. An annual prize examination in Greek. Although it is an extra subject in the Remove, nonetheless, Ogilvy, Vernon Smith and, obviously, Linley enter. (252).

NORTH, Thomas, (Tom). He is in the Sixth Form at Greyfriars. A prefect, he is comparatively light handed with discipline, and so is popular amongst the juniors. He is the First Eleven goalkeeper.

NORTON. A fag in the Second Form at Greyfriars.

NOSEY. One of the ruffians hired by Poynings to kidnap Coker to prevent exposure of Poyning's blackmail of Coker's Uncle Henry. (982).

NOSEY. The driver of the furniture van, supposedly belonging to Jones & Co. of Weymouth, used by a gang of smash and grab raiders. Bunter, who was lost, took a lift in the van and so was able to give information to the police which led to the arrest of the crooks and a reward for Bunter. (1531).

NOSEY CLARK. See Clark, Compton.

NOSEY PETE. The jailer in the town jail at Packsaddle. He was tricked into leaving his post so that Barney Stone's associates could effect his escape. (1579).

NPONG. The juju, or medicine man, of the village wherein was hidden the ivory hoard sought by Captain Corkran. Npong was leading the religious ceremony leading up to Nugent's death when Bunter overcame his funk and made the village idol speak. It ordered the release of Nugent, and the death of the witch doctor. (772).

NUGENT, Miss Ada. Sister to Mr Nugent, and maiden aunt to Frank and Dicky. She lives with the family and spoils Dicky outrageously. (881).

NUGENT, Amy. Sister to Frank and Dicky. Like her sister, Cissy, she is overcome with awe and admiration for the Famous Five. (881).

NUGENT, Cecilia, (Cissy). Younger sister to Frank and Dicky. (881).

NUGENT, Francis, (Frank). The nom de plume behind which the historian of Greyfriars hides his real identity. He was the first of the Famous Five to go to Greyfriars and, when Harry Wharton arrived befriended him, despite Harry's efforts to be contrary. Castigated as a milksop by Bunter, in reference to his good looks, he is in fact quite capable of looking after himself, (unless up against the top fighting men). The patience he demonstrates towards his closest friend, Harry Wharton, is amazing, and when the occasional rift occurs in the Co., Frank is the last to fall out. He is a fair sportsman, although only good enough for a reserve place most of the time. All too often Vernon Smith hopes that Wharton will put Nugent in the team so as to be able to accuse him of favouritism. Frank's one blind spot is his inability to see the manipulative power of his minor - and so the rest of the Famous Five put up with Dicky Nugent under protest.

NUGENT, Mr Henry. Father of Frank, Dicky and their sisters. He is a would be stern parent who insisted that the spoilt Dicky went to Greyfriars. He has, however, no idea of how to cope with his wife's softness and sentimentality.

NUGENT, Mrs. Mary. A doting mother who can see no wrong in any of her four children. So much so that, even when Dicky was threatened with expulsion for throwing a stone at Wingate Major, she was certain that he had been victimised.

NUGENT, Matilda. Marjorie Hazeldene, to demonstrate her acting abilities, took in all of Greyfriars by pretending to be Frank Nugent's non-existent Aunt Matilda ! Despite intense embarrassment, Frank showed her round the school. When Ionides was rude to her, Marjorie responded with her umbrella - to his head ! (106).

NUGENT, Richard, (Dicky). At first a wayward, spoilt brat who, because he could not have his own way, came very near to expulsion. However, after an unusually tough start to school life, he settled down to become the undisputed leader of the Second Form. (Except of course for the inevitable power struggles!). The possessor of a good mind, he refuses to use it, preferring to get his major to do the work for him. Despite regular trouble in class on this score, he never seems to learn that this sort of behaviour does not pay.

NUTTY NIXON. See Nixon, Nutty.

O.

O BO, Mr. Uncle to Wun Lung. Not having been blessed with a male child to supervise his obsequies when the time comes, he was desperate to persuade Wun Lung's father to permit him to adopt Wun. By the Old Chinese religion, it is essential to have a son to set you on your way to heaven. To ensure this, he tried to kidnap Wun, (other methods having failed). But for Bob Cherry, who mistrusted Mr O, he might well have succeeded. (HBE 43).

O NO, Mr. The confidential servant to Tang Wang. He was placed in charge of the imprisoned Friars. A kindly gaoler, he permitted such freedom to his charges as he could. When they escaped, thanks to Ferrers Locke, rather than face death, he murdered the Mandarin. (HBE 25; HBE 25a).

OAK LANE. About three miles from Greyfriars and one mile from Highcliffe, this lane lies between the Lantham Road and the River Sark.

OAK TREE FARM. Is run by Mr Bunce, who is a tenant of Sir Hilton Popper. He caught Mick the Gipsy cooking a poached rabbit. It took all Bob Cherry's persuasive powers to make Sir Hilton show his gratitude for Mick having pulled him out of the river, and let him off. (819).

OAKS, The, Nr. Amesbury, Wiltshire. The home of the Nugent Family. It a small pleasant house lying in the Wiltshire country side, but is far too crowded for comfort with the size of family and number of relatives who live here.

OAKSHOTT, Kent. The village where Tinker Wilson lived for a time with Tatters. The school inspector discovered the boy and sent him to the local school. (1195).

OAKSHOTT, Captain James, (Jimmy). He was picked up by Ponsonby and Co. while on holiday. He was a gambler and a thief. Having disguised himself he robbed Mr Monson, (his host), but luckily, Johnny Bull, who had been tied up by Pon. & Co., saw him removing his disguise and the Famous Five were able to recover the stolen wallet. (1648).

OAKSHOTT SCHOOL, Essex. A Public School from which James Warren was expelled. Price, to further his feud with Jim Warren, persuaded Warren's former study mate, Bullivant, to come to Greyfriars for the day to see if Warren was an imposter, (as Price was convinced). The plan fell through because Jim Warren had been injured by Loder and was unable to leave his study. (HBE 38).

OAKWOOD, Sir Giles. An old friend of Colonel Wharton. He is uncle and guardian to Gilbert Tracey. He found it impossible to control his ward and so he asked his old school friend Mr Quelch for advice. Following this to the letter, he sent Gilbert to Greyfriars. An indulgent man, he at first allowed Tracy as much pocket money as he desired. As this had no effect on his behaviour, Mr Quelch had to ask Sir Giles to limit Tracy's resources, thus increasing his hatred of Greyfriars. (HBE 12; HBE 15).

OAKWOOD PLACE, Wharton Magnus, Surrey. The home of Sir Giles Oakwood. The property adjoins that of Colonel Wharton. (1590).

ODD FELLOWS OF GREYFRIARS. (Title HBE Volume 79). A collection of unrelated incidents from the annals of the old school. From the mystery of the schooner Castille, to Captain Holsten's attempted revenge against Colonel Wharton.

OGILVY, Donald Robert. The youngest of a large family of brothers. They hail from Inverness in Scotland. His brothers, (all six of them), are, or were, in the forces. Oggie shares Study No 3 in the Remove with Russell, and is an average member of the form who is usually required for the Form teams.

OKE, Dave. A fisherman with a wooden leg who lives alone on Blackrock Island in an old shanty built of driftwood. He acts as watchman and caretaker to the island and its ruined castle. (HBE 50).

OKEHAM, Devon. A country town in Devon. Behind the town lies Blackmoor, on the edge of which is Blackmoor Prison. Also on the edge of the moor lies Hilton Hall. Mr Elias Rance, with whom

Mr Vernon Smith did a lot of business had his office in Okeham, and spent much of his time in the town's chief hostelry, The Okeham Arms. There is a Public School in the town - Okeham School- at which Messrs. James Loder and Stephen Lagden taught.

OLD OAK INN. Barely half a mile from Wharton Lodge, Harry Wharton and his friends are well known to the landlord, Mr Hodge. They often have a ginger beer, sitting outside under the trees in the summer. Vernon Smith, on one occasion, persuaded the landlord that Mr Smedley, (a guest at the time so that he could spy on Smithy), was a wanted criminal. (1367).

OLD CLO', The nickname given to Mr Abrahams, a Friardale rag and bone man. (729).

OLD POMPOUS. The nickname given to Mr Prout. Unkind it may be, but it is certainly appropriate !

OLD RED HOUSE, The. A fair sized house in a lonely part of the countryside some few miles from Hawkscliff. It is about a quarter of a mile inland. The house was rented by Mr Knowles as a prison in which to keep Arthur Durance while his son was impersonating him at Greyfriars. (1130).

OLD SAL. A crone in Slummock's Alley who used to look after Skip, when Barney the Binger, (who had stolen him as a child), was out on a "job". (1554).

OLDCROFT SCHOOL, Sussex. The Public School which Christopher Carboy was asked to leave after taking the blame for a prank committed by the Headmaster's son, Dick Holroyd. (HBE 23).

OLDWOOD SCHOOL. The school which Otto von Tromp attended before going to Greyfriars. He had already been demoted from his prefectship for brutality before he was expelled. (1169).

O'NEIL, Barney. One of Dick Trumper's friends at Courtfield Grammar School. He is an Irishman who will fight his best friend if there is no-one else with whom to scrap ! (146).

O-O-LOLUO. The shark god of the cannibal island on which the "Greyfriars Adventurers" were shipwrecked. Bunter persuaded the islanders to make him chief by using his ventriloquism - thus saving himself from the cooking pot ! (HBE 12).

OPERATIC SOCIETY. Before the arrival of Wibley at Greyfriars and the formation of the Remove Dramatic Society, the Remove's chief exposition of the arts was in the form of Music Hall entertainments.

ORRIS, James. Valet to Mauleverer. A compulsive gambler, he tried to extort money fom his employer by leaving threatening notes. When that failed he held Mauly prisoner to try to make him pay a large enough sum to liquidate his debts. Thanks to Bunter's prying, the truth was discovered and Orris was arested. (1244-1246).

OUED TAHAR. The oasis in the Sahara Desert from which Ali ben Yusef's tribe takes its name. (GBC 12).

OWEN. A one time scholar at Greyfriars. He was probably in the Remove. (2).

P.

PACKER. The butler at Popper Court. (820).

PACKINGTON. On his return from Australia, where he was wanted by the police, he obtained the post of butler at Ravenspur Grange. Former associates of his came to the house seeking "Black Edgar", only to be murdered, as were two policemen investigating the crimes. When Ferrers Locke solved the case, it was discovered that Packington was both "Black Edgar" and Sir Richard Ravenspur's brother, Edgar. (HBE 36).

PACKSADDLE. A moderate sized township in Texas. It is important as the Stage Coach post for the Rio Frio Valley. It lies some fifteen miles from Mr Vernon Smith's ranch the Kicking Cayuse. (HBE 32).

PAGET, Mr Freddy. A young man who made friends with Vernon Smith and stayed with him at Riverside Bungalow, Wimford. A sporting gentleman, he not only encouraged Vernon Smith to gamble, but abused his host's hospitality by robbing the bank in Wimford. Bunter was hiding in the surrounding woods and, seeing Paget change out of his disguise, identified him to the Famous Five who captured him. (1260).

PAGET, Percival Spencer. Tubbs greatest friend and his lieutenant in the leadership of the Third Form. Paget, somewhat uncharacteristically for a Third Former, considers himself something of a dandy !

PALM LEAF. Mr McTab's yawl. He took Mauleverer and the Famous Five, (and Bunter too, who had stowed away!), on a cruise. Ysabel Dick and Van Dink managed to sneak on board while the Greyfriars party were anchored off Turtle Reef. They then drugged the ship's company, with the exception of Wharton, and wrecked the vessel on Baloo, a cannibal island. Ysabel Dick had second thoughts about their actions and came to the Friar's aid in driving off the attacking natives. Harry Wharton, meanwhile, adrift in the sea, was picked up by Ken King who altered course to take the party off Baloo. (1598) .

PAN SHAN. A city in the Kwang-Si province of China. It was the headquarters of Tang Wang, wherefrom he plotted to gain the Emperor's Throne, empty since the revolution. Wharton, Cherry and Bunter were taken prisoner by Tang's men and conveyed to Pan Shan. Rescue from here was difficult but, between Ferrers Locke who managed to pass himself off as a member of Tang's household, and Wun Lung, Bull, Nugent and Hurree Singh who had taken a sampan into the city, it was successfully achieved. (HBE 25) .

PANDY DIN. Colonel Wharton's khitmugar, or batman, when on active service. He returned to his officer's service to help him when taking Hurree Singh to Bhanipur. A tower of strength and loyal beyond belief, he more than once saved the party from attacks and ambushes.   (GBC 4) .

PANHANDLE. A cow puncher on the Kicking Cayuse Ranch. He was one of Barney Stone's men, and actively engaged in rustling the owners' cattle. When Vernon Smith began to suspect the truth, Stone and Panhandle kidnapped Bunter in mistake for Smithy who had changed beds with Bunter. Panhandle was fired by Bill Buck, (made foreman after Stone's arrest), and almost certainly arranged Stone's escape from jail. Knowing him to be Stone's aide, Smithy took Panhandle back on the payroll and used him to trap Stone and the rest of his gang. (HBE 32) .

PARIS. The capital city of France. It was the setting for several adventurous holidays. Mr O tried to separate Wun Lung from the Famous Five so that he could take him back to China, but he was foiled - mostly through Bob Cherry. When on holiday with Bunter as host, Tiger Bronx made several attempts to "persuade" Bunter to return the fortune he thought was rightfully his. (HBE 43; HBE 64) .

PARKER. Clerk to Mr Pilkins the Estate Agent in his Combermere office. He was not satisfied with the explanation he received to explain his employer's mysterious disappearance. When he went to Bunter Court as Captain of the local cricket team, Combermere Rangers, he made his suspicions clear to the Famous Five. (HBE 3).

PARKER. Private secretary to Lord Cavandale. An ardent bibliophile, he made use of his time at Cavandale Abbey to study the old manuscripts and learn the secret passages so that he could attack his employer. As he was a compulsive gambler who had bet his all on the second favourite in the Lantham 1,000 guineas, he wanted the favourite, the Earl's horse, to be withdrawn. Ferrers Locke trapped him, and effected his arrest. (HBE 22).

PARKER. Animal attendant in Muccolini's Circus. He normally helps Marco with the lions but, for a time, he was relieved of these duties when Bunter became, briefly, Bunto the Boy Tamer. (HBE 55).

PARKER, Inspector. Stationed at Dorchester, he was called in after Jack Drake had disappeared from Cherry Place - presumed kidnapped by Jimmy the Fox's gang. (He had been chloroformed and placed in a trunk believed to be Bunter's, which was awaiting collection. As Bunter had also been abducted, a message apparently from him did not arouse suspicion). (1420).

PARKER, Mr. Mate in the Aloha. When Soames took over the vessel, he knocked out the mate and had him thrown to the sharks to make the Kanaka crew obey his orders. Needless to say, this show of strength was successful. (1022).

PARKER, Pedlar. A brutish lout who found Ragged Dick wandering the roads after his father's death. He took him up and used him as a vent for his ill-humour. When Dick had left him for his "Grandfather", Parker, convinced that he was an impostor, tried to blackmail Sir Henry Compton, but only received a thrashing. (HBE 80; GL 3).

PARKER, Alfred Albert. Having stolen Sir Hilton Popper's wallet, he ran into Greyfriars to evade capture, and hid his booty in Temple's Guy Fawkes effigy which was in the woodshed. His efforts to regain the wallet were in vain. It was discovered, fortuitously, when the Famous Five saw, and took exception to, Temple's guy. In destroying this, the wallet fell to the ground. (1238).

PARKER, Bud. Chick Chew's "side-kick" in his efforts to kidnap Putnam van Duck. A true "Yank", he was uncomfortable away from Chicago, and so was of little use to his boss. When Chew was arrested, Parker was glad to return home. (HBE 45).

PARKER, Cyrus. Head of Enterprise Pictures, Hollywood. Incensed at Mr Fish's "capture" of Mauleverer, he tried, successfully, to lure him to his own studios. What he did not realise was that Bunter was wearing Mauly's hat, and as usual acknowledged, as seems right and proper to him, being addressed as "My Lord" ! The imposture did not last long, and Bunter had a hot time escaping Parker's wrath ! (1097).

PARKER, Nobby. Slim Jim's lieutenant. He acted as gaoler to Mr Quelch at The Old Moat House and, later, at Sea View. Distrustful of visitors he soon had a running battle on his hands against the Remove, and Vernon Smith in particular, who suspected the house and its air raid shelter of concealing a secret. But even Smithy did not realise his Form Master was imprisoned there, as he discovered after outwitting Parker. (HBE 29-30).

PARKINS. Hatters and Outfitters, Courtfield. They are the appointed suppliers of hats and accessories to Greyfriars School. The shop is in the High Street, near the Bun Shop.

PARKINSON. A lesser light of the Sixth Form. He does not play in either School or Form teams.

PARKINSON. A chauffeur working for Chunkley's Car Hire Department, from whom Jarvish hired a Rolls Royce with chauffeur for Bunter. As is usual amongst aristocrats of Bunter's type, he could never remember the driver's name ! (HBE 64).

PARKINSON. Butler to Mr Skelton. (1037).

PARKINSON, General. After a robbery at Parkinson Place the General had to sell many of his belongings to pay for a valuable, but uninsured, necklace. A chair which Harry Wharton bought for Study No 1 was one of the lots sold. Bunter worked out, by a method known only to himself, that it was his chair, and in the struggle to get it to his study, broke it - wherein was discovered the necklace. In gratitude, the general paid the £15 owing for the purchase of the chair, (not 15/- as Bunter thought!), as well as getting it repaired. (1311).

PARROTT. A member of the Second Form at Greyfriars.

PARSONS, Jim. The lookout man for Cobb's illegal casino on the Haunted Island. (149).

PARSONS, Captain Peter, (Dandy). Owner and Master of the Sea Cat. An unscrupulous blackguard who tried to shoot a deserting crew member, (Popoo, who then joined the Friars). After Ysabel Dick and Van Dink had scuttled the Flamingo they were picked up by "The Sea Lawyer of Lukwe". They then prevented Parsons from picking up the

Greyfriars party who were adrift on a raft. In fact he ran them down later when they were trying to get back to Kalua by canoe from the cannibal island on which they had been shipwrecked. Mauleverer managed to trap the Sea Cat in the lagoon around Koo-Koo's island, and Parsons had to concede defeat. (HBE 12).

PAUL DALLAS AT GREYFRIARS. (Title GBC Volume 6). After his father had been presumed dead in South America, Paul Dallas was sent to a charity School. Mr Vernon Smith had been lent a large sum of money by Mr Dallas, which he had not been able to repay before the latter's death. In settlement of the debt, Mr Vernon Smith traced the boy and sent him to Greyfriars. Vernon Smith was convinced that Dallas was trying to oust him from his position as son and heir. In typical Bounder style he would not be persuaded that this was totally untrue. There followed a long and bitter feud on Smithy's part. Dallas, a thoroughly good-hearted man, tried to keep the peace but Smithy fell out with everyone, including Tom Redwing. Dallas was on the verge of expulsion when Ferrers Locke proved that Vernon Smith had planted evidence incriminating him. Vernon Smith, himself under threat of expulsion unless he mended his ways, finally had to retract his position when Mr Jim Dallas reappeared on the scene and took Paul with him to South America.

PAWLINGS. The steward in the S.Y.Sea Nymph, Captain George Cook's yacht. (HBE 61).

PAWSON. The butler at Gadsby Croft. He insisted that the "Greyfriars Hikers" camped in the grounds so that they would be obvious suspects of a robbery he had planned with Bates. Luckily Vernon Smith, staying with Gadsby, overheard their plotting and was able to warn the Friars. (1339).

PAYNE, Dr. Dr Pillbury's predecessor as Medical Officer to Greyfriars. (178).

PAYNE, Mr. A bogus assistant to Dr Woods of Leyford, played by Packington in disguise. His object was to deliver a poisonous mixture into the house so that Sir Richard Ravenspur's murder could be effected without suspicion. Captain Ravenspur suspected the man and checked with Dr Woods. (1123).

PEAL of BELLS, The. An inn on the outskirts of Courtfield, near the Common. It is frequented by visitors to the town, (such as circus folk), as well as being the "local" for the Popper Court staff.

PECOS PETE. A member of Barney Stone's cattle rustling gang. He was so called because he came from the area of the same name beyond Squaw Mountain, Texas. (1579).

PEDRILLO. A famous acrobat in Zorro's Circus. While giving a performance at Friardale his trapeze broke and, being injured, he was taken to the sanatorium by the Famous Five who had been forbidden to go to the show. Pedrillo was placed in the school by Dr Locke as Zorro refused to have anything to do with an injured artiste. Hobson and Pedrillo became great friends, against Sir James Hobson's explicit orders. To prevent his son learning that Pedrillo had in fact been kidnapped at Sir James' behest to ensure Peter's fortune for himself, Pedrillo was again kidnapped by Zorro. Harry Wharton forced Sir James to free him and acknowledge him as his nephew. (HBE 77).

PEDRO. A Spanish thief who led Coker and Co., (lost thanks to the great Horace's sense of direction!), into the clutches of his leader Carlos Alvaro. The gang found plenty to steal from Coker, and then left the Fifth Formers tied up in the forest above Gibraltar. (1315).

PEEK, Dr. Medical Practitioner of Seahill, Sussex. He was called in to treat Vernon Smith, after he had received a head injury from Nessuno. (1524).

PEGG, Kent. A fishing village on Pegg Bay near the mouth of the River Sark. It lies five miles down the coast from Hawkscliff. The village is a popular resort for Greyfriars on half holidays when it is within bounds. An out of the way spot, it is reached from Greyfriars through Friardale and then along Pegg Lane. The village boasts an excellent inn, The Anchor, which is near the jetty, and also a tea house on the cliffs above the village on Cliff Road, (Cliff Garden).

PELHAM. A member of the Fourth Form at Highcliffe. He follows Ponsonby's lead, and sometimes joins in ragging Greyfriars. (572).

PENFOLD, Mr. The hard working, hard up, father of Dick Penfold. He is the local bootmaker and, as such, is well known to all Greyfriars. A thrifty man, he once was tempted by the thought of money making schemes, and bought some worthless shares. Newland fell out with Dick so that he could recover Mr Penfold's money without his best friend knowing what had happened. (843).

PENFOLD, Richard, (Dick). The son of the Friardale cobbler, who won a scholarship to Greyfriars. The cads and snobs of the Remove, as usual made what capital they could out of his going to a Public School, but his innate honesty, decency, as well as his lack of brilliance academically, and his ability as a sportsman, soon allowed him to settle into the Remove. He shares Study No 9 with Newland, Treluce and Trevor. His chief hobby is photography, at which he excels. He is also the "poet of the Remove", being a more than adequate rhymester.

PENGARTH, Cornwall. A derelict property on the north Cornish coast. It was in Chancery for many years, until Sir Reginald Brooke persuaded the Court to release the title to its rightful owner, Sir Jimmy Vivian who, visited the house with a party of friends, (See The Mystery of Pengarth). (GBC 33).

PENGARTH BAY. It is a secret, sinister place, surrounded by cliffs, on the north Cornish coast. The only house overlooking the bay is Pengarth House, which is said to be haunted. (GBC 33).

PENGELLY, Dick. A Cornish fisherman from Polpen. He directed Sir Jimmy Vivian and his friends to the house when they arrived in Cornwall. Cardew of St Jim's, searching for Sir Jimmy who was lost, hired Pengelly's boat to search the caves in Pengarth Bay. (GBC 33).

PENMAN, Mr. A business man of Canterbury, Kent, for whom Wally Bunter works. An Old Saint himself, he sent Wally to his old school in gratitude for his preventing a robbery in the office. (569).

PENNY. A member of the Upper Fourth Form at Greyfriars.

PENRUDDDY. A village in Cornwall. Mr Rance told Vernon Smith that he had instructions to take him to his father who was staying there. En route, he had Smithy kidnapped by Big Bill Harker and Peter Coot. The story was entirely credible, as Smithy knew that his father was buying Penruddy Manor. (1627).

PEREIRA, Captain. Captain of the S.S. Ganso, a "rusty dusty old steamer", in which Captain Corkran and his party of Friars travelled from Lagos to Banana. While on board, Casco tried to obtain the secret of the whereabouts of the ivory hoard Corkran was seeking. His attack on the Greyfriars party, aided by some of the native crew, was repulsed by Bunter making a native idol talk. (770).

PEREZ. A relative of Vino, the foreman on the Boa Vista. Together they had imprisoned Sehor Manoel Caminho in a hut on the lake in the plantation. Their plan was to swindle the owner out of the sale moneys. Mr Vernon Smith, the prospective purchaser, astute as he is, suspected nothing. Bunter saw Perez practising Caminho's signature, and Smithy then figured out the truth. (1230).

PERFECTION FILM SYNDICATE, The. The film company in which Mr Fish is a majority share holder. Foiled by refusals from all the major Public Schools, including Greyfriars, Mr Fish hit upon the idea of taking a party to America on an "educational" tour. They would end up in Hollywood and make the film he planned about English Public School life. (GBC 20-21).

PERICLES. One of Marco the Lion Tamer's lions in Muccolini's Circus. (HBE 55).

PERKINS. A fag in the Third Form at Greyfriars. (9).

PERKINS. One of Mr Vernon Smith's footmen. He acted as butler and "man" to Vernon Smith while he was holidaying at Riverside Bungalow. (1261).

PERKINS. The grocer in Combermere. In common wih the other trades folk of the town, he was owed a fortune in unpaid bills run up by Bunter during his tenancy of "Bunter Court". Mauleverer eventually heard about the situation and paid all the accounts. (HBE 3).

PERKINS & SONS. Fruiterers of Courtfield. The shop, (which is owned by Henry Perkins), is sited off the High Street. (751).

PERKINS, Henry. He bought a fruiterers and greengrocers business in Courtfield. Timothy Perkins, putting on airs at Greyfriars as Algernon de Vere, felt strongly that his uncle should sell up and leave the town, rather than offend his, (Timothy's), sensibilities by having a relative in trade ! (751).

PERKINS, Lawrence. A complete outsider, complete with loud checks, yellow boots, and a striking, clashing colour scheme in his outfit. It is hard to know whether he or his cousin Timothy is the greater bounder. Larry, knowing how de Vere felt about his relations, blackmailed him with undisguised glee. (752).

PERKINS, Thomas, (Tom). The son of Henry Perkins. Shortly after moving to Courtfield from London, he became a member of the Courtfield Junior Eleven, for whom he is the star bowler. He is a thoroughly pleasant chap, and is absolutely at a loss to understand his cousin's standoffish behaviour. (751).

PERKINS, Timothy. Son of William Perkins. After his father made his fortune, he changed his name by deed poll to Algernon de Vere and as such, entered Greyfriars. An arrant snob, he won instant dislike by his treatment of everybody, and Linley and Penfold in particular. It was a pity that he had not learnt humility, as he is a first class cricketer, (and would, therefore, have been welcome to the Remove). True to his colours, he made friends with Angel. Having discovered that his uncle had bought a shop in Courtfield, he tried to buy him out, in order to avoid any casual interpretation on family likenesses. The final straw was, for him, when his outsider of a cousin, Larry, came on the scene and proceeded to blackmail him. Too much for Algernon, he left Greyfriars suddenly; a sadder and, hopefully, wiser man. (GBC 35).

PERKINS, William. Father to Timothy. By listening to financial tips while waiting at table in his capacity as butler at Holly House, he made himself a fortune. Leaving employment, he changed his name to de Vere, and bought de Vere Manor. Maintaining the "family history" he sent his son Algernon to Greyfriars. (GBC 35).

PERKINS FAMILY. Cousin Lawrence blackmailed Algernon de Vere by threatening him with introducing some of his less eligible relations to Greyfriars; ie Aunt Eliza, a washer woman; Uncle Peter, who keeps a fish shop; Cousin Bert, who is a barman; and "Aunt Martha, whose husband drinks". Worthy folk, but they all felt, quite rightly, that they owed William, (de Vere's father), a grudge for his stuck up behaviour. (752).

PERNAMBUCO, Brazil. Taking a trip ashore while on their way to Rio de Janeiro to meet Jim Valentine, the Famous Five and Bunter were horrified to meet O Lobo whom they believed to have been left in the Canary Islands. His efforts against them were easily thwarted. (1463)

PERSECUTION OF BILLY BUNTER, THE. (Title HBE Volume 78). When Mr Quelch decided that Bunter needed to learn something, he arranged to give extra tuition to the dunce of his form - whose knowledge would disgrace the worst fag in the Second. Failing to keep his appointment with Mr Quelch, Bunter found himself in the Punishment Room. Locking his Form Master in his place did Bunter no good - a flogging and more "Punny" ! When Mauleverer and Marjorie Hazeldene were locked in the vaults by Ponsonby, the Famous Five needed all the help they could get from their Highcliffian friends to bring Pon. up to the mark. Sending him a white feather succeeded where a direct challenge had failed.

PET LAMB, The. The nickname given by the Remove to Mr Lamb. A somewhat infelicitous choice as it did not reflect his character at all. (HBE 29-30).

PETER. The porter at Wharton Magnus Station. (723).

PETER. A footmen at Portercliffe Hall. (1436).

PETER. A Yorkshire terrier belonging to Dr Locke. Bunter provoked an outburst from Mr Lamb, (who is petrified of dogs), when he imitated the dog in class. (1666).

PETERS. Coachman to Lord Mauleverer. As eccentric as ever, Mauly had "tooled" down to Greyfriars to make a sensational arrival ! Peters had been left to make his own way there. His lordship was most displeased to be kept waiting two minutes by his coachman ! (184).

PETTIFER, James. A cheekier than average fag in the Second Form, who is not above imitating the Head in the August Presence ! (949) .

PETULENGRO. A gipsy to whom Caffyn gave Coote the carrier's horse "to hold for ten minutes" in the full knowledge that he would steal the animal. (1408) .

PHANTOM SPANIARDS, The. The legend of Pengarth relates how the ghosts of Spaniards, drowned off Pengarth after the Spanish Armada, haunt the house. It was a story used to good effect by Scaife and his gang, for no-one local would go near the house after dark; nor in daylight if he could help it. (GBC 33) .

PHILPOTT, Mr. The Fifth Form Master at Oakshott School, Essex. The fact that he had been up at Oxford with Mr Hacker led the latter to invite him to Greyfriars to expose Jim Warren, whom Hacker disliked. Mr Philpott had no cause to like James Warren, an insolent, lazy and now ex-member of his form. However, when Mr Philpott went to Warren's study he found James there who was the same as ever. In a towering rage Philpott left Greyfriars without Hacker knowing which Warren it was. (HBE 38-39) .

PHIPPS. A member of the Sixth Form at Greyfriars. He is not normally to the fore in school affairs, but he took an active part in the "Sixth Form Rebellion". (745) .

PICKERING, Mr. A retired schoolmaster who ekes out his meagre pension by tutoring during the holidays. He lives at Sea Cliff Bungalow, Ampinge, Kent. Vernon Smith was to have spent some time with him but, instead, went to the continent with Ponsonby and Co. He bribed Bunter to go in his place. When Mr Vernon Smith visited his son, there was quite a scene; Bunter getting his usual allowance of boot leather ! (1365) .

PICKFORD, Inspector. The Scotland Yard officer into whose custody Ferrers Locke delivered Biter and Jenkins, members of Jimmy the Fox's gang, after he had apprehended them. (1421) .

PICKINGS. Sir Geoge Tipton's "man". A long suffering, good humoured, and loyal member of his staff, who puts up with his employer's tantrums and crotchets. (1646) .

PICKLE JAR. The son of Brass Pan, he was the bosun on the Ganso. Captain Pereira was about to shoot him for having followed Casco in an attempted mutiny; however, he was saved by Harry Wharton, and became Harry's faithful servant. After the Famous Five and Bunter were captured by cannibals, Pickle Jar led Captain Corkran to the village where they were being held. He returned to England determined to serve Wharton. His arrival at Greyfriars, breathing vengeance on all who threatened the supremacy of his beloved Massa Harry caused quite a furore ! Sadly, he returned to the Congo when a real English winter proved too much for him. (GBC 12).

PIEFACE. The elephant in Swinger's Celebrated Circus. (1160).

PIERRE. A French smuggler and acquaintance of Rawlings, the steward in the Firefly. With Louis, he tried to capture the Famous Five, so that Compton and his uncle could be forced into continuing their life of smuggling. (1508).

PIETRO. Shipped in at Port Said as a replacement for a deserting fireman in the M.V. Fanny Jones. It was he who disabled the ship so that Baji Rao's agents could attack the ship and try to prevent Hurree Singh's return home to supress a coup d'etat. (964).

PIETRO. A Venetian gondolier paid by Tiger Bronx to deliver Bunter into his hands on the felucca Colombo. Lord Conway in the Silver Foam came to the rescue. (1386).

PIETRO. An Italian smuggler in Villefranche. A contact of Rawlings, he was to have snatched a tennis racket with contraband hidden in the handle. Vernon Smith suspecting this, prevented the theft of the racket by throwing it into a lake. (1509).

PIETRO. An Italian brigand in the pay of Dr Sin. After the Famous Five had been captured, Pietro took Wun Lung away from the rest of the party to take him to his uncle. (1544).

PIGEON, The Very Old and Benevolent. The name of Mr O's aeroplane. (1543).

PIKE, Poker. A Chicago ex-gangster employed by Mr Vanderdecken Van Duck to protect his son, Putnam, from the attentions of Chick Chew on the principle of dog eat dog. When his charge expressed a desire to go to Greyfriars he was permitted to go on the condition that his guardian angel went with him. The Remove had much fun with Mr Pike, encouraging him to take the class in Mr Quelch's absences and teach them about gunmanship ! For all the fun poked at the gum-chewing, hard-bitten gangster, he was alert and more than once saved Putnam. He finally got his man. (HBE 44-45).

PIKE, Richard. When convict 33 escaped from Blackmoor Prison he terrorised the house guests at Hilton Hall during the Christmas holidays. After his capture, it was learned that he was Walsingham's half-brother who had been trying to make the butler help him in his escape. (HBA 6).

PIKE, The. Also called locally "The Black Pike", this large outcrop of rock forms one of the arms of Pegg Bay. It is on the Hawkscliff side of the bay, and is a popular picnic spot in the summer. Not far out to sea, to the east of the Pike, lies Black Rock Island.

PIKE LANE. The lane that runs the several miles from Courtfield Bridge up to the Pike. (1369).

PIKER, Mr. The owner of a farm neighbouring Friardale Lane. Stacey set fire to his barn while smoking an illicit cigarette and almost managed to get Harry Wharton blamed for the damage. (HBE 16-17).

PILLBURY, Dr. General Medical Practitioner of Friardale. He is Medical Officer to Greyfriars School.

PILKINGTON. The butler at Cavandale Abbey. (HBE 22).

PILKINS, Mr. An Estate Agent with offices in Courtfield, Lantham and Combermere. His rival in business, Mr Stummer, seems to do only a fraction of the business carried out by Mr Pilkins.

PILKINSON, Pug. An ex-boxer who is now a trainer. When he thought that Mr Lascelles was going to fight "The Game Chicken", he tried several times, unsuccessfully, to beat up the Greyfriars mathematics master so that he would be unable to box. However, Lascelles skill had not deserted him. (1321).

PILVERTON, Devon. Lying some six miles inland, it is the nearest town to Polpelly. (1453).

PIMBLE. A member of the Shell. He is not a leader in form affairs, but in common with his form mates, he disapproved of Coker's promotion. (145).

PIPER. The school porter at Cliff House School.

PIPER. A fag in the Second Form at Highcliffe. By what means is not clear, Ponsonby and Co. manage to persuade him to fag for them on occasions. (147).

PIPER, P.C. The local "Bobby" in Wharton Magnus. He was sent for by Mr Hodge, the landlord of the Old Oak Inn, to arrest a guest on information received from Vernon Smith. The "wanted man" was Mr Smedley who had been trailing Smithy to gather any facts that might discredit him. (1367).

PIRANDELLI, Signor. The landlord of the Osteria Aquilla Nera in Umbria, Italy. When Bunter's plane made a forced landing, the Famous Five stayed here while their host enjoyed even worse conditions as a guest of Tiriddu, a kidnapper! (1387).

PITU. An island in the Kalua group. The first clue Mauleverer had to his cousin's whereabouts was a begging letter post marked from here. (HBE 12).

PLOUGH INN. Above Oxford on the Thames. The crew of the Water Lily camped here one night and gullibly paid thrice for their camp site! Inspector Jones took pity on them and forced the "owners" to repay the rent. (1650).

POINDEXTER, Elias J. An American "share pusher" who floated phoney companies and sold shares in them to small investors - including Mr Prout. He was chased by Mr Reginald Wilmot who had the intention of shooting him for his fraudulent activities. Poindexter went to ground in Wimford Mill from which he was rescued by the Famous Five after Wilmot had fired the place. For his embezzlement, Poindexter received a long prison sentence. (1207-08).

POINTER, Captain. A "Bunco-booth" expert in the Three Thimbles con trick, with which he made £20 out of Mauleverer who was on his way to Blackpool for a Bank holiday outing. (234).

POKER BLAKE. The nickname of Jad Blake, one time owner of the Circle O ranch. He had gambled his stock away, and was glad to sell the land to Vernon Smith, on his father's behalf, to pay his debts. (1580).

POLK, Myron. The leading actor at Perfection Studios, and one of the greatest "box-office draws" in the business. Unfortunately, he is a self-opinionated, paranoid coward. While a party of Friars were in Hollywood, Polk kept up two feuds. One against Coker; the other against Harry Wharton. In both cases he was lucky to escape gaol - considering he could have faced a charge of attempted murder against Wharton. Also a bootlegger, he was actually arrested for this, but managed to avoid being sent to the "stone jug". (GBC 20-21).

POLLY. A parrot belonging to Bomoo, Mr McTab's head house boy. Bunter made it "talk" in revenge for McTab taking Bunter's intended eat! It mattered not to Bunter that the parrot was in the chair. It did not take long for the Famous Five to realise the origin of the insults, and they rewarded the "speaker" - liberally! (1592).

POLPELLY, Devon. A derelict estate in Devon bought by Mr Vernon Smith who intended searching the land for tin. The house dates from

Tudor times and lies on Polpelly Cove, overlooking the Atlantic. The squire in 1588 captained a vessel in Drake's fleet and captured the San Pietro, (the Italian contingent's treasury ship), which later sank in Polpelly Cove. Polpelly is some 30 miles as the crow flies from Barnstaple, (although 50-60 by road), and six miles from the nearest town, Pilverton. There are extensive caves beneath the house wherein Captain Marco Zero, the Italian Captain, was held prisoner. Nugent and Bull were imprisoned in the same dungeon and, in trying to dig an escape tunnel, found the treasure. The house is said to be haunted by the ghost of the Elizabethan squire searching for the hidden treasure. (HBE 39).

POLPEN. A Cornish fishing village on the opposite side of Pengarth Bay to Pengarth itself. The house is about half a mile from the village across the bay or one mile by the footpath. Sir Jimmy Vivian and his friends had tea at the village inn, The Rose Inn, before going on to the house when they first arrived in the area. (811).

POMPEII. Stopping off on their way to Egypt, Sir Reginald Brooke's party visited this ancient Graeco-Roman town. Harry Wharton became separated from the rest of the party, and was attacked by Kalizelos' men trying to obtain the Scarab of A-Menah. (1278).

PONCET, M. A French business friend of Mr Vernon Smith whom the latter was visiting in Le Bosquet-dans-le-Foret. At the same time, Smithy was there with Ponsonby and Co. when he should have been studying with Mr Pickering. Smithy was wounded saving his father from an attack by a cut throat Apache pickpocket. This action saved him from being disowned. (1366).

PONG, Mr. A clerk to Mr Wun Chung Lung in Hong Kong. He was a member of The Red Dragon Tong who tried to persuade Ferrers Locke to send Wun Lung to "his father's house" in the Peak District. Locke would not permit this and was instead taken prisoner himself and sentenced to death by Tang. Luckily, Bunter trespassed in Tang's garden and was able to free Ferrers Locke from a nasty death by slow drowning. (1181).

PONS, M. A passenger on the R.M.S. Comet confined to his cabin with rheumatism. Bunter decided that he had to be O Lobo waiting his chance to "get at" the Friars on board. Raising the alarm of fire, Bunter discovered that M. Pons was really an innocent passenger ! (1463).

PONSONBY, Colonel. Younger brother to Sir Cecil and uncle to Ponsonby of Highcliffe. He lives at Ponsonby Park. Bunter claimed that he had obtained permission for "The Greyfriars Hikers" to camp on the Colonel's land; they were ordered off and, in the ensuing argument, the Colonel fell into a nearby river. Saved by Harry Wharton, (the Colonel did not swim), he changed his mind and, making Ponsonby and Co. promise that they would not harm the Friars, offered them the hospitality of his house. (1336).

PONSONBY, Cecil. The one time Captain of the Fourth Form at Highcliffe is the son of Sir Cecil Ponsonby. Devoid of any good, let alone having any virtue, this scion of the nobility has affection for none save himself. His "friends" are bound by fear of what he would do to them if they were to eschew their leader, rather than by affection. There can only be one reason why he has never been expelled from Highcliffe - snobbery on Mr Mobbs' part and wordly weariness on Dr Voysey's. For the former, a pretended word of welcome from Pon.'s Uncle the Marquis will suffice to purge almost any contempt; for the latter no concern about events in his school, or the outside world can shake him out of his lethargy. To catalogue Ponsonby's crimes, (and make no mistake they are crimes), would take for ever. Suffice it to say that gambling and smoking are as breathing; the beating up of solitary opponents, drink; and any "fixing" of persons or events by drugs, imprisonment, torture or coercion - meat. Cowardice is his cloak, and even Satan must blench at such a recruit to his numbers.

PONSONBY, Sir Cecil, Bart., of Ponsonby Hall. The unworthy sire of an unworthy son. An expert manipulator in the city, he was created baronet, making one wonder who got burnt in the process. The depths of his son's depravity are hinted at in the father who got himself appointed advisor to the governors of Greyfriars. He would have then quite happily ruined the school, had not the Remove, together with a good number of other forms, threatened to make their parents take them away from the school if Sir Cecil's measures were implemented. A man who obeys his son's dictates is either a rogue on the same scale or a weak fool. The latter type never made it big in the city.

PONSONBY, Sir Gerald. The owner of the Lancashire factory wherein Mark Linley worked before going to Greyfriars. Sir Gerald is an acquaintance of Gussy D'Arcy, who almost committed an unforgivable solecism when he first met Mark. (103).

PONSONBY, Walter. A thoroughly decent man, working in a bank in Bowdsley, Linley's home town. Pon., his cousin, sent him a letter, addressed to Harry Wharton, for posting from that town. It was not until Linley, expelled for theft, saved him from being run over, that the depths of "Dear Pon.'s" plotting became apparent. Having as much liking for his cousin as the Famous Five, he gladly helped to clear Linley of this accusation. (939).

PONSONBY HALL. The home of Ponsonby of Highcliffe. Its precise location is not revealed. (1338).

PONSONBY PARK. The home of Ponsonby's uncle. It is an estate set in the Warwickshire countryside. (1336).

POOKS, Mr. The landlord of the Golden Pig Inn at Hoad. As hospitable as he is plump, he has a profitable side line in conveying tourists to see the nearby haunted castle. (1191).

POOTING. A railway station on the line betwen Lantham and Ashwood, Surrey. Bunter was, as usual, bilking the railway company and hiding under the seat when he came to Lord Cavandale's aid. He persuaded the Earl to pay his fare, (and to give him a lift), after the Earl had been attacked. (1191).

POP. See Popper, Cecil.

POP. A bulldog hired by Mauleverer to protect "The Greyfriars Hikers" from Herbert Higgins. The expected night attack resulted in a convincing victory for Pop! (1334).

POPLARS, The, Wimford. A solitary house lying about half way between Wharton Lodge and Wimford. Fisher T. Fish had disappeared - kidnappped by Barney McCann. Wharton had a long chatty letter from his Aunt Amy in which, amongst the local gossip, was a tale of a rude, invalid American renting the house. The coincidence set Harry wondering and, obtaining permission for an exeat for the Famous Five, went to Wharton Lodge for a few days. Their suspicions were correct and they were able to effect Fishy's rescue. (1165).

POPOO-LO-LINGA-LULO. A Tongan seaman, more usually called Popoo. He deserted from Captain Parsons' vessel The Sea Cat and was invited aboard the Mindanao by Bunter who looked on him as his "faithful nigger" - mistakenly! However, when the Friars were castaway on Yo'o he proved an invaluable aide in obtaining food for them. (HBE 12).

POPPER, Archibald, (Archie). Nephew to Sir Hilton who, in his usual autocratic way, decided to send Archie to Greyfriars. He then changed his mind, sending him to sea instead. Wibley, awaiting sentence from the Head, took the telephone message to this effect. Expelled for guying Mossoo, Wib decided to return to school as Archie and launch a campaign for his own reinstatement. (See Expelled from Greyfriars). (HBE 57).

POPPER, Cecil. Sir Hilton's younger brother had worked in a circus. After his death, as his uncle would not help, the circus owner brought the boy up as his own. He became a renowned acrobat – Pop. When Pop came into an inheritance, Sir Hilton claimed the boy as his nephew, (to be more precise, Sir Hilton claimed the fee for guardianship), and placed Pop, a misfit, at Greyfriars. Pop, realising that the circus was no longer doing so well, rejoined the show against orders. He even escaped from the punishment room to perform. After making a fool of his uncle in the ring, he was allowed to remain with his friends in the circus. (GBC 25).

POPPER, Cecily. Niece of Sir Hilton Popper. While out for a walk with her nurse one day, she wandered into the path of an oncoming train at Friardale. Bob Cherry, who was cutting detention, saved her, and had to watch Bunter take the credit he did not deserve. When Bunter tried to charge Sir Hilton for damaged clothes, Cherry admitted that he had broken detention and seen the rescuer, who was not Bunter. He did not claim the credit and so was sentenced to a flogging. Marjorie Hazeldene told Mr Quelch the truth, so that everyone came by their just deserts. (431).

POPPER, Sir Hilton, Bart., J.P., O.F., Chairman of the Board of Governors of Greyfriars School. A blustering, overbearing landlord; a local magistrate whose contempt for the law is seen in his enclosing "Popper's Island" as his own – despite it being common land; a meddler who cannot leave his old school to be run in its quiet way by its modest Headmaster; a meddler who can blackmail a widower into joining the army with promises of caring for his son should he fall, and then forgetting his word. Yet a man who can on occasion be generous – as when he placed Mick the Gipsy at Greyfriars, and "Nap" Fanfair at Rookwood. A man who can demean himself by walking his acres to catch trespassers; a man incapable of choosing men worthy to work at Greyfriars – ie Brander, Jeffreys, Sharpe – or of realising that discipline does not mean floggings and an iron rule. He is a man so blinkered that he seems incapable of learning from each monumental mistake, but continues the tempestuous path he has set himself. Impoverished, intensely proud, he is in the hands of the money lenders. He refuses to modernise his estate and will not acknowledge that he needs help. Withal, a sad relict of a past so distant that it is a tragic figure he casts.

POPPER COURT. The hereditary home of the Popper family. It is situated near Friardale, Kent. The estate is bounded by the River Sark on one side, and Courtfield Common on the other. The estate is heavily mortgaged through the obstinate mismanagement of the present owner, Sir Hilton Popper, who refuses to move with the times. Although there are public rights of way through the estate, the owner prevents their use – an illegal act – but, as a magistrate, he feels that he is above the law.

POPPER COURT HOME FARM. The part of the Popper Court estates managed by Sir Hilton himself. One of the major crops is fruit which Bunter regularly "scrumps". Sir Hilton, visiting the school one day, led Bunter to believe that he had been caught – he confessed and was sent to Mr Quelch for punishment. All very unfair – to the sufferer ! (820).

POPPER COURT WOODS. A large part of Sir Hilton's estate is game preserve, jealously guarded by his gamekeepers. These preserves are a favourite short cut for Friars, and make good places for illicit smoking parties, or hiding from authority.

POPPER ISLAND REBELS, THE. (Title HBE Volme 46) . When Bunter was expelled for boasting of a crime committed by Fisher T. Fish, he was believed innocent by some of the Remove who, nothing loathe to leave school, barred themselves out on Popper's Island. Efforts to storm the Island or starve out the rebels by siege failed. Mr Quelch found his loyalty to Dr Locke strained, since he believed in Bunter's innocence; and it was he who finally prevailed upon his chief to allow him to mediate and solve the crisis.

POPPER PRIZE. A prize endowed by Sir Hilton open to all Friars below the Shell. The prize is awarded for the best paper in Greek Literature. Its value is £10. Disappointed at not winning it one year, Mark Linley, desperate for money to send home to his family, helped "Uncle" Clegg with his income tax return, amid suspicion from some people as to the origins of the money he had. (1116-17) .

POPPER'S ISLAND. The name givn in sarcastic derision to an island lying some half mile upstream from Greyfriars. It is in fact commonland. However, Sir Hilton, autocrat that he is, maintains that he owns the island, and claims to have the title – although no-one has ever seen the deeds ! To prevent trouble, Dr Locke long since placed the island out of bounds to all Friars, although this rule is more honoured in the breach than the observance ! It is a regular picnicking place for all.

PORRITT. The butler at Monson Chalet. He was most upset at Ponsonby's behaviour when the Famous Five brought a message from Mr Monson after he had been robbed. (1648) .

PORSON. The butler at Mauleverer Towers. (1244) .

PORTER. One of Dick Trumper's closest friends at Courtfield County School. Like his leader he is always ready for a rag with the Remove although, in reality, a good friend of theirs.

PORTERCLIFFE, The Right Honourable the Earl of. The present title holder is the nephew of the late Earl. He arrived back in England just in time to prevent Mr Fish making off with the treasure, (150,000 golden sovereigns) - in fact his late uncle's fortune. The Famous Five found him to be a pleasant friend with whom they spent an enjoyable holiday after the departure of the Fishes - Senior and Junior. (HBE 34).

PORTERCLIFFE HALL, Kent. Set in extensive park land, the house is one mile from Margate. After the death of the late Earl, the new lord had to let his home to defray expenses. The late Earl, mistrusting banks had put all his money into gold coins, and hidden them around the house. To find this fortune, Mr Fish rented the Hall one holiday. The house is said to be haunted - a tale made use of by Chandos the butler in his search for the fortune. (HBE 34).

POTKELLY, Devon. A tiny fishing hamlet reached by footpath, (there is no road). It lies at the base of some cliffs, huddled in a small coombe. It was from here that Mr Tregelly rowed the Famous Five and Bunter to Blackrock Island. (HBE 50).

POTTER, George. With Greene he shares Study No 4 in the Fifth Form under the quasi-leadership of Coker. Like his friend Greene, he will take any insult or order so as not to miss out on the largesse of Aunt Judy or Coker himself. This apart, he is a good sportsman and is on the fringe of the First Eleven.

POTTS LANE. A small unadopted road about three miles from Greyfriars. It is one and a half miles long and runs from the Redclyffe Road towards Wapshot. It was on this lane that Count Zero used an old army hut to hold Vernon Smith prisoner. (1456).

POWSER. A chauffeur at the Courtfield Garage, and a longstanding crony of Vernon Smith. Powser often helps Vernon Smith in his illicit escapades. No doubt the largesse he receives helps considerably in sealing his mouth ! He even took the Famous Five and Bunter to Devon as Smithy's "guests" at Blackrock Castle. To be fair to Powser, he did try to warn the Famous Five that all was not as it seemed.

POYNINGS. Sir Henry Compton was surprised at the extent of Ragged Dick's literacy, considering his life on he road. However, he had learned much from a Master of Arts from Oxford - himself on the road. His name was Poynings, known to the other gentlemen of the road as "Spouting Billy". (HBE 80; GL 3).

POYNINGS, Mr. Secretary to Mr Henry Coker. Having found an incriminating letter, he proceeded to blackmail his employer. He kidnapped Horace Coker to prevent his going to his Uncle's for

Christmas, but the Famous Five came to the rescue. At Holly House, Bunter, hiding as usual, discovered that Poynings was poisoning Mr Coker. It did not take long, under threat of his own poison, for Poynings to return the letter. (GBC 29).

POYNINGS, Lieutenant Arthur. At one time he was a reckless officer under Colonel Wharton's command. After the war he forged a cheque and, when out of prison, he changed his name and became a chauffeur. Colonel Wharton recognised him and promised not to reveal his true identity unless circumstances dictated otherwise. Poynings did not keep his promise of going straight. (He was known as Barnes, Dr Locke's chauffeur). He was eventually, amid much excitement, exposed as The Courtfield Cracksman and, as a result of his crimes, is now serving a long prison sentence. (HBE 5).

POYNINGS, Mr Edgar. A relative of Cecil Ponsonby. He seems to maintain the family tradition of evil. Like his cousin is, he was at Highcliffe School. He tried to blackmail Mauleverer while working on Sir Reginald Brooke's yacht, the Silver Scud. When letters failed, he proceeded to violence. He was finally exposed as Gideon Gaunt by Harry Wharton and received a seven year prison sentence for his crimes. (GBC 35).

PRAIRIE BENDS. A railway town in Texas. Vernon Smith and his party of friends left the train here to travel overland to the Kicking Cayuse Ranch. (HBE 31-32).

PRATT. One of the chauffeurs at the Courtfield Garage. (1321).

PREFECT. Senior men, traditionally in the Sixth Form, appointed by the Headmaster to positions of authority within the school, to maintain discipline. The term derives from the latin - praefectus - a minor governor in the Roman Provinces.

PREFECTS' BEATING. For offences of unusual seriousness that can be kept from higher authority, a Prefects' beating is administered. It is the prefects' equivalent of a flogging. As no prefect can give more than six strokes of the cane, (very occasionally a double six is given), the effect of six from each prefect can be gauged.

PREFECTS, List of. The present praefectorial body is composed of, (in approximate order of seniority):-
> Wingate,(Major), Head of School.
> Gwynne
> North
> Loder
> Sykes
> Walker
> Carne
> Parkinson
> Faulkener
> Hammersley
> Tremaine.

PRICE. A fag in the Second Form.

PRICE, Stephen. The study mate of Cedric Hilton. After Loder, with whom he is an uneasy ally, he has to be the shadiest character at Greyfriars. Hating exertion in any form, (unless that form is horses, cards or billiards), it seems strange that he should have been treasurer of the Fifth Form Games club. His friendship with Hilton is tinged with more than a trace of contempt for his easy going wealthy chum, who seems to be more a banker than a pal.

PRIDE of KENT. Mr John Redwing's boat. His son Tom, Vernon Smith and the Famous Five had planned to take her for a sail, but Skinner and Co., with Ponsonby and Co., stole her and wrecked her on Shark's Tooth Island. Mr Redwing would not allow his son's friends pay for the damage, but Smithy was able to fathom the truth, and gain recompense for the owner. (922).

PRIMROSE, Miss Penelope. The headmistress of Cliff House School, Pegg. A gentle lady who hides behind a mask of severity, necessary in the handling of her high-spirited charges! A close friend of Dr Locke and his family, whose sister was for many years her deputy at the school.

PRINCE OF GREYFRIARS, THE. (Title GBC Volume 40). When von Rattenstein, a minor German Prince, arrived at Greyfriars, he took no time at all in demonstrating his arrogant, overbearing behaviour. The worst type of Prussian, he delighted in dividing friend against friend. His stay at Greyfriars was, luckily, brief, and he left, publicly flogged and expelled, after forging a letter in Harry Wharton's hand to Joe Banks.

PRIORY, The, Wold, Wiltshire. The home of Jimmy Silver of Rookwood. It is only three or four miles from Nugent's home. (881).

PRIORY, The Old. Originally part of the Monastery, this building in Friardale Woods has fallen into ruins since the 16th century. It is, nonetheless, an extensive building, with many original features still discernible. Used as a field centre for archaeology and architecture for outdoor lessons, the only salient feature that interests Friars is the secret passage between the Priory and the school. This is "well over half a mile long". It starts behind the panelling in Mr Quelch's study and runs to the vaults beneath the Priory. It is dangerous and, therefore, out of bounds.

PROUT, Captain Eustace, O.F. An ex-army officer who was wounded on active service. In deep financial trouble he borrowed a sum from Sharp & Co. and left a cheque as security. Unfortunately, he forged the signature. Using this, a Mr Tighe tried to blackail Mr Prout, Eustace's uncle. Always in dire straits, Mr Prout later planned to send his nephew £10. This he mislaid, and Wilmot was accused of stealing it. Happily, this was proved untrue. (1133; 1469)

PROUT, Mr Paul Pontifex, M.A., (Oxon) . The portly, pompous, pachydermatous, pedantic pedagogue of the Fifth Form. With a progress to make a Pouter Pigeon appear puny, his over-weening pretentiousness is proof against the slings of his fellows in the Common Room, and the barbs of his pupils without. The claimant to the crown of Nimrod, he has dusty heads and guns upon his study wall to give credence to his panegyrics of puisne derring-do in pursuit of Ferae Naturae. Not for Don Pomposo is the simple phrase - grandiloquent, polysyllabic circumlocution is his forte; and woe betide the man who tries to muzzle Mnemosyne when she is in full flood! Only Coker in class, and Mr Quelch out of class, can stem the prolix perjorations. The first by assinine insistence in his mentor's erring in matters classical and orthographical; and the second by walking "Quenbus Flestrin" off his feet!

PUCCI, Signor. The private secretary to Cardinal Colonna. After the Famous Five had gone to the aid of Brother Antonio, (a scene witnessed by the Cardinal), Signor Pucci was sent by His Eminence to show the Friars the sights of Rome, using the Cardinal's car. (1388) .

PUG. See Pilkinson, Pug.

PUGG. A retired professional footballer, and now barman at The Cross Keys. Still only twenty five, he was forced into premature retirement because he arrived for a match drunk. He is an acquaintance of Vernon Smith who invited him to play for "The Greyfriars Crusaders" against Wharton's Team. Needless to say, being in a class of his own when sober, he ran rings round the opposition who lost 6-3. (249) .

PULTENEY, Sir Fulke, Bart., of Edgecombe Towers, Wiltshire. A creation of the fertile, romantic brain of Montague Snooks, (a one time member of the Remove). Living in a fantasy world, he created Sir Fulke to prove to the Remove his aristocratic connections ! Temple, owner of a copy of Debrett, discovered the baronet's non-existence; but it was left to Wibley to cure Snooks by making up as Sir Fulke and "coming down" to Greyfriars ! (814).

PUNCE. The station Master at Friardale. (184).

PUNISHMENT ROOM, (Punny). With bars to both door and windows, the room is in a distant part of the school, on the top floor. In here are placed boys under sentence of expulsion awaiting their final ignominy. It is also used as solitary confinement for the punishment of really serious offences. In the past, "Punny" was used extensively but, nowadays, it is rarely used.

PUNTER, "Professor". Almost certainly the possessor of false degrees and titles, he came in answer to Vernon Smith's advertisement for a hair-restorer for Mr Prout. (763).

PUNTER, Mr Bernard R. A city business man of dubious morals who sent his son to Greyfriars to search for the legendary Greyfriars Treasure, buried at the time of the Dissolution of the Monasteries. Bunter, tying his shoelaces, (or something!), found out their secret. (952).

PUNTER, Wilfred. The son of Mr Bernard Punter. He was sent to Greyfriars to search for the Greyfriars Treasure. Gradually, his father sent him more and more details about the hiding place. By this time, Skinner and Co. had "got in on the act", and solved yet another false trail laid by the crafty monks, before fleeing the King's wrath. (952).

PURKISS. A ruffianly brute who begs under the guise of an ex-corporal, (in fact he was never in the army). He also poaches game in the Wimford area. He received a prison sentence for assaulting Wun Lung one Christmas. (47).

PURKISS. A regular at The Feathers Inn who was "put up" to going to Greyfriars to discredit Levison. Thrashed for his pains, he later tied up Levison to prevent him playing in a match; but again he got a thrashing ! (799).

PURKISS. An old retired fisherman of Pegg, to whom the Remove sometimes take discarded clothes or gifts of food. (1068).

PURKISS. One of the Bowery toughs who kidnapped Coker in New York, and held him for $10,000 ransome. Bunter was, himself, lost the next day, when he stumbled on Coker, and freed him. (1094).

PURKISS, Smudge. A bicycle thief who found Mauleverer's bike in Redclyffe Wood. He repainted it and sold it to Bunter who bought it on the "never-never"! Discovering the true owner, Bunter demanded, and got, a reward of £1 for "finding" it! (1659).

PYCROFT, Mr. The mate in the S.Y.Sea Nymph, Captain George Cook's yacht. (1312).

PYLE, Mr. A one time Master of the Second Form.

PYNSENT, Mr. Private tutor to Harry Wharton before he was sent to Greyfriars. He was obviously an ineffectual man, as his charge was allowed to do as he pleased; which most certainly was not schoolwork! (1).

Q.

QUADRANGLE, The. Approaching the school from the Main Gate, the first view is of the imposing Quadrangle. Built at the start of the 18th Century, the Quadrangle, (or Quad, for short), is a three-sided structure, the front of which is open. In one corner, beneath ancient trees, is the old Abbot's House, now converted into the School's Tuck Shop. The grass in the courtyard is reminiscent of the Oxford Backs. One side of the Quad, on the ground floor, contains the Sixth Form Studies - in front of which is "Sixth Form Green". The central cobbled area is enhanced by the statue of the Founder, King Edward VIth, erected in 1851 to celebrate the School's 300th Anniversary. On the other side of the Quadrangle are the Masters' Studies and Common Room. On the first floor, surrounding the Quad, are many of the boys' Studies, while the second floor is devoted to dormitories. The central part of the building contains the imposing Archway leading to the Close, which lies behind. To the side of the arch is the main entrance of the school, leading to the Hall and Dining Hall.

QUELCH, Miss Cora. Mr Quelch's niece.

QUELCH, Mr Henry Samuel, M.A., (Oxon) . The Master of the Remove. As was said of Dr Temple, Headmaster of Rugby, Mr Quelch is a "beast – but a just beast". With an austere, unforgiving exterior, ever mindful of the rigid path of duty, Mr Quelch belies himself more often than not. He seems always to be aware of the truth, always aware of problems besetting any of his charges and, if he can, he will always give them the benefit of the doubt. Even when the impulsiveness and hot headedness of Harry Wharton come to the forefront, "Quelchy" will always proffer an olive branch – that it is refused cannot be said to be his fault. Mr Quelch is the archetypal, dedicated teacher whose life is given to his beloved classics, Greyfriars and his form. Not a believer in the rose path, he will put away his manuscript of his "History of Greyfriars" if duty calls. For him a masters job is twenty four hours a day until the term is over. For relaxation, there is nothing better to him after a long hard walk, (usually exhausting Mr Prout), than to settle down with his typewriter or to read one of his favourite classical authors – or perhaps discuss for hours some minute, arcane point in Aeschylus with Dr Locke, his life long best friend. His intense loyalty to his chief has on occasions been strained; and it must hurt deeply to choose to support Bunter in preference to the Head.

QUELCH, Roger. The nephew of Mr Quelch, and probably brother to Cora, as there is no mention of Mr Quelch having two brothers. He is at High Coombe School, in Devon, where he shines on the sportsfield, but not in class. In view of his continuing bad reports, he was sent to Greyfriars, at his uncle's suggestion, to try to bring him up to the mark. Roger, however, had other ideas ! With his propensity for practical jokes, he exceeded even his uncle's tolerances, and was soon sent back to High Coombe. (GBC 15) .

RABBIT. One of "Captain Flash's" accomplices in a big jewel robbery. The "Captain" was arrested, but his jewels were not found – he had hidden them in a caravan which Harry Wharton and Co. rented for a holiday tour. Rabbit tried to find the cache but was arrested with Stokes, his accomplice. (GBC 22).

RABY, George. A member of "The Fistical Four" at Rookwood School. They share Study No 8 in the Classical Side. Sporting rather than academic, Raby is a regular member of the school's Junior teams.

RACKSTRAW, Cyril. Sir George Cholmondely's grandson, and heir presumptive to the title. The heir apparent, Cecil Cholmondeley, had long ago disappeared. Once rediscovered, Rackstraw, (the engineer of the disappearance), tried all ways to remove "Tatters" from first Greyfriars and, later, his home. The idea was that, if Tatters could be taken abroad, he, Rackstraw, would in time become the heir. This would ease his financial burden as the moneylenders, to whom he was deeply in debt, would then wait on his expectations before demanding repayment. To gain his ends, Rackstraw even blackmailed Carne into helping him with his plots. But Carne, faint-hearted, proved a broken reed. Ponsonby, also proved of no use. Finally, thoroughly disgraced, Rackstraw fled the country. (GBC 19).

RAFIA, The. A Corsican secret society. Sir William Cherry's father, (Bob Cherry's grandfather), stumbled across a meeting and, in order to avoid death, joined the society. Thirty years later they demanded "their rights" – £40,000. Sir William's refusal almost led to his death by poison administered through the wearing of his father's ring, sent back to him by the society. Bunter, hiding in the wrong car was caught by the society. He managed to free himself, and as a result saved Sir William's life, and caused the breaking up of the English Lodge. (1108).

RAG, The. The popular name of the Junior Common, (or Day), Room. It is the communal meeting place for forms below the Shell. It is used for meetings, debates, form trials, as well as, as the name suggests, for rioting! Usage has made it the Common Room for the Remove. The Shell keeping themselves entirely to their studies; the Upper Fourth likewise, to a great extent; while the Third and Second Forms use their classrooms as common rooms.

RAGGED DICK. A waif who tramped the byways of southern England after the death of his father, (Robert Compton), who had left home after his brother refused to help him. He had married against his parent's wishes and then, after the death of his wife, become a tramp. Dick was taken in by Sir Henry Compton to be made into his grandson – little realising that he was, in fact his nephew – to prevent Roger Compton succeeding to the title and estate. (HBE 80; GL 3).

RAILTON, Mr Victor, M.A. The Housemaster of the School House at St Jim's School. He is an immensely popular man who enlisted as a private rather than take the proffered commission during the war. He was invalided out of the army after receiving a shoulder wound.

RAINY FACE. A Wolf-Apache Indian Chief in league with Barney Stone's gang of cattle rustlers. After taking part in the abortive kidnapping of Bunter, in mistake for Vernon Smith, he led his band in an attack on Vernon Smith and the Famous Five and, managing to lasso Smithy, took him prisoner. (HBE 32).

RAJAH. The elephant in Muccolini's Circus. After making himself unpopular with Scipio, the trainer, Bunter found himself on board the beast, unable to control him ! However, he finally succeded, and then made the elephant duck Bob Cherry in a pond. (HBE 55).

RAKE, Richard, (Dick). He shares Study No 6 in the Remove with Desmond, Wibley and Morgan. A lesser light of the form, he is, nonetheless, a keen sportsman who only rarely gets a place in the Form Team.

RALEIGH. The Junior Captain of Topham School. His wallet was stolen while playing in a match at St Jude's and Wilmot accused of the theft.

RALPH. See Cooper, Ralph.

RAMON. A Mexican member of Gomez' bootlegging gang. His attempted kidnap of Mauleverer was foiled by Leonora La Riviere, who pulled an (unloaded) gun on him. After the arrest of the leader of the gang, Ramon was involved in the kidnap of Harry Wharton by Myron Polk. (GBC 21).

RANCE, Mr Elias. (Young Mr Rance). He inherited his father's firm of Rance & Co. Estate Agents, Valuers and Auctioneers, of Okeham, Devon, and proceeded to squander his birthright in drinking and gambling. In a desperate effort to raise money he tried to fool Mr Vernon Smith, of all people, who was buying property in the area. It did not take long for his criminal activities to become obvious and so, he had Mr Vernon Smith kidnapped, and later Smithy. His price for their freedom was £100,000 and their silence. After the rescue of the prisoners from the sea cave on Blackrock Island, Mr Rance found himself indicted for embezzlement of client's and the firm's moneys, as well as kidnapping. (HBE 50).

RANDALL, O.F. A recent leaver from the School, he was in Harry Wharton's early days "the fattest and best natured prefect at Greyfriars". (49).

RANSOME. The accomplice of Captain Spencer. After the loss of the proceeds of a robbery at a Lantham Bank, Ransome attacked the Captain in an attempt to convince the police of Spencer's innocence. He and his leader used the same disguise at the same time; while Ransome appeared in one place, Spencer robbed a bank in Courtfield. Vernon Smith, having seen through the play acting, was instrumental in Inspector Grimes's arrest of Captain Spencer. Ransome, however, managed to escape justice. (HBE 75).

RAT. The accomplice of Slim Jim who acted as goaler to Mr Quelch while he was being held prisoner in The Old Moat House at Wimford. After Jack Drake had worked out the secret of the Moat House, Rat made his escape with Slim Jim. (HBE 29).

RAT, Jimmy The. See Jimmy the Rat.

RAT HANKEY. See Hankey, Rat.

RATTY. One of the ruffians hired by Captain Reynham to kidnap and transport "Lord Reynham". (HBE 14).

RATTY the ROGUE. A member of "Slimy" Sugden's gang. He was captured by Dick Lancaster after a bank raid at Courtfield whom, in order to preserve his "cover", Lancaster had to help escape, but not too obviously. After Harry Wharton had discovered the truth about Lancaster, Ratty helped to kidnap Wharton. He was finally arrested in the act of attempting to murder Ferrers Locke. (HBE 7).

RAVENSPUR, Captain Cecil. Youngest brother of Sir Richard Ravenspur. He lives at Ravenspur Grange with his brother. He disbelieved the Famous Five's tale of a murdered man outside the house. As he had on a bloodstained coat he was their prime suspect in the crime. This was heightened the next day when he came out of the house carrying a revolver just after Sir Richard had been shot. However, he was cleared of suspicion after Inspector Cook's murder, since he was, at that time, in Leyford Nursing Home, having taken poison intended for Sir Richard. He is a hard headed, reckless cynic, despite his affection for his brother. He invited the suspicion fixed upon himself, and this may well have made the case harder to solve. (HBE 36).

RAVENSPUR, Edgar. The son of Sir Richard Ravenspur's younger brother, (who had died in the war). He went to the bad at an early age and emigrated to Australia. There he became a Queensland Bushranger known as "Black Edgar". Escaping from justice, he returned to England and changed his name. Hunted by two of his former accomplices, he murdered them to keep his identity secret. A master of disguise, his intention was to murder Sir Richard and then reappear as the lost heir. His plan failed and he was arrested by Ferrers Locke, to the dismay of his uncle, who could not believe that his butler would try to take his life. He escaped the penalty of the law by taking his own life. (HBE 36).

RAVENSPUR, Colonel Sir Richard, Bart. The present title holder. The oldest of three brothers and one sister, (now Mrs. Nugent). His life was attempted by his heir, Edgar Ravenspur, several times. The attempts failed due to a combination of luck and watchfulness on the part of his surviving brother, Captain Cecil, and the Famous Five. (HBE 36).

RAVENSPUR GRANGE, Leyford, Oxfordshire. The house lies about half a mile from the village, and three miles from the town of Ley. It is the home of Sir Richard Ravenspur. Here, Nugent's mother, (the baronet's sister), spent her childhood. It is an old house, built in the days of secret passages, one of which ran from a hunting lodge to the house, allowing the murderer access to the house. The Famous Five, on their way to visit Nugent's uncle, found themselves embroiled in a murder mystery that taxed even Ferrers Locke. (HBE 36).

RAWLINGS, Edward, (Ted). The steward in the S.Y. Firefly, and a partner of Captain Compton in his smuggling business. A thoroughly bad man who tried to rob Senhor Gugman Diaz of his wallet after he had been rescued at sea, but was foiled by Harry Wharton. When he realised that the Famous Five suspected that all was not well on board the ship, he tried to lose them in the woods above Marseilles - unsuccessfully. He then used Bunter as a carrier for smuggled goods, and when Valentine Compton persuaded his uncle to give up smuggling, Rawlings led a mutiny with Swain the mate. They then marooned the Captain and his nephew; Rawlings ensuring that their water bottles were empty and the containers empty of food. (HBE 48).

RAWSON. He is in Study No 5 in the Classical Side at Rookwood. (739).

RAWSON. The steward in the S.Y. Silver Star, Ferrers Locke's yacht, which was used to take Wun Lung and a party of Friars to China. (1179).

RAWSON, Captain. The Captain in the S.S. Sunderbund, travelled in by Mauleverer's party from Singapore to Suva. (1589).

RAYLEIGH, Bernard Sefton, O.F. He is still remembered today with awe and reverence for his batting in a St Jim's match in the 1890's. Going in at about 30-4, and needing 313 to win, he made 166 not out - one of the highest scores recorded by a Friar. (795).

REBEL. A nickname, soon discarded, given to Piet Delarey on his arrival at Greyfriars. The name originates from his having the same name as a famous South African rebel against Colonial rule. The name was enhanced by Delarey's initial behaviour.

REBELLION OF HARRY WHARTON, THE. (Title HBE Volume 2). Loder, as "down" on Harry Wharton as ever, put him many times in the wrong. Hot-headed impetuosity worsened the situation so that Mr Quelch came to believe in his head boy's wrong doing. On the basis of "cap fit, cap wear" Wharton went all out, it seemed, to prove them both right. Finally, on the verge of expulsion, he ran away from school. Mr Quelch searching for Harry, got himself into trouble, and was saved from the sea at Pegg by Harry who was then, begrudgingly, reinstated. It took all of the Christmas holidays, and much of the next term, to regain the ground he had lost in his Form Master's opinion.

RED COW INN, Elmbridge, Surrey. An Inn frequented by the racing fraternity when the races are on there. Joe Banks is a regular guest. (1368).

RED COW INN, Friardale. Near the church on the edge of the village, it is the nearest pub to the school and, probably for that reason, not frequented by the "gay dogs".

RED COW, Wharton Magnus. An inn near Wharton Lodge. (1491).

RED DRAGON TONG. A Chinese secret society. At one time it was presided over by Tang Wang who used its members as a private army to initiate his campaign of rebellion to make himself Emperor of China. As a money raising scheme, he threatened rich merchants, Wun Lung's father included. His methods of persuasion included attempted kidnapping, as well as murdering his victims families. Hence the idea of Ferrers Locke taking Wun Lung home to China to the safety of his home. (HBE 24-25; HBE 25a).

RED EARL, The. One of Mauleverer's ancestors who, arraigned for high treason, hid in the turret of Mauleverer Towers - where he perished. Since then his ghost has been said to appear to the title holder just before his death. Brian Mauleverer made use of the legend to try to frighten Mauly one Christmas. He was finally exposed through Bunter's usual dishonest behaviour. (474).

RED EARL of PORTERCLIFFE, The. An Elizabethan nobleman who got his name from his murderous activities. Eventually meeting a violent death himself, his ghost is said to haunt Portercliffe Hall. When Mr Fish saw the ghost it seemed real enough to the treasure hunter – particularly when exposed as Chandos the butler! (HBE 34).

RED FLARE, The. A saloon in the town of Packsaddle. (HBE 32).

RED KELLY. The Irish proprietor of the Red Flare Saloon. (1578).

REDCLYFFE, Kent. A village some five or six miles from Greyfriars. It is on the railway line between Lantham and Courtfield. The school, (Redclyffe School), plays matches against Greyfriars at all levels. Redclyffe Manor House was the scene of one of the Courtfield Cracksman's daring robberies.

REDGATE, Surrey. A few miles from Reigate, and twenty miles from Wharton Lodge, it is the home town of the Bunter family, and the postal adress of Bunter Villa, (or Court, as Bunter insists!).

REDMAY, Mr. A farmer who owns Redmays Farm, on the Greyfriars side of Redclyffe Wood. Chasing Bunter, whom he believed had thrown a turf at him, Mr Quelch trespassed on the farm and was forced onto the roof of an outhouse by the farmer's apparently ferocious dog. However, Bunter overheard the farmer and, learning to the contrary, "saved" Mr Quelch from the dog, and himself a lot of trouble! Bunter received a box of chocolates as a reward for his bravery. (1566).

REDWING, Mr John. The seaman father of Tom. He lives at Hawkscliff in a tiny cottage of incredible neatness. His pride in his son's prowess knows no bounds. A simple, honest soul who is more of a gentleman than Bunter could ever hope to become, he welcomes eagerly any of his son's friends to his home. As a seaman, he is absent from home a great deal of the time but, like all seamen, home is still the best place to be.

REDWING, Thomas, (Tom). Shortly after saving Vernon Smith's life, he came to Greyfriars posing as Clavering. From gratitude grew Smithy's great friendship, and the scholarship Tom won to stay at Greyfriars was founded by Mr Vernon Smith. Modest and unassuming, he never changed his outlook on life even when he bcame wealthy in his own right. His tolerance and patience are a byword in the Remove, for not only does he have to contend with Smithy's tantrums and outbursts of blackguardism, but also the gibes of the Skinner brigade. That he is one of Mr Quelch's favourites is not surprising since he is consistently near the top of the form academically, as well as being a good man at sports.

REGENCY BOARDING HOUSE, Brighton. The hotel at which Eric Carlow was bootboy. One summer he saved Sir George Cheyne, a guest, from drowning, and was rewarded by being adopted by the baronet. Coker had also stayed here, and recognised Carlow when he went to Greyfriars. (1239).

REMOVAL OF HORACE COKER, THE. (Title GBC Volume 31). Relates not only how Aunt Judy persuaded the Head to promote Horace to the Fifth Form, but also the arrivals at Greyfriars of Sammy Bunter, Johnny Bull and Fish.

REMOVE, The. More properly the Lower Fourth Form but, following the Charterhouse tradition, this intermediate form has became known as the Remove. Presided over by Mr Quelch it is the bane of the other masters who simply do not have the necessary stature to control the large and varied, but mostly high-spirited members. By weight of force, as well as ability, they have become the recognised leaders of the Junior School, even over the Upper Fourth, and the official Junior Team of Greyfriars in representative matches. The Head of the form and Captain of its teams is Harry Wharton, ably asisted by his lieutenants, the rest of the Famous Five.

REX. A wolfhound bought on a whim by Mr Bunter. Proving too much for a suburban household, the dog was given to Bunter's Uncle Ted, who was going on a Big Game Hunt to Africa. Skinner obtained the letter telling Bunter the news and, altering the word "Rex" to "you", gave Bunter the idea of borrowing Mr Prout's gun for target practice ! To Bunter's dismay, Skinner's perfidy was discovered - he was not to leave Greyfriars ! (1091).

REYNHAM, Captain Rupert. Cousin and heir to Lord Reynham. Shortly after returning from abroad he suggested that, in order to prevent attempts on the Earl's life, the Earl should return home with a private detective as guard, in order to trap, or capture, the would-be kidnappers. As it was the Captain plotting to ensure his own succession to the title, the plan nearly succeeded. Bunter had impersonated the Earl, thus flushing out the Captain whom Harry Wharton had discovered to be the prime instigater of the crime. The Captain was allowed to leave England rather than face his trial with its attendant publicity. (HBE 14).

REYNHAM, William, The Right Honourable The Earl of. A sickly youth who had been removed from his home to a place of safety by his guardian and uncle, Sir Peter Lanchester. To try to discover and arrest the would-be kidnappers, (or worse), Bunter stayed at Reynham Castle in the guise of the Earl for a Christmas holiday. Several attempts were made to kidnap him - the last one successful. The Famous Five had been invited by Bunter to stay, and Harry Wharton, who had suspected Captain Reynham of being the kidnapper kept a close watch on him, and was able to effect Bunter's release before he was transported abroad. The real Lord was then able to enter into his rightful place. (HBE 14).

REYNHAM CASTLE, Near Castlewood, Sussex. An ancient battlemented pile built in the middle ages, it stands in an extensive park, the drive of which is one mile long. Set on the Sussex Downs, the castle is about a mile from the little town of Castlewood. It is the seat of the Earls of Reynham. (HBE 14).

RIDINGS SCHOOL, Brighton. "A Childrens' Boarding School" at which Miss Bullivant, (now of Cliff House School), once worked. She was able to place her young brother at the school. He was stolen away by "Barney the Binger", (better known to the police as Barnabas Crake), the former butler at the school. He had been caught stealing by Miss Bullivant and, in revenge, took the boy who later went to Greyfriars under the name of Skip. (HBE 63).

RIGG. A money lender in Lantham from whom Mossoo borrowed £20 to help a sick niece. After paying back the principle and interest of £10, Mossoo was blackmailed into paying a further £10, or losing his post at Greyfriars. Harry Wharton overheard the threat and, with Mauleverer's help, raised the money, which they sent anonymously to M. Charpentier. (951).

RIO de JANEIRO. The Brazilian port at which Harry Wharton and Co. disembarked on their way to visit Jim Valentine. While in the city, O Lobo made a daring daylight attempt on Jim Valentine's life. (1463).

RIO KID, The. A young American outlaw, chased and harried for crimes he did not commit. One of his hiding places is in the Squaw Mountain near the Kicking Cayuse Ranch. While "holed up" there he helped Vernon Smith several times, culminating in the capture of Jad Blake. (HBE 32).

RIO REXO. A navigable river in Brazil, on the banks of which is Mr Peter Valentine's coffee plantation. A desolate spot, only reached with much difficulty across country or, more easily, by using the river itself as a highway. The river is the route by which the plantation produce is taken to market. (HBE 44).

RIVER LODGE, Kingston. Until his arrest on a variety of criminal charges, this was the home of Mr Ulick Driver and, his cousin and ward, Jim Lee. (784).

RIVERSIDE BUNGALOW, Near Wimford, Surrey. A bungalow downstream from Wharton Lodge. It was taken by Mr Vernon Smith on his son's behalf one holiday. He stayed here with Tom Redwing and a wastrel, Mr Freddy Paget. Persisting in a feud begun the previous term, the Famous Five and Vernon Smith continued their warfare. The first round went to the Famous Five and Bunter, when Bunter identified Paget as a bank robber. The second round, with Ponsonby and Co. in Smithy's corner, was intended to see the "sacking" of Wharton, followed by his being marooned on Monk's Island. In the dark, Pon. and Co. got Tom Redwing who was returning from warning Wharton. As a result of lying out on the island all night, Redwing was ill for quite some time. (1260-61).

RIVERSIDE INN. Lies on the bank of the River Sark between Greyfriars and Popper's Island. It is a pleasant rural spot patronised by Friars when out boating, since it's tea garden and restaurant are within bounds. (1112).

ROBERT. A footman at Wharton Lodge.

ROBERT. Trotter's predecessor as pageboy at Greyfriars. (6).

ROBERT. A footman at Eastcliff Lodge. (1679).

ROBINSON. One of Lord Mauleverer's chauffeurs.

ROBINSON, (Minor). A fag in the Third Form at Greyfriars. (927).

ROBINSON, Mr. An alias used by Mr Gooch when, in the guise of a racing man, he successfully gave Bunter illicit cigarettes and got him to make bets. However, with Wibley dressed a la Bunter, all he received for his pains was a plastering of mud! (1571).

ROBINSON. William Waggs' groom on his Little Puddleton farm Bunter, lying as usual, claimed to have given the "Greyfriars Hikers" packs to a carter of this name to take to the village. (1333).

ROBINSON, George. An alias used on several occasions by Ferrer Locke. He used the name when getting work in Muccolini's Circus a an animal hand and, again, when posing as the Head's chauffeur, in vestigating the capture of Mr Quelch by Slim Jim. (HBE 56; HBE 29).

RODNEY, Richard, (Dick). A one time member of the Remove (682).

ROGERS, Mr. The mate in the S.Y. Silver Foam, Lord Conway's yacht. (1386).

ROGUE OF THE REMOVE, THE. (Title HBE Volume 68). Named after the impersonation of Arthur Durance by Ulick Stone, this volume also relates how Coker tried to "wedge" into the First Eleven; as well as the theft of the Moonstone from Popper Court.

ROLLO. "The Fattest Man on Earth". The name by which he appears in a side show in Swinger's Circus. He invited Bunter to join his "Wild Weird Freaks", as the act is called. To Bunter's indignation he was to be billed as "The Fattest Boy on Earth" – fancy anyone thinking Bunter fat ! (1160).

ROMAYNE, Sir William, Bart. A deaf, eccentric "scientific jintleman", (sic), who lives in "The House on the Heath". A large, mixed party descended on him one Christmas after a railway accident. Their unwelcome intrusion, (to Crawley), led to the capture of Ludwig Wolf, a Prussian spy. (461).

ROME. The capital of Italy. Its ancient monuments make it an attractive holiday resort. The Famous Five have visited the city several times, and had many exciting adventures here. (1388; 1543).

ROOK, Esau. A most appositely named gentleman. The director of "Phenomonal Films" of San Pedro Street, Los Angeles. He exists by extorting money out of aspirants to film stardom with the promise of making both a film and a name for the hopeful. Bunter managed to escape his snare by having no money ! (1107).

ROOKWOOD SCHOOL, Coombe, Hampshire. A Public School against whom Greyfriars play regular fixtures at all levels. It is some 70-80 miles from Canterbury, and to get there involves a long, cross-country route.

ROPER. A Highcliffe Sixth Former, prefect and member of the First Elevens. It was he whom Loder "crocked" when he actually played for Greyfriars First Eleven. Wingate ordered Loder off the pitch. Loder's hatred of Wingate was heightened by this, and he set to work to depose Wingate as Head of School. (923).

ROSE INN, Polpen. Prevented from reaching Pengarth, Sir Jimmy Vivian's party went to the Inn for tea, and directions as to how to reach the house on foot. (811).

ROSE & CROWN INN, Courtfield. The Inn at which Mr Perkins, (de Vere's uncle), stayed while looking for a business opening in the town. (751).

ROSENBLAUM, Herr. The owner of Beechwood School and, for a time after its bankruptcy, German Master at Greyfriars, while he tried to raise the money to open another school – his Foreign Academy. He is a pleasant friendly but most ineffectual man with no financial sense. It would be most surprising if his dreams come to fruition.

ROTTINGDEAN, Near Brighton, Sussex. Mr Hazeldene, who lives nearby, rented a bungalow on behalf of the Famous Five, on holiday at the time Bunter was lording it in Muccolini's Circus. While performing here as "Gugliemo" he told Hazeldene the winner of a race. As the horse came no-where, this jape nearly led to Hazel stealing. (1486).

RUCTIONS AT GREYFRIARS. (Title HBE Volume 66). Recounts the happenings at Greyfriars during the term after the Famous Five and Smithy returned from Safari.

RUDGE, Dr. A former Headmaster of Greyfriars whose tyranny led to open revolt. As a result of this he was asked to resign. (1170).

RUNNING WATER. A Wolf-Apache Indian and horse thief whom Vernon Smith saved from a horsewhipping, or worse, at the hands of the cowboys on the Kicking Cayuse Ranch. In gratitude he saved Smithy's life when Barney Stone misdirected him into a quicksand instead of the ford over the river. He also came to Smithy's help when he had been captured by Apaches at Barney Stone's behest. (HBE 32).

RURITANIA, R.M.S. The Cunard liner, upon which Mr Fish's party of Friars sailed from Liverpool to New York on their way to Hollywood. (1093).

RUSSELL, Richard, (Dick). He shares Study No 3 in the Remove with Ogilvy. He is not one of the leading lights of the form, but is nonetheless handy with his fists. Unfortunately, he can frequently be found in Bulstrode's camp of bullies.

RYLCOMBE, Sussex. A "pleasant little rustic village in the heart of Sussex". It is the nearest village to St Jim's School.

RYLCOMBE GRAMMAR SCHOOL. The great rival establishment to St Jim's. Its juniors are led by Gordon Gay who, soon after his arrival instituted matches against the Remove at Greyfriars.

RYMER, Inspector. Stationed at Winchester, he led the investigation into the threats made against Mauleverer by Brian, his cousin. (1245).

St BEDE'S SCHOOL. A lesser Public School which Skinner's cousin attends. Their last Headmaster was Mr James Carnforth, who came from here to Greyfriars, for a time, after Sir Hilton Popper had forced Dr Locke to resign. (743).

St JAMES' COLLEGIATE SCHOOL. More commonly known as St Jim's, this famous school at Rylcombe in Sussex has close associations with Greyfriars in all sporting fields. All St Jim's-Greyfriars matches are considered major fixtures.

St JUDE'S SCHOOL, Near Redclyffe, Kent. A Public School which is some ten miles from Greyfriars by road, although the short-cut through Redclyffe Wood shortens the journey to half an hour on bicycle. The Remove certainly play matches against their junior team and, although there is no mention of senior fixtures, they presumably do take place.

St KIT'S SCHOOL. Although the location is not mentioned, this is one of the schools that Greyfriars play at football.

St OLAF'S SCHOOL. A Public School in the Midlands which Arthur Carter attended and which he was asked to leave for persistant and flagrant rule breaking. He managed to get a place at Greyfriars after this. (1569).

SAINT. The name by which any member of St Jim's School is known.

SALOMAN, Mr. After Mr Quelch had been concussed by Chick Chew, a Mr Saloman was sent down by Leggett & Teggers Agency as a locum. He was kidnapped and then impersonated by Chick Chew who succeeded in abducting Putnam van Duck. Luckily Poker Pike was alert and able to arrest the kidnapper. (1478).

SAM. A carter by profession and a ruffian by nature, he assisted Mr Purkiss tie up Levison to prevent him playing in a cricket match against Highcliffe. (799).

SAM. Potman and "chucker-out" at the Cross Keys. (923).

SAMPSON. The strongman in Muccolini's Circus. He is a close friend of Marco the lion tamer and Tip the clown. (HBE 56).

SAN PIETRO. The treasury vessel of the Italian contingent in the Spanish Armada. She was captured, and later sank in Polpelly Cove. (1452) .

SANATORIUM. Greyfriars School maintains a well equipped Sanatorium within the school grounds where boys requiring nursing or medical care are looked afer by the fully qualified Nursing Sister, under the direction of the School's Medical Officer.

SANDEMAN, Mr. The grocer in Friardale. (48) .

SANDERS, Dandy. The leader of a gang of crooks. Jerry the Rat had hidden the proceeds of a bank raid in Study No 1 in the Remove. After Jerry's arrest, the boss himself directed operations to recover the loot. However, Carne had found it and so his search was in vain until, led by Bunter, he found both the plunder and the law ! (HBE 53) .

SANDERS, Soapy. A racing tout and hanger-on at the Three Fishers. He took bets from Friars, (ie Hazeldene), and found Stacey a ready customer. He even went so far as to send a fake telegram on Stacey's behalf to discredit Wharton. While Warren was at Greyfriars, he was willing "for a quid" to "knock" him so that Loder could get into the First Eleven. Sanders cetainly has a police record for theft. (1413; 1430; 1448) .

SANDERS, "Two-Gun". A Texan "gun-slinger" who came to England to persuade Vernon Smith not to visit his father's ranch The Kicking Cayuse - unsuccessfully. Once back in the U.S.A., he made several more attempts that all failed to "get" Smithy. After he was captured, his boss, Barney Stone, freed him, but he was recaptured, and wounded in the process by Smithy and the Famous Five. (HBE 32) .

SANDERSON, Mr. The owner of a sea-going motor boat, used in the landing of contraband from the Firefly. (1506) .

SANDY. The strongman in Swinger's Circus. (1160) .

SANKEY, General. A friend of Colonel Wharton, who lives at Sankey Hall, a mile from Wharton Lodge. He was the owner of a famous collection of Indian jewels which were stolen by the Courtfield Cracksman. (1141) .

SANTLEY. A one time member of the Remove. He was a reasonably good cricketer and played in the match between Bob Cherry and Harry Wharton to decide the captaincy of the Remove. (GBC 3) .

SARAH. Mrs. Bunter's maid at Bunter Villa. (1352) .

SARK, Mr James. After he had run away from Greyfriars, believing his father to be bankrupt, Vernon Smith expended his last 6d on a saveloy and coffee for himself and a waif named Alf Johnson. Before he could leave the all-night stall whereat they had eaten, Smithy was arrested for the theft of Mr Sark's gold watch. It was found in Smithy's pocket and he was sentenced to borstal, but soon released when it was discovered that Johnson was the thief. (933) .

SARK, River. A navigable waterway, at least as far as Courtfield by barges. It runs through Friardale, Courtfield and Redclyffe. Meandering through this part of Kent, it is bordered by mostly good arable land. Popper's Island and The Haunted Island lie in the river in the vicinity of Greyfriars. The river is used for rowing and swimming by the local schools and it is also used by many tourists for pleasure excursions.

SARK ABBEY. A ruined abbey on the bank of the River Sark, up the river from Highcliffe. It is in a better state of repair than many ancient monuments in the area. Mauleverer used the Abbey as the setting for getting a confession from Ponsonby that it had been he who had stolen the Cliff House girls' boat - an act for which the Famous Five had received the blame. (1530) .

SARLE, Mr J. Former solicitor to Miss Judith Coker and one time guardian to Edgar Caffyn. He used his position, and ward, to try to get Miss Coker to change her will in Caffyn's favour. At first he found his ward an apt pupil but, under the influence of his cousin, Horace Coker, he changed his attitude, and eventually confessed to his Aunt Judy. As a result, Mr Sarle found himself dismissed as her legal adviser, and received a drubbing from her into the bargain ! (HBE 9) .

SARRAIL, M. Gaston. A French friend of Mr Quelch. As they had not met for twenty years, it was easy for "The Gentleman Pincher" to impersonate the Frenchman, so that he could enter Greyfriars and burgle the place at leisure. However, he was recognised as an impostor by Vernon Smith who had met and cheeked the real M. Sarrail. "Mr Brown" was, therefore, soon arrested, and M. Sarrail freed. (1264) .

SASSO, Signor. The Captain of the Venetian felucca, The Colombo, hired by Tiger Bronx to kidnap Bunter. Once the Captain realised that Lord Conway had given chase and would easily catch him, he hoved to and surrendered his prisoner. (1386) .

SASSO, Guiseppi. A Maltese sailor picked up from the sea by the Silver Star. It was discovered that he had been hired by Tang Wang's son to attack Wun Lung. Bunter, in uncharacteristic mood, showed great bravery ! (1179) .

SCAIFE, Mr. For many years he led a gang of drug smugglers operating from Pengarth, (Sir Jimmy Vivian's Cornish property). Safe while the house was in Chancery, he tried to kidnap Vivian once he came into his inheritance. Having imprisoned Vivian and his guests in the sea caves at Pengarth, he thought he was safe, but he had not counted on the perspicacity of Cardew of St Jim's who rescued them - thus leading to the arrest of the gang. (GBC 33).

SCHEMER OF THE REMOVE, THE. (Title HBE Volume 9). Coker's cousin Edgar Caffyn was sent to Greyfriars at the suggestion of Mr Sarle, Miss Judith Coker's solicitor. His plan was that Caffyn should get Coker expelled so that he, Sarle, could share Aunt Judy's estate with Caffyn. One of the most thorough going rascals ever to be in the Remove, Caffyn, (soon nicknamed "The Snipe"), was an apt pupil of his guardian. That his efforts failed was due largely to luck - for Coker, in his usual way, played into the plotters' hands. However, Caffyn eventually realised the wrong of his efforts, aided by his cousin's boot, and told his Aunt everything.

SCHENK. Crawley's real name, before he took out papers of naturalisation. (461).

SCHOOL BOATMAN. The nephew of Mr Jones, one of the Friardale boatmen. He is known to all as Joe, but his surname in not mentioned. (1528).

SCHOOL BOUNDS. Although Friardale, Courtfield, Pegg and Lantham are within bounds on half holidays, during the rest of the week the bounds are set at the tow path on the one hand, and Oak Lane on the other.

SCHOOL CAPTAIN. At present George Wingate, (Major). This post of Captain of Games is elected by the school; every man having a vote.

SCHOOL COLOURS. Adopted at the inception of the school under its present Charter in 1716, the School colours are blue and white.

SCHOOL NUMBERS. On only one occasion can we find reference to the actual size of the school. This was at the time of an election in which the following votes were polled:

For Courtney:	152
For Carne:	62
Abstentions:	1
Candidates:	2
TOTAL	217

Absentees are most unlikely, as elections are taken seriously at Greyfriars. The only possible non-voters being men in the Sanatorium. (428).

SCHOOLBOY CARAVANNERS, THE. (Title GBC Volume 22). Hiring a caravan from Mr Lazarus, the Famous Five, with the inevitable Bunter, planned a holiday tour. They discovered that the van had been used as a cache by "Captain Flash" for stolen goods. Once they had disposed of the other members of his gang who were trying to obtain the loot, they met an escaped convict, Bert Gunner. Jack Drake, whom they met by chance, recaptured him. The party then went over to France for the remainder of the holiday, where, apart from Bunter selling the van, a good time was had by all!

SCHOOLBOY SMUGGLER, THE. (Title HBE Volume 47). Captain Compton, an Old Friar, sent his nephew, Valentine, to Greyfriars, knowing that the secret passage leading from Smugglers' Cave at Pegg to Greyfriars could be used to land contraband. The Captain was confused and dismayed to discover that the goods were not reaching their destination. Vernon Smith had found out their secret and was sending the parcels to the police. The end of the mystery is retailed in "Bunter's Christmas Party".

SCHOOLBOY SPECULATOR, THE. (Title GBC Volume 39). After Snoop had unsuccessfully tried to blackmail Hazeldene, using a faked photograph, Fish "cornered" woollens with the idea of making a "killing". Happily he lost £30! Colonel Wharton's trophy for inter-form football was won by the Remove. Finally Fish threatened Mr Quelch, only to find that Ferrers Locke had been summoned to expose the criminal.

SCHOOLBOY TOURISTS, THE. (Title HBE Volume 61). Invited by Bunter for a cruise on his cousin's yacht, The Sea Nymph, the Famous Five, Wibley, and Coker and Co. accepted. It was not until they were well out to sea that they found out that Bunter had omitted to mention the price! The immediate benefit of this was to lose Fish's company, (he had stowed away on board, with visions of a free holiday!). After recovering from the shock, an eventful and enjoyable time was had, (by most chaps).

SCHOOTZ, Mr Rigg. The producer at Perfection Films, Hollywood. While the Greyfriars party was here he was making two films: "The Lord of the Desert", starring Myron Polk; and a film about English Public School life, starring the Friars. (GBC 20-21).

SCHWARTZ, Mr. After Mr Quelch had been suspended from duty by Mr Carnforth, Mr Schwartz was appointed by the new Head to be in charge of the Remove. Typical of all petty tyrants, he was crueller than his master. The Remove barred themselves out, and rid Greyfriars of their new master by removing him bodily from the school and shaving him until he consented to leave! (GBC 27).

SCIPIO. The elephant handler in Muccolini's Circus. An African gentleman, to whom Bunter was as rude as usual. However, he gained his revenge by making Rajah, the elephant, take Bunter off on a long ride. (1483).

SCOTT, James Kenneth. He shares Study No 5 in the Upper Fourth with Tomlinson Minor. He is a regular member of the Form teams, and is certainly better at games than his Captain, Temple!

SCROOGE, Billy. The comedian in Mr Whiffle's pantomime company in which he played a cat. Mournfully, he declared that his part was dead! (409).

SEA CAT, The. The lugger owned by Captain Peter Parsons. Popoo, a Tongan sailor, deserted from her and joined the Greyfriars party for a time. After leaving the Flamingo helpless at sea, Van Dink and Ysabel Dick were picked up by The Sea Cat and, when they sighted the Friars, drifting on a raft, Van Dink forced Parsons to leave them to their fate. The Sea Cat was shipwrecked after the Friars managed to escape from a cannibal island by over-powering Van Dink and Ysabel Dick. (HBE 12).

SEA CLIFF BUNGALOW. On the cliffs near Pegg, overlooking the Channel, the house was rented by Nosey Clark to keep Harry Wharton hostage and force Colonel Wharton to return Jim Valentine to Clark. As Valentine was at Greyfriars, he could not comply – but Valentine managed to rescue Harry. (1298).

SEA CLIFF BUNGALOW, Ampinge. The home of Mr Pickering, a tutor employed by Mr Vernon Smith to teach Smithy one holiday. (1365).

SEA NYMPH, M.Y. The vessel bought by Captain George Cook for use as a cruise vessel. His first cruise was with a party of Friars, inveigled on board by Bunter, who had omitted to tell then they had to pay! (HBE 61).

SEA VIEW, A chalet-style house with a large garden on the Cliff Road between Pegg and Cliff House. Sheltering here from a rain storm, the Famous Five found themselves in trouble with Mr Lamb for trespassing. Vernon Smith, conducting a feud against the temporary master, was convinced that he had some secret hidden here. As indeed he had; Mr Quelch was being kept a prisoner in an air raid shelter. (HBE 29-30).

SEAGULLS CAVE. A cave near Pegg whose mouth is covered at high water. Harry Wharton, in trouble with Mr Quelch, ran away from school rather than be expelled. Mr Quelch, searching for the truant, was cut off by the incoming tide and, helped by Wharton, climbed above the high water mark. As a reward for this bravery, the sentence of expulsion was lifted. (1296).

SEAHILL PARK, Sussex. The holiday home belonging to Mr Vernon Smith. Set in a large estate, it has its own private beach, and is a beautiful place at which to spend the summer holidays. Smithy had planned a "doggish" time with Ponsonby and Co. but reckoned without Bunter, who invited the Famous Five to protect him against the Highcliffians. It was lucky he did, for it required Smithy and the Famous Five to save Mr Vernon Smith from the attentions of "Nessuno". (HBE 37).

SEATON D'ARCY PRIZE. An annual examination open to the Remove. It consists of a paper in Latin of the candidates own choice, followed by a viva voce examination by the Head. Harry Wharton had entered soon after his arrival at Greyfriars. Hazeldene thought he had ensured the prize for himself by cutting off a button from Harry's jacket, with which Wharton was wont to fiddle while being tested. Caught out by Nugent and Cherry, Hazeldene confessed and the examination results were altered so that Harry won. (3).

SECRET PASSAGES. Being an ancient building, Greyfriars has many secret passages which seem to have been extended as the buildings were added to. They run from Mr Quelch's study, the Remove Box-room and the Vaults, to outside places such as The Friar's Oak, Smugglers Cave at Pegg, and The Abott's Cell in the Spinney. They were used for escaping on occasions but, mostly, for nefarious activities, such as smuggling or self-indulgence. As indeed they are to-day!

SECRET SEVEN, The. The name given by Vernon Smith to the society he founded to "put down" Mr Prout and Loder. (HBE 42).

SELIM ben MUSTAPHA. He is in charge of Hilmi Maroudi's caravans that traverse the deserts. Knowing Sheik Abdurahman, on Maroudi's instructions, he went to the sheik to persuade him to change his allegiance from Kalizelos to Maroudi. (1284).

SEVEN ELMS. A village some five miles cross country from Greyfriars. Tatters was held prisoner in a cottage in Seven Elms Lane by Tinker Wilson. He was found there by Messrs. Quelch and Prout after they had lost their way while out for a walk. (1197).

SHADOW OVER HARRY WHARTON, THE. (Title HBE Volume 27).
Harry had been left a fortune by a distant relation, Mr Cortolvin.
Captain Marker, also a distant relative, an impoverished, compulsive
gambler and wastrel, determined to obtain the fortune for himself.
The condition precedent of the will was that Harry Wharton should
not be expelled from his school, as had Marker. Marker, therefore,
sent da Costa to Greyfriars with instructions to cause Wharton's expulsion. Aided by a dishonest solicitor, Mr Gedge, he set out to do just
this but, realising that his prey was a decent sort, changed his mind
after several of his schemes had gone wrong.

SHARK, The. A boat once owned by Captain Van Dink. He had obtained her by murder and theft and, with Ysabel Dick, had poached
pearls and run slaves. She was probably lost by shipwreck. (1593).

SHARK'S TOOTH ISLAND. A small rocky islet between Pegg and
Hawkscliff. Ponsonby and Co., out with Skinner, wrecked
Mr Redwing's boat on the island and then bribed Jim Sparks to lie
about their whereabouts. Vernon Smith outbid Ponsonby's bribe and
got at the truth. (922).

SHARP, Mr. One of the music masters at Greyfriars. He is a part
time member of staff, who was not old enough to avoid conscription
during the war. (525).

SHARP, Seargeant. A deserter from the German army who was later
discharged from the British army with dishonour. He was then
brought to Greyfriars by Sir Hilton Popper to "bring some discipline
into the place". A cowardly bully, he made the entire school's life a
misery until he was tarred and feathered, (a fate almost shared by Sir
Hilton too). He then demanded the expulsion of Coker and Harry
Wharton; nearly all the school walked out in protest. It was not until
Colonel Wharton, who knew the man, came down to school that order
was restored. Sir Hilton resigned from the Governing Body after this.
(392).

SHARP, Superintendant. Having discovered that Mr Quelch could
identify him, Slim Jim impersonated a police officer so that he could
kidnap Mr Quelch and keep him prisoner until he had finished working the Courtfield area. Meeting Mr Quelch on the common, Sharp,
alias Slim Jim, captured him, watched by Bunter, who was hiding in a
bathing hut by the pond. (1660).

SHARPE, Mr. A representative of the Christmas Dinners Association,
(C.D.A.), who was sent to Greyfriars to examine the bona fides of
Bunter as a provider of Christmas Dinners ! Needless to say,
Mr Sharp, and the Head, found Bunter wanting ! (148).

SHARPE & KEENE. Solicitors to Major Cherry. They were briefed by him when Bob was faced with expulsion after Heath had forged his signature to Nugent's Postal Order. (173-174).

SHARPE BODDY, Mr. The representative of World Wide Assurance who brought the news to Gosling of his windfall of £1,000. (763).

SHARPER, Nick. The leader of the gang of toughs hired by Mr Jeffreys to put down the "Sixth Form Rebellion". (505).

SHARPLES, Miss. An angular, acid lady who was not pleased to discover that her services were not required to cure Mr Prout of his baldness! (763).

SHARPLEY'S. The firm of private detectives hired by Sir George Cholmondely to find Tatters. (1195).

SHEIK OF GREYFRIARS, THE. (Title GBC Volume 8). Ali ben Yusef succeeded to the rulership of his tribe on the death of his father. Determined to gain power, Mustapha ben Mohammed through his son, Bou Saoud, captured Ali and took him from Greyfriars, (where Major Cherry had hoped he would be safe), to North Africa. Major Cherry in his efforts to find Ali was captured, as were Marjorie Hazeldene and Clara Trevlyn. Tracked across the Sahara by Harry Wharton and Co., they were finally rescued after much hardship and many bitter battles, and Ali restored to his rightful place.

SHEPCOT FARM. On his way to Wharton Lodge Mr Quelch's taxi was involved in a road accident. He lost his way in the fog, and meeting Jim Valentine, they wandered together until, by chance, they found themselves here, some five miles from Wharton Lodge. Mr Quelch, convinced that Valentine had saved his life, rewarded him by persuading Dr Locke to allow him to enter Greyfriars. (1297).

SHEPHERD, Reverend. A distant relative of Leonard Clavering with whom he lived after his father had been killed in action, and by whom he was tutored. After Clavering and Redwing had changed identities, Mr Shepherd's intended visit to Greyfriars caused consternation to Redwing, but Vernon Smith made use of Ponsonby and Co. to tie up Redwing so that he could not meet "his tutor" and so be exposed. (GBC 28).

SHIP INN, Crewey, Devon. Vernon Smith made certain that Count Zero heard his plans to leave Polpelly but, instead of returning to London as announced, he and his guests stayed here. (1454-55).

SHOOK, Mr. A Chicago multi-millionaire who, near death, changed his will to exclude his nephew, Tiger Bronx, and, instead, left his fortune to James Jarvish, his valet. Unbeknownst to Jervish, he again changed his will, leaving the entire estate to an animals home ! (1384) .

SHORT, Dr. Medical Practitioner of Friardale. It is not clear whether he was Dr Pillbury's predecessor, or whether they are partners.

SHORT, J. High Street, Ramsgate. Bootmaker and Repairer. Having received an account from them, Bob Cherry, as requested, gave Bunter "his note for 10/-" ! (1682) .

SHORT, Sam. The grocer's boy in Friardale who is always grateful when Alonzo Todd offers to carry his basket for him ! (137) .

SHOULDER, The. A rocky outcrop at one end of Pegg Bay. Unless the wind is from that quarter and extremely strong, the Shoulder acts as a shelter to the village and its harbour.

SHUTE, Inspector. Stationed at Castlewood, Sussex. He was called in to arrest "The Smiler" after his capture by the Famous Five. He had been overpowered by the crook's rescuer and was then released by Captain Reynham. The Inspector was relieved to discover that the Famous Five suspected that this might happen, and so kept watch outside to recapture him. (1559) .

SHYLOCK OF GREYFRIARS, THE. (Title HBE Volume 72) . Julian Devarney did not make many friends at Greyfriars when he announced that he barred Monty Newland on account of his father being ruined by a dishonest Jew in the city. Before he left Greyfriars he had changed his outlook - since the "Jew" was in fact his uncle in disguise ! Mr Tighe, (alias many other names), tried to blackmail Mr Prout - knowing that public knowledge of his nephew's forgery would lead to Mr Prout's enforced resignation. Coker recognised Tighe as a man who had swindled his aunt and, in handling him, recovered the forged cheque Mr Prout so badly wanted. Coker, due for a flogging for an imposition not done, was reprieved.

SILVER, Jimmy. The Junior Captain at Rookwood School. He shares Study No 8, (The End Study), with Lovell, Newcome and Raby. He lives with his parents at The Priory, a few miles from Nugent's home.

SILVER FOAM, M.Y. Lord Conway's yacht. Luckily for Bunter she was taking a party of Saints on a cruise and had called in at Venice when Bunter was abducted by Tiger Bronx. Conway was able to run down the felucca in which Bunter was being held, and force the Colomba to heave to and release her prisoner. (1386) .

SILVER SCUD, M.Y. Sir Reginald Brooke's yacht in which he took a party of Friars for a cruise one holiday during which "Gideon Gaunt" demanded money with menaces from Mauleverer. (GBC 35).

SILVER SPOON, The. One of the saloons in Packsaddle, Texas. After being forcibly ejected from the Red Flare, Running Water tried to get a drink here. (1578).

SILVER STAR, M.V. The vessel owned by Ferrers Locke and captained by himself. He took Wun Lung and a party of Friars to China in her. (HBE 25; HBE 24a).

SIMMONDS. The doorman at Magic Films, Hollywood. It is his job to keep out unauthorised tuft hunters, as well as would-be stars. For a time he had to suffer Bunter but, after the the exposure of his incompetence as an actor, and his taking-in of the director, he took great pleasure in kicking Bunter off the lot ! (GBC 20-21).

SIMMONDS, Inspector. He was called in by Lord Portercliffe to investigate the disappearance of Mr Fish and his son after Chandos has incarcerated them in a hidden chamber in the Hall. (1439).

SIMMONS, Mr Longford, O.F. The junior partner in the law firm of Merrill & Simmons of Melford. He had been Walker's fag-master when at School, and was a great favourite of Mr Quelch. However, his apparent embezzlement of £2,000 from Walker's Aunt did not enhance his reputation in his old school. Even the explanation of his well-meant actions did not do him a great deal of merit. (953-955).

SIMPSON. One of Colonel Ponsonby's keepers at Ponsonby Hall. (1336).

SIN SONG, Mr. Secretary to Mr O Bo. It was he who put into effect his employer's orders to take Wun Lung by force so that he could be taken back to China, and there adopted as Mr O's son. His urbane suavity never left him no matter what the circumstances, and his philosophical, good-natured acceptance of defeat must have puzzled the Famous Five. (HBE 43).

SING SING. Ferrers Locke's Chinese servant in Baker Street.

SINGAPORE. The far Eastern port visited thrice by the Famous Five. On their visits to the Pacific with Redwing and Mauleverer; and on their way to China with Ferrers Locke.

SINGH, Jam Bahadur. Uncle to Hurree Singh, and Regent of Bhanipur during his nephew's minority. A kindly man who has known Colonel Wharton for many years, both as a soldier and as a friend. He is always delighted to welcome Hurree Singh's friends either to his country or to Her Embassy in London.

SINGH, Hurree Jamset Ram, Nabob of Bhanipur. To see him in the Remove at Greyfriars one would never guess that he is the absolute monarch of his Himalayan country. Indeed, when there with "Inky", his friends hardly recognised him for the placid, easy going schoolboy he is. Orphaned, he was brought to England at the request of his uncle, the Jam Bahadur, (Regent during Hurree Singh's minority), by Colonel Wharton, who stands in loco parentis. Running away from Beechwood Academy in favour of Greyfriars, Inky, (so called because of his complexion!), soon became a close friend of Harry Wharton's and eventually a member of the Famous Five. His English, taught him by the wise moonshee, Mook Mookerjee, is enough to make the angels weep, (with laughter!), and for all the good Mr Quelch's castigations do, he might as well give up! Hurree Singh fools many people as to the depth of his thinking and the power of his intellect, but manys the time that he finds solutions not apparent to his chums. Incapable of a dishonest or disloyal thought, it was only he who saw through da Costa and his treachery when Captain Marker wanted Harry Wharton expelled.

SIT-IN STRIKE AT GREYFRIARS, THE. (Title HBE Volume 35) . Appointed temporary Head in Dr Locke's absence, Mr Hacker soon proved his petty tyrannical nature. Determined to resist the expulsion of seven Removites, the whole form, under the direction of Mauleverer, barred themselves in the tuckshop, and fought off all comers – including an "army" of toughs employed by Mr Hacker. It was not until the Head returned, and sat in calm judgement on the accused, that the situation was resolved.

SIX BOYS IN A BOAT. (Title HBE Volume 11) . Hiring a boat for the summer holidays, the Famous Five, with Bunter in tow, set out from Kingston-upon-Thames to explore the Thames. Chased by "Shifty" Spooner, who was a willing ally in Ponsonby and Co.'s villainy, they had an eventful holiday. Bunter by accident discovered Spooner's interest in the Water Lily – a valuable cache of stolen goods, placed there by Spooner who was trying, after his release from prison, to repossess the boat and her cargo.

SIXTH FORM. The senior form at Greyfriars is composed of the oldest members of the school, (except for Reggie Coker, the most brilliant scholar) . From its ranks are selected the School Prefects. Most "Bloods" are Sixth Formers, although there are a few in the Fifth.

SIXTH FORM GREEN. Amongst the privileges enjoyed by Sixth Form men is that of strolling on Sixth Form Green – a fenced off portion of grass in the Quad. Any lesser mortal who crosses the Rubicon can be certain of six from the nearest prefect!

SIXTH FORM REBELLION, THE. (Title GBC Volume 36). When Sir Hilton Popper forced Dr Locke into resigning, he had already selected his ideal replacement - a Mr James Carnforth. A man whose idea it was to belittle even the Head of School publicly, as well as cane prefects, (even if it was Loder!). It is not surprising that Wingate, unable to tolerate such behaviour, led a rebellion against his authority. Nothing loathe, the Remove soon joined in, despite orders to the contrary from Wingate.

SKELTON, Mr Sempronius. An eccentric millionaire to whom Bunter gave his umbrella, (it was raining), and his watch, (he looked poor), in an aberrant moment of generosity, brought on by reading Dickens' Christmas Carol. As a result of this, Bunter was invited to spend Christmas with Mr Skelton. Not, as he imagined in feasting, but in giving alms. The millionaire's family, worried about the dwindling fortune, persuaded him to go abroad, thus ending Bunter's dreams of a luxurious holiday. (HBE 58).

SKEPPLETON, General Frederick. A lifelong friend of Colonel Wharton who rented Hawkscliff House one summer. He invited Harry Wharton and Co. for a picnic. Bunter opened the letter in the hope of finding money and took a party for tea, without reckoning that the General would be able to recognise the Famous Five. Almost arrested as would-be burglars, Bunter and his party were glad to escape with only a taxi fare! (693).

SKIMSON, Mr. The tutor employed by Mr Penman to prepare Wally Bunter for St Jim's. What he must have thought of the change in personality when WGB changed places with Wally is a matter of no conjecture! (570).

SKINNER, Anthony. Brother of James, and cousin to Harold. As nasty a piece of work as his brother and cousin, he is as equally at home in a shady card game or a vicious jape. (513).

SKINNER, Harold. Sharing Study No 11 with Snoop and Stott, this mean, vicious snob can be guaranteed to play any trick on any man to either belittle, demean or disgrace him. Nothing is too low. He is Greyfriars answer to Ponsonby with whom he delights in allying himself against his chief enemies, the Famous Five. Any new man not possessed of wealth or a title can be sure of feeling the rough edge of Skinner's so-called humour. His one talent is drawing and he has the makings of a fine cartoonist. Unfortunately, this talent is used to show his envy and hatred which, if he uses, will be in the worst of political cartoons - assuredly lacking in any taste.

SKINNER, James. Brother of Anthony, (cf). (513).

SKIP. A pickpocket who had lifted the Famous Five's wealth but failed to do the same to Coker. The latter determined to reform the waif, and persuaded his Aunt Judy to pay Skip's fees at Greyfriars. Here, he found life more than difficult; on the one hand, the Famous Five, determined to believe in him and, on the other, the "bad hats" equally resolved not to. Vernon Smith, especially, had a down on him and, despite Skip saving him from expulsion, he continued to hound Skip. Vernon Smith even accused him of stealing a locket, containing Miss Bullivant's picture, which was his one possession. This act, evil in intent, led directly to Skip's identification as Miss Bullivant's brother, Richard, who had been stolen as a child. (HBE 62-63).

SLANEY. A hand in Whiffle's circus who had been sacked for cheeking the manager, Mr Dance. He was reinstated by Bunter, resplendent in the owner's wig and clothes. As a result Slaney proved loyal to Bunter - chucking out many Friars who dared take objection to the "owner's" insults! (1069).

SLEUTH OF GREYFRIARS, THE. (Title HBE Volume 33). Mr John Hazeldene, despite his innocence, had fled rather than face police questioning, after a robbery at the bank where he works. He hid near Greyfriars and, as the stolen notes were being passed in that area, the search for the guilty man was centred here. Coker, who can do all things best, determined to find the criminal, but only succeeded in enraging Colonel Hazeldene, (Mr John's father), who had lately arrived to prove his son's innocence! Following the arrest of the robber and the proving of Mr Hazeldene's innocence, the Famous Five went to London to celebrate the Jubilee. This was almost spoiled for them by the pursuit of Jack Drake by Jimmy the Fox, whose arrest in Oxford Street was a highlight of the Royal Day.

SLICK FLICK. A gunman from New York and lieutenant to Barney McCann. He came to England with his boss to kidnap Fisher T. Fish in the wake of Mr Fish "cornering pork". He first took Bunter for Fishy, an understandable mistake, since Bunter was carrying a letter which began "Dear Fisher"! He later held the Head at gun-point, but was arrested by Harry Wharton. (GBC 25).

SLIM JIM. A master burglar of renown about whom the police knew nothing until Mr Quelch, late one night, saw him without his mask. Mr Quelch was kidnapped and the Remove taken by Mr Lamb, the replacement for Mr Woose. After a long and bitter feud between Mr Lamb and Vernon Smith, it transpired that Mr Lamb was Slim Jim. (HBE 29-30).

SLIM JIM. Vernon Smith, in one of his periodic feuds against Harry Wharton, announced that he was cutting games practice. As though this was not enough, he persuaded Mr Quelch to give him extra tuition for the Head's Latin Prize, but did not do the exercise set by Mr Quelch. Still as rebellious as ever, he refused the proffered olive branch and got Joe Banks to hire Slim Jim and Jerry the Pug to beat up Wharton. Remorseful at last, he came to Wharton's rescue. (1013).

SLIM JIM. Bunter had not been allowed to return to school following his running away and impersonating Mr Whiffles. However, return he did, and in the process was instrumental in the capture of Slim Jim who was burgling the Head's safe. Bunter was reprieved for raising the alarm. (1076).

SLUMMOCK'S ALLEY. A thieves' kitchen in London where Skip spent much of his youth. It was here that Barney the Binger taught him to pick pockets. (1545).

SMALL GAME. The school term for the Second Form Games and the ground whereon they are played. (1501).

SMEDLEY, Mr Charles. Uncle to Mr Eustace Smedley. He had been up at Oxford with Mr Prout, a lifelong friend of his. When Mr Prout announced that he knew Eustace, the temporary master was most put out, until he discovered that Prout had not seen him for many years. However, Mr Charles Smedley, writing to Prout, told him that his nephew was teaching in Canada. A story that did not entirely convince the Fifth Form Master. (HBE 51-52).

SMEDLEY, Mr Eustace, M.A., Oxon. A professional school master who was on the books of Leggett & Teggers. Offered the post of temporary master at Greyfriars he accepted with alacrity, only to have Teggers offer him a permanent position in Canada. Obviously preferable to a "temp", he jumped at the chance, little realising that Teggers intended to use his name and go to Greyfriars as "Smedley". (HBE 51-52).

SMILER, The. One of the gang employed by Captain Reynham to capture Lord Reynham. After attempting Sir Peter Lanchester's life, he led several attempts at kidnapping Bunter, who was playing Lord Reynham. He was captured, promptly escaped, only to be recaptured by Tomlinson, a private detective. (HBE 14).

SMILEY. In the employ of "Mr Knowles", with whom he kidnapped Arthur Durance. (1130).

SMILEY DICK. An habitue of the Cross Keys. (494).

SMILEY JOE. Having served five years in prison through the work of Ferrers Locke, his first thought on his release was to "get" the man who had been the cause of his sentence. Paul Dallas, contemplating running away from school was able to warn Ferrers Locke of his attacker, and so win himself a valuable friend who could clear his name of an offence for which he would otherwise have been expelled. (1002).

SMILEY JOHNSON. Employed with "Nosey" by Poynings to kidnap Coker. They successfully carried out their part of the business and kept Coker captive in Hillcrest Bungalow, near Cliff House. (GBC 29).

SMILEY'S STORES, Courtfield. A small grocers shop outside which Coker busked in his war effort to cheer people up. Like Queen Victoria, the audience "were not amused"! (528).

SMITH, Edward William, (Major). He shares Study No 2 in the Fifth with Fitzgerald.

SMITH, Henry, (Minimus). The youngest of three brothers, he is a fag in the Second Form.

SMITH, Robert Fortescue, (Minor). The second of three brothers. He is in the Remove where he shares Study No 8 with Elliott. He is not in the forefront of form affairs, either sporting or academic.

SMITH, Skid. Micky the Sprat's accomplice in a smash and grab raid on Mr Lazarus' shop. Unlike Micky, he escaped to their rendezvous, The Black Bull at Lantham. Micky tried to get word to Skid about the hiding place of the loot by sending Bunter with a Holiday Annual containing a coded message. However, he was arrested before the message arrived. It was this Holiday Annual that interested Ponsonby so much when he harrassed "The Greyfriars Hikers" during their holiday. (1331).

SMITH, Soapy. A disreputable racing tough who hangs around the public houses in the Courtfield and Friardale area, and especially the Three Fishers. He certainly took bets from Gilbert Tracy while he was at Greyfriars. He still acts as bookmaker for Vernon Smith when Jerry Hawke and Joe Banks are absent.

SMITHSON. A staunch supporter of Courtney at Highcliffe.

SMUGGLERS' CAVE, Blackrock. A large cave which, legend tells, was used by smugglers on Blackrock Island. It was here that Young Mr Rance held Mr Vernon Smith and, later, Vernon Smith, captive in an effort to recoup his gambling losses, and to replace the clients' money he had spent. (HBE 50).

SMUGGLERS CAVE, Pegg.   Under the rocky promontory to the north of the village are many small beaches and caves accessible only from the sea.   The largest is known as Smugglers Cave.   Extending many hundred yards into the cliff the entrance is covered at high tide, although much of the cave is above the highwater mark.   A secret passage runs from here to the school and was used by Captain Compton to land contraband.   The same cave was used by Soames to imprison Tom Redwing when he tried to force him to yield his fortune.

SNAITH, Cecil.   "A weak cowardly cringing", character who had been expelled for theft while in the Shell at Greyfriars.   He ran away from home and tried to blackmail Vernon Smith without success. (418).

SNELL, Sid.   A member of Lantham Speedway who, with Joe Banks, the bookmaker, fixed both the races and the odds to their mutual benefit.   Shown up by the astuteness of Vernon Smith he received a sound thrashing at the hands of Boy McLaren, once their scheming had been exposed. (1220).

SNIGGERSON.   He stole a valuable diamond pin from Mr Isaacs who was visiting Wharton Lodge on business.   To avoid arrest he sold it to Bunter for 1/- who, in turn, sold it to Fish for £2/10/0.   Fishy, as cute as ever, saw a fat profit, but instead, found himself trying to explain to Mr Grimes how he came to be in possession of stolen goods ! (HBE 8).

SNIKE & SNAGGS.   A firm of stockbrokers in the city.   Their advertisement persuaded Mr Penfold to invest his all in one of their fraudulent schemes.   But for Sir Montague Newland "persuading" them to buy back the shares, Mr Penfold would have lost his nest egg. (843).

SNIPE, The.   A most appropriately unpleasant nickname for a most unpleasant type – Edgar Caffyn. (HBE 9).

SNIPEY.   With Pug Pilkinson, he tried to dissuade Mr Lascelles from meeting The Game Chicken.   This was all a misunderstanding created by Bunter who had answered Larry's phone and given the wrong answer ! (1321-22).

SNOOKS, Mr.   Father of Montague.   He brought his son to Greyfriars in the hope of curing his romantic fantasies. (814).

SNOOKS, Alfred. Having worked in the Dionysius Motor Tricycle Factory, he knew that part of "Methusalah", Bob Cherry's "Bargain", was made of platinum and, thus, worth far more than the price paid for the machine. He, therefore, followed the Famous Five on their holiday tour, with the intention of stealing the trike with the aid of Bill Harris. (HBE 36).

SNOOKS, Montague Wilfred. He was sent to Greyfriars to cure him of his romantic fantasising. For example, he insisted that his uncle was Sir Fulke Pulteney! Disbelieved by all, he was shown up as a liar by Temple who owns a Debrett's, (he would!). To cure him of his dreams, Wibley dressed up as Sir Fulke and gave him the fright of his life. It is to be hoped that he profitted from the lesson. He left school almost immediately after this - to avoid embarrassment of the exposure. (814).

SNOOKSON, Jane. The very ordinary name, (but real!), of Leanora La Riviere, now Mrs. Peter Carter. (GBC 20-21).

SNOOP, Mr Josiah. The father of Sydney James. An entrepeneur whose geese did not lay the expected golden eggs, he found himself serving a sentence of three years for embezzlement. He escaped from prison, and was helped to flee the country by Vernon Smith. He then enlisted, and his sentence commuted for bravery in action. A weak character like his son, but without the viciousness, he is one of fortunes forgotten ones who always fails. After his demobilisation he went to Canada with his brother-in-law, Mr Higgins, for whom he now works.

SNOOP, Sidney James. With Skinner and Stott he pollutes Study No 11 in the Remove. He is not as bad as his leader, Skinner but, nevertheless, goes along with any plot hatched by that arch Macchiavelli. He has managed twice to amaze the world, and probably himself most of all. The first time when he defied his uncle, (who pays the bills), and met his father; and the second when he saved Joyce the woodcutter's son from the river. One could hope from these two episodes that there is a future for Sidney James but, as weak as his father, it seems that the downward path is his choice.

SNOPE, Inspector. One of the previous Inspectors of police at Courtfield before Mr Grimes' days. After receiving a tip from Bunter, he stopped Melchior and Barengro's caravan, and was amazed to discover Harry Wharton and Co. in charge of the situation, having overpowered the gipsies who had kidnapped Marjorie Hazeldene. (5).

SNUFSON, Mr. A Lantham stamp dealer who pronounced that Desmond's Sandwich Island 2c stamp was not an original but merely a facsimile. (425).

SO FAT. Secretary to Mr Wun Chung Lung in Canton. He was a pleasant companion to the Friars, and proved an excellent guide to the sights of the city. (1183).

SOAMES, James. The ever suave master crook who having made and lost a fortune slave-trading in the Pacific, entered Mr Vernon Smith's service as his valet. Abusing the trust placed in him, he was prepared to stick at nought to prevent Tom Redwing finding his uncle's treasure. Ever endowed with the proverbial luck, he escaped his just deserts on this occasion - as he did when he went to England to try to gain his revenge. Next he sank to theft and, robbing Lantham Post Office with Rat Hankey, had yet another encounter with the Famous Five - this time seeking a cigarette case containing a secret message as to the whereabouts of the plunder. When the Famous Five went to Eastcliff Lodge as "Sir William Bird's" guests, they little realised they would meet their old enemy again, (he had returned into service). Yet again he escaped justice. For all his chicanery and dishonesty, there can be litle doubt that Harry Wharton and Co. have a great respect and, possibly, a sneaking admiration for him. (GBC 11; HBA 4; HBE 41).

SOAPY JONES. See Jones, Soapy.

SOAPY SMITH. See Smith, Soapy.

SOLEIL D'OR. An auberge, (or Inn), some ten miles inland from Marseilles. Rawlings, the steward in the Firefly, suggested a trip there to take lunch. His idea was to strand Valentine Compton's guests so that the ship would be free of encumbrances and, therefore, able to continue with her smuggling. Bunter became separated from the rest of the party and so inadvertently was able to effect their rescue with Valentine's help. (1508).

SOO. Mr O's steward in his aeroplane, The Ancient and Benevolent Pigeon. (1544).

SOO. The Tongan steersman on Barney Hall's lugger. His thick hair saved him from a nasty injury when Ysabel Dick hit him in an attempt to escape from the boat. (1591).

SOUARAD DIN, Sheik. Chief of the Oued Nail tribe who was paid by Tiger Bronx to keep Bunter's party captive while he "worked" on Bunter to make him hand over his fortune. Bob Cherry managed to free his hands and overpower the gangster, so that the Friars could escape unscathed. (1389).

SOUTHEND. On their return from the Pacific, helping Tom Redwing find his fortune, Skinner put about the story that the Famous Five had in fact only been to Southend for their holidays! He followed this up by forging a paragraph in the Southend paper. Mr Quelch, known to be a "downy bird", did not take long to uncover the origin of the rumour. (1027).

SOUTHGATE SCHOOL. Hurree Singh's cousin, Dhoolah Das, is at this school, which is some distance from Greyfriars. Without a fixture one day, they arranged a football match, only to discover that their rules differed from the visitors – as did the shape of the ball! (306).

SPADGER, The. A great friend of Sir Jimmy Vivian's from his days in Carker's Rents. When the Spadger visited Greyfriars, Skinner tried to frame him for the theft of Vernon Smith's wallet. Smithy had given it to Skinner so that he could prove the waif's innocence, having expected something of this nature. After a much interrupted study tea, it was Smithy who had the idea of trying to "place" the Spadger, and accordingly persuaded his father to help. (491).

SPANIARDS CAVE. One of the largest caves under Garth Cliff, wherein Scaife imprisoned Vivian and his Greyfriars guests. (812).

SPARKINSON, Professor. A more than eccentric inventor and explorer. He rented The Willows, a house on Courtfield Common, for a time. He amazed everybody with his virility, agility and strength; all due to an invention of his – The New Elixir. He gave some to Alonzo Todd whom he saw being ragged by Ponsonby and Co. Alonzo used the elixir to try to reform the Remove, until Bunter stole the bottle. After a short stay in England, the professor left on an expedition to Central Africa. (HBE 20).

SPARKS, Jim. A longshoreman from Pegg. When Ponsonby and Co. with Skinner stole Mr Redwing's boat and wrecked her, it was Sparks who took them off Shark's Tooth Island. Well paid for his trouble, he then tried blackmailing the knuts. But for Vernon Smith who paid more for the truth than Sparks got for silence, the facts might never have come out. (922).

SPENCER, Captain Eric, O.F. Robbing the bank at Lantham on his way to stay with the Head at Greyfriars, he was seen removing his disguise by Vernon Smith. As he was out of bounds at the time, it was only the presence of the stolen money in his pockets that led Mr Quelch and the Head to believe Smithy's story. Even then they did not, and would not, believe that Captain Spencer was the robber. Indeed, Smithy's persistence in this accusation led him to the Punishment Room. Eventually, the Captain was arrested, and Smithy lost no time in rubbing salt in Mr Quelch's wounds caused by his disbelief in the Bounder! (HBE 75).

SPENCER. Chauffeur to Sir George Cholmondely. (GBC 19).

SPEZZI, Orlando. A variety artiste who performs a hypnotism act. He convinced Coker, if nobody else, of his powers and this gave the aspirant to the Form Eleven the idea of hypnotising Blundell to make him put Coker in the Team ! Blundell went along with the idea, but Coker's experiences of being used as a football rid him, for a while, of further sporting ambitions ! (834).

SPOFFORD, Mr. A supply teacher who was to have taken the Remove during Mr Quelch's absence with a cold. Instead, he went to Rookwood for a spell. Wibley, who had taken a message to this effect impersonated Mr Spofford, and kept his word to thrash the Famous Five. He was exposed when Mr Prout described the locum to Mr Quelch. Wibley barely escaped capture by the Head and the Prefects. He was not so lucky with regard to his form mates ! (1341).

SPOONER, Shifty. Released from prison after serving a two year sentence for robbing Popper Court, he tried to buy back his old boat, The Water Lily, wherein was hidden his plunder. Failing in this, he tried many times, while the Famous Five were sailing up the Thames in her, to steal the boat. He fell in with Ponsonby and Co. who were ragging the Friars, and each found the other a useful and willing weapon in their respective endeavours. However, he failed and ultimately, (after Bunter had found the cache), was arrested by Inspector Jones. (HBE 11).

SPOOPHEM, Mr. Purporting to be a member of the College of Heralds, this man will trace your family tree, and ignoring the truth, find it to be of great antiquity – as he did with the Bunters'. (897).

SPOUTING BILLY. The name by which an itinerant Master of Arts of Oxford was known to other Gentlemen of the Road. (HBE 80; GL 3).

SPRAT, Micky the. See Micky the Sprat.

SPRAT, Mr Joseph. A bookmaker who sometimes patronises the Cross Keys. He was bribed by da Costa to write to Harry Wharton and implicate him in betting. Faced with trouble from this accusation, Wharton was saved by Bob Cherry who had the idea of making Spratt identify his client; which he was unable to do. (1063).

SQUAW MOUNTAIN. One of the highest peaks to the west of the Kicking Cayuse Ranch in Texas. A lonely barren area, it is one of the Rio Kid's hideouts. While here, he was able to help Vernon Smith capture Jad Blake. (HBE 32).

SQUIDGE, Mr Thomas, (Tommy). A racing tout who frequents the Cross Keys. His failure to blackmail the Famous Five did not deter him. A terrified Angel gave his name as Wharton and a promise to pay £5. Squidge was invited to the school by Mr Quelch and, as he could not point out Wharton, he left in dudgeon. Angel did not escape so lightly! (1613).

SQUIFF. The aptly obvious nickname given to Field, on his arrival at Greyfriars. It is not difficult to see its origin: Sampson **Q**uincy **I**ffley **F**ield.

SQUINNEY. So called because of his affliction, he made, with "Nosey", a successful smash and grab gang. However, Bunter, who had been stranded by Vernon Smith, saw the furniture van they used, and overheard their conversation. This led, not only to their arrest but, also, and more important to Bunter, a large reward! (1531-2).

SQUINTY. A member of a gang of poachers, one of whose members, Bill, had been imprisoned by Sir Hilton Popper. Vowing vengeance, Squinty, George and Fred, set upon Sir Hilton. The Famous Five, out of bounds on Popper's Island, went to the rescue, and were rewarded by a form prize. (1309).

STACEY, Inspector. Stationed at Wimford, he was in charge of several cases involving Friars. ie Elias Poindexter and the burning of The Old Mill; and the robbing of a Wimford bank by Freddy Paget.

STACEY, Captain A, O.F. He was married, according to Colonel Wharton, to "a sort of second or third cousin" of the Colonel and Miss Wharton, and had been "unfortunate in some respects". The Colonel tried to help the adventurer, (to whom any method was legitimate in making ends meet). The Captain permitted the Colonel to pay his son Ralph's fees at Greyfriars, until he found another venture in which to involve himself. An ungrateful man, he was an unregenerate cynic. (HBE 16-17; HBE 18).

STACEY, Ralph. The only son of Captain Stacey. He is identical in appearance to his distant cousin, Harry Wharton, and was sent to Greyfriars by Colonel Wharton. He took a prompt dislike, (fired by jealousy), to his relative. Taking advantage of their similarity, he did not care if he was caught in any of his nefarious activities - particularly as Harry Wharton seemed always to get the blame. The more so since Stacey, notably a brilliant sportsman, and also a "toady", soon had himself made both Head of Form and Junior Games Captain. He was seen through after a while by some of the form, but it took a long time, (and a perilous one for Harry Wharton), before Mr Quelch finally learned the truth, purely by chance overhearing Fish blackmailing Stacey. Faced with expulsion, he remained the same cool customer, unrepentantly leaving school to go abroad with his father. (HBE 16-17; HBE 18).

STACEY SPECIAL. (Title HBE Volume 18). More correctly "The Greyfiars Double", this volume contains the full saga of the Stacey-Wharton feud. (See also "Harry Wharton's Enemy"; and "The Black Sheep of Greyfriars").

STACLIFFE-by-SEA, Sussex. Invited to stay at The Firs by Ponsonby and Co. Mauleverer, unable to find the house, met the Famous Five. This proved as well, since Pon. and Co. were intending to fleece Mauly at cards. Despite his efforts not to gamble, his hosts insisted. A predicament from which Mauly was rescued after a battle royal between Friars and Highcliffians. (706).

STAFF. The Common Room is at present composed of the following members:

Dr. Locke,	Headmaster and Sixth Form.
Mr. Prout,	Fifth Form,
Mr. Hacker,	Shell,
Mr. Capper,	Upper Fourth Form,
Mr. Quelch,	Remove,
Mr. Wiggins,	Third Form,
Mr. Twigg,	Second Form.

Other members of staff include:

Mr. Lascelles,	Mathematics and Games,
M. Charpentier,	French,
Hr. Gans,	German,
Mr. Flatt,	Music,
Mr. Sharp,	" ,
Mr. Woose,	Librarian.

STATTON, Mr Arthur. An old friend of Mr Henry Coker. After he had been made scapegoat for a city swindle, Mr Coker helped him to escape overseas. Poynings obtained possession of a letter from Mr Statton to Mr Coker and used it to blackmail his employer, until he was "persuaded" to part with the letter by Coker and the Famous Five. (984).

STEELE, Mr. A magistrate in the Strand Court who sentenced Vernon Smith to three years in Borstal after Alf Johnson had placed a stolen watch in Smithy's pocket. This harsh sentence was reported in the newspapers. These were seen by Tom Redwing, (to be precise it was Smithy's photograph Tom recognised), and he went to London, with the Head, to help free his friend. (933).

STEELE, Mr Richard. Inspector of Police at Scotland Yard. He was in charge of the Courtfield Cracksman Case. As he had trained as a schoolmaster before joining the police force, he was able to enter Greyfriars without suspicion, in charge of the Remove by day, while hunting the Cracksman by night. His nom-de-guerre was a clever pun on his real name - Irons ! Harry Wharton discovered his real identity, as did Bunter. Since the latter could not be trusted to keep his own counsel, he was rusticated for a time until the case was completed. (HBE 5) .

STENSON. Footman to Sir George Tipton. (1646) .

STERNDALE, Dr. Headmaster of Greyfriars during the eighteenth century. He burnt his cane and birch because he was against corporal punishment. However, he proved a tyrant as vindictive as Mr Brander in many ways. Such as bread and water diets for weeks on end for malefactors; impositions that took a term to write; and scrubbing floors. "His unhappy charges soon found themselves sighing for the return of the birch and the cane" !

STEVENAGE. The famly name of the Earls of Trant. (1526) .

STEWART, Edward. A member of the Shell and usually in the Form teams.

STIMSON. Chauffeur to Mr Vernon Smith. (1222) .

STODGES "CAVALIER RELIQUES". A learned tome written in 1724 containing family histories and the coats of arms of the oldest English families. There is a copy in the Greyfriars Library, and to Bunter's delight it mentions the de Bonterres, his Norman ancestors, (except that the original bearer of the name died without issue!) . (897) .

STOKES. An erstwhile member of "Captain Flash's" gang. When Harry Wharton and Co. hired the Captain's caravan from Mr Lazarus who had bought it, Stokes and Rabbit tried to steal it so that they could search for their leader's cache of stolen jewels. (704-705) .

STONE, Barney. Prior to Mr Vernon Smith's purchase of the Kicking Cayuse Ranch in Texas, he held undisputed sway. He made a more than comfortable income out of rustling the cattle in his charge and splitting the profits with Pete Corcoran, (the head of the rustling gang) . Vernon Smith suspected the foreman after he had given Smithy the wrong directions, which led, not to the town of Hatchet, but into a quicksand. The same quicksand in which the previous owner had met his death. Smithy had a hard time proving his case against the foreman but eventually, with the help of Captain Hall of the Texas Rangers, he trapped Stone. (HBE 32) .

STONE, Ulick. A former pickpocket, and son of "Mr Knowles". He was sent to Greyfriars in the place of Arthur Durance, whom his father had kidnapped, so that he could lay claim to the fortune left by Durance's mother. Stone was exposed when Vernon Smith managed to engineer Durance's escape. In the confusion that followed the revelation of the truth, Stone managed to escape. Even had Smithy not realised the truth, it is unlikely that Stone would have lasted long at Greyfriars, since he is used to a life of cigarettes and no discipline. (1130-31).

STONEVILLE, H.M.P. The London prison to which Vernon Smith was sent pending the finding of a Borstal place for him, after he had been found guilty of the theft of a gold watch that Alf Johnson had stolen. He was luckily not in "The Stone Jug" for long, as Tom Redwing was able, with Dr Locke's help, to secure his release. (933).

STORK, "Pop". The proprietor of the Pack Hotel, Packsaddle, where Vernon Smith and friends stayed on their way to the Kicking Cayuse Ranch. (1580).

STOTT, William. The least member of Study No 11. He will enter into Skinner's plots but, on occasions, (rare though they be), he will refuse to go to the extremes planned by his leader.

STRAUS, Mr. A moneylender in Courtfield. Snoop, in deep financial trouble, had borrowed money from him to pay his gambling debts. Nugent, soft-heartedly, lent Snoop the Cricket Club funds to pay the moneylender. Smithy, as cynical as ever, realised the origins of Snoop's windfall, and the roots of Nugent's apparent theft of the cricket moneys and, therefore, gave Snoop the cash, (under vows of secrecy), to replace the missing funds. (434).

STUBBS. A bicycle dealer in Courtfield to whom "Honest" George Jobson claimed he had offered de Courcy's bicycle, but was unable to get a good price. Mr Stubbs is well known to all Friars for obtaining spare parts and for doing major repairs to their "jiggers". (1056).

STUCE, Inspector. Stationed at Seahill, Sussex, he was in charge of the case against Nessuno who made several attempts on Mr Vernon Smith's life. (1525).

STUDIES. All members of the school in the Remove and above have a study. Members of the Sixth Form each have a Bedroom-cum-Study to themselves; while lesser mortals have to share. Their chief function is, (as their name suggests!), for study, but they are also used for the preparation and consumption of "feeds". A privelege not lightly bestowed, the withdrawal of which is viewed with more than dismay by the punished. (For study lists see Appendix 2).

STUMMER, Mr. An Estate Agent in Courtfield from whom, to his amazement, Mauleverer bought High Oaks for use as a school after the Remove had walked out in protest at Mr Quelch's dismissal by the Head. (1044).

SUGDEN, Dandy. He entered Sir Hilton Popper's sevice as valet using forged credentials in order to steal the Moonstone. This he gave to Bunter for safe keeping while he was "taking a dip". Having been arrested on suspicion of the theft, Sugden sent J. Judson to Greyfriars to get the jewel from its guardian. (1157).

SUGDEN, Sylvester. Posing as a wealthy city businessman with a country home, Beech House, in Surrey, Sugden was actually the head of a gang of thieves, as well as being a "fence" and moneylender. Dick Lancaster's late uncle had been one of the gang's main assets, until his death through drink. By that time, however, he had taught Dick all he knew so that he, in turn, became the gang's major asset. Sugden, to whom Sir Hilton Popper was deeply in debt, forced the baronet to enter Lancaster at Greyfriars where he was to serve Sugden's nefarious ends. When "The Wizard" rebelled against his past, Sugden tried all sorts of pressures to keep his protege off the straight and narrow. After Harry Wharton had unmasked Lancaster, Sugden had him kidnapped. This led directly to the latter's arrest, as Ferrers Locke was called in to help solve the mystery of Wharton's disappearance. (HBE 7).

SULEIMAN the SEER. A sand diviner in Biskra. He told Bob Cherry of his father's fate and that of the accompanying escort of French soldiers. It is most likely that Bou Saoud or Mustapha ben Mohammed paid the seer to pass the message as part of their plan to obtain the "Eye of Ahmed". (866).

SULOO. The steersman in Parson's boat the Sea Cat. He was assaulted by Ysabel Dick to prevent Parsons picking up the "Greyfriars Adventurers", adrift in the Pacific. (1594).

SUNDABAND, M.V. Homeward bound from China, the Silver Star picked up the sole survivor, Vanderpeck, after she had struck a reef and sunk. Ferrers Locke suspected what had happened, and so was able to save the Captain, despite the mate's efforts to dissuade him. (1186).

SUNDERBUND, S.S. The ship travelled in by Mauleverer and his party from Singapore to Suva in Fiji, on their way to Kalua. It was while on board that the Friars first met, and fell out with, Van Dink - to whom the name of Mauleverer was obviously known. (1589).

SUTCLIFFE, Mr John. A temporary master who was on his way to Greyfriars when he was kidnapped and walled up in a cave in the Pike, without a care for his survival, by Gentleman Jim. Luckily, the Famous Five were around and were able to free him. (992).

SUTTON, Sir James. The owner of Sutton Manor, a large house facing Courtfield Common. Ferrers Locke had just begun his case against Slim Jim and was keeping a midnight vigil in the hope of gaining information. He followed a man who turned out to be on his way to rob the Manor. The fact that he had prevented a robbery was poor consolation to Mr Locke for losing Slim Jim. (1663).

SUVA, Fiji. The capital and main port of Fiji. Mauleverer and his friends arrived here in the S.S. Sunderbund on their way to look for Mauly's Cousin Brian. The night before they docked, Van Dink tried to throw Mauly overboard. (1589).

SWAIN, Mr William, (Bill). The mate in the Firefly. An ill-tempered man, he was a shareholder with the Captain, Jim Compton, and Rawlings, in the smuggling business they carried on from the yacht. When Captain Compton was hesitating about giving up smuggling, Swain followed Rawlings' lead in a mutiny which led to the Comptons being marooned on an island off Corsica. However, he had no part in their being left without food or water. (HBE 48).

SWEET, Mr. The caterer in Friardale. Miss Primrose hired him to provide refreshments at a dance held soon after Cliff House School opened. Ionides, who had gone uninvited to the function, was taken by Miss Primrose to be one of his waiters, and she complained bitterly to Mr Sweet about the standard of service ! (59).

SWINGER'S CELEBRATED CIRCUS. While the show was at Woodend, Bunter was invited to join the circus. His visions of stardom faded when he realised that he was to join the "Weird Freaks" ! Indignation followed but, as he had cheeked Mr Quelch, his way back to school was hazardous, to say the least ! As usual, luck was on his side - he disturbed a burglar as he tried to get into school. (1160).

SYKES. A Sixth Former and a prefect. A good sportsman who shines on both football and cricket fields. He is particularly noted as a bowler. When Bunter crocked Sykes' wrist just before a big fixture, the dismay can be imagined. Sykes is a friend of Wingate and is popular with nearly all the school. He is a fair man who does not over-indulge in the use of the cane.

SYLVESTER. An Old Friar who was ill on the occasion of one of the Old Boys matches. His replacement, Westbrook, arrived too late for the match, but in time to identify "Chester" as an imposter. (844).

SYLVESTER, Roderick. The unspoilt son of Mr Abraham Sylvester, an American millionaire. He is a fag in the Second Form, where he is particularly friendly with Hop Hi. He is a far better specimen of humanity than Fish, (although any comparison with Fishy is odious!).

T.

TADGER. A local ruffian hired by Loder to prevent some of the First Eleven playing in a match at Lantham against the Loamshire Regimental Eleven. Potter, Courtney, North, Valence and Greene were left behind. (The first three, team members; the others, reserves). (435).

TADGER. A member of "Slimy" Sugden's gang. With the Weasel he assaulted Ferrers Locke in a final bid to avoid the arrest of the gang. When Tadger was about to pull trigger on Mr Locke, Dick Lancaster was just in time to save the detective's life at the expense of a serious wound to himself. It was his going to the rescue like this that persuaded Ferrers Locke to advise his being "let off". (1219).

TADGER, Montgomery. The actor who played the Title role in Puss-in-Boots in Mr Whiffles' pantomime at Lantham. (409).

TADPOLE. The nickname of a Highcliffe Junior whose name is not mentioned. He caught Ponsonby and Co. trying to blind Tubb with mirrors so that he would steer the Remove Eight into a bridge and so lose a race against Highcliffe. (918).

TAGGLES. The St Jim's School porter. He is about as crusty and perverse as Gosling !

TALBOYS. In the Fourth Form at Highcliffe and an occasional member of Ponsonby's gang. He helped Vernon Smith in his bid to oust and get expelled the Famous Five and Linley. His part was in the capture and tying up of some of the Remove so that they would lose a Scouting contest. (247).

TALUPA. The Tonganese cook on board the Aloha. When Soames put Bunter under him in the Galley, he took delight in using the ropes-end on the man who knew how to deal with "niggers" and servants! When the Friars regained control of the boat, Bunter got his revenge! (GBC 11).

TAMINAHO. The cannibal chief of an island at which the Golden Arrow stopped to buy fresh fruit. He bid ten women and fifteen fat pigs for Bunter whom he fancied for a feast! (1021).

TANG LAO. The son of Tang Wang. He hired Guisppe Sasso to make an attempt on Wung Lung's life. When this failed, he went up in an aeroplane which attacked the Silver Star while she was steaming through the Red Sea. A sudden storm arose and caught the plane which crashed, killing all on board. (HBE 25; HBE 25a).

TANG SING. The young son of Tang Lao. (1183).

TANG WANG. A Chinese Mandarin and a descendant of the Ming Dynasty. He had pretensions to the Chinese Throne. To raise funds for his rebellion he demanded money of all the rich merchants, Wun Chung Lung included. His refusal to pay led to attempts on Wun Lung's life, and an increase in the demand from 3,000 to 20,000 Taels. Tang's persistent efforts to persuade Wun Chung Lung led to the capture of some of the Friars when they went to China to take Wun Lung to his father. They escaped and, Tang's secretary fearing, (rightly), for his life, murdered him. Tang was the head of the Red Dragon Tong, and used its members to his own ends. With agents all over the world, and in every Chinese city, he had no trouble in his continued assaults on the Greyfriars party. A ruthless tyrant, he held no value on human life, and executed anyone who displeased or failed him. (HBE 25; HBE 25a).

TANGANYIKA. The East African country which was the home of Ludwig Krantz the slave trader. (1229).

TARANAKI. Tom Brown's home in North Island, New Zealand.

TATTERS. Abducted by his cousin, Cyril Rackstraw, and given to "Tinker" Wilson, he led the life of a drudge - beaten and starved by his evil mentor to force him into crime. To this he steadfastly refused to stoop. He met the Famous Five and Bunter and was, soon after, found by his grandfather, Sir George Cholmondley. He was then sent to Greyfriars in the family tradition. Rackstraw, in desperate financial straits, used first Ponsonby, and then Carne, to try to get Tatters expelled. Ponsonby's attempt to accuse Tatters of assault almost landed the Highcliffian in court. After Rackstraw, the heir presumptive, had been exposed and thrown out of the family home,

Tatters left Greyfriars to continue his education with a private tuto:
(GBC 19).

TATTERS OF THE REMOVE. (Title GBC Volume 19). See Tatters.

TATTON, Rowland. A fag in the Second Form.

TED. A regular at the Red Cow Inn. Joliffe the landlord sent him t
Greyfriars with a note for Levison – as a direct consequence of whic
Levison was expelled. (46).

TED. One of Sugden and Joe Judson's gang. He kidnapped Harr
Wharton by pretending to be a Wimford taxi-driver. (1157).

TED. One of Archie Valence's team of ex-boxers intended as sparrin
partners for Mr Lascelles when Valence thought his cousin would re
enter the ring. In the event, he and his colleagues had to kidna
Larry to try to make him change his mind. A ploy that failed. (1322)

TED, Uncle. A relative of Bunter's. Although it is not certain t
which side of the family he belongs, judging from the tone c
Mr Bunter's letter to his son, one would assume that he was on the dis
taff side. Sent by his firm to West Africa, Bunter thought, thanks t
one of Skinner's jokes, that he was to go too! He, therefore, borrowe
Mr Prout's gun and scared Farmer Grabble and his donkey! Th
truth of the matter was that Uncle Ted was to take Rex, a dog wh
proved too much for the corpulent Bunters to exercise! (1091).

TEGGERS, Luius, B.A., Oxon. A cousin of Vernon Smith's. He
about 28 years old. After leaving Oxford and doing some teaching, h
became junior partner in a scholastic agency – formerly Legget – no
Leggett & Teggers. He learned that Mr Vernon Smith would disow
his son if he did not behave himself and, that he, Teggers, would be
come the millionaire's heir. In desperate financial toils, (to just on
bookmaker he owed £215/16/0d), he saw the disgracing of his cousin a
his salvation. He, therefore, removed Mr Eustace Smedley to Canad
so that he might take his name and post at Greyfriars in locum tener
to Mr Quelch. Determined to get Vernon Smith expelled, "Smedley
followed, spied upon, and even fabricated evidence against, Smith
At first by luck, and later by guile, Smithy escaped the net woven fc
him. Soon nicknamed "The Creeper and Crawler", Teggers even as
saulted Mr Quelch to delay the latter's return to school. Finally h
was exposed by Mr Vernon Smith and left Greyfriars, unrepentant c
his actions. Some time after this, when Captain Vernon was plottin
against Vernon Smith, he contacted Teggers for help in his plan
(HBE 51-52; 1632).

TEMPLE, Cecil Reginald. Son of Sir Reginald Temple, he is the Head and Captain of the Upper Fourth Form. He is very full of his own importance. An aspiring dandy, he spends a fortune on clothes, although, all too often they, with Temple inside, end up in a puddle! He is convinced of his superiority at games - a view endorsed with varying degrees of acclamation by his study mates, Dabney and Fry, with whom he shares Study No 2. His conceit leads to many feuds with the Remove, who usually win! This same conceit leads to the conviction that he should Captain the Junior Teams at Greyfriars; but as his team rarely, if ever, beat even a weak Remove Team, this idea is laughed at. For all this, he is not a bad sort, and is certainly generous and will help anybody down on his luck.

TEMPLE, Sir Reginald, Bart., Governor of Greyfriars School. The doting father of Cecil Reginald. His home is in Grovesnor Square, London. A wealthy man, he gives his son generous tips on the slightest pretext.

TENERIFFE. One of the Canary Islands. The Famous Five were visiting the Peak when O Lobo managed to separate Harry Wharton from the rest of the party. His plan was to murder him, so that the rest of the party would not visit Brazil. Fortunately, Herr Blitz was also on the Peak that day, and able to come to the rescue. (1462).

TERROR OF THE TONG, THE. (Title HBE Volume 24). See "Billy Bunter in China"; and "The Kidnapped Schoolboys".

TEXAS. The Lone Star State of America where Mr Vernon Smith's ranch The Kicking Cayuse is to be found. Vernon Smith and a party of friends visited the State on Mr Vernon Smith's behalf. (HBE 32).

TEXAS BILL. The bronco rider in Whiffles' Circus. In common with the rest of the circus, he believed that the enraged, bald headed man was an escaped lunatic, and not Mr Whiffles! After all the boss was in front of him! (1070).

THAMES, River. The principal waterway of England. Navigable from the North Sea to Lechlade, it makes an ideal holiday route by water. Starting at Kingston-upon-Thames, the Famous Five and Bunter camped and rowed and sailed their way up-stream in the Water Lily, pursued by "Shifty" Spooner. (HBE 11).

THAMES NOOK. The home of Major Loder, uncle to Gerald Loder. Having rented a camp site, as they thought, the Famous Five had a battle royal with Loder and friends who tried to evict them. Crestfallen, the crew of the Water Lily retired, bloodied but not beaten! (1645).

THATCH END. A secluded farm one mile from Lantham on the Greyfriars side. It was an ideal spot to make a training camp, and that is exactly what Archie Valence did to prepare, as he thought, Mr Lascelles for the ring. When Larry refused to box, it made an excellent prison! (1322).

THEATRE ROYAL, Courtfield. The Theatre which "put on" Little Red Riding Hood for its Christmas show with Paula Bell as the leading lady. (200).

THEATRE ROYAL, Lantham. Harry Wharton and a crowd of friends found employment here taking various parts in Puss-in-Boots to raise money for the troops. (409).

THOMAS. A particularly unsavoury cat belonging to Mrs. Kebble, and the apple of her eye. His nocturnal wailings make hideous the night and, no doubt, one day Wun Lung really will put him in a Chinese stew!

THOMAS. The pageboy at Wharton Lodge. A distant relative to Wells the butler, his secure position seemed in jeopardy when a series of thefts appeared to have been committed by him. However, as Bunter was "stowing away" at the time, his good name was speedily restored. (HBE 8).

THOMAS. One of the footmen at Bunter Court. His avarice, and Bunter's generosity with other fellows notes, made master and man allies of sorts. When Walsingham had "to go to London", Thomas was promoted to butler in his place. (HBE 3).

THOMAS. One of the long-suffering staff at Tipton Lodge. (1646).

THOMPSON. The name under which Soames was operating when Rat Hankey robbed Lantham Post Office. "Thompson" was waiting at Pegg with a motor boat to take them to safety. As Hankey was injured, he gave Bunter a cigarette case containing a message to deliver to Pegg. Arriving there, intending to tea at the Anchor, Bunter was appalled to recognise Soames. (1609).

THOMPSON. In the guise of an A.R.P. officer of this name Mr Brown, (or Herr Braun, more accurately), endeavoured to kidnap Wibley disguised as Sir William Bird. Bunter, who was spying as usual called for help, but Brown unfortunately avoided capture. (1682).

THOMPSON, Mr. An assistant in the Nairobi Stores whereat Bunter spent a small fortune on safari equipment which was returned by Mr Vernon Smith. Upon asking what had happened to his order

Thompson, piqued no doubt by the loss of his commission, gleefully held the door while the manager kicked Bunter into the street ! (1231) .

THORPE, Mr John. A former Master of the Remove. He had died while still at Greyfriars, and had hidden his will somewhere in the vaults. "His old friend", Mr Bright had obtained an invalid will leaving Thorpe's money to him, thus dispossessing Mr Levison, the nephew. To ensure his safety, Mr Bright sent his son, "The Toad" to Greyfriars to find and destroy the true will. This was found in a secret passage off Mr Quelch's study, after the Toad had lost himself and Levison in the vaults. (GBC 26) .

THREE FISHERS, The. A disreputable public house up the tow path from Greyfriars. One entrance is on the tow path itself, while the other is in Oak Lane. A large rambling place, its out-houses are used for illegal prize fights and cock-fighting. The short cut to school, through the grounds, is out of bounds but, nonetheless, frequently used. The landlord and Joe Banks obviously make a packet out of gambling and, as such, encourage Friars to patronise the place.

THRESHER, Major. He lives next door to Greyfriars, and is known well by all the staff. He is particularly friendly with Mr Capper. When his house was burgled, Angel, who was out of bounds, accused his Form Master of the robbery, which had been committed by man similar in appearance. (918; 974) .

THRESHER, Phyllis. Niece to Major Thresher. Out for a row one day, they received a ducking when Ponsonby ran their boat down. After rescuing uncle and niece, the Famous Five ducked Pon. ! (918) .

TIGHE, Mr. A blackmailing money lender who extorts many times the principal from people who cannot afford to have their financial problems made known. He also operates under the names of Brown, Buzzard and Sharp. (1333-34) .

TIN BONG. The priest of a Chinese Temple where Wharton, Cherry and Bunter sheltered from Tang Wang. Promising to help them get to Canton, he betrayed them to Chang Lo, one of Tang's men. He died when a part of the Temple fell on him. A just end for a treacherous priest. (1184) .

TIP, Tippity. The clown in Muccolini's Circus. He also runs a side show wherein he ventriloquises with two dolls. His closest friend is Marco the lion tamer. Bunter was most contemptuous of Tip's abilities as a ventriloquist and caused havoc amongst circus staff and audiences by interfering with Tip's practices and performances. For a time, Tip had his side-show taken away from him, and Bunter, instead, did his own money spinning turns. He was fired through Bunter's blackmailing Muccolini but, when the owner had been arrested, Marco, the new boss, reinstated Tip who was in the van to give the erstwhile Circus star the boot ! (HBE 55-56) .

TIPTON, Sir George, Bart. The uncle of Stephen Price who lives at Tipton Lodge, on the Thames between Mapledurham and Whitchurch in Berkshire. Caught in a downpour, the crew of the Water Lily took shelter in his summer house. They were driven off and were trying to gain some respite from the storm when they recovered property stolen from Sir George by "Shifty" Spooner. From an irrascible martinet, Sir George became an hospitable host, to the fury of Price and friends whose efforts to drive off "the fags" met with the Baronet's wrath. (1646) .

TIRIDDU. An Italian bandit who kidnapped Bunter after he had run away from a plane crash. Holding him to ransome, Tiriddu gave himself away by spending money too freely. Tiger Bronx realised the facts, (helped by Jarvish' duplicity), and took the Billionaire prisoner himself. But he was outsmarted by the Famous Five. (1387) .

TO SUN. A gardener to Tang Wang in his house in Pan Shan. Ferrers Locke took his place after doping him with opium, so that he could help the captive Friars escape. (1185) .

TOAD, The. The nickname give to Edgar Bright. It summed up his character most succinctly. (GBC 26) .

TOAD OF THE REMOVE, THE. (Title GBC Volume 26) . Mr Esau Bright sent his son, Edgar, to Greyfriars to search for the last will and testament of Mr John Thorpe. By this document, he had left his money to his nephew, Mr Levison. By a former will, which Mr Bright had found, the estate had been left to Mr Bright. Searching the school, when not engaged in his hobby of cruelty to animals, Bright tried to find the will before Levison, (at Greyfriars for the same purpose) . Levison saved Bright from the vaults wherein he was lost and, in reaching safety, found the will.

TODD, Alonzo Theophilus, (Lonzy) . An orphan brought up by his Uncle Benjamin and Aunt Selina. From the former he has acquired a philosophy which Alonzo will share with everyone at every opportunity. He is perhaps as much of a dunce as Bunter, (one of his study mates), but Alonzo can never be devious, mean or show duplicity. His honest simplicity shines out so that, no matter what he has done, it is always with the purest of motives. Even when made to do a mean trick by Skinner, such is his basic integrity that it is impossible to punish such a man.

TODD, Mrs. Belinda. Aunt to Peter and Alonzo. It is with her that Alonzo gains his athletic prowess – by playing crocquet ! (1344).

TODD, Mr Benjamin. Uncle to Peter and Alonzo. He is Alonzo's guardian and fount of all wisdom to that youth. At any opportunity Lonzy will quote his uncle's morality to the Remove until they are not sure if they wish to scrag uncle or nephew the more ! It was Uncle Benjamin who gave Alonzo his favourite book "The Story of a Potato – from Seed to the Pot".

TODD, Ernest. No relation to Peter or Alonzo, he is a fag in the Second Form, and the form's expert in practical jokes. Not that they always go right. When Hop Hi arrived, Todd tied an inkwell to Hop's pigtail. The astute Chinee made sure that the jokers got the ink and not himself !

TODD, Peter Hastings. The self-appointed leader of Study No 7 is the son of a Bloomsbury solicitor, and intends to join the parental law firm. As honest as his cousin, he has a far greater intellect, a sense of humour, and a native wit that saves him from his form-mates barbs. His mission in life is to save his study mates from their follies; his cousin from fatuousness; and Bunter from dishonesty. His ever ready cricket stump awaits either mens' actions. For Tom Dutton, he reserves a confidential tone that can be heard most of the way to Friardale !

TODD, Selina. Daughter of Mr and Mrs. Benjamin Todd, with whom Alonzo often plays croquet.

TOFOLOKO. The king of the Mateli tribe in the upper reaches of the Congo. It was to him that Ludwig Krantz sold the Greyfriars Safari party as slaves. All except Bunter who was destined to be fattened for the table ! A tyrannical autocrat, he sentenced Vernon Smith to death for striking him. Kikolobo and Captain McCann were able to rescue the Friars, who had tied up the king prior to making their escape. (HBE 65).

TOM. Mr Coote, the carrier's horse. Caffyn had been soundly thrashed for catapulting the beast and making him bolt. In revenge, he gave the horse to a gipsy. Coker's efforts to obtain a new animal from Banks almost led to his expulsion. For betting ! (1408).

TOM REDWING'S TRIUMPH. (Title GBC Volume 28). When Tom Redwing saved Vernon Smith from a stormy sea, he never thought he would see him again but, a few weeks later, persuaded by Clavering to change places, Tom was to go to Greyfriars. Vernon Smith knew that there was a reason behind his actions and, not only kept his counsel, but also saved Tom on several occasions from exposure. When the truth came out - Clavering had thrashed Sir Hilton Popper for remarks about his dead father - Redwing left Greyfriars. To return shortly as the first holder of "The Memorial Scholarship" founded anonymously by Mr Vernon Smith at the insistence of his son.

TOMASSO TOMSONIO. The stage name of Tommy Thompson, the trapeze artiste in Whiffles' Circus. (HBE 28).

TOMLIN. Clerk to Mr Elias Rance. He helped his employer throw Vernon Smith out of the office after he had accused Mr Rance of lying about his father's whereabouts. (1628).

TOMLIN, Mr. A boatman who hires out rowing boats from his yard by Courtfield Bridge. The Famous Five had hired a boat from him the day they were accused of "sacking" Loder through the deceits of Ponsony and Co. (1586).

TOMLINSON. Chauffeur to Mr Vernon Smith.

TOMLINSON, Dr. Consultant physician from Courtfield. He was called in by Dr Monroe to examine Sir William Cherry after he had been poisoned by the Rafia. (1108).

TOMLINSON, Mr. A private detective employed by Sir Peter Lanchester to catch the would-be kidnappers of Lord Reynham. He is a taciturn, curt man who posed as Sir Peter's secretary. After the Famous Five had captured "The Smiler", Tomlinson was drugged so that he might escape. However, Tomlinson soon trapped and recaptured him. When the Famous Five were about to leave Reynham Castle, fed up with Bunter's behaviour, it was Tomlinson who persuaded them to stay. (HBE 14).

TOMLINSON, Edward Edwin, (Teddy), (Minor). The younger brother of Thomas, he shares Study No 5 in the Upper Fourth with Scott. He is somewhat on the stout side !

TOMLINSON, Thomas Trotter, (Major). The older brother of Teddy, he is in the Fifth Form, and is probably in Study No 5.

TOMMY. The potman and billiards marker at the Three Fishers. (1264).

TOMONGO. The witch doctor in Koo Koo's tribe. An evil, shrivelled old man, he had charge of Bunter after his capture by the cannibals. It was his job to fatten him for a feast. Bunter soon had him grovelling when he made the island's god speak. When chosen as chief, by divine intervention, (!), Bunter expelled him from the village. (1595).

TOODLE, Mr. He succeeded Mr Kelly as Master to the Second Form. He seems to have been a kindly, but ineffectual, man. (183).

TOOLEY'S WHARF. Situated in the East End of London, this derelict building was used by the Rafia as their headquarters. It was here that they held Bunter prisoner, and from where he escaped after befriending the dog left to guard him. (1108).

TOOTHY. Mr Redmay's apparently ferocious mastiff. Mr Quelch had been chased onto the roof of a barn by the dog, from where he was bravely rescued by Bunter, who had heard the farmer joke about the dog's actual gentleness! (1566).

TOPHAM, Mr. A master at Redclyffe School. The soul of tact and discretion, he gave Wingate a message about his minor being at the Cross Keys as privately as possible. (925).

TOPHAM, Mr Jabez. A rich stockbroker and acquaintance of Mr Vernon Smith. He lives at Topham Croft, some four miles by road from Greyfriars. Vernon Smith and Skinner were returning from a midnight joy-ride, when their car crashed near the house which was in an uproar as the Courtfield Cracksman had just robbed the safe. Vernon Smith saw him hide his booty and persuaded Wharton to return the stolen bonds. In so doing he discovered Mr Steele's true identity. (1148).

TOPHAM & TUKE. A firm of turf accountants in Taftesbury Avenue, London, to whom Orris, Mauleverer's valet, owed a large sum. Bunter picked up a letter to Orris from them. His attempts at bluster got him put in the well at Mauleverer Towers by the valet. (245).

TOPHAM SCHOOL, Surrey. A Public School from which Eric Wilmot was expelled for theft during a school match at St Jude's. After Crawley, the real thief, had been exposed, Wilmot returned to Topham. The Greyfriars First Eleven play against Topham, but there is no mention of junior fixtures.

TOTO. A deck hand in the Brig Mindanao. He took his lawyer cane to Ysabel Dick after he had knocked down Captain Jarrack. (1590).

TOTO TOTO. One of Koo Koo's islanders. It was he who captured Bunter, but later became a servant to the temporary chief. He helped the Greyfriars Castaways escape by blocking the channel, so that they could take over the Sea Cat. (HBE 12).

TOTUA. The cook in the Flamingo. He managed to get off in the ship's boats when Ysabel Dick and Van Dink scuttled her. (1593).

TOWER, The Old. A derelict and dangerous ruin at the back of the main school buildings. It dates from monastic times and was the belfry for the Abbey Church. Because of its state, (all openings are boarded), it is out of bounds. Nonetheless, it is used for surreptitious smoking parties. Its finest hour was when Bob Cherry held his barring out here with the rest of the Famous Five to get their's and Mark Linley's expulsions, engineered by Vernon Smith, rescinded.

TOZER, P.C. The Friardale policeman. A real "village bobby", he seems more interested in his garden than his work but, probably, in common with his kind, he knows everybody with "form" in the area. In his meetings with Greyfriars he usually comes off second best because, all too often, he is called in to deal with events that are beyond his duty.

TRACY, Captain, O.F. Father of Gilbert. He had spent a long time in Nursing Homes as a result of a war injury. A contemporary of Colonel Wharton's at Greyfriars, the Colonel tried to help Gilbert for his father's sake. In the event it was the Captain's recovery and discharge from medical care that led to Gilbert's repenting of his former ways. (HBE 15).

TRACY, Gilbert. The spoilt nephew of Sir Giles Oakwood. He was sent to Greyfriars at the suggestion of Mr Quelch, Sir Giles' old friend, to try to instil some discipline. Gilbert was determined not to stay at school and tried constantly to get himself expelled. However, Mr Quelch was alive to this, and steadfastly refused to recommend this, going so far as to argue with the Head on the subject. Even after he had been locked in the Punishment Room by Gilbert, he did not let him go. When Tracy learned that his father was due to leave hospital, he reformed, somewhat belatedly, and went abroad with him. (HBE 15).

TRAILL, Arthur. A somewhat delicate youth who, after recovering from a long illness, was sent to Greyfriars. Ragged unmercifully by the caddish element of the Remove, he began sleep walking, which led to rows and unpleasantness in the form until Harry Wharton discovered the facts. Considered unfit for the hurly-burly of boarding school life, he left after only a couple of weeks. (1317).

TRANT, The Right Honourable the Earl of. He lives at Trant Elms, Sussex, and Trant House, London, S.W.1. While staying at Seahill Park, Bunter picked up a letter which began "Dear William", and was signed by Lord Trant. Bunter claimed him as a relative. Vernon Smith and the Famous Five were amazed to be welcomed to Trant Elms! And even more astonished to hear the Earl invite Bunter with his friends to his London house for the Coronation. What even Bunter did not realise was that he had accidently saved the Earl from a footpad ! (1526).

TREASURE HUNTERS, THE. (Title GBC Volume 11). When Ben Dance brought a carved map of a Pacific Island, purporting to show the hiding place of Tom Redwing's uncle, Black Pete's treasure, everybody hoped it would enable Tom to ease his and his father's positions. Nobody realised the dangers they would have to face in the Pacific, thanks to the plottings of Soames, Mr Vernon Smith's valet. Entrusted by the financier to look after the Friars while he conducted business, Soames took them towards Caca Island. But then, showing himself in his true colours, he attempted to get the treasure for himself. Losing their boat and drifting in the ocean after having found the treasure, (and in the process having to escape cannibals and a volcanic erruption), they were picked up by The Golden Arrow. In the excitement, Soames escaped unpunished.

TREGELLIS, Mr. Landlord of the Rose Inn, Polpen, where Sir Jimmy Vivian and his friends tea'd before arriving at Pengarth, which is about a mile from the village. (811).

TREGELLY, Mr. A boatman of Potkelly who rowed Bunter and the Famous Five out to Blackrock Island on their way to stay, as they thought, at the Castle. (1626).

TRELUCE, Anthony. A lesser light of the Remove who shares Study No 9 with Penfold, Newland and Trevor.

TREVELLY, Inspector. Stationed at Okeham, Devon, he was in charge of the search for Convict 33 – Richard Pike – who had escaped from Blackmoor Prison while Bunter and The Famous Five were staying with Hilton for Christmas. (1402-1403).

TREVLYN, Clara. The tomboy of the Cliff House Fourth Form, and one of Marjorie Hazeldene's closest friends. Not for her is the decorum of the young lady. Rather the boisterous high spiritedness of the only girl in a family of men ! One cannot but suspect that Bob Cherry is her favourite Removite, though she would be torn by wild horses before she admitted that Marjorie's friend was her choice. She will, like Bob Cherry, do anything to get outside rather than froust inside.

TREVOR, Herbert Beauchamp. The son of a Lancashire manufacturer. His closest friend is his study mate, Treluce. A one time member of the Remove Form Teams, he has been superceded by better players, and is now one of the reserves.

TROTTER, Mr Ebenezer. Late uncle to Trotter the pageboy. Upon his death, he left his nephew £100. The cadgers of the Remove's endeavours to get a share in the legacy were frustrated by the discovery that the money and the interest were not to be touched until Trotter's 21st birthday! (1010).

TROTTER, Theophilus Frederick. The Greyfriars pageboy has wisely dropped his first name. Ostensibly employed to run errands for the Head and to announce visitors, he is in fact at the beck and call of the entire school. In addition, he helps Mrs. Kebble in the kitchens. He is willing, for a tip, to perform what services he may for anyone. A cheerful soul, he is for ever at war with the housekeeper, trying to avoid work, and instead read his beloved penny dreadfuls!

TRUMPER, David, (Dave). A fisherman from Pegg. He is a great friend to most of Greyfriars and Cliff House, and often hires out his boat to them.

TRUMPER, Richard Arthur, (Dick). The son of Dave Trumper, he is the acknowledged leader of the Courtfield Grammar School Juniors, Captain of their teams, and a firm friend to the Famous Five, despite the inter-school rivalries. He will never miss the chance to score over the Friars; a good example being when he and his friends disguised themselves as Cliff House girls for a snowball fight!

TRUMPINGTON, Dr. The Headmaster of Greyfriars during George IIIrd and IVth's reigns. One reference is made to his being Head during the great rebellion in the time of William IVth. A case of Homer nodding in Mr Quelch's History. It seems safe to suggest that he ruled the school from about 1810-1830. To quote Mr Quelch's History of Greyfriars: "The Head was arbitrary and tyrannical. It is painful to write such words of the Headmaster of Greyfriars, but it is the undoubted fact. His tactless interference between masters and boys earned him both dislike and contempt". It was this behaviour that led to the great rebellion of 1828. When Skinner gave this quote to Dr Locke it caused the High Oaks Mutiny. (HBE 10).

TRUMPINGTON SQUARE, London. The London address of the Jam Bahadur. It is most likely the official residence of Bhanipur in London, and is probably used as the High Commission. It was here that the "Christmas Candles" were lit, after their recovery by Jack Drake, to reveal Hurree Singh's Christmas presents to his friends. (723).

TUBB, George. In the Third Form, he is the acknowledged leader of the fags. He is scruffy and good natured, and has the misfortune to be Loder's fag – a task master who rewards with the cane or the boot rather than a jam tart! Tubb's one ambition is to beat the Remove at football – a goal about as unattainable as getting to the moon without a space ship !

TUCK SHOP. The old Prior's House of Monastic days has been converted into the tuckshop with accomodation for the manageress, Mrs Mimble and her family. It is a separate building in a corner of the Quadrangle, shaded by some of the ancient elms. Apart from many hours spent in window shopping by Bunter it is a popular resort for the school. Whether sitting in the shop, or the inner sanctum reserved for Bloods and the Sixth Form, or, on summers days sitting under the trees, Mrs. Mimble's ginger beer, home-made pies and cakes are old and tried favourites always to be enjoyed. The Remove, under Mauleverer's generalship, used the shop for a barring out against Mr Hacker. Not only is the place a stronghold, but is is also well provisioned to withstand a siege !

TUCQUET, M. Alphonse. One of the French gentlemen with whom the Famous Five and Bunter shared a camp site while caravanning in France. (709).

TUDOR, Miss Mirabel. The actress who played the Prince in Little Red Riding Hood at the Theatre Royal, Courtfield. (200).

TUNSTALL. A member of the Upper Fourth.

TUNSTALL. In the Fourth Form at Highcliffe, he is, as it were, a reserve for Ponsonby when he requires reinforcements against Greyfriars.

TUPPER. The Rookwood pageboy. He was named in error for Trotter on one occasion – in Magnet No 1394.

TURNBULL, Mr. A brutal locum for Mr Quelch in the days when Dick Chester was in the Remove. Chester led a barring out against his behaviour and, after the Head caught him flogging a fag, he was dismissed on the spot. (844).

TURNER, Maurice. In Study No 3 in the Upper Fourth.

TURPLE, Mr. He was involved in a fight on a train returning from the races at Wapshot. He threw his winnings, £500, out of the window, rather than give them to his assailant. Bunter picked up the roll of notes and, spreading a tale about largesse from home, spent twice as much as he said he had been given. When Peter Todd caught him with the one note whose number was known, Todd and the Famous Five arranged for the money to be returned to Mr Turple. (1014).

TURTLE REEF. A small island mid-way between Baloo and Kalua. Mr McTab took the "Greyfriars Adventurers" here on a sailing trip. They met Ysabel Dick and Van Dink on the island. Soon after this, Van Dink drugged the Friars, with the exception of Wharton who managed to escape for help. (1598).

TURVEY. The Captain of Tyneside Rovers Football Club who played a match against Lantham. Wibley and the Remove dressed up Tyneside Rovers and played against Trumper's Team!

TWIGG, Mr Bernard Morrison, B.A. The master of the First Form when Greyfriars still took pupils so young. Since this practice has stopped, Mr Twigg has left Greyfriars, presumably to work in the Greyfriar's Preparatory School.

TWIGG, Mr Eusebius, B.Sc. Brother to Mr Bernard Twigg, he is the long suffering master of the Second Form, whose charges never desire to acquire knowledge.

TYNESIDE ROVERS. A professional football team, and members of the Football Association. They are in the same league as Lantham Argyll. (918).

TYRANT OF GREYFRIARS, THE. (Title HBE Volume 21). Determined, no matter how, to succeed Dr Locke as Headmaster, Mr Brander had his nephew, Otto von Tromp, knock out the Head, so that he was forced to leave. Making his bullying, caddish nephew Head of School, the pair proceeded to upset all the tradition and peaceful running of the school. Eventually the floggings became too much, and the Remove barred themselves out. Brander, making false promises to stop the rebellion, proved himself to be as unspeakable as all thought - so the rebellion went on to its bitter end, culminating in the revelation of the methods used by uncle and nephew to get into the school. Their departure can hardly be said to have been dignified!

TYRRELL, Paul. Cousin to Bob Cherry. He was always sponging on Major Cherry, who asked Colonel Wharton's advice. This was that he could "not be expected to bear for ever, the burden of a selfish, ungrateful nephew". Harry Wharton saw this and, assuming that it referred to himself, went into one of his rebellious moods. (HBE 6). Shortly after this, a warrant was issued for the arrest of Tyrrell on a charge of forgery. Coming to Greyfriars, he tried to persuade his cousin to help him. It was Vernon Smith who gave him the money he required to flee the country and make a fresh start, convinced that he would, from then, go straight. (1268).

U.

UMBRIA. A province of Italy in which Bunter's aeroplane was forced to make an emergency landing during a storm. Bunter, in a panic, ran off from the rest of the party, (the Famous Five and Jarvish), and was kidnapped by Tiriddu who, spending the money stolen from Bunter too freely, led Tiger Bronx to the billionaire, who also tried to kidnap Bunter. The attempt was foiled by the Famous Five. (1387).

UNCLE TED. See Ted, Uncle.

UNDER BUNTER'S THUMB. (Title HBE Volume 73). When Henry Crumm came to Greyfriars, no-one could understand the Head's reason for admitting him. But then, neither could they understand why they performed unaccountable acts ! Mauleverer realised, and made the hypnotist son of a world renowned hypnotist promise to mend his ways. When Bunter found a letter from Loder to a Bookmaker he, as usual, made everyone's life, from Loder downwards, a misery until Hurree Singh found and returned it. For a time, Loder and the Famous Five were "Under Bunter's Thumb".

V.

VALDEZ, Chico. A Mexican who first met the "Greyfriars Filmstars" as he was "Riding the Cars", (in Bunterian terms he was bilking the railway company!). Mauleverer paid his fare for him. He is the descendant of an old Mexican family who used to own much of the land on which is now built Hollywood. In gratitude for Mauly's help, he warned the Friars of an impending attack on Coker. He was badly injured in going to Coker's aid. (1098).

VALENCE, Archibald, (Archie). Cousin to Mr Lascelles. He is a professional gambler who has tried many ways of earning a living. One of them was to promote boxing. Without his cousin's consent, Valence put Larry up to fight "The Game Chicken". He telephoned the school; Bunter took the call and agreed to Archie's request ! Valence could not understand the subsequent refusals ! So, he kidnapped Lascelles to make him change his mind. Vernon Smith was convinced that Larry's refusals were false and followed him to prove it and, finding him a prisoner, freed him in time for Larry to play in a county cricket match in which he had permission to play. (1321-22) .

VALENCE, Rupert. A one time member of the Sixth Form. He was a gambler and worse than Loder or Carne at their worst. Deeply in debt to Jerry Hawke, he forged a cheque in settlement. He then went to the Cross Keys to steal back the cheque, and was trapped in the building when it was hit by a bomb. He was saved by Courtney at the cost of the latter's life. Valence then left the school rather than face expulsion, and enlisted in the army.

VALENCE, Violet. Sister to Rupert and as different a character as possible. She and Courtney were more than friends and, soon after his death, Violet herself died. (520) .

VALENTINE, Jim. Determined to reform his way of life, "Dick the Penman" fled from his former associates. Wandering in a fog, he met Mr Quelch, also lost, and, guiding the master to safety, persuaded him to allow him , (Valentine), to go to Greyfriars. Hounded by Nosey Clark, the leader of the gang, Jim had a hard time. He earned Vernon Smith's enmity by letting a pickpocket, (Kicky the Pincher), escape. Vernon Smith, in his usual shrewd manner, put two and two together, and exposed Valentine to the police. However, Mr Peter Valentine, Jim's uncle, had arrived from Brazil, and was able to get him away to safety. He went to Brazil and now works on his uncle's coffee plantation, where they were visited by the Famous Five and Bunter, who found themselves up against O Lobo. (GBC 9; HBE 44) .

VALENTINE, Mr Peter. Uncle and only relative to Jim Valentine. Formerly with the Brazilian Air Force, he now owns and runs a coffee plantation on the Rio Rexo in the country of his adoption. (GBC 9; HBE 44) .

VAN DINK, Captain. A Dutchman who worked in the islands of the Pacific. He had lost his boat by shipwreck, probably when drunk. He recognised Mauleverer and set out to murder him and any of the other Friars who got in his way. He tried to throw Mauly overboard; stranded the Friars on a cannibal island; and, in a final attempt, drugged the party,(except for Wharton), so that their boat would founder. Luckily Harry escaped and brought help. Van Dink brought the news to Brian, Mauly's cousin, that he had succeeded to the title and fortune, and that he, Van Dink, expected to share it. They fell out, and in the ensuing fight, Van Dink was killed by a shark. (HBE 12) .

VAN DUCK, Mr. The assistant director of Perfection Pictures, Hollywood. He had charge of the film in which the Greyfriars party starred about English Public School life. (GBC 20-21).

VAN DUCK, Putnam. The only son of a Chicago Millionaire, he was fed up with his chaperon, Poker Pike. So Van Duck left his father's luxury yacht on which they were cruising, and stowed away on the R.M.S. Bayford Castle. He had already made friends with the Famous Five in Rio, and had decided to join them! He went to Greyfriars, and at his father's insistance, Poker Pike accompanied him to protect him from Chick Chew who wanted to kidnap him for a ransom of $500,000. The ructions caused by Pike in the classroom, and Chew outside, meant that the term was more than exiting! After many attempts, Chew did kidnap Van Duck – only to be arrested by Pike who had followed him. Once the threat of kidnapping was lifted, Van Duck returned home to Chicago, leaving many friends in the Remove. (HBE 44-45).

VAN DUCK, Mr Vanderdecken. A Chicago multi-millionaire, and father of Putnam. To protect his son from kidnappers, he hired the services of a Chicago ex-gangster, Poker Pike. (1471).

VAN HORN, Mr. A New York detective hired by Mr Fish to find Coker after he had been kidnapped by Ulick Burke and Co. (1094).

VAN SCHUYLER, Mr Ralph. A sharper who made Vernon Smith's acquaintance on the train from New York to Chicago. Realising that there were two birds to pluck, he persuaded Vernon Smith and Mauleverer to go for a drive around the city. They were held up and robbed. Vernon Smith of $60, Mauly of $5 – he had suspected van Schuyler, and left his money at the hotel! The following night, van Schuyler took Vernon Smith to a speakeasy and gaming house, where he was fleeced of a large sum of money and left in the lurch by his friend when the place was raided by the police. (1095).

VAN TROMP, Otto. He managed, somewhat mysteriously, to enter the Sixth Form at Greyfriars and, immediately, showed himself in his true lights as a bully and a coward. He tried to fag and cane the Remove, but was stopped by Wingate. When he struck the Head, forcing him to leave the school, his uncle Mr Brander became Head, and promptly made Van Tromp Head of School. After this, his cruelty knew no bounds. He flogged everyone from Wingate down, until the Remove, driven to rebellion by uncle and nephew, barred themselves out in their dormitory. Van Tromp was conspicuous by his retreating rather than his bravery in the melees that ensued! He was finally made to admit that it was he who had struck down the Head, and was kicked out of school – by Coker! (HBE 21).

VANDERPECK, Mr Jan. Mate in the Sundabund who was found drifting alone in a dinghy after his ship had gone down. Ferrers Locke suspected that he had been involved in foul play. Suspicions that soon proved correct. He had stolen the Captain's money belt and thrown him into the sea. He was clapped in irons on the Silver Star and taken to France. He tried to escape and received a bullet in his knee; followed by a prison sentence for his crime. (1186).

VASCO, Senhor Jaoa. A Portuguese interpreter employed by Mr Vernon Smith to translate some documents about the N'Gombo Concession that the financier was contemplating buying. On his way to Seahill Park, Vasco was waylaid and tied up by Nessuno who went to the Park with the intention of obtaining the papers for himself. Luckily Vasco was found by Vernon Smith and the Famous Five who were in time to save Mr Vernon Smith from the Italian's murderous attack. (1525).

VASELINE. The nickname given to Hazeldene in his early days at Greyfriars. It was a pun on the hair oil he uses and his fawning deceitful ways.

VAULTS. Beneath the original buildings at Greyfriars is an extensive area of cellars and vaults, used in former times for storage. Out of them lead secret passages; and both passages and vaults are out of bounds. This notwithstanding, the vaults have been used on many occasions for secret smoking- and card-parties by the black sheep of succeeding generations of Friars.

VAVASOUR. One of Ponsonby's closest allies at Highcliffe against both Courtenay and Greyfriars. He is one of Pon.'s regular bridge partners, and willingly takes part in any illegal enterprise, whether it is playing billiards at the Three Fishers or an en-masse ragging of a solitary Friar.

VENICE. This beautiful Italian city was visited by the Famous Five with Bunter as their billionaire host. While here, Tiger Bronx made several attempts to kidnap Bunter helped by Jarvish, whose actions became suspicious to the Famous Five, (not that Bunter would listen!) Lord Conway, on a cruise with a party of Saints, was able to lead an exciting chase across the Adriatic to rescue Bunter from the American gangster. (1386).

VERDE. A small town some thirty miles down stream from the Valentines' plantation to which they take their coffee-harvest by river. Bunter had been left behind by the Famous Five when he decided to follow them in a canoe. As incapable as ever, he stranded himself on a bank. Chico gave him directions to free himself. He had barely set out for home when O Lobo lassoed Chico. Bunter's rescue of the Indian hunter, for the second time, further raised him in Chico's estimation. (1465).

VERNON, Captain. A retired Indian Army officer and a poor relation of the Vernon Smiths'. He decided to place his nephew, Bertie, at Greyfriars, having worked out a scheme to substitute his worthwhile nephew for the black sheep. To this end, he rented Lantham Chase, and fitted up the Turret Room as a prison, in which he eventually trapped Vernon Smith. His plans went awry when Bertie Vernon decided that he could not go through with the imposture, after the Captain had also imprisoned Tom Redwing. Although criminal, his plans and actions were based on a desire to help Bertie. (HBE 54-55).

VERNON, Bertie. Cousin to Vernon Smith. He and his uncle, Captain Vernon, looked down on the "Smiths" as parvenus, refusing to recognise their full name. A double to his cousin, whom he hates as much as his cousin hates him, he is as different as is possible in every other way. As bright in class as Vernon Smith, he does not smoke, drink or gamble; while on the cricket field he is a brilliant bowler. When he was sent to Greyfriars by his uncle, the cousins promptly barred each other, and fought and feuded at all times. His contempt and detestation for Vernon Smith led him to acqiesce in his uncle's plans for him to impersonate his cousin after he, (Vernon), had been removed from school "to prevent further trouble". For a time he played this charade, but when he realised that Tom Redwing, (with whom "Smithy" had fallen out), had also been imprisoned by his uncle, he could not continue, and persuaded his uncle to give up the game. It is probable that, after leaving Lantham Chase, Bertie and his uncle left England to return to India. (HBE 54-55).

VERNON SMITH, Herbert Tudor. The only son of the Cotton King, Mr Samuel Vernon Smith, of Courtman Square, London. He more than astounded the natives by arriving at Greyfriars drunk! Ever contemptuous of authority, "Smithy", will never lose the chance of any daredevil act that will aggrandisise him in the eyes of his fellow men. When the mood is on him, woe betide any man who tries to stop his recklessness; as Harry Wharton and Co. have found out to their cost: to cross Vernon Smith means Big Trouble. When not engaged in his flagrant defiance of authority, Vernon Smith can be one of the best men in the Remove. Highly intelligent, good at all sports and, surprising to some, often ready to help a lame dog. His friendship with Tom Redwing, his study mate, surprises some, but no-one doubts Tom's influence for good. Sadly, even this is not always proof against "The Bounder's" worse nature, and Tom has had to admit on occasions that Smithy's character seems irredeemable.

VERNON SMITH, Mr Samuel. Known as the Cotton King to his associates in the city, this self-made millionaire will only put aside business if his son requires help. He is a hard man but is, nonetheless, capable of acts of generosity - and not always for self gain. He founded The Memorial Scholarship anonymously, rather than let Tom Redwing know the origins of his benefactor at Greyfriars. Mr Vernon Smith's empire stretches world wide. To the Far East, where his shipping line carries much of the freight between China and the USA, as well as the produce of his rubber plantations. To the Pacific, where he owns vast copra interests. To the USA, where he owns at least one enormous "spread". Honest, according to his own lights, he dislikes being beholden to any man. Hence his paying Paul Dallas' fees at Greyfriars until his father returned, unexpectedly, from South America. On the other hand, he did let Tom Redwing pay the cost of the Aloha after she sank, and Tom had found his treasure.

VERNON SMITH'S RIVAL. (Title HBE Volume 54). Relates how Bertie Vernon, under the direction of his uncle, came to Greyfriars with the intention of taking Vernon Smith's place as son and heir to the financier's fortune. Smithy and Bertie Vernon were to be swapped, and Smithy taken out of the country. Who would believe the impoverished nephew of a millionaire when he laid claim to the position of son? So went the Captain's thinking. And the plan very nearly worked.

VERNON TRACEY, Mr Arthur. One of Vernon Smith's many cousins. A wealthy man who backs theatrical shows in order to ingratiate himself with the leading ladies. He is a nasty specimen of the genus Stage Door Johnny. He was trying to impress Paula Bell but was knocked down by Wingate, and then the Remove. (The former with his fists; the latter with snowballs!). Once Miss Bell had had an offer from a London director, her fear of the man evaporated for herself; although she still worried what he might do to Wingate. In the event it was Wingate who thoroughly thrashed Mr Vernon Tracey sending him back to London to nurse his wounds, both to body and pride. (200).

VERNON TRACEY, Richard, (Ginger). Cousin to Vernon Smith. He is at Hexham School in Northumberland. When the school closed down because of a 'flu epidemic, he visited Greyfriars. Smithy had had his suggestion of playing Ginger in the Remove Team turned down but, after Smithy fell in the river and found himself in the sanatorium, Wharton had no option. Wibley, however, thought he had a prior claim to a place in the eleven and so, having pulled Ginger out of the River, (after he had crashed his motor cycle), Wib had the idea of taking Ginger's place in the team. "Ginger" did not shine in the match, and Smithy was heading for the ragging of a life time when the real Ginger came on the scene. Needless to say, Wibley got that ragging! (1308).

VICAR of FRIARDALE. See Lambe, Reverend Orlando Beale.

VILLA des FLEURS. The villa rented by Mr Hazeldene for his North African holiday. While out riding one morning, Marjorie Hazeldene and Clara Trevlyn were taken prisoner by Bou Saoud as additional persuasion on Ali ben Yusef to yield the Eye of Ahmed. (865).

VILLA LUCIA. Mr O's house on the outskirts of Rome. He had the Famous Five's car held up just outside the villa, in an effort to separate them from Wun Lung, so that he could get Wun back to China. However, Mr O had not reckoned on the fighting abilities of the Remove ! (1543).

VILLA MIMOSA. A house on the outskirts of Biskra, rented by Major Cherry while he was searching for Ali ben Yusef who had been abducted by Bou Saoud. When the Major failed to return, the Famous Five, too, left the safety of the town to search for both the Major and Ali. (865).

VILLAGE SHOP, The. The name of Mr Clegg's shop in Friardale. It is a general grocery store; but so far as Greyfriars is concerned, it is a confectioners and bakers ! At times, however, there is quite a run on his "fresh" eggs for use as ammunition against the local or other rival schools.

VINEY, Mr. Solicitor to Sir Reginald Brooke. Scaife knew this and came down to Greyfriars pretending to be Mr Viney's representative. By seeing Sir Jimmy Vivian, he could then kidnap him at a later, favourable opportunity, and so prevent him coming into his inheritance of Pengarth. He instead saw Bunter who was running an errand in Sir Jimmy's place ! (809).

VINO, Joaz. The foreman on Senhor Caminho's plantation, The Boa Vista, in Kenya. With a relative, Perez, he had made the owner a prisoner and, with Perez impersonating Senhor Caminho, they tried to sell the estate to Mr Vernon Smith. Their efforts were foiled by Vernon Smith and the Famous Five realising that something was amiss when they were prevented from bathing in the lake. (1230).

VISITOR'S ROOM. Sited at the end of the Master's passage, it is an infrequently used room, except for prospective parents awaiting interview with the Head. Whereas relatives are free to go to a man's study, unknown visitors to the school wait here for their host. Bunter, hiding here from well deserved bootings or stumpings, picks up morsels of information which frequently turn out to be of great moment !

VIVIAN, Sir Brandon. "A sort of uncle's cousin or cousin's uncle" to Sir Jimmy Vivian. He was a roystering, hard drinking man who met his end in a boating accident at Pengarth. After his death, his manservant Keeley remained as caretaker to the establishment which was placed in Chancery until the heir to the baronetcy, (Sir Jimmy), came of a suitable age to inherit the property. (811).

VIVIAN, Sir James, (Jimmy), Bart. The cousin of Herbert, Earl Mauleverer, he was brought up in Carker's Rents, a London slum, from which he was rescued by Sir Reginald Brooke and sent to Greyfriars. His less than Chesterfieldian manners would have brought tears to Mauleverer's eyes had it not been too much fag to weep ! Inevitably from his upbringing, Sir Jimmy is as tough as they make them, and supplies the brawn his cousin affects to lack in Study No 12. He is a keen but merely average sportsman and, with his cousin, a great friend to the Famous Five.

VON RATTENSTEIN, H.E. Prinz Rupprecht. The son of a naturalised Briton, an ex-German minor nobleman, he has to be one of the worst characters ever to go to Greyfriars. Delighting in acts, both petty and grand, bordering on the criminal, he first split friend against friend. When this failed, he forged Harry Wharton's hand in a letter to Joe Banks. Luckily Bunter, prying as ever for tuck, found the proof of his villainy and so von Rattenstein was expelled. (GBC 40).

VOYSEY, Dr. The Headmaster of Highcliffe School. A man of past retirement age, (it is rumoured that he is 70 years old!), he is totally disinterested in the school and its running which he leaves to anyone who may take an interest. And that is only a few men like Courteney. He is quick to take offence when any one at the school is accused of a wrong act. He seems to support those with titles, or titled relatives, like Ponsonby, rather than the side of justice. He owns a Rembrandt which is said to be worth a fortune. This is more than likely, since it was stolen by "The Wizard", but retrieved immediately by Harry Wharton, (who was out of bounds to give Pon. a deserved thrashing!).

W.

WADDON. The station for Holly House – Mr Henry and Miss Judith Cokers' home. (984).

WADE, Mr. The owner of Wade's Bookshop in Courtfield High Street. Harry Wharton had been accused of going to the Three Fishers on the evidence of his raincoat, found in that resort by Mr Quelch. Bunter had borrowed it one rainy afternoon and followed Stacey to the pub to play billiards. Seeing Mr Quelch approach, Bunter ran, leaving the evidence. When accused in front of the Head, Wharton had the supported alibi of having been in Mr Wade's shop. He is obviously a frequent customer since he had spent the better part of that afternoon talking with the owner. (1426).

WADHAM. It is not certain if he is the senior footman, or whether he was brought in as a temporary replacement during Well's absence one Christmas at Wharton Lodge. It is possible that, if Sir Giles Oakwood was abroad at the time, he may have lent Colonel Wharton his butler's services. (1038).

WADHAM. Sir Giles Oakwood's butler at Oakwood place. (1601).

WAGGS, William. An old farmer of Little Puddleton, Sussex. The "Greyfriars Hikers" visited the village to find it in an uproar. The old gentleman had refused to pay his tithes and, as a result, had his livestock distrained to be sold to pay his dues. The local farmers, enraged at this, had barricaded the village to prevent the auctioneer holding the sale. Knowing that the money would be obtained eventually, Mauleverer paid Hunker, (the Bailiff), the sum due – £25/15/0d. (1333).

WALKER, Mr. Uncle to James Walker. He visited the school one day. In the hope of extracting a "fat tip" from him, Walker persuaded Bunter, (with the promise of six tarts!), to entertain his uncle with a ventriloquial show. Unimpressed, Mr Walker dismissed Bunter who, enraged, gained his revenge by making it seem that Walker was cheeking his uncle. Exeunt Bunter and "Tenner"! (GL 1).

WALKER, "Honest". A tramp who lost his hat in a fracas with the Famous Five. Now, Bunter had hidden £5 belonging to Mr Quelch in his hat band, (in revenge for an impot); Skinner had stolen the hat and thrown it on the village rubbish dump, (in revenge for a "licking"), and Walker had "totted" the hat! Eventually the fiver was recovered, although the hat, it had to be admitted, had seen better days! (1226).

WALKER, Mrs. Hubert. Aunt to James Walker of the Sixth. A somewhat crusty lady who would not listen to her solicitor, or his advice about investing her money. By what was, in law, embezzlement, Simmons saved her money. (954) .

WALKER, James. A Sixth Form prefect who, after Valence left unlamented, went some of the way to repairing his murky behaviour. Nonetheless, going about with Loder and Carne inevitably means that he is not one of the best in the school. However, on occasions, he does try to be straight, and can, sometimes, make a place in the first Eleven.

WALKER, Mr Jimmy. The owner of "Walker's World Renowned Circus", a small show which was dependant on "Pop" for most of its income. Pop, an orphan, had been saved from the workhouse by Mr Walker. When Pop was forced to leave the circus, the gates fell dramatically. Despite this, Walker struggled on, determined that his one time ward might better himself. An honest, loyal and true friend to Pop, he received him back with open arms when he rejoined the show. (GBC 25) .

WALKER, William. A tramp who persuaded Alonzo Todd, (not a difficult task), that he was about to sign the pledge. To help him, Alonzo allowed Walker to stay in the Remove box-room. Only Alonzo was surprised that Walker had raided food and money !

WALKER'S WORLD RENOWNED CIRCUS. A small travelling show which fell on hard times when its star attraction left to be "made a gentleman". When they were performing at Friardale, Pop, "The Boy Acrobat" and star of the ring, left school, against explicit orders, to help the circus' falling receipts. Discovered by Sir Hilton Popper, literally in the act, Pop was disowned, and returned to his true home and first love - the ring. (GBC 25) .

WALLABIES, The Three. Three Australian Juniors at Rylcombe Grammar School. ie Gordon Gay, the leader and Captain of Form and Games, and the brothers Jack and Harry Wootton. (118) .

WALLIS, Dr. General Medical Practitioner in Waddon, and doctor to Mr Henry Coker. He was perplexed by the symptoms shown by his patient which, it transpired, were due to the poison administered by Poynings. (984) .

WALSH, Mr. The owner of Friardale Grange. (939) .

WALSH, Ethel. The daughter of the owner of Friardale Grange who fell through the ice while skating against parental orders. Fearful of being found out, she made Mark Linley, her rescuer, promise to keep silent. This he did, and in the process was accused of being a funk. When Miss Ethel confessed to her father it started a train of events leading up to the reinstatement of Linley, who had been expelled through Ponsonby's plottings. (938-939).

WALSINGHAM. The butler at Combermere Lodge. Convinced by Mr Pilkins, the Estate agent, of Bunter's bona fides, (reinforced by Bunter himself, telephonically, imitating the Estate Agent's voice), he was disarmed for a time by promises of large cheques to meet the expenses. He was horrified to discover the Estate Agent locked in the wine cellar – where he too was trapped by the wily Bunter. Unable to wreak the vengeance he desired by reason of his tenant bolting, he was only placated when Mauleverer came to the rescue, taking the blame for the fraud, since it was he who had asked Bunter to view the house. Placated by largesse, Walsingham became the deferential man-servant. As usual ! (HBE 3)

WALSINGHAM. The final proof to Bunter of the magnificent holiday in store for him at Blackrock Castle was the mention, by Vernon Smith, of the butler. However, Walsingham proved as ephemeral as the Castle ! (1626).

WALSINGHAM, Francis. The butler at Hilton Hall. His normal urbane manner was severely tried when his half-brother, Richard Pike, proved to be an escaped convict from the nearby Blackmoor Prison. Terrified by the threats made, Walsingham tried to help, albeit unwillingly, and was more than relieved when the convict was recaptured. (HBA 6).

WALTERS. Chauffeur to Sir Philip Angel. (822).

WAPSHOT. A small county town, at least one and a half miles beyond Friardale. It is a garrison town which, after serving as an initial training camp for the army, became an important air field for Strategic Air Command, (and as such was photographed by Muccolini to obtain military secrets). On the outskirts of the town is Wapshot Race Course, a small unimportant track, whose only claim to fame is the Wapshot Cup, run in January. The town is served by a railway station, near which is found the Wapshot Hotel.

WARDLE, Mr. A solicitor from Penruddy in Cornwall. Mr Vernon Smith who was buying property in the area, (using Mr Rance as his agent), inquired of Mr Wardle about the deeds to Penruddy Manor, and discovered Mr Rance's fraudulent conversion of clients' money. (1627).

WARING, George. Half brother to Mr Eric Gilmore. He escaped from Blackmoor Prison and, making his way towards Dover with the intention of fleeing the country, met Bunter near Wharton Lodge. The next term, Bunter was convinced that the temporary master, Mr Gilmore, was the escaped convict ! As Greyfriars lay on his route, Waring took refuge in the school and asked Gilmore for help. A request that was refused. In desperation, Waring struck down his half-brother and imprisoned him, leaving him to his fate, about which he cared nothing. But for the perspicacity of the Famous Five, Mr Gilmore would have perished. Waring was soon after recaptured. (1039) .

WARREN, Sir Arthur, Bart. A widower, he is in the diplomatic service. On furlough in England, prior to a posting to China, he met Harry at Colonel Wharton's request. The colonel is an old friend of Sir Arthur, (who named his son after the Colonel) . When his son was asked to leave Oakshott School, Sir Arthur asked the Colonel to keep an eye on him. (1440) .

WARREN, Captain Bernard. The younger brother of Sir Arthur Warren, he walks with a limp as a result of a war injury received on active service. Like his brother, he is a widower, and also has a son named James, (usually abbreviated to Jim), also named after Colonel Wharton his old Commanding Officer. An angry man used to action, he fretted at the forced inactivity his wound caused. When his nephew, James, refused to go to Greyfriars, he sent his son Jim instead – without any intention of defrauding anybody; after all the fees had been paid ! Realising that his son could not continue at Greyfriars for more than one term, he was glad to accept a post as military adviser and instructor in Abyssinia. (HBE 38–39) .

WARREN, James. The son of Sir Arthur Warren. He is a bully and a braggart. Expelled from Oakshott School, Essex, he continued his wayward behaviour, bullying Harry Wharton and Hurree Singh, and then ducking Wharton in the lake at Warren Croft. Refusing parental orders to go to Greyriars, (after his father had left the country), he continued his shady life. To his cousin Jim's discomfort he stayed as a guest of Clarence Cook at Popper Court. Loder, mistaking the facts, wrote to Captain Warren to inform him that an impostor was at Greyfriars while his nephew was at Popper Court gambling ! James did not enjoy his uncle's visit. He was soundly thrashed by the Captain for his behaviour and was sent home, in charge of a constable, to await being sent to his maternal uncle who is "a tough nut". (HBE 38–39) .

WARREN, James, (Jim) . The only son of Captain Bernard Warren. He took the chance of a term at Greyfriars with alacrity. His cousin James had refused to go, vowing that he would be expelled if he went. The Captain's plan was that Jim should present a clean sheet for James, so that he could go to Rookwood the following term. At

Greyfriars, Jim was placed in the Fifth Form. He proved immensely popular and was soon in the First Eleven. Loder was convinced that Jim had taken his place. Hearing a rumour to the effect that Jim was an impostor, (Bunter inevitably!), Loder tried to expose him. Effort after effort failed, until he overheard Bunter on the telephone. As it was James and not Jim he showed up in his true lights, his plotting cannot have been said to have been successful. Jim, as honest as the day, indulges in none of his cousins vices, (and they are legion), and, if truth be known, Jim was glad when the truth came out. He accompanied his father to Abyssinia with the intention of becoming a coffee planter. (HBE 38-39).

WARREN CROFT. A country house some five miles from Wharton Lodge. It is the home of Sir Arthur Warren. For some years his younger brother, Captain Bernard, acted as estate manager, a form of charity which irked. (1440).

WASH, Mr Job. The owner of the store in Packsaddle, Texas, where the Kicking Cayuse buys its provisions. (1575).

WATER LILY, The. A river craft navigable by rowing or sail, (given a favourable wind). She used to belong to "Shifty" Spooner. Sold when he was sent to prison, she was bought by Mr Baker of Friardale who, in turn, rented her to the Famous Five for a cruise up the Thames. Mr Baker had her transported over-land to his nephew's boatyard at Kingston-upon-Thames. Unbeknownst to the Famous Five, or the police, Spooner had hidden his stolen goods in a secret compartment on the boat. A fact which, when it was known, explained Spooner's persistence in following the boating party and his continued efforts to steal her. (HBE 11).

WATERSIDE INN, The. This was a disreputable resort, about half a mile downstream from Greyfriars, frequented by Carberry and his cronies. They inveigled Dicky Nugent to accompany them, soon after his arrival at Greyfriars. Thinking they had heard the Head order them to return to school, (it was Bunter imitating his voice), they made up a story to exonerate their presence here. Enmeshed in his lies, Carberry was caught out and expelled. (107).

WATKINS, Timothy. The Estate Agent at High Hoad. An impoverished man, he saw a fortune for himself if he could bring the market value of Hoad Castle to rock bottom. By then purchasing it himself, he could develop the land. To this end he resurrected the ghost of Hoad Castle, and frightened all and sundry, (including Ponsonby and Co.). Harry Wharton and Co. who were not so easily intimidated, caught him out and exposed his plans. (1335).

WATSON. One of the chauffeurs at the Courtfield Garage. He is frequently employed by Vernon Smith on his nocturnal forays.

WATSON. Chauffeur to Lord Cavandale. (1195).

WATSON. Chauffeur to Lord Mauleverer. (1277).

WATSON. The name given to Bates by Pawson, the butler at Gadsby Croft, when speaking to him in front of the Famous Five. It transpired that they were planning to rob the house and use the Friars as scapegoats. (1339).

WATSON, James. The alias used by Philip Darke when, in escaping from justice, he hypnotised Mr Quelch. As Harry Wharton had recognised his photograph in the newspapers, his ploy did not work, and he was soon arrested. (1517).

WAYLAND. A town in Sussex. Its station is the junction whereat it is necessary to change for Rylcombe, the village and station for St Jim's.

WEASEL, The. A member of Slimy Sudgen's gang. It was his job to reconnoitre houses prior to their being robbed by The Wizard, and to act as lookout during the crime. He would then take the stolen goods to Beech House. When Harry Wharton discovered Lancaster to be The Wizard, the Weasel helped kidnap him. Shortly after this, when the gang was being rounded up, he made a desperate bid to delay the inevitable by attacking Ferrers Locke. An attempt which failed thanks to the intervention of Lancaster. (HBE 7).

WEIR. Built across a tributary of the River Sark below Baker's Mill it serves to create a head of water to power the mill. It is a dangerous spot and is out of bounds to all Friars below the Fifth Form. It was here that Eric Carlow saved Dicky Nugent from a watery grave after he had gone punting against school rules.

WELLS. The butler at Wharton Lodge where he has worked man and boy; graduating to become the head of the domestic staff. The archetypal butler, he is stately, urbane and taciturn, with an impeccable manner - although even his shoulders have been known to shake when Bunter is more than usually fatuous!

WEST, Bill. A rider with Lantham Speedway. Boy McClaren lent him his motor cycle after his own machine had failed. (1220).

WESTBROOK, Captain, O.F. Being short of a man for an Old Boys match, the Captain sent Westbrook a telegram to the United Services Club asking him to play. He arrived too late for the match and, when told of the fantastic goalkeeping of Dick Chester, amazed everyone by his announcement of Chester's death in action. (844) .

WESTMOOR SCHOOL. No mention is made of its location, but the First Eleven have played matches against the school in the past, and presumably still do. (200) .

WHARTON, Miss Amy. Sister of Colonel Wharton and aunt to Harry. She is a gentle, kindly soul who had so much trouble in handling her nephew at one time that the colonel, on his return from India, found him unmanageable. This is all in the past now; and she is not one to bear a grudge. She will never refuse a plea for help, no matter who asks. So soft-hearted is she that she has even sent Harry money when specifically asked not to by her brother. She will, and does, do anything for Harry and his friends; keeping an ever open, welcoming house for them. When in trouble, Harry frequently asks her for advice - he finds it easier to take her gentle admonitions than his uncle's outbursts. Many is the time that Miss Wharton has acted as peacemaker between uncle and nephew. With all her meekness of mien, she is an astute lady who can often sense when something is wrong. As happened when Fish was being held prisoner at The Poplars.

WHARTON, Harry. The only son of Colonel Wharton's late brother and sister-in-law. He was initially brought up by his doting Aunt Amy. Appalled by the results, the colonel sent Harry to Greyfriars. After a more than inauspicious beginning, he became the recognised leader of the form, Junior Games and the Famous Five. Proud, often wilful, sometimes headstrong, Harry Wharton can be stubborn and refuse to take the diplomatic way out of impasses. But, whatever his faults, there is no way in which he will lie, or be guilty of any dishonourable act. If he thinks something is right, he will never shirk unpopularity in the execution of his duty.

WHARTON, Colonel James, (Jim), J.P., O.F., Governor of Greyfriars School. Harry Wharton's uncle and guardian. Upright and totally honest, he is too like his nephew for a quiet life to exist between these two friends. All too often the one, (Harry usually), takes umbrage at some imagined offence, and this leads to a temporary estrangement. Both are inarticulate and find it difficult to swallow their pride and apologise. The colonel is the owner of Wharton Lodge in Surrey, over whose acres he wields a benevolent seigneury. A Justice of the Peace, he is lenient or stern as circumstances dictate - and like his nephew he is never affeared of popular opinion in the face of duty.

WHARTON, Margaret. Sister to Colonel and Miss Amy Wharton. Her married name has not been mentioned. She is a widow living in Bournemouth. When his uncle and aunt had to help her recuperate one Christmas, Harry was glad to have been omitted from the invitation. He has only stayed with her once, and found her a formidable and terrifying lady. So, an invitation to Cavandale Abbey seemed a better alternative ! (1192) .

WHARTON ARMS. Just over the road from Wharton Magnus station this residential inn is the usual place to find a cab for hire.

WHARTON LODGE. Situated in the county of Surrey, the house is some 8-10 miles to the west of Reigate. It lies about a quarter of a mile from Wharton Magnus station. The house is typical of many of the houses in this part of Surrey. It is surrounded by a wooden paling fence enclosing its woods. The extensive grounds also include a formal garden, game preserve and a lake, upon which Harry and his friends boat in the summer and skate in the winter. Wharton Lodge is the home of Colonel and Miss Wharton and their nephew Harry. As befits a military man, the house is a well run, orderly establishment, organised by Wells - supreme below stairs. The house is said to be haunted by the ghost of a Wharton of Carolean times, killed by Cromwell's men who razed the house to the ground. The present house is built upon the same site.

WHARTON MAGNUS. A small hamlet whose name derives from the nearby house. It probably got its name in medieval times when the Manor House still stood. Although there is something of a railway station, the village is now little more than a suburb of Wimford. Despite which it does boast a cottage hospital.

WHEATFIELD LANE, Wharton Magnus, Surrey. The lane in which are to be found both The Bunch of Grapes, (by Mr Hodge), and Wharton Lodge. (1209) .

WHEATSHEAF INN, Cowgate, Surrey. The rendezvous chosen by the "Greyfriars Hikers" to start their holiday. This was somewhat spoilt by the sight of Ponsonby and Co. who had discovered the address by tricking Bob Cherry. (1332) .

WHITEBRIDGE. Some ten miles from Greyfriars, this town is known for its small race course. Bunter, having "conned" £1 from Miss Wharton, "went to the races" here. In fact, having had an expensive tea, he tried to leave the restaurant without paying, but was prevented by "Pop". (1166) .

WHIFFLES, Mr Montague Montmorency. The owner-manager of a pantomime company that performed in Lantham one year. Having helped Mr Whiffles out of a snow drift, Harry Wharton and Co. plucked up courage to ask for parts in the show. Their aim was to earn money to send comforts to the troops in the front line.

Mr Whiffles was amazed to discover that not only could the Removites act, but that they were good. Good enough for Harry Wharton to get a principal part. Apart from the occasional lapse due to Nugent falling in love, the Friars pleased the manager well with their efforts. (409).

WHIFFLES, Mr Montgomery St Ledger. An incredibly pompous man who might be taken for Malvolio, so vain is he ! Totally bald, he sports a wig, and a "full-set" – a closely guarded secret. Until, that is, Bunter saw him bathing in the Sark and, recognising his clothes, borrowed them and thus the circus owners identity, to avoid trouble at school. The bald headed fat man who alternately skulked behind bushes and ranted openly was taken for a madman by his circus hands ! He was more than glad of the imposture when he discovered that Bill Huggins was after him with a grievance to settle. Mr Whiffles finally got back his wig, beard, clothes and personality and, with them, his circus. He found himself considerably the poorer, due to the depradations of Bunter and his ex-manager, Dance. (HBE 28).

WHIFFLES' CIRCUS. See Billy Bunter's Circus.

WHOOF, Mrs. The Rottingdean, (near Brighton), lady who "does" for several holiday bungalows. The Famous Five had asked Mr Hazeldene to arrange the rental of "Chez Nous" on their behalf. Mrs. Whoof would come in daily to do housework and prepare an evening meal for them. (1486).

WIBLEY, William Ernest, (Wib). This future Olivier of the Remove has his being in greasepaint to the exclusion of all else, (including, all too often, his work). His study mates, Desmond, Morgan and Rake, put up as good-naturedly as possible with a room overflowing with the Remove Dramatic Society's props. Wib's greatest ally is perhaps Mr Lazarus who enters wholeheartedly into the creation of a new role. Sadly, Wibley is convinced of his prowess on the games field – a misconception that leads often to rows between him and the Famous Five.

WICKERS, William. One of Solly Lazarus' and Dick Trumper's friends at Courtfield County School, and a member of Courtfield Junior Team.

WIDGERS, Bartholomew, (Barty), O.F. Expelled some years ago for studied impertinence to his Form Master, Mr Prout, he swore to return and "give him six". He returned, but was prevented by the Famous Five from fulfilling his promise. Mr Prout, whose pride was hurt by the gossip, had got the Famous Five "six" each for an imagined slight and so, under Bob Cherry's direction, they captured Mr Prout, (as they thought), to return the compliment. When Mr Prout came on the scene, they found out that they had been whopping Widgers! This was sufficient to make him leave the school! (1237).

WIGGINS, Mr Herbert, M.A. The Master of the Third Form at Greyfriars. He is not amongst the more prominent members of the Common Room, nor is he as strict as many of his colleagues in class; but he is more of an authoritarian than Mr Twigg or Mossoo! His chief hobby is photography for which he has some first class equipment. Bunter had decided to win a photographic prize and so he "borrowed" Mr Wiggins camera. While taking a snap of the owner asleep, Bunter was butted by a bull, and lost the camera in the river.

WILDRAKE, Kit. A member of the Fourth Form at St Jim's. (738).

WILKINSON. Thinking him to be an ex-serviceman down on his luck, the Famous Five allowed him to tag along with them on a caravan tour. When they were joined by Jack Drake, he recognised "Wilkinson" as Bert Gunner, an escaped convict. (707).

WILKINSON, Edward, (Teddy). The most studious member of the Upper Fourth. Unusually, he has a study to himself. But for the fact that he is a good goalkeeper, life would be unbearable for him. When Bob Cherry had to study for the Head's Latin Prize, (his father thought he needed knowledge!), he fell out with the Remove and moved into Wilkinson's study. A move that proved unpopular to both forms.

WILLIAM. A footman at Popper Court.

WILLIAM. The assistant to Mr Grimes, a Courtfield Auctioneer. Bunter had bid to "put some life into things", and found himself the proud owner of a four-poster bed! His efforts to explain to William that he had not bid for it were not successful. (729).

WILLIAM. One of Sir George Tipton's men-servants. (1646).

WILLIAM. Footman at Monson Chalet. (1648).

WILLIAMS. Under chauffuer to Mr Vernon Smith. (1523).

WILLIAMS. The Head's chauffeur. When he was called up, his place was taken by Ferrers Locke, (posing as Robinson), to prosecute his search for Mr Quelch who had been taken prisoner by Slim Jim. (1663).

WILLIAMS, Bill. A platelayer on the L.M.S. Railway. He was working near Crewe when Jerrold Drew threw the secret of

Mr McAlpine's dyeing process out of a train window. The envelope hit him in the face; and he kept the letter until Harry Wharton recovered it. (672).

WILLIAMS, Bill. Marco the lion tamer's real name. (1481).

WILLOW LANE, Wimford. This road leads from the main road towards the River Wyme. Riverside Bungalow is to be found along here. (1261).

WILLOWS, The. An old house with a large walled garden, between Courtfield Common and the river. It is about one mile from Greyfriars and half a mile from Courtfield. This is the house Professor Sparkinson rented for the duration of his stay in England. (HBE 20).

WILMOT, Eric. Mr Hacker's nephew. Amongst the leaders of Topham School, he received a jolt to be accused and sentenced for a theft committed while playing football at St Jude's. His uncle persuaded the Head to admit Eric to Greyfriars - where he went most ungraciously. Mr Hacker tried to help him, but this was neither wanted nor required. This help convinced many of the Remove that Wilmot was a "toady", and led to an increase in his churlish behaviour. He settled down after a time, only to revert to his old ways when Crawley of Topham started to threaten him. Eventually it came out that Crawley was the thief, and Wilmot returned happily to his own school. Not the easiest part of this whole nightmare for Wilmot was trying to keep the facts of his expulsion secret from his widowed mother. (1457-60; 1469-70).

WILMOT, Mr Reginald. Deranged by the swindling activities of Elias J. Poindexter, he swore vengeance on the American sharepusher. He followed Poindexter to Greyfriars, and because the Famous Five saved the Con-man from Wilmot, the latter presumed that there was a connection between the Famous Five and the swindler. This was borne out by Bunter who, in order to get a lift, glibly announced that Poindexter was Harry Wharton's American uncle! Wilmot followed the Famous Five to Wimford Mill where it is hard to say if the Famous Five or Atropos was the more astonished to find Poindexter hiding there! In a bid to flush his quarry, Wilmot fired the mill. However, he was arrested for his crimes and received a prison sentence. (1207-08).

WILMOT-SNELL SCHOLARSHIP. Open to juniors and worth £50 to the winner, the examination consists of two papers covering the Classics, Geography, English, Mathematics and History. Hazeldene, in debt, copied the questions, but the Head, realising that the papers had been tampered with, slightly altered the questions, thus catching out the culprit. Hazel confessed before an inquiry was held and so saved himself from expulsion. Linley, who won the prize that year, gave Hazel the £10 he needed to "square Mr Killip". (949).

WILSON. One of the Popper Court keepers. (1381).

WILSON. An under keeper at Wharton Lodge. (1610).

WILSON, Mr. Sir George Cholmondley was not amused to be told by the Famous Five that they knew a Wilson. The Wimford Postmaster! (1195).

WILSON, Slick. After being taken prisoner by Gomez, Bunter escaped by making Wilson fall out with another member of the bootlegging gang. After Gomez had failed to kill Harry Wharton on the Hair Trigger, Wilson shot at him. The bullet missed and the ricochet hit Myron Polk. Wilson made several blundering attempts to get Wharton for Polk, before finally being arrested by Peter Carter when posing as Mr Fish's chauffeur. (GBC 21).

WILSON, Tinker. A ruffianly brute who made more of a living out of theft than tinning. He had been paid by Cyril Rackstraw to take Tatters and bring him up as a waif. Tatters was constantly maltreated and thrashed because he would not steal. When he managed to escape from the tinker, Wilson followed him to Greyfriars, and twice managed to take him back. The first time was foiled by Mr Quelch and Mr Prout; the second by the Famous Five who tied up Wilson before handing him over to the police. (GBC 19).

WIMFORD. A town in mid-Surrey, lying on the main Sussex to London road. It is barely ten minutes from Wharton Lodge, ie about three miles. The River Wyme flows southward through the town. The town boasts two cinemas - The Wimford Picture Palace and The Imperial Cinema. There is a railway station outside the town on the Wharton Lodge side. To the west of the town on a piece of high ground used to stand Wimford Mill. It was said to be haunted by the ghost of the last miller who hung himself. The mill was destroyed by arson when Mr R. Wilmot fired it in a crazed attempt on Elias J. Poindexter's life, (and co-incidently, the Famous Fives'). The town is the shopping centre for Wharton Lodge, and is presumably more than adequate in this respect, since there is no mention of Miss Wharton shopping in Reigate - some ten miles away.

WINGATE, Captain Bert. The cousin of George and Jack Wingate. He is in the Loamshire Regiment and is in charge of recruit training. As such, he was persuaded, by George, to arrange a match between the regiment and Greyfriars. Loder, who had a bet on the result of the match, tried to "fix" the outcome but, the Famous Five, who had been given leave to watch the game, provided the match-winners - leaving Loder to find £25 to settle the outstanding half of his bet with Banks. (435).

WINGATE, George Bernard, (Major). The second son of Mr Wingate, lately of Surrey and now of Cheshire. He is the Head of School and the Captain of Games. His popularity is complete, (even Loder and his cronies have to admit a begrudging respect for him). The benign firmness of his rule endears him to all - masters and scholars alike. His integrity is such that when his minor was seen at a pub, Wingate resigned rather than continue as many others would.

WINGATE, John, (Jack), (Minor). Not wishing to go to Greyfriars, he tried to make use of his brother's position when he first arrived. For a while he was as unpopular as is possible, and his early days in the Third Form were hard. Eventually, however, he settled down. Perhaps by way of revolt against being the brother of the Head of School, he is not averse to a cigarette or a flutter.

WIZARD, The. The nickname of a famous safe cracker and thief - Dick Lancaster. Until his exposure by Ferrers Locke, there was no clue to his identity. (HBE 7).

WODEHOUSE SCHOOL. The school attended by Mr Eric Gilmore and his half brother, George Waring, (Convict 19). Their similarity was such that they were known as "The Siamese Twins". When accused of being Waring, Mr Gilmore gave his old Headmaster as a character reference. (1040).

WOLD. The Wiltshire country town near Nugent's home and, incidently, not far from Jimmy Silver's place.

WOLF, Ludwig, Lieutenant. A prisoner of war held at Wapshot where there was, for a time, a concentration camp. He escaped and evaded the local search parties. A large party of Friars and Highcliffians had been stranded by a blocked railway line and, in their search for shelter, saw Wolf, "a good 15 miles from Wapshot". They found and forced an entry to "The House on the Heath". After an adventurous night, during which several of their number disappeared, they found and caught the German who was being hidden by Crawley, the owner's secretary. (461).

WOOD, Dr. A general medical practitioner of Leyford, Oxfordshire. He was called in to treat Sir Richard Ravenspur after he had received a gun shot wound. Captain Ravenspur suspected the bona fides of the assistant whom Dr Wood was said to have sent with medicine for Sir Richard, and was poisoned by the draught. The Captain was admitted under the care of Dr Wood to the Leyford Nursing Home. (1122).

WOOD LANE. Runs through Friardale Wood into Friardale Lane. It is little more than a cart track. When the Famous Five were caught in a downpour they sheltered in a car parked in the lane - and blocking it. It proved to belong to the man guilty of the bank robbery for which Mr John Hazeldene found himself the prime suspect. (1417).

WOODEND. A village five miles or so from Greyfriars, in the opposite direction to Courtfield. Swinger's Circus was pitched here when Bunter was asked to join the Wild Weird Freaks. Captain Spencer, when Vernon Smith suggested he had been visiting the hiding place of his loot, claimed to have cycled "round by Woodend". Although only a village, it does have a railway station.

WOODFORD, Kent. A village about two miles from Hawkscliff, through which it is necessary to travel if going to Hawkscliff by car. It is otherwise off the beaten track so far as Greyfriars is concerned; Friars usually take the cliff path to visit Redwing's home. (1088).

WOODFORD, Surrey. A few miles from Wharton Lodge, this village is the terminus of the local railway line from Elmbridge via Wharton Magnus to Woodford, where it is possible to connect with the main line to Redgate. Bunter, leaving Wharton Lodge, caught the local line from Wharton Magnus and, on his journey, purchased a "paste" diamond from a Mr Sniggerson. (1352).

WOODHURST, Surrey. Some three miles from Wimford Common. Muccolini sent Bunter with a false message to the inn here. The idea was that Jimmy Guggs would assault him en route. Zara, out for a ride, came to his rescue as he crossed Woodhurst Heath, just outside the village. (1485).

WOOSE, Mr. He first came to Greyfriars when Mr Prout had sacked Mr Quelch. He was nicknamed the Squeaker almost as soon as he arrived. He was "a quiet well-mannered little gentleman who peered rather like an owl from large glasses". He was often late, made many mistakes and did not succeed in impressing the Remove the least little bit. After the reinstatement of Mr Quelch, he was kept on by Dr Locke in the joint capacities of librarian and Headmaster's secretary, as well as art Master. Posts that suited him much better than teaching the Remove! After he left Greyfriars to work in one of the war-time ministries, his place was taken by Mr Lamb.

WOOSEY, Mr. One of the names given to Mr Woose by the school because of his absent minded behaviour. It is a slightly unkind play on words! Because of his mildness of manner, the joke spread throughout the school, from Dr Locke down, until it is probable that he was not certain of his own name!

WOOSTER, Mr. The casting director of Magic Films. Disbelieving the interminable list of Bunter's capabilities and self-awarded superlatives, he tried to cast him as a comic waiter to the future star's fury! Discovered to have wedged his way in by fraud, Bunter soon got the boot. (1099).

WOOSTER, Mr. The tailor in Ashwood whom Bunter employed to make several suits. In his usual aristocratic way, he ordered more than he needed and put the bill to somebody else's account — this time Lord Cavandale's. (1192).

WOOTTON, Jack and Harry. A pair of Australian brothers at Rylcombe Grammar School. With Gordon Gay, they make up the unholy trinity of the Three Wallabies! (118).

WORST BOY AT GREYFRIARS, THE. (Title GBC Volume 1). Not realising that his uncle was off on a dangerous mission, Harry Wharton played football rather than meet him for tea. Remorse soon turned to bitterness as Bunter spread tattle to the effect that Wharton preferred footer to saying goodbye to his uncle. A succession of misunderstandings, compounded by Wharton's pride, led to his downfall and demotion from the Form captaincy. Continuing his wayward behaviour he faced expulsion, only to be reprieved at the eleventh hour by Dr Locke.

WORTH, Major. The governor of H.M.P. Stoneville who was absent when Dr Locke tried to see him about obtaining Vernon Smith's release from prison. (933).

WRIGGLES. The contortionist in Muccolini's Circus. Friendly with Marco and Tip, he too had to bear the cheek of Bunter. (HBE 55-56).

WU, Mr. One of Tang Wang's emissaries. He followed Ferrers Locke's party through France with the unwilling and unwitting help of Bunter. As the Silver Star was about to sail from Marseilles he was taking aim to shoot at Wun Lung when Ferrers Locke beat him to the draw. (1178).

WUN CHUN LUNG, Mr. A rich Chinese merchant from Canton. Following the fashion of Westernisation prevalent among a large section of his countrymen, he sent his sons, Wun Lung and Hop Hi, to Greyfriars. When Tang Wang demanded money of him for his rebellion, Mr Wun refused to make the required contribution. His eldest son, (perhaps the most important person in the household, after the oldest), was threatened. To contain the threat, Ferrers Locke was asked to escort his son to Canton for safety which, after many dangers, he finally did. Full of gratitude, Mr Wun gave all the Friars valuable presents. Like all Chinese of his generation, Mr Wun is a mixture of autocrat and child. Autocratic to his household and children, (albeit a gentle autocrat); he goes in fear and trembling of his father, Wun Ko, whose every word is law to him.

WUN HOP HI. Wun Lung's younger brother by their father's Number Two Wife. He is, if possible, even more mischievious than his older brother. He is certainly adept at turning practial jokes against the perpetrators! After standing a feed of gigantic proportions to the Second on his arrival at Greyfriars, (he knew he could not fight them!), he soon became a popular member of the form.

WUN KO, Mr. The father of Mr Wun Chun Lung, and the undisputed head of the family as befits the eldest and most venerable member. When Mr Wun tried to stop Wun Lung and friends going to free the Friars captured by Tang Wang, Grandfather Ko fairly "roasted" father Chung for not letting his son do his duty to his guests, irrespective of the dangers. (1176).

WUN LUNG. The oldest son of Mr Wun Chung Lung, and older brother of Hop Hi. He shares Study No 13 with Bob Cherry, Hurree Singh and Mark Linley. One of the craftiest men at Greyfriars, he often lies shamelessly, and can usually be trusted to turn a situation to his advantage. If a feed is stolen, it is discovered to the discomfort of the "guests", that it was cat or dog stew! His sleight of hand equals that of Wibley but, unfortunately, all too often, he uses it for malicious jokes. The one person he will never jape is Bob Cherry, whom he has idolised since Bob stood up for him on his arrival. It was also Bob who mistrusted Mr O and Dr Sin when they tried to abduct Wun to take him back to China to become Mr O Bo's adopted heir. Not having a son himself, Mr O was desperate to adopt Wun in order to have someone to oversee his last rites and funerary pomp, which if not performed by an eldest son means a spirit unhappily haunting the earth unable to reach heaven. When Wun's life was threatened by Tang Wang it took all of Ferrers Locke's ingenuity and cunning to get him to the safety of his father's home in Canton. When Wun heard that three of his friends had been captured by Tang, he persuaded his Grandfather to order his father to allow him to go in search of them. Thus, for all his oddly childish behaviour, Wun is as plucky as the best of the Remove.

WUN SAN. The daughter of Mr Wun Chung Lung by his Number Three Wife. (1176).

WYATT, Mr. The Headmaster of St Jude's School. He is a scholarly man and is on good terms with Mr Quelch. When the Remove, booked for a match against St Jude's, were detained, Vernon Smith got Bunter to imitate Dr Wyatt's voice and invite Mr Quelch to meet him to discuss a paper written by Mr Quelch. As the match was at St Jude's the Remove were more than embarrassed to be ordered back to school by their irate Form Master. (1269) .

WYME, River. The river from which the town of Wimford takes its name. It meanders through that part of Surrey in a series of slow bends and ox-bows. Some idea of these meanders can be gauged from the fact that, although it is three miles by road from Wharton Lodge to Wimford, it is six or seven miles by river. The river is nearly a mile from Wharton Lodge, and Riverside Bungalow is some three miles down stream, with Monk's Eyot, (or Island), about half way between them.

WYNN, Fatty. A Junior at St Jim's. Despite being more than rotund, he manages to be a first class goalkeeper and bowler. For all his size, and a gargantuan appetite, he is not the glutton and liar to which the Bunters and Trimbles of this world aspire.

X.

XERO, Silvio. A half-caste from the Pacific. He murdered Black Peter in a beach brawl on one of the islands, and then followed Ben Dance to England to try to steal the carved map showing the whereabouts of Black Peter's treasure. When Vernon Smith's party next met him, in the Pacific, he had taken Dance prisoner to force him to reveal the hiding place. Luck favoured Xero, for he found the chart after Tom Redwing had thrown it in the sea rather than allow Soames to gain possession of it. He made his way to Caca Island and, having been made prisoner by the Friars, was freed by Talupa. Rather than make an immediate escape, he tried to murder Ben Dance, who shot him in self-defence. A thoroughly evil man, who boasted of twenty or thirty murders, his death was mourned by no-one. (GBC 11) .

Y.

YATES. A Fourth Former at Highcliffe and a staunch supporter of Courtenay.

YEO, Mr. The landlord of the Ship Inn at Crewey where Vernon Smith and his friends stayed after making Count Zero believe that they had left Polpelly for good. (1454).

YO'O. A tiny Pacific island no more than half a mile at its widest. Its population has all been "blackbirded". Mauleverer and Co. were stranded here when Ysabel Dick stole their boat, after he had escaped from custody in Barney Hall's boat. They managed to cover the twenty or so miles back to Kalua by building themselves a canoe. (1591).

YORKE. The Junior Captain at Redclyffe School. (253).

YSABEL DICK. An outcast of the Pacific - alcoholic, lazy, defiant of authority and a beachcomber. He was deported from Kalua soon after Mauleverer's party arrived, but still contrived to try to kill Mauly on many occasions. Van Dink, with whom he used to sail, was his evil genius, and persuaded him to try harder to get Mauly. It was not until informed by Van Dink that Mauly was dead and that, having succeeded to the title and fortune, he, Van Dink, wished to share it with him, that Brian Mauleverer, (for it was indeed him), realised the evil of his ways. After Van Dink's death, (which he was in part responsible for), he was more than relieved to find his cousin still alive. (HBE 12).

YUBA DICK. One of the ranch hands on the Kicking Cayuse. He was not involved in Barney Stone's cattle rustling activities. (HBE 32).

YUMA BILL. A member of the Mexican bootlegging gang run by Gomez for Myron Polk. He played a part in kidnapping Harry Wharton in Polk's final bid to remove the Friar whom he saw as a threat to his continued stardom. (1107).

YUSSUF. An arab member of Ludwig Krantz's slave trading gang. Smithy had been captured by Krantz and was being guarded by Yussuf when he tried to escape, only to be re-captured immediately. Yussuf was almost certainly one of the eight or ten members of the gang killed by Kikolobo in his pursuit of Krantz to free the Friars. (1234).

ZAMPA. The Italian engineer in the M.V. Fanny Jones, the vessel chartered by Colonel Wharton to take Hurree Singh and Co. to India. It was Zampa who realised that the propeller had been sabotaged by Pietro when the ship broke down in the Red Sea. (964).

ZARA. Known as "The Queen of the Ring", she is the bare-back rider in Muccolini's circus. A fiery, passionate lady who believes in the "sight", and so gave Bunter credence when he claimed to have seen and heard her father in Zara's crystal ball. She took Bunter's word that it was he who had gone to her rescue when her horse bolted; and so for a time he basked in her approbation. But when she discovered that he was a fraud, she was as implacable a foe as she had been a generous friend. After Marco took over the running of the Circus, she married him and became Mrs. Bill Wiliams. (HBE 55-56).

ZERO, Count. Determined to find the treasure hidden by an ancestor in Polpelly, he kidnapped Vernon Smith. The price of freedom was to be the handing over of Polpelly by Mr Vernon Smith who had bought the property. Thwarted by Bunter freeing his prisoner, he followed the Greyfriars party to Devonshire. There he tried to frighten them away by haunting the house. He captured Nugent and Bull, intending to add all the other Friars to his tally, but was outwitted. Firstly, Vernon Smith managed to trick and trap him, and secondly, Nugent and Bull found the treasure. Magnamanious for once, Vernon Smith let him go. (HBE 39).

ZERO, Captain Marco. Count Zero's ancestor who was captured after the Spanish Armada and held prisoner in Polpelly. While there he managed to hide the treasure which his ship, the San Pietro, had been carrying. (1453).

ZEUS, M.Y. Kalizelos' luxury yacht. (1277).

ZORRO, Juan. The owner of Zorro's Spanish Circus. He is a ruffianly, cruel brute. Sir James Hobson had paid him to keep Pedrillo in his circus. However, when the acrobat was injured in a fall, he washed his hands of him - an injured acrobat was no good to him. When Sir James heard that Pedrillo was at Greyfriars, he was furious and ordered Zorro to take him back by force. Harry Wharton suspected the truth and made Sir James "rescue" his nephew Peter from the circus owner.   (HBE 77).

APPENDICES.

1) Greyfriars School Form Lists.
2) Greyfriars Study Lists.
3) Magnets reproduced to June 1982.
4) Howard Baker Editions published to June 1982.
5) Greyfriars Book Club Volumes published to May 1982.
6) Holiday Annuals reproduced to June 1982.
7) Greyfriars Library Editions published.
8) Miscellaneous Greyfriars publications by Howard Baker.

APPENDIX 1.

Greyfriars School Form Lists.

We know that there are over 300 scholars at Greyfriars School. This list includes all those mentioned to date, and totals 158.

Sixth Form.

Bancroft.
Barnes.
Benson.
Bentley.
Carford,   (Ma).
Carne, A.
Coker, R. (Mi).
Datchett.
Dempster.
Dodds.
Doone.
Faulkener,   L.
Gwynne,   P.
Hacker.
Hammersley,   V.
Laurence.
Loder,   G.
Lang.
Longley.
Lucas.
North, T.
Parkinson.
Phipps.
Reynolds,   R.
Sykes.
Tremaine,   C.
Walker,   J.
Wingate, G, (Ma)
Yates, G.

Fifth Form.

Bland, E.
Blundell, G.
Coker, H, (Ma).
Fitzgerald, T.
Giddy.
Greene, W.
Higgs.
Hilton, C.
Potter, G.
Price, S. (Ma).
Smith, E, (Ma).
Tomlinson,T,(Ma).
Wavery, F.

Shell.

Carr, A.
Chowne, C.
Churchill,   L.
Clancy.
Gilbert.
Hobson, J.
Hoskins, C.
Jackson, P.
Jones, (Ma).
Longe, A.
Maddison.
Miles, S.
Milsom.
Mole.
Pimble.
Rayner, N.
Robinson, J.
Stewart, E.

Upper   Fourth Form.

Angel, A.
Bates.
Blane.
Carford,   (Mi).
Castle.
Dabney, W.
Doone, P, (mi).
Fitzgerald, P.
Fry, E.
Giddy.
Kenney, P.
Lorne.
MacDougall,   R.
Murphy, S.
Penney.
Phipps, C.
Scott, J.
Temple, C.
Tomlinson,E,(Mi).
Tunstall.
Turner,   M.
Wilkinson,   E.

Remove.	Third Form.	Second Form.
Bolsover,P,(Ma).	Bolsover, H,(Mi)	Bilsby.
Brown, T.	Bolton, O.	Bunter, S, (Mi)
Bull, J.	Conrad, L.	Castle, T.
Bulstrode, G.	Grant.	Carey.
Bunter, W, (Ma).	Lunn, H.	Diggs.
Cherry, R.	O'Rourke, T.	Gatty, G.
Delarey, P.	Perkins.	Green. Gunn.
Desmond, M.	Robinson, (Mi).	Hop Hi.
Dupont, N.	Paget, P.	Lankester.
Dutton, T.	Simpson, J.	Legge.
Elliott, N.	Tubb, G.	Marsden, E.
Field, S.	Wingate, J,(Mi).	Monson.
Fish, F.		Myers, E.
Hazeldene, P.		Norton.
Hilary, R.		Nugent, R, (Mi).
Kipps, O.		Parrott.
Linley, M.		Pettifer, J.
Mauleverer, H.		Price.
Morgan, D.		Smith, H, (Min).
Newland, M.		Spring, C.
Nugent, F, (Ma).		Sylvester, R.
Ogilvy, D.		Tatton, R.
Penfold, R.		Todd, E.
Rake, R.		
Redwing, T.		
Russell, R.		
Singh, H.		
Skinner, H.		
Smith, R, (Mi).		
Snoop, S.		
Stott, W.		
Todd, A.		
Todd, P.		
Treluce, A.		
Trevor, H.		
Vernon Smith, H.		
Vivian, J.		
Wharton, H.		
Wibley, W.		
Wun Lung.		

APPENDIX 2.

Greyfriars Study Lists.

Unfortunately, there is not as much information about study occupants as is needed to compile a complete list. This problem is compounded by the practice of changing studies at the start of term. This list is, therefore, to some extent conjectural.

Sixth Form

Study-Bedrooms are allocated to each member of the form. There is no mention of any of them being numbered.

Fifth Form.

No. 1. Bland & Blundell.
No. 2. Fitzgerald & Smith, (Ma).
No. 3. Wavery.
No. 4. Coker, Greene & Potter.
No. 5. Hilton & Price.
No. 6. Higgs & Tomlinson.

Shell.

No. 1. Carr & Miles.
No. 2. Chowne & Churchill.
No. 3. Rayner & Stewart.
No. 4. Jackson & Robinson.
No. 5. Hobson & Hoskins.
No. 6. Lange.

Upper Fourth.

No. 1. Murphy.
No. 2. Dabney, Fry & Temple.
No. 3. Turner.
No. 4. Fitzgerald & MacDougall.
No. 5. Wilkinson.
No. 6. Angel & Kenney.
No. 7. Doone.
No. 8. Scott & Tomlinson, (Mi).

Remove.

No. 1.   Nugent & Wharton.
No. 2.   Bulstrode, Brown & Hazeldene.
No. 3.   Ogilvy & Russell.
No. 4.   Vernon Smith & Redwing.
No. 5.   Hilary & Kipps.
No. 6.   Desmond, Morgan, Rake, & Wibley.
No. 7.   Bunter (Ma), Dutton, Todd (A), & Todd (P).
No. 8.   Elliott, & Smith, (Mi).
No. 9.   Newland, Penfold, Treluce, & Trevor.
No. 10. Bolsover (Ma) & Dupont.
No. 11. Skinner, Snoop, & Stott.
No. 12. Delarey, Maulverer, & Vivian.
No. 13. Cherry, Linley, Singh, & Wun Lung.
No. 14. Bull, Field, & Fish.

Third and Second Forms

The Third and Second forms do not have studies, but instead have to use their Form Rooms for both recreation and preparation.

APPENDIX 3.

A complete list of Magnets reproduced by the Greyfriars Press up to June 1982

Abbreviations used in the Table:
         A ... Greyfriars Holiday Annual
         B ... Howard Baker Edition
         G ... Greyfriars Book Club
         H ... Howard Baker Annual
         L ... Greyfriars Library

From	To	Vol		From	To	Vol		From	To	Vol	
1	10	G	3	487	494	G	24	779		G	37
1		H	4	496	498	G	27	781	784	G	37
11	20	G	42	501	505	G	27	787		G	37
21	30	G	43	507	508	G	27	789		G	14
31	40	G	44	510	511	G	27	793	799	G	14
43	50	G	13	513		H	12	806	812	G	33
59		G	13	517	522	G	28	814		G	33
100		A	27	525	526	G	28	819	823	G	34
100	107	G	30	528		G	28	826		B	82
117	125	G	18	530	533	G	28	828	830	G	34
137		H	14	569	572	B	67	834		B	70
144	151	G	31	584		H	6	841		G	38
145		A	28	585		B	67	843		G	38
173	174	A	20	597		H	11	844		B	76
176	184	G	16	649		H	16	846		G	38
200		H	13	651		H	16	848		H	15
234		H	2	672		H	12	853	855	G	38
247	254	G	7	682		G	22	858	860	G	38
288		H	13	689		G	22	862	869	G	8
306		A	25	693		G	22	874	877	B	82
392		H	13	704	709	G	22	"	"	L	1
401		H	16	715		G	22	879	888	G	1
407		H	16	723		H	10	893		H	15
409		H	12	729	730	G	36	896		H	15
412	413	G	39	737	739	G	36	897		B	80
415	416	G	39	743	745	G	36	898		B	83
418	420	G	39	748		G	36	899	900	B	80
422	423	G	40	749	753	G	35	904		B	83
425		G	40	755	759	G	35	906	909	B	80
428		G	40	760	761	B	82	"	"	L	3
429		H	11	763	765	G	37	910	917	B	3
431		H	11	766		G	12	918	922	B	71
433	435	G	40	768	774	G	12	923	931	G	2
461		H	5	776		G	12	932	933	B	71

From	To	Vol		From	To	Vol		From	To	Vol	
935	936	B	83	1050	1052	B	73	1190		B	13
938		B	76	1053		B	79	1191	1194	B	22
939		B	81	1054		B	74	1195	1203	G	19
940		B	76	1055		B	79	1204		B	22
942		B	77	1056	1057	B	70	1205		H	12
944		B	81	1058		B	74	1206		B	22
945	948	B	77	1059	1067	B	27	1207	1208	H	9
949		B	81	1068		B	73	1209	1219	B	7
950	951	B	77	1069	1076	B	28	1220		B	76
952	955	B	81	1077		B	79	1221	1223	B	63
956	957	L	4	1078	1082	B	23	1224	1225	H	10
956	959	B	78	1083		B	76	1226		B	13
960	970	G	4	1084	1086	B	23	1227		B	21
971		B	78	1087	1089	H	4	1228	1236	B	65
972		B	83	1090		B	73	1237	1243	B	66
973		B	78	1091		B	74	1244	1246	H	2
974		B	74	1092	1099	G	20	1247	1254	B	4
975	979	G	29	1100	1107	G	21	1255	1261	B	6
980		B	83	1108		B	74	1262	1263	B	53
981	984	G	29	1109		B	7	1264	1268	B	58
985	990	G	15	1110		B	72	1269		B	6
991		B	83	1111	1117	B	69	1270	1275	B	53
992		H	14	1118	1125	B	36	1276		B	58
"		A	35	1126	1128	B	72	1277	1284	B	1
993		B	79	1129	1131	B	68	1285	1296	B	2
994	995	G	15	1132		B	61	1297	1307	G	9
996		H	14	1133	1134	B	7	1308	1310	B	60
"		L	2	1135		B	66	1311		B	13
997	1004	G	6	1136		B	72	1312	1316	B	61
1005		H	13	1137		B	73	1317		B	13
1006		B	74	"		L	2	1318		H	1
1007	1013	B	75	1138	1151	B	5	1319	1320	B	61
1014		B	74	"	"	B	5a	1321	1322	B	63
"		L	2	1152		B	79	1323	1324	H	8
1015		B	73	1153		B	76	1325	1327	B	31
1016		G	26	1154	1155	B	68	1328		B	13
"		L	2	1156		H	10	1329	1330	H	5
1017	1026	G	11	1157	1158	B	68	1331	1340	B	19
1027		B	78	1159		B	13	1341	1342	B	20
1028	1029	G	26	1160		B	60	1343		H	7
1030		B	79	1161	1168	G	25	1344	1348	B	20
1031	1034	G	26	1169	1174	B	21	1349	1353	B	8
1035		B	70	1175	1177	B	24	1354	1358	B	24
1036	1037	B	58	1178	1185	B	25	1354	1358	B	24a
1038		H	8	1175	1185	B	25a	1359		B	8
1039	1041	B	70	1186		H	9	1360	1367	B	51
1042		B	64	1187	1188	B	13	1368	1373	B	52
1043	1049	B	10	1189		B	79	1374	1382	B	46

From	To	Vol		From	To	Vol		From	To	Vol
1383	1389	B	64	1485	1490	B	56	1575	1582	B	32
1390	1397	B	42	1491		H	3	1583	1584	B	52
1398	1400	B	43	1492		B	56	1585	1587	H	7
1401	1403	H	6	1493	1497	B	47	1588	1599	B	12
1404	1412	B	9	1498		B	56	1600	1608	B	15
1413	1417	B	33	1499	1501	B	47	1609	1612	H	1
1418		B	34	1502	1509	B	48	1613	1614	B	57
1419	1421	B	33	1510	1517	B	35	1615	1622	B	49
1422	1427	B	16	1518	1525	B	37	1623	1630	B	50
1428	1433	B	17	1526	1530	B	40	1631	1638	B	54
1422	1433	B	18	1531	1532	B	3	1639	1642	B	55
1434	1439	B	34	1533	1535	B	40	1643	1650	B	11
1440	1447	B	38	1536	1540	B	57	1651		H	3
1448	1455	B	39	1541	1544	B	43	1652	1659	B	26
1456		B	31	1545	1552	B	62	1660	1667	B	29
1457	1460	B	14	1553	1555	B	63	1668	1675	B	30
1461	1468	B	44	1556	1559	B	14	1676	1682	B	41
1469	1470	B	16	1560		B	57	1683		H	1
1471	1478	B	45	1561	1568	B	59				
1479	1480	B	17	1569	1572	B	60				
1481	1484	B	55	1573	1574	B	31				

APPENDIX 4.

Howard Baker Editions.

The complete list of Volumes of Magnets published by The Greyfriars Press up to June 1982. Note that Volumes marked * are out of print. This list is correct at the time of going to press.

No.	Title.	Source.
1.	Billy Bunter in the Land of the Pyramids....	.1277-1284.
2.	The Rebellion of Harry Wharton...*.	1285-1296.
3.	Billy Bunter of Bunter Court..... .	910-917.
4.	Billy Bunter & the Terror of the Form.....	.1247-1254.
5.	Billy Bunter & the Courtfield Cracksman...*.	1138-1151.
5a.	Billy Bunter & the Courtfield Cracksman...	.1138-1151.
6.	The Downfall of Harry Wharton.'....	.1255-1261;1269.
7.	The Greyfriars Pretender.........*.	1209-1219.
8.	The Mystery of Wharton Lodge.....*.	1349-1353;1359.
9.	The Schemer of the Remove........*.	1404-1412.
10.	Billy Bunter & the Greyfriars Mutiny......*.	1043-1049.
11.	Six Boys in a Boat............... .	1643-1650.
12.	The Greyfriars Adventurers....... .	1588-1598.
13.	Bunter the Ventriloquist.........*.	1311;1317;1159;1328 *.1226;1187;1188;1190
14.	My Lord Bunter....................	.1556-1559;1457-1460
15.	Calling Mr. Quelch...............*.	1600-1608.
16.	Harry Wharton's Enemy...........*.	1422-1427;1469-1470
17.	The Black Sheep of Greyfriars....*.	1428-1433;1479-1480
18.	The Greyfriars Double............*.	1422-1433.
19.	The Greyfriars Hikers...........*.	1331-1340.
20.	Alonzo the Great................*.	1341-1342;1344-1348
21.	The Tyrant of Greyfriars........*.	1169-1174;1227.
22.	Billy Bunter's Christmas........*.	1191-1194;1204;1206
23.	The Joker of Greyfriars.........*.	1078-1082;1084-1086
24.	The Kidnapped Schoolboys;.......*.	1354-1358. The Terror of the Tong..........*.1175-1177.
24a.	The Mysterious Mr. Kranz........*.	1354-1358.
25.	Billy Bunter in China...........*.	1178-1185.
25a.	Greyfriars Chums in China.......*.	1175-1185.
26.	A Bargain for Bunter............*.	1652-1659.
27.	The Shadow over Harry Wharton....*.	1059-1067.

292

APPENDIX 5.

Greyfriars Book Club.

Listed are all the Volumes in this library, not only Magnets, to May 1982. Volumes marked * are out of print.
Abbreviations: M = Magnet.
                G = Gem.
                B = Bullseye.

Greyfriars Book Club Editions.

No.	Title.	Source.
1	The Worst Boy at Greyfriars	*.M. 879- 888.
2	Loder for Captain	*.M. 923- 931.
3	The Making of Harry Wharton	*.M. 1- 10.
4	Harry Wharton & Co in India	*.M. 960- 970.
5	Tom Merry's Schooldays	*.G. 1- 15.
6	Paul Dallas at Greyfriars	*.M. 997-1004.
7	The Greyfriars Crusaders	*.M. 247- 254.
8	The Sheik of Greyfriars	.M. 862- 869.
9	Dick the Penman	*.M.1297-1307.
10	The First Ten Bullseyes	*.B 1- 10.
11	The Treasure Hunters	.M.1017-1026.
12	Harry Wharton & Co in Africa	.M. 766; 768- 774; 776
13	New Boys at Greyfriars	.M. 43- 50; 59.
14	Levison's Return	.M. 793- 799; 789.
15	The Boxer of Greyfriars	.M. 985- 990; 994- 995
16	Cock of the Walk	.M. 176- 184.
17	Outcast of the School	.G. 759- 767.
18	The Bounder of Greyfriars	.M. 117- 125.
19	Tatters of the Remove	.M.1195-1203.
20	Harry Wharton & Co in Hollywood.	.M.1092-1099.
21	The Greyfriars Film Stars	.M.1100-1107.
22	The Schoolboy Caravanners	.M. 682; 689; 693; 704- 709; 715.
23	The Toff of St. Jim's	.G. 334- 341; 351- 353
24	The Fall of the Bounder	.M. 487- 494.
25	Action at Greyfriars	.M.1161-1168.
26	The Toad of the Remove	.M.1028-1035.
27	The Flogging Judge Jeffreys	.M. 496- 498; 501- 505 507; 508; 510; 511
28	Tom Redwing's Triumph	.M. 517- 522; 525; 526; 528; 530- 533

295

APPENDIX 6.

Holiday Annuals Published to June 1982.
The reprinted Greyfriars Holiday Annuals are not given
Library Numbers. Volumes marked * are out of print.

No.	Title.	Year.	Magnets
	Greyfriars Holiday Annual.........1920.*.		173- 174.
	Greyfriars Holiday Annual.........1921..		
	Greyfriars Holiday Annual.........1925.*.		306.
	Greyfriars Holiday Annual.........1927..		100.
	Greyfriars Holiday Annual.........1928.*.		145.
	Greyfriars Holiday Annual.........1935..		992.
	Greyfriars Holiday Annual.........1941..		942.
1	Greyfriars Press Holiday Annual...1973..		1318;1609-1612
	.... .1683.		
2	Howard Baker Holiday Annual.......1974..		1491;1651.
3	Greyfriars Holiday Annual.........1974.*.		234;1244-1246
4	Greyfriars Holiday Annual.........1975.*.		1;1089.
5	Greyfriars Holiday Annual.........1976.*.		461;1329-1330
6	Greyfriars Holiday Annual.........1977..		584;1401-1403
7	Howard Baker Summer Omnibus.......1977..		1343;1585-1587
8	Greyfriars Holiday Annual.........1978..		1038;1323-1324
9	Howard Baker Easter Omnibus.......1978..		1186;1207-1208
10	Greyfriars Holiday Annual.........1979..		723;1156;1224
	.........1225.		
11	Billy Bunter's Own Collection.....1979..		429; 431; 597
12	Greyfriars Holiday Annual.........1980..		409; 513;
	.........672;1205.		
13	Greyfriars Holiday Annual.........1981..		200; 288;
	.........392;1005.		
14	Collector's Pie No. 1.............1981..		137; 992; 996
15	Greyfriars Holiday Annual.........1982..		848; 893; 896
16	Collector's Pie No. 2.............1982..		401; 407; 649
	....		651.

APPENDIX 7.

Greyfriars Library List.

Only four volumes have been published in this series.

Note: SOL = Schoolboy's Own Library.

No.	Title.	Source.
1.	Billy Bunter gets the Boot...SOL No. 286.	
2.	Bunter the Bad Lad...........SOL No. 237.	
3.	Billy Bunter's Tramp.........SOL No. 253.	
4.	Bunter's Rebellion...........SOL No. 143.	

APPENDIX 8.

Miscellaneous Greyfriars Publications.

Greyfriars Wall Map.
Greyfriars Map Book Mark.
Greyfriars for Grown Ups, by Laurie Sutton.
The World of Frank Richards by W.O.G. Lofts and D.J. Adley
The Greyfriars Companion, 1977.
The Men behind Boys' Fiction, by W.O.G. Lofts
and D.J. Adley.